AESTHETIC TECHNOLOGIES OF
MODERNITY, SUBJECTIVITY, AND NATURE

AESTHETIC TECHNOLOGIES OF MODERNITY, SUBJECTIVITY, AND NATURE

Opera • Orchestra • Phonograph • Film

Richard Leppert

UNIVERSITY OF CALIFORNIA PRESS

University of California Press, one of the most distinguished university presses in the United States, enriches lives around the world by advancing scholarship in the humanities, social sciences, and natural sciences. Its activities are supported by the UC Press Foundation and by philanthropic contributions from individuals and institutions. For more information, visit www.ucpress.edu.

University of California Press
Oakland, California

Library of Congress Cataloging-in-Publication Data

Leppert, Richard D., author.
Aesthetic technologies of modernity, subjectivity, and nature: opera orchestra phonograph film / Richard Leppert.
pages cm
Includes bibliographical references and index.
ISBN 978-0-520-28737-2 (cloth : alk. paper) — ISBN 978-0-520-96252-1 (ebook)
1. Music—Philosophy and aesthetics. 2. Modernism (Music)—History—20th century. 3. Opera—Social aspects. 4. Motion pictures—Social aspects. 5. Sound recordings—Social aspects. 6. Nature in music. 7. Nature in motion pictures. 8. Puccini, Giacomo, 1858–1924. Fanciulla del West. 9. Fitzcarraldo (Motion picture) 10. Days of heaven (Motion picture) I. Title.
ML3845.L44 2015
780.9′04—dc23

2015009826

Manufactured in China

24 23 22 21 20 19 18 17 16 15
10 9 8 7 6 5 4 3 2 1

The paper used in this publication meets the minimum requirements of ANSI/NISO Z39.48–1992 (R 2002) (*Permanence of Paper*).

CONTENTS

ILLUSTRATIONS

MUSICAL EXAMPLES

ACKNOWLEDGMENTS

I wish to express deepest gratitude to the several colleagues and friends who read various chapters and offered insights, corrections, and encouragement during the long gestation of this project: Hisham Bizri, James Currie, Daniel Goldmark, Helen Greenwald, Berthold Hoeckner, Lawrence Kramer, Charles Kronengold, Sherry Lee, Alice Lovejoy, David M. Lubin, Susan McClary, Jeannie Poole, and Gary Thomas. Peter Franklin and Mitchell Morris patiently read all of it and provided me with a great deal of invariably thoughtful, critical engagement. Joey Crane handled putting all of the musical examples in order; to say the very least, I very much appreciate his attention to detail, timeliness, and skill.

As always, Mary Francis, my long-time editor at the University of California Press, provided invaluable advice and moral support throughout the six years of the book's gestation; to her I owe a special note of gratitude. Anne Canright, who copy-edited the manuscript, was attentive to the smallest detail and, in that regard, saved me from more than a few embarrassing lapses. Bradley Depew and Rose Vekony saw to all the details of putting the book into print.

The staff support at the University of Minnesota Libraries was, as ever, professional, tireless, and cheerful, and no matter the numbers of requests for closed-stacks materials. I'm deeply grateful kind assistance provided by John Pennino, Archivist for the Metropolitan Opera, and the several staff assistants in the New York Public Library's Billy Rose Theatre Division at Lincoln Center.

Chapters 1, 2, and 4 are based on the following previously published essays; they have been revised and expanded for inclusion in this volume:

"The Civilizing Process: Music and the Aesthetics of Time-Space Relations in *The Girl of the Golden West*." In *Musical Meaning and Human Values*, ed. Keith Chapin and Lawrence Kramer, 117–50, 203–17. New York: Fordham University Press, 2009.

"Opera, Aesthetic Violence, and the Imposition of Modernity: *Fitzcarraldo*." In *Beyond the Soundtrack: Representing Music in Cinema*, ed. Daniel Goldmark, Lawrence Kramer, and Richard Leppert, 99–119. Berkeley: University of California Press, 2007.

"Two Notes, One Ending (Three Operas) at the Boundary of the Great Divide; or, Aesthetic Meanderings of the Sonic Psyche." *Opera Quarterly* 31, nos. 1–2 (2015): 71–99.

INTRODUCTION

This is a book about music, opera especially, the phonograph, and cinema centered on questions concerning modernity, subjectivity, and nature emerging in the years immediately preceding 1910 and following in the next decade or so thereafter. The cultural practices of my concern either date from those years (three chapters) or are constituted by late-twentieth-century looking back at that time period. Along the way, I pause the main narrative to take up related issues in two freestanding excurses. I'll characterize the subject matter of the individual chapters and excurses in due course.

The governing idea for what follows developed over a number of years, but the seed for it was a well-known (at least to literary scholars) text by Virginia Woolf, writing in 1924, where she noted: "On or about December, 1910, human character changed."[1] A few years ago, the by-then dim memory of Woolf's remark, which I initially encountered decades ago in an undergraduate class on modern British literature, came to mind for whatever reason. I'll return to Woolf's text presently, but suffice to say for now that her date for fundamental change coincides with the December 10, 1910, premiere at the Metropolitan Opera of *La fanciulla del West,* Puccini's initial, if tentative (but hardly insubstantial), genuflection to modernism, a score well noted for its dynamic aggressiveness and harmonic discord. I've thought about this opera for many years. I bought a recording when I was in high school, around 1960, and very much liked it from the first hearing. The link between Woolf's remark and Puccini's opera, however arbitrary, set me to thinking what it was about the opera that had for so long appealed to me. Considering the matter led me down a number of different paths (among the pleasures of any sort of research), and the result is this volume, the totality of which at times moves quite far beyond this opera, regarding which I would be less than frank were I to assume that the connective tissue shared by the chapters and excurses will seem entirely evident simply by the names I've given to each of them. However, if I've succeeded in the task I set for myself, by the time you finish reading what follows, the historical, social, cultural, and aesthetic homologies should be clear. Individually or taken together, in any event, I'm confident that the cultural artifacts and practices I've considered are historically and culturally significant: that much as the minimum.

Woolf's concern in 1924 (coincidentally the year of Puccini's death) looking back to 1910 was the changing state of English literature, which faced new aesthetic demands in the twentieth century; in brief, her concern was modernism. Writers, as she put it, "tried to compromise" (like Puccini, of which more later), but compromise wasn't up to literature's cultural task. "And so," she wrote, "the smashing and the crashing began." And here, though speaking about literature, Woolf provides a vivid series of explicitly *sonic* metaphors that mark quasi-epistemic cultural change: "Thus it is that we hear all round us, . . . the sound of breaking and falling, crashing and destruction. It is the prevailing sound of the Georgian age—rather a melancholy one if you think what melodious days there have been in the past . . . if you think of the language, and the heights to which it can soar when free, and see the same eagle [now] captive, bald, and croaking."[2]

Taking a different but related tack a few years later, the Futurist (later fascist) poet F. T. Marinetti celebrated modern noise as the fitting harbinger for a modernism allegorized in this instance as an apotheosis of violence. He wrote to his friend and fellow Futurist Luigi Russolo about the sonorities of what he had heard at the battle of Adrianapolis, Turkey, in October 1912. In an orgasmic ecstasy of words piled atop one another, he took unambiguous pleasure in the sonic (and olfactory) chaos that gave him pleasure *as music:* "What a joy to hear to smell completely *taratatata* of the machine guns screaming a breathlessness under the stings slaps *traak-traak* whips *pic-pac-pum-tumb* weirdness leaps 200 meters range Far far in back of the orchestra pools muddying hyffing goaded oxen wagons." To which Russolo drily responded, "We want to give pitches to these diverse noises, regulating them harmonically and rhythmically."[3]

Ezra Pound succinctly got at something similar to Woolf and Marinetti in his two-line poem "L'art, 1910," appearing in his 1916 collection *Lustra;* here he celebrates not sound but color while nonetheless replicating hints of violence:

> Green arsenic smeared on an egg-white cloth,
> Crushed strawberries! Come, let us feast our eyes.

These three textual citations encapsulate tropes that organize the chapters that follow: human character and its representation, modern technology, violence, acute sensitivity to a sound world, a hint of altered nature (crushed strawberries), and the place of music and visual/visualized culture as both a reflection and agent of fundamental, even shocking change. There is in these citations a solicitation of modernity filtered through the lens of modernism, still somewhat out of focus, variously perceived, but giving the sense that there was no turning back. On balance, optimism is apparent, though the path ahead is uncertain. Woolf: "We must reconcile ourselves to a season of failures and fragments. We must reflect that where so much strength is spent on finding a way of telling the truth, the truth itself is bound to reach us in rather an exhausted and chaotic condition"; and she concludes: "Tolerate the spasmodic, the obscure, the fragmentary, the failure. Your help is invoked in a good cause."[4]

CRUSHED STRAWBERRIES! COME, LET US FEAST OUR EYES

Reference to nature in the remarks by Woolf, Marinetti, and Pound is absent or minimal, but nature lurks in the shadows as the silenced other to modern culture. The distinctions established between nature on the one hand and culture (and its cousin civilization) on the other were not news in 1910 any more than during the heyday of the early modernism represented by the Enlightenment, when the dialectic emerged as an issue of both theoretical and practical importance, some sense of which is readily apparent in the obsessions put to paper by Rousseau. There's hardly a better place to look than his (in)famous 1750 *First Discourse* on the question "Has the restoration of the sciences and arts tended to purify morals?" Rousseau's essay, which was awarded the prize from the Academy of Dijon that had posed the question, fixated on modern (enlightened) learning, whose social benefits he doubted. Modern knowledge production in his view—articulated with characteristic attention-getting hyperbole—in the end has increased inequalities, limited human emancipation, and (a particular bugaboo for Rousseau) made people soft. I'm less interested in the details of his extended argument; it's this that matters for my purposes: "Peoples, know once and for all that *nature* wanted to keep you from being harmed by knowledge just as a mother wrests a dangerous weapon from her child's hands; that all the secrets she [nature] hides from you are so many evils from which she protects you, and that the difficulty you find in educating yourself is not the least of her benefits."[5]

Rousseau sets nature against modern culture/civilization, whose access to knowledge privileges the few at the expense of the many. Nature is constituted as a good, in opposition to (modern) culture, posited as an evil. In other words, Rousseau defines the difference between the two as a moral distinction. Living rightly engenders responsibility to the law of nature, a form of right that precedes and trumps all others, at the heart of which, for Rousseau, are two foundational principles that he articulates in his *Second Discourse,* "On the Origin and Foundations of Inequality among Men" (1755): nature provides us our ardent desire for well-being and self-preservation; it likewise gives us empathy ("a natural repugnance to see any sensitive being perish or suffer, principally our fellow men").[6] And then he gets to his larger point: "It is from the conjunction and combination that our mind is able to make these two principles, without the necessity of introducing that of sociability, that all the rules of natural right appear to me to flow: rules which reason is later forced to re-establish upon other foundations when, by its successive developments, it has succeeded in stifling nature."[7] What are we to observe, he asks: the law of nature or the "sole law of the strongest"?[8]

Concern with the nature of nature and nature's relation to humankind did not diminish after Rousseau; indeed, it became an *idée fixe* of Romanticism, as has been well been traced across the arts. My principal concern, the sound world represented in music, found distinctive and affecting ways to engage the social implications of our relation to nature. Along the lines Rousseau envisioned, no musician paid the matter greater heed than Wagner, especially in the *Ring;* indeed, Rousseau's emphasis on the nature/culture dialectic, engaged through a discussion of the decline of morality, is echoed in Wagner's epic tetralogy.[9] I'd like to take a brief look at Wagner's account of the supposed origin of his idea for the *Ring,* and the articulation of nature that opens *Rheingold,* as regards the *sounding* of nature, which in turn has implications for what follows—both thereafter in the cycle and in this book.[10]

THE RIVER RHINE

The setting is near Venice: "After a night spent in fever and sleeplessness," Wagner writes,

> I forced myself to take a long tramp the next day through the hilly country, which was covered with pine woods. Returning in the afternoon, I stretched dead tired, on a hard couch, awaiting the long-desired hour of sleep. It did not come; but I fell into a kind of somnolent state, in which I suddenly felt as though I were sinking in swiftly flowing water. The rushing sound formed itself in my brain into a musical sound, the chord of E flat major, which continually re-echoed in broken forms: these broken chords seemed to be melodic passages of increasing motion, yet the pure triad of E flat major never changed, but seemed by its continuance to impart significance to the element in which I was sinking. I awoke in sudden terror from my doze, feeling as though the waves were rushing high above my head. I at once recognized that the orchestral overture to the *Rheingold,* which must long have lain latent within me, though it had been unable to find definite form, had at last been revealed to me. I then quickly realised my own nature; the stream of life was not to flow to me from without, but from within. I decided to return to Zürich immediately, and begin the composition of my greatest poem.[11]

These remarkable and notably self-aggrandizing remarks from *Mein Leben* take up an account of the composer in a state of near-total physical exhaustion. Having gotten himself out of Venice for a day, he seeks relief from the city's noise in what he terms "the absolute calm" of a village (Spezia). He sleeps there but poorly, and the next day he forces himself into the woods for a solitary walk, but he finds no relief. Returning to his lodgings, he stretches out on a sofa and falls into a quasi-dream state. His dreaming is slightly nightmarish but hardly unique; not least, it's immensely productive. Wagner slips beneath the waves; it's as though he's drowning—indeed, he tells us that he awoke in a sudden terror. The dream he describes is musical, and in a key (and who else but Wagner would recount musical dreams of such specificity?). He is submerged in the flow of a river—a primordial soup, a river of life, whose movement slowly "progresses" toward history itself. The river is trying to "say" something in its reechoing broken forms; melodies of increasing motion try to break through. The E-flat major chord never changes. This changelessness, as Wagner puts it, "seemed by its continuance to impart significance to the element"—water—in which he was sinking.

In the dream narrative, Wagner and water are each distinct and yet the same, the confirmation of which comes at the end of the quoted statement. In the river, wholly at one with it, Wagner recognizes that the *Nature* external to him—the flowing water—was also latent within him: what he describes as "my own nature; the stream of life." In his dream Wagner is momentarily reconciled with nature, hence reconciled with his own nature (though the experience produces a terror so startling that he awakens). The strikingly productive result, so Wagner is keen to tell us, is the *Ring,* which is, after all, very much about nature, including human nature. As Wagner put it elsewhere in his autobiography, "It was in this great prelude that [the] foundations of the entire [*Ring*] had to be laid."[12]

The 136 bars on E-flat at the beginning of *Rheingold,* evoking the Rhine, unfold like an inexorable sonoric current gradually increasing in intensity, its momentum functioning as a metaphor of creation as regards both the opera's narrative and its musical undertow. That is, the E-flat Prelude, in all its purposeful monotony, constitutes an ur-motive for the opera as a whole, the musical germ, as it were, from which is derived the music that will follow. The audience may not actually hear precisely when the music starts, deep in the double basses and quietly, as though it were always "there," below consciousness: that which simply *is*—Nature itself.[13]

The Rhine is the locus of forces, literal and allegorical, that will drive a complicated myth of creation and, ultimately, destruction. Wagner gives us a foretaste of its energy in the opening, which seems always already to have been present, the terrestrial analogue to music of the spheres. The E-flat pedal sounding in the double basses throughout the Prelude, and the very slow unfolding of quasi-melody, doesn't so much take us out of time as never permit us into time in the first place—until the very end. The music's energy gradually increases, and as the Prelude abruptly is interrupted at its dynamic and harmonic climax, something else, wholly new, wholly different, bursts forth via an abrupt shift to an A-flat chord: the human voice comes onto the scene, at first, and only momentarily, vocalizing linguistic nonsense (Weia! Waga!), followed immediately by the introduction of recognizable language and its unique discursive power. Language emerges, as it were, from nature but will ultimately serve the needs of humankind's war on nature in Wagner's tetralogy, as an instrumentalized device to advance cunning and guilt—which will become evident within the opera's first few minutes when the Rhinemaidens employ language as a foil against the sexual desire of the ugly Alberich. Once love is out of reach, Alberich turns to power and plots successfully to steal the gold that designates agency over everything—in essence, over nature itself. Warren Darcy aptly puts it thus: "The tragic events of the *Ring* ensue exactly because humanity loses touch with its natural origins."[14]

The conventional account of the orchestral opening of *Rheingold* draws attention to a telos of sorts, specifically the transformation that occurs in the quasi-evolutionary move from nature to a notably dystopian history. Time, in its relation to progress, as part of the myth of modernity, is critical to modernity's realization. Yet time in any ordinary sense as it's experienced in nineteenth-century music is all but absent from the ponderous opening of this music drama. Nonetheless, what matters most about the *Rheingold* Prelude is, indeed, still time; but it matters, as it were, precisely by its absence.

Or—not quite. There is a better way to describe what Wagner is up to. The *Rheingold* Prelude is "about" time's (relative) absence, but in a specific dialectical relation to musical *space*. It is the spatial quality of this music that is so striking, and not its temporality. Time dramatically makes its sonoric entrance only at the point at which the Prelude is, in effect, abruptly cut off, that is, when the voice (the human) and language (the human subject) are first heard. Moreover, it's only with the voice that the possibility of modernity (broadly conceived) emerges, to the degree that the human voice will define human dominion over nature, this dominion providing the central demarcation for the modern (by which I mean history) and not least for the formulation of the human subject—or, to put the matter within the culture of modernity, and to borrow from Foucault, for the invention of Man.[15]

Arthur Schopenhauer, in *The World as Will and Idea,* commented: "In the deepest tones of the harmony, in the basso continuo, I recognize the lowest levels of the objectification of will, of inorganic nature, of the mass of the planet." He suggested that "the basso continuo is thus for us in the harmony what inorganic nature is in the world, the crudest mass upon which all things rest and from which all things rise and develop." As for melody, "in the upper, singing main voice—directing the whole and, with unfettered volition, displaying a whole in the uninterrupted, significant interconnection of a *single* thought progressing from beginning to end—I recognize the highest level of the objectification of will, the thoughtfully aware life and striving of the human being."[16] Schopenhauer held that what he termed "the phenomenal world, or nature, and music [are] as two different expressions of the same subject matter."[17] He further insisted that, unlike other art forms, which merely represent the world, music was connected with the inmost nature of the world and our own self, and hence is universal. Music, he claimed, is "just as *immediate* an objectification and image of *will* as a whole as the world itself is, indeed just as much as the Ideas whose multiplied phenomenon constitutes the world of individual things. Thus music is in no way, like the other arts, an image of Ideas, but *an image of the very will* of which Ideas are also the objectivization."[18]

Schopenhauer—to whom, not coincidentally, Wagner sent the text of the *Ring* in 1854—recognized in music the sonoric trace of a wholeness, and a creative force, upon which life itself depends, as is clear in remarks that summarize his argument: "The inexpressibly inner element in all music, by virtue of which it is to us in its passage like a so entirely familiar and yet eternally distant paradise, so entirely intelligible and yet so inexplicable, rests on the fact that it reproduces all the stirrings of our innermost essence, but entirely apart from actual reality and far from its torments. . . . Its object is immediately will, and this is in its essence the most serious thing of all, as that upon which all things depend."[19] I draw attention to a single phrase from these remarks: music, Schopenhauer, insists, floats through our consciousness as the vision of an "eternally distant paradise, so entirely intelligible and yet so inexplicable." Music, that is, lets us see something—a vision—in which we believe but cannot reclaim for lived experience; music posits a utopian reconciliation with nature, that which is us.

PARADISE EVER DISTANT

Terrence Malick's extraordinary film *The New World* (2005), structured around the (historically uncertain) John Smith and Pocahontas story of the early-seventeenth-century Jamestown Colony in Virginia, readily and directly engages the collision between a technologically advanced world (ships, cannon, guns) and the natural splendor of the New World attentively filmed (using 65 mm film stock) to produce in both long shot and close-up a nearly overwhelming sense of beauty, and at the same time to engender a comprehensive sense of intrusion and even violation of the setting that attends the appearance of European colonizers. The New World "already" has human inhabitants, the Powhatans, who, as Malick relates, live in harmony with nature to which they are highly sensitive, experiencing it and themselves as part of one organism. The Europeans refer to them as "the naturals." I mention this film only to speak briefly about its opening sequence employing the *Rheingold* Prelude (in fact one of three quotations of the Prelude in the film).[20] The narrative describes the disruption of the harmony of apparent oneness among the native people and the implications that result for them and the colonizers, but also of course for us.

Robert Sinnerbrink suggests that "*The New World* explores the potential for cinema to enact alternative forms of world-disclosure, aesthetically revealing, through cinematic art, new ways of being, of dwelling, within a world-context and relationship with nature that is more than ever under pressure from a destructive rationalism, reductive instrumentalism, and imperialist violence."[21] The title sequence thus opens with the sounds of an abundance of birds both near and distant, to which is then added the soft sound of rippling water. After a few seconds the first image appears, a nearly smooth water surface reflecting a cloud-laden blue sky, accompanied by more sounds of life forms, insects and maybe amphibians, and at this point we hear the initial voiceover of Pocahontas: "Come, Spirit. Help us sing the story of our land. You are our Mother, we field your corn. We rise from out of the soul of you." Shot from below, we have our first glimpse of her, standing and reaching to the sky, arms raised over her head. At this juncture, roughly a minute and a half into the film, the title sequence begins, accompanied by bird sounds and the

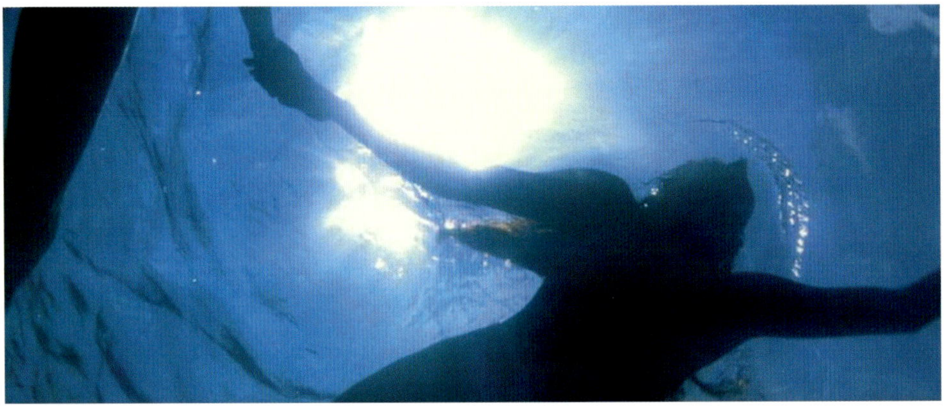

FIGURE 1
Terrence Malick (director), *The New World* (2005): open water sequence with Wagner's *Rheingold* Prelude (4:14).

title music composed by James Horner. The *Rheingold* Prelude is first heard near the end of the credits (3:04), overwritten at the start by the animal sounds that are soon silenced.

Malick then shoots an extended underwater sequence, the screen mostly blue, variously showing native Indian swimmers (their naked bodies entirely under the water), all young: three women for part of it, and otherwise a young man and young woman (fig. 1). At the start of this sequence, Pocahontas continues her voiceover while we watch a single woman in the water: "Dear Mother, you fill the land with your beauty. You reach to the end of the world. How shall I seek you? You, the great river that never runs dry." The camera, still shooting from below, moves upward, closer to the water's surface, sufficient for us to see three young native men, posed in a stance signaling alarm, pointing outward to the sea as they first sight the arrival of a new temporality. The camera then rises to a position just above the water's surface, angled so that we see the ships transporting the English colonists. An onscreen textual reference locates the moment: "Virginia 1607." The Prelude continues, but music that had mostly been heard in the absence of other sounds, apart from the brief voiceover, is now accompanied by the racket of the colonists preparing their ships for the landing. Medium and close-up shots of shipboard details document the process. Malick cuts to a shot of Powhatans, their mostly naked bodies painted and decorated with feathers, running to see the arrival; they do so silently, except for a high-pitched whistle pipe with which one young man sounds the alarm (figs. 2 and 3). The music gradually fades only when the Englishmen set foot on shore, warily, to begin their initial exploration, nearly swallowed by a green sea of abundant flora. As Wagner's music subsides, the natural sounds of the New World take its place.

In 1831, two centuries and more after the Jamestown colony was established, Alexis de Tocqueville and his friend Gustave de Beaumont set off to America, officially to study

FIGURE 2
Malick, *The New World:* Powhatan man signals alarm (6:16).

FIGURE 3
Malick, *The New World:* Powhatans witnessing arrival of colonists' ships (6:34).

its prison systems but with Tocqueville's own larger, long-term political ambitions foremost in mind. They stayed nine and a half months, traveling widely as far west as Wisconsin, north into Canada, and south to New Orleans, and by every means then available on land and water. That July, they undertook a foray into the American backcountry of Michigan Territory and as far west as Green Bay in what is now Wisconsin; Tocqueville's account when published was called "Two Weeks in the Wilderness," a principal goal being, as he put it, "our search for savages and wilderness."[22]

I'll conclude by citing two distinct impressions that Tocqueville imports to his memoir. The first:

> The only feelings one has from passing through these deserts in flower where everything, as in Milton's *Paradise,* is ready to welcome man, is a quiet admiration, a gentle and

> melancholic emotion, a vague disgust for civilized life, a sort of savage instinct which inspires painful thought that soon this delightful solitude will have assumed a different appearance. In fact, the white race is already marching through the woods which surround it and, in a short number of years, the European will have cut down the trees reflected in the clear waters of the lake and forced the animals inhabiting its banks to retreat toward new wilderness.[23]

The second:

> One looks down upon them [the Indians] with a melancholic pleasure; somehow there is an urgency to wonder at them. The idea of this natural and wild grandeur, which will come to an end, blends with the imperious images evoked by the triumphant progress of civilization. One feels proud to be a man and one experiences at the same moment some kind of bitter regret for the power which God has granted us over nature. The soul is disturbed by ideas and opposing feelings, but all the impressions received are magnificent and leave a deep mark.[24]

The pages that follow will pursue what's at stake for late-modern subjects living within the parameters of the nature/culture dyad articulated in these passages, and the ways that sonic and visual cultural practices and artifacts reflect and engage the actuality and operationality of this long-prevailing dialectic.

CHAPTER OUTLINE

Part 1 of what follows, "Modernity and Opera; Nature and Redemption," consists of two chapters. Chapter 1, "The Civilizing Process: Music and the Aesthetics of Time-Space Relations in *The Girl of the Golden* West," considers David Belasco's 1906 play and Puccini's 1910 opera as instantiations of the West of the imagination addressed via time-space relations in a state of crisis. The play and the opera are situated within California's Sierra Nevada, perhaps the most dramatic landscape in the American West. The setting more or less constitutes a character in its own right, one of overwhelming power that shapes both action and people. Nature, that is, is the organizing metaphor of both Belasco's play and Puccini's opera. The two works, literally and figuratively, are also travel stories: literally so, to the extent that the characters are very much on the move, having traveled across the seas and the continent to get to California to participate in the gold rush; figuratively, to the extent that the characters journey toward moral redemption—though redemption is a more fundamental trope in Puccini's opera than in Belasco's play. The Sierra Nevada for Belasco and Puccini alike is a material site, inhabitable. It is likewise a psychic site, existing within the realm of the imagination as an ethereal reality.

The melodrama and the opera both heavily invest in modernist ideologies that govern what Norbert Elias has called the civilizing process, as manifested in the characters' locus in history, place, and, above all, nature, perceived in its seemingly "most natural" state, an imagined nature in which human beings are unwelcome intruders. Both Belasco and Puccini saw the American West as a space defined by its relation to time—historical time and the now-time of early-twentieth-century modernity. Both addressed the cultural displacements of modernity, looking back in time to a defining phenomenon of modernity, the American westward expansion and the formation of an imagined sublime. Both envisioned a paradise, but a modern one in which presence is already marked by the promise of absence and expulsion. Nevertheless, their narratives stage reconciliations, however momentary, of subject to object, man to woman, and culture to nature.

Belasco's play, enormously successful, emphasized naturalism above all else. Every theatrical resource at his disposal was put to use in an effort to capture what he regarded as the essence of the place and time represented. His often hoary plays, now notable for the strikingly old-fashioned tropes conventional to melodrama, were staged and acted out with the precision afforded by the most modern of stage technology. Above all, Belasco was known for his innovative, inventive use of electricity, particularly as regards lighting but also to produce highly realistic sound and visual effects, such as howling wind, blizzard-driven snow, crackling fire, and the like. Most important, Belasco employed modern technology in order to elicit a sense of nature's overwhelming power on the one hand and its putative spiritual essence on the other.

The natural space—indeed, the natural paradise—of Puccini's West, like Belasco's, is mediated by the rawest form of cultural modernity, registered in class distinction, ethnic and racial tension, economic destitution, jealousy, hatred, loneliness, greed, violence, and injustice. That is, in this opera the eternal sameness of a would-be perfect nature is confronted by modern history in sonic form, in regard to which Puccini employed tonality as a kind of sonic geography, a historical map tracing modern subjectivity and desire. But in *La fanciulla del West,* he exploited tonal instabilities, laying bare his self-consciousness about the limits of conventionalized musical practice to represent the modern world. Sonically speaking, he recognized tonality's closing frontier and moved, however tentatively, toward the outer boundary of the familiar, seeking the energy available at the margins of acoustic modernity.

Among the musical devices that define the opera's allegory, one in particular stands out. Puccini evoked the vast California wilderness by producing for his audience a sense of sonic distance, in order to articulate not only space but also—crucially—time and memory. Puccini's West, that is, evokes time through space; it is this relation that controls his understanding of the West's essence.

Chapter 2, "Opera, Aesthetic Violence, and the Imposition of Modernity: *Fitzcarraldo,*" considers the same historical moment scripted by Belasco and Puccini but from the perspective of the late twentieth century. Werner Herzog's 1982 film tells the story of the film's namesake, an Irish colonialist who intends to build an opera house in the remote Peruvian rainforest town of Iquitos and to have Enrico Caruso to perform there.

The money for the undertaking would come from a rubber plantation he hopes to exploit, provided he can reach it by traversing dangerous rivers and hostile native people, and by pulling his river boat over a hill to access a different river that will allow him to lay claim to the lands: all of this effort in the name of art, to be as much imposed on the Indians as offered to them. Fitzcarraldo himself is operatically larger than life, and a man obsessed to hear life sung; every narrative element in the film revolves around this urgent need.

Herzog's *Fitzcarraldo* connects the Peruvian Amazon to an incomplete, timeless space seemingly caught in the ahistoric moment of its creation. Nature is perceived by the film's characters as nearly overwhelming, and as such it serves as the de facto foil for the culture Fitzcarraldo will provide them via live opera and its substitute, Caruso recordings played on a lotus-horn gramophone at several key moments throughout the film. The logical "impossibility" that lies at the heart of opera organizes the film's logic and is exploited by Herzog. Indeed, epic-quality improbability constitutes the film's cultural logic, a point Herzog is keen to establish from the very start, notably including an enactment of a performance of Verdi's *Ernani* in the opera house at Manaus, Brazil, itself the product of rubber-baron cultural aspiration. Caruso performs the title role, while actress Sarah Bernhardt mimes the role of his lover, Elvira, all of it staged as the first cousin of music hall, the absurdity standing in, precisely, for what matters most about opera, the manifestation of a world where life is only sung. The point, obviously enough, is that Werner Schroeter, who directed this scene for Herzog, staged opera as a carnival-mirror reflection of modernity whose truth lies precisely in distortion. Opera is the film's form and its content. Opera determines the narrative, defines the antiheroic hero, and, not least, provides a commentary to the story of which it is a determinant.

Opera as Culture writ large, and as the means by which to acculturate Amazonian peoples, is understood by Fitzcarraldo to depend upon a confrontation with nature, something of an impersonal demon of which the Indians are its offspring. In brief, Fitzcarraldo will rescue them from themselves and do it with song and by means of the new technology of sound recording. Caruso records will first pacify and then enlighten, or so he thinks. Fitzcarraldo is convinced that his form of colonialism is better by far than the colonialism of his peers, vulgar men merely in it for the money. Fitzcarraldo, in contrast, is in it for aesthetics. The looniness of the undertaking is built on a dream riddled with contradiction: art results from privilege and exploitation; as such art convicts itself of being that to which it stands in opposition—the world as it is. Nevertheless, warts and all, and social to the core, art attempts the expiation of its own sins by pointing to something better and beyond itself.

Part 2 of this book, "Voicing Subjectivity," consisting of an opening excursus followed by two chapters, considers opera in two guises. The excursus, "Opera, Monumentality, and Looking at Looking," concerns the institutionality of opera, centered on the architectural actuality of the opera house as a spatial enclosure within which was staged a semblance of the social totality, determined in part by the seating arrangements and the visibility of the audience to itself: altogether, a regime of scopophilia directed both toward the performers and—as much—toward the audience surveilling (or cruising) itself. Looking—foundational to the experience of opera—is what matters, far more than looking at anything in particular. Everything looked at mirrors back. As viewers, looking at looking while at the opera raises the stakes of the specific site where scopophilia is stimulated and maybe also sated. Opera as an experience of hearing marks just half of the equation, although this protocol gradually changed through a new cultural pedagogy promoting listening, the subject of the next chapter.

Chapter 3, "Caruso, Phonography, and Operatic Fidelities: Regimes of Musical Listening, 1904–1929," considers what happens when the dimension of sight is removed from the equation of experiencing opera (or music more generally) with the advent of sound recording. Phonography, in brief, required a recalibration of the sight/sound relation. As it happened, and surprisingly so, a substantial component of that recalculation employed opera recording as the means by which to rethink and promote a new world of sightless (acousmatic) sound, and it did so in significant part by playing off established principles of elevated aesthetic taste associated with opera, never mind that the taste for popular musics vastly outweighed the interest in classical musics of any sort, alike at the earliest history of phonography as today. This fact notwithstanding, opera became the measure of the worth of sound recordings and, for that matter, the domestic ownership of the playback equipment. The story is a multifaceted mix of would-be aesthetics, industrial competition, business acumen, advertising and marketing, education, technophilia, ideologically inflected pedagogy, and, perhaps above all, capitalist economics.

Opera recording served as the linchpin of phonographic promotions articulating democratic principles of an imagined universal access to the best of musical art. In this regard, the major recording labels promoted classical music, opera especially, by replicating discourse inaugurated in nineteenth-century cultural aesthetics combined with popular principles about self-improvement and public (democratic) education.

The chapter addresses the industrial-musical production of two companies, Edison's National Phonograph Company and the Victor Talking Machine Company, notable for the phonographs they manufactured and the enormous numbers of opera recordings (mainly arias and ensembles) each company produced—machines and recordings consistently and vigorously promoted by rival claims to superior sound fidelity and under the banner of the cultural worth of opera.

Opera for Victor meant Caruso, their star of stars, with whom the company had an exclusive contract, a successful pairing that was never matched by Edison. Caruso became a textual-visual advertising code for singing itself and all that vocal music could "do" for its auditors. Company claims on behalf of recorded sound linked the permanence afforded by the new technology on the one hand with the preservation of cultural treasures, classical music and opera especially, on the other. Victor and Edison likewise insisted that their recordings were a fine substitute for experiencing live opera, with the added advantage that Caruso and other such stars, via recordings, made themselves available to listeners in their own homes and at any time they might wish to hear them. Recordings allowed listeners to control recorded time—use it, archive it, discard it, at will.

The chapter concludes with a look back to the early modernity of the seventeenth century to consider two visual representations of the sense of hearing, each structured on a trope about hearing music, but music of very different sorts, encompassing two rigidly distinct class pedigrees, one privileged, the other not. The epistemology underwriting these images is distinctly modern; like record collecting (avidly promoted by Edison and Victor), such paintings characteristically mark the pleasure of excess consumption, linking it directly to power/wealth when sound cultures associated with privilege are involved. The advertising campaigns of early phonography fundamentally replicate this discourse.

Chapter 4, "Aesthetic Meanderings of the Sonic Psyche: Three Operas, Two Notes, and One Ending at the Boundary of the Great Divide," is principally an investigation of opera perceived as a site where subjectivity could be staged, witnessed, and celebrated both visually and aurally. As regards subjectivity, and to express matters with some hyperbole, what audiences saw and heard enacted in opera was the unruliness of desires whose realization was characteristically self-suppressed or else experienced only at great cost. The chapter investigates the problematics of articulating the social and personal actuality of wounded subjectivities and unfulfilled desires that found voice, an audible trace, on stage and for the delectation of the audience by way of sonically induced transference.

The operas I consider maintain gestural allegiance to a musico-Freudian language while traversing the border separating late romanticism from modernism, beginning in 1896 with *La bohème* and following with Bartók's *Duke Bluebeard's Castle* (1911–17), hence a bit before and just after the 1910 date of Virginia Woolf's concern. The argument is structured around a semiotic micrology of two singular pitches—grace notes sung by Rodolfo in the third act of the Puccini opera and a high C employed just once, sung by Judith, in Bartók's opera—read within the specific contexts of their usage as sedimentations of the history of subjectivity, and especially under fraught circumstance. I conclude with a few related remarks about a late-modern musical rewriting of the ending of another opera seventy-five years (and a lot of history) after its premiere.

For Mimì and Rodolfo, Puccini employs grace notes as the aural expression of desire emergent in elocutions associated with love in its various forms, including in particular its manifestations encompassing states of abjection. The act three grace notes are assigned a distinct, one might say heavy, function that simultaneously runs in two directions, toward profound regret and loss on the one hand, and on the other marking an effort to vocalize these emotions in an attempt to heal the wound through reconciliation with the estranged beloved. The grace notes assigned to Mimì fall within established convention; Rodolfo's do not. His grace notes are semiotically out of bounds with the bourgeois male ideal of emotional self-control already well in place by the mid–nineteenth century.

Bartók's one-act opera represents a modernist rejection not only of the pleasure principle that opera had provided by means of tonal harmony but also, and more importantly, of the socio-cultural semiotics that tonality promoted. It's fair to say that by 1911 too much history had intervened for the old musical language to be retained in good conscience. Judith's one high C occurs at the moment when the fifth of the seven bolted doors is opened, painfully blinding her as sunlight for the first time penetrates the castle's gloom, triggering her vocal outburst, and immediately leading to the opera's dramatic highpoint, though one very unlike what Judith's high C might seem to promise. Bluebeard speaks of his vast kingdom that stretches out before her, now all hers, proclaimed with the support of a nearly overwhelming orchestral tonal/tonal-hybrid underscore. What matters most, however, is Judith's subsequent response to Bluebeard's pronouncement. Indeed, she all but ignores him, as though deaf to both him and the blasting orchestra supporting his declaration. It's as if the urgency of the situation was beyond what major-mode tonality was capable of. In its place, Bartók gives us a kind of tonality *in extremis.*

The chapter concludes with a brief consideration of the new ending for Puccini's *Turandot* provided by Luciano Berio at the start of the current century. Berio's ending leads Puccini away from the acoustic culture of the Grand Tradition, a departure that he was clearly moving haltingly toward but didn't complete. Berio's ending attacks both certainty and musical historicism, taking advantage of cultural and musical history subsequent to 1924, a "final" moment read as the last gasp of Opera writ large.

Part 3, "Modernity, Nature, and Dystopia," also includes an excursus and two chapters. The excursus, "Natural Beauty/Art Beauty," as the title suggests, addresses the relation between the two aesthetic types, principally within the context of the philosophy of Theodor Adorno emerging from his last monograph, *Aesthetic Theory,* not quite finished at the time of his death in 1969. My concern is the historicity of the concept of nature and its functional agency when set against culture on the one hand and human subjects on the other. Adorno perceived the relation as one of eternal and unresolved conflict, even as he insisted on the centrality of nature to human conceptions of wholeness and future hope. Our longing for nature—for example, as expressed in ecological regard and wilderness preservation, but also and in particular art, in Adorno's argument—is a projection of a lack. Adorno insisted that art worthy of the name is shot through with what he termed truth content (social truth, aesthetic truth) that could provide a semblance (but only that) of utopia, the realization of which was dependent on a reconciliation with what resided in nature: natural beauty. Art acknowledges the natural beauty that the human subject has otherwise degraded yet nonetheless desires in its non-extant "perfect" state; art, that is, reflects on this fact.

The excursus historicizes nature/culture/aesthetic conjunctions through a discussion of early-modern Western European paintings on nature themes. Western art has long been tasked with visualizing the cultural complexities of the human relationship to nature, the response to which was characteristically riddled with contradiction. By the seventeenth century, hence at the dawn of modernity, however, tropes representing the domination and othering of nature were legion, though the costs were aesthetically disguised. Three of these tropes are of particular interest to me: Orpheus Charming the Animals, Bird Concert, and Gamepiece (hunting still life) paintings, discussed in ascending order of the frankness each embeds regarding human fantasies of control over nature, beginning with aesthetic coercion and concluding with bloody violence.

Art, for Adorno, is the site where the engagement with this contradiction (the otherness of the subject) occurs, the point being that art addressing this urgent task both confronts and, *in appearance* (hardly in reality), allows at some level of imaginative experience the de-othering of our otherness: reconciliation, a closing of the gap between subjects and their others. Closing of the gap requires, for Adorno, a rethinking of the conjunction that joins natural beauty to art beauty. Natural beauty makes promises, which is precisely why we seek it out; its purported and readily apparent difference from what it is *not* offers consolation at a minimum, which is neither concurrent with nor antagonistic to the concept of reconciliation, in regard to which the excursus concludes with comments by Adorno (and others) about the nature of the American West. It is here where filmmaker Terrence Malick fittingly makes his entrance.

Chapter 5, "Sound, Subjectivity, and Death: *Days of Heaven (promesse du bonheur),*" concerns Malick's *Days of Heaven* (1978), which is structured around the conflicted relationship in late modern society of culture to nature as played out in the lives of characters living in desperate existential circumstances in the early twentieth century on the American Great Plains. Much of the story is related through the life of one of the story's four main characters, a teenage girl who recalls the events at some temporal distance from when they occurred. The film marks a fundamental dialectic between the natural world, timeless but threatened, and modernity, shown at its height of self-confidence in the immediate lead-up to World War I, defined by industrialization, mechanization, technology, speed, restlessness, and freneticism, all of it driven by rampant social inequality.

My remarks focus in particular on the film's cinematography of the natural world and its sound design. Defamiliarization of the familiar is a hallmark of Malick's cinema and a gateway to his engagement with modernity and its troubles. The soundtrack at the film's opening employs the "Aquarium" section of Camille Saint-Saëns's *Le carnaval des animaux* to help evoke this trope. I suggest that the use of "Aquarium," for the title credits and elsewhere in the film as well, to say nothing of Ennio Morricone's original score, functions as a sonoric realization of confinement and limitation mirrored by the life experiences of the film's principal characters as they attempt to rebuild their lives from the point of misery that defined them at the opening of the narrative.

Among the numerous visual and sonic references to the winds that perpetually blow across the prairie, none carries more weight throughout the film than that of the wind-driven electric generator atop the Victorian house that rises like a totem on the treeless plains. The generator whirrs throughout the film, sometimes only as a sound, other times as a sight; its *sound* presence is made insistent at fraught moments in the narrative, something like a mechanized Greek chorus to the unfolding narrative. Sound in *Days of Heaven,* distinct from dialogue (of which there is surprisingly little), is employed as a category of the philosophical; the sounds that matter most help at once to articulate and engage the nature/culture relation. The emphatic acoustic presence of wind throughout the film, far more than as a mere supplement to its visual phenomenology, not only transmits a sonic insistence on temporality, change, and the impermanence of everything except change, but also at the same time functions as an aural demarcator of the space of the prairie and the significance of spatiality in the larger metaphorical sense. Sound, as Malick employs it, has sign value in excess of its ties to the logic of the unfolding narrative.

The natural beauty surrounding the film's characters in the American western setting bears no necessary relation to their quotidian concerns or comforts. The days of heaven, lived out in a stunningly beautiful setting sharply distinct from the miseries of urban degradation, are in fundamental ways more or less wholly imagined, and in any event the heavenly days are few, ending violently. Nature might offer the appearance (and to some extent the reality) of providing for what is otherwise missing in these people's lives, but this is not to say that nature somehow has their interests at heart. Instead, what Malick offers is a profound contrast between the striking beauty of the natural world and the equally striking suffering of human beings who instrumentally exploit and degrade nature, even while recognizing that the natural world points toward some semblance of an alternative. One of the most significant accomplishments of this extraordinary film is the degree to which its impact accrues not from the images captured on film—gorgeous as they often are—but from the sound effects and nondiegetic musical underscore.

The Conclusion, "Acoustic Invocations of Crisis and Hope," revisits the terms that make up the book's title (technologies, subjectivity, and nature) through brief looks at a dream, two pieces of music, and a scene from a film. The dream, at once erotic and about opera (in ruins, literally), was experienced by Adorno during the Second World War; I consider the dream in relation to his sustained love of and antipathy toward opera.

The first of the two musical compositions is Mahler's Third Symphony, the third movement scherzando, read through Adorno, particularly with regard to his account of Mahler's concern with nature. I relate the movement to an image from the early decades of the nineteenth century celebrating high-speed travel by horse-drawn coach and the employment of the posthorn as a signaling device in both this artwork and Mahler's score. My concern is the relation between, on the one hand, the posthorn solo as a sonic reference to the approach of human beings into a natural paradise of birds and, on the other, the reaction of the birds, standing in for nature more generally, to the new presence. I consider the posthorn as an aesthetic technology of considerable semiotic import in this symphony.

The second composition is Charles Ives's *The Unanswered Question,* again engaging the relation of human subjects to nature as fundamental to the question of existence. I finish, thus, with a look at the use of Ives's piece in Terrence Malick's World War II film

The Thin Red Line (1998), where it is heard, in excerpt and in adaptation, during one of the film's most important scenes. Malick's film revisits the consequences of the nature/culture dialectic, at the same time voicing hope for reconciliation in the face of horrific violence. Nature imagery and music together constitute the principal means through which Malick develops tropes of damnation and redemption.

PART I

MODERNITY AND OPERA; NATURE AND REDEMPTION

1

THE CIVILIZING PROCESS

Music and the Aesthetics of Time-Space Relations in *The Girl of the Golden West*

> There are days which occur in this climate, at almost any season of the year, wherein the world reaches its perfection; when the air, the heavenly bodies and the earth, make a harmony, as if nature would indulge her offspring.
>
> RALPH WALDO EMERSON, "NATURE" (1836)

GETTING CIVILIZED/GOING NATURAL

In 1907 Puccini made the first of two visits to New York, to supervise the first performances of *Manon Lescaut* and *Madame Butterfly* at the Metropolitan Opera. He was also in search of a subject for his next project. Accordingly, while in the city, and despite his very limited English, he attended numerous plays, including three by David Belasco, whose *Madame Butterfly* he had seen staged in London in 1900. One of the Belasco productions caught his eye, *The Girl of the Golden West,* which is the general subject of this chapter.[1] In particular, I am interested in exploring some of the ways that Belasco's play and Puccini's opera invest in modernist ideologies governing what Norbert Elias called the civilizing process.[2] To get at the issue, I take a concentrated look at how both Belasco and Puccini envisioned time-space relations, with specific regard to how each understood their characters' place in history (hence time), place (hence space), and, above all, nature, which I want to consider as both a problem for, and opportunity within, the civilizing process.

Belasco's play and Puccini's opera are situated within California's Sierra Nevada, perhaps the most dramatic landscape in the American West. The setting more or less constitutes a character in its own right, one of overwhelming power that shapes both action and people. Nature, that is, is the organizing metaphor of both the play and the opera—and as Michel de Certeau remind us, metaphors "are spatial trajectories."[3] Both works, literally and figuratively, are also travel stories: literally so, to the extent that the characters are very much on the move, having traveled across the seas and the continent to get

FIGURE 4
"The Mammoth Trees *(Sequoia gigantea)*, California (Calaveras County)" (c. 1860), chromolithograph published by A. J. Campbell, Cincinnati. Washington, D.C., Library of Congress, Prints and Photographs Division.

to California to participate in the gold rush; and figuratively in that the characters journey toward moral redemption—though redemption is more a fundamental trope in Puccini's opera than in Belasco's play. The Sierra Nevada for Belasco and Puccini alike is a material site, inhabitable. It is likewise a psychic site, existing within the realm of the imagination as an ethereal reality.[4]

In late-nineteenth-century America, no landscape received greater attention than the West, particularly the mountain West of the Rockies and the Sierra Nevada. The California mountains especially claimed a central place in the American imaginary, not least because of the imposing challenge to cross them to get to the promised land. The fate of the Donner Party during the winter of 1846–47, whose history quickly passed into legend, drove home the point. The gold rush, which quickly followed the discovery of gold in January 1848 at Sutter's Mill, fully established the Sierra Nevada in the forefront of national consciousness, creating new western mythologies fueled by the promise of fortunes literally waiting to be scooped up from the gravels of the American River.

The actual mountains and their unimaginably gigantic trees produced particular awe (fig. 4), with Yosemite (early on known as Yo-Semite) serving as the focal point of the larger whole. Indeed, the mountain West's visual splendors seemed to defy the human imagination, though hardly for want of trying to come to terms with them. In 1864, Lincoln designated Yosemite as a wilderness preserve, the nation's first; it was made a national park in 1890. In the decades that followed, Yosemite was endlessly written about, painted, photographed, and of course visited as a major tourist attraction. Currier and Ives produced lithographs marking a sense of Yosemite's spatial vastness, just as photographers produced stereographs of views carefully selected to exploit the three-dimensional effects of the medium—a kind of vicarious substitute for the reactions of awe commonly experienced by visitors.[5] In the immediate aftermath of the Civil War, Yosemite took on greater significance as a site of healing and reconciliation—a park in place of a battlefield, in the parlance of Frederick Law Olmsted.[6] The writings of John Muir (1838–1914) in particular best expressed the spiritual impact of the Yosemite landscape.[7]

The American West had its dystopian realities, of course, as the fate of Custer demonstrated to a shocked nation in 1876, the news reaching the East, ironically, during the July 4 centennial celebrations. But the promise of American singularity on the whole played well against inconvenient arguments to the contrary, as the reception history of Frederick Jackson Turner's famous paper read to the American Historical Association in Chicago in 1893, "The Significance of the Frontier in American History," makes clear. "American social development," Turner wrote, "has been continually beginning over again on the frontier. This perennial rebirth, this fluidity of American life, this expansion westward with its new opportunities, its continuous touch with the simplicity of primitive society, furnish the forces dominating American character. The true point of view in the history of this nation is not the Atlantic coast, it is the Great West."[8]

The sublime drama of Turner's Great West was ably captured by painters, among whom Albert Bierstadt (1830–1902) had few equals, though his fame was short lived and his critics, from the start, many.[9] From his hand came monumental imaginings of a western Eden. As with Belasco and Puccini, three tropes in particular organize Bierstadt's visionary representations: monumentality, unimaginably vast space (the effect of both often amplified by the enormous size of some of his canvases, the largest being nine and a half feet high and fifteen feet wide), and light (figs. 5 and 6). These tropes served as metaphors for the untrammeled purity of a world in a state of nature and as signs of nature's redemptive agency for man after the fall from grace. In nationalist terms, Bierstadt's images visually certified claims to the mythologies of American singularity. Here was a landscape at once aged and yet at the seeming moment of its creation, a visible sign of the "divine endorsement of American progress."[10]

The West did not actually look like what Bierstadt painted, not least on account of the multiple perspectives encompassed in his canvases, a visually jarring effect that invites the eye to search out a compositional unity that does not in fact exist (a fact that sorely irritated his contemporaneous critics, who regarded the violation of convention as mere incompetence). But whatever his shortcomings as a painter, Bierstadt pedagogically led

FIGURE 5
Albert Bierstadt (1830–1902), *Among the Sierra Nevada, California* (1868), oil on canvas. Smithsonian American Art Museum, bequest of Helen Huntington Hull, granddaughter of William Brown Dinsmore, who acquired the painting in 1873 for "The Locusts," the family estate in Dutchess County, New York. Photo credit: Art Resource, New York.

viewers toward a particular way of seeing the western mountains. In the words of Lee Clark Mitchell, Bierstadt "imagined the West as a dramatic (and therefore moral) terrain rather than a geographical one."[11] His vision was of a spectacular and visually magnetic western sublime, whose results he put on display in exhibition galleries in the East and also made available in mass-produced prints.[12]

Anthropologist Mary Douglas points out that societies are imagined to have form, boundaries, and margins; in short, they have structure. But where society's energy concentrates is "in its margins and unstructured areas," precisely where "any structure of ideas is vulnerable."[13] It is this vulnerability that Belasco and Puccini confront via the liminal terrain of the American West, specifically the imagined boundaries separating civilization from its absence, and culture from nature.[14] Both men perceived the West as a space defined by its relation to time—historical time and the now-time of early-twentieth-century modernity. Time—like nature, like space—as the product of history, is "a social institution."[15] Elias marks modern time as "the symbol of an inescapable and all-embracing compulsion."[16] Time in modernity has a life of its own; it reaches beyond our capacity to control it. Belasco and Puccini confronted modernity, despite the conservatism and even regression evident in their work. Their West was at once in the past, as a narrative of the gold rush, and a present, the literal reality of two worlds in stark

FIGURE 6
Albert Bierstadt, *Cathedral Forest,* oil on canvas. Private collection. Photo credit: Art Resource, New York.

opposition: the East of frenetic, ultra-modern Midtown, and a West whose wildness was by then *in actuality* already well tamed apart from a few sanctioned sites set aside as national parks for eternal preservation, in regard to which Michael Johnson marks what he terms "postfrontier anxiety": "A manifold phenomenon, it involved as well remorse, envy of forefathers, doubts about the nation's democratic spirit and masculinity, misgivings about the future of industrial civilization—but most strongly that nostalgia for a return to nature. And nature meant, eminently, the West, a place now conquered, much of its wildness lost and gone forever."[17]

Modernism, Stuart Hall has suggested, is "modernity experienced as trouble."[18] Belasco and Puccini were reluctant, conflicted modernists, both romanticists at heart yet well aware of the new cultural world as articulated by Virginia Woolf. Modernist Belasco virtually fetishized electricity for what it offered the theater; modernist Puccini, who collected fast cars and speedboats, experimented with post-Romantic sonorities learned from Debussy and Strauss. Belasco left California for New York as a young man and rarely returned to his wild western roots; Puccini, whose life as an opera composer demanded endless journeys to urban centers, could never get back to his country estate fast enough to keep him happy.[19] Both men, in their lives and in their work, were deeply ambivalent about modernity—an ambivalence that was manifested in the internal contradictions marking their respective settings of *The Girl of the Golden West.*

Belasco and Puccini both addressed the cultural displacements of modernity; both looked back in time to a defining phenomenon of modernity, the American westward expansion and the formation of an imagined sublime. They envisioned a paradise, but a modern one in which presence is already marked by the promise of absence and expulsion. Nevertheless, their narratives staged reconciliations, however momentary, of subject to object, man to woman, and culture to nature. Each sought to bind what Adorno called nature's wound, though in the end the wound continued to bleed, which is precisely what guarantees their work a degree of historical, modernist authenticity.

The Girl of the Golden West was something of a cultural phenomenon in the early years of the twentieth century. The play itself was highly successful in the years following its 1905 opening (fig. 7). In 1911, Belasco produced a novel based on his play, a year following the première of Puccini's opera (fig. 8).[20] The book remained in print for some years thereafter and was reissued again in 2007. Its first printing included four colored illustrations of important scenes; later printings replaced the illustrations with stills from a now-lost film of the same title released in 1923 (fig. 9). In fact, between 1915 and 1938 four American feature films followed in the wake of Belasco's play. The first, in five reels, shot in eight days in California in 1915, was by Cecil B. DeMille, then working in only his second year as a director.[21] The 1923 silent in seven reels, directed by Edwin Carewe, starred popular actress Sylvia Breamer; and this film was remade in 1930 with sound, in ten reels, with Ann Harding in the title role (fig. 10). The 1923 film had a popular-music spin-off, a tune called "The Girl of the Olden West" (fig. 11), its cover sheet reproducing Breamer's face hovering over a mountainous landscape.[22] Other music publishers readily cashed in with songs whose titles closely approximated the title of Belasco's play (figs. 12 and 13). The 1938 film was a Nelson Eddy–Jeanette MacDonald musical, the score by Sigmund Romberg.[23] (There were other gold rush films throughout this period, Chaplin's 1925 film concerning the Yukon Klondike narrative being the best known.) In sum, *The Girl of the*

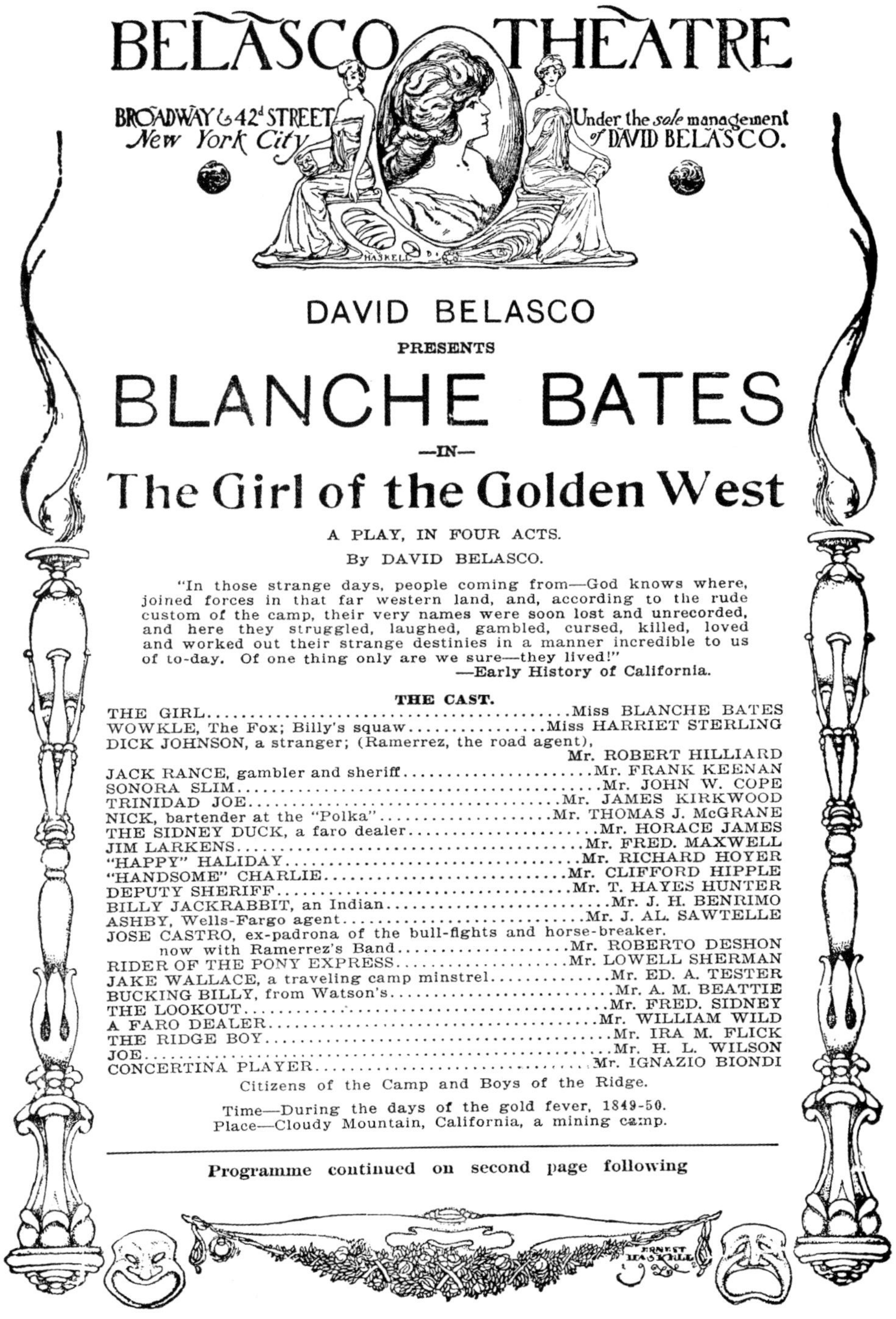

BELASCO THEATRE

BROADWAY & 42d STREET
New York City

Under the *sole* management
of DAVID BELASCO.

DAVID BELASCO

PRESENTS

BLANCHE BATES

—IN—

The Girl of the Golden West

A PLAY, IN FOUR ACTS.

By DAVID BELASCO.

"In those strange days, people coming from—God knows where, joined forces in that far western land, and, according to the rude custom of the camp, their very names were soon lost and unrecorded, and here they struggled, laughed, gambled, cursed, killed, loved and worked out their strange destinies in a manner incredible to us of to-day. Of one thing only are we sure—they lived!"

—Early History of California.

THE CAST.

THE GIRL..Miss BLANCHE BATES
WOWKLE, The Fox; Billy's squaw................Miss HARRIET STERLING
DICK JOHNSON, a stranger; (Ramerrez, the road agent),
Mr. ROBERT HILLIARD
JACK RANCE, gambler and sheriff......................Mr. FRANK KEENAN
SONORA SLIM...Mr. JOHN W. COPE
TRINIDAD JOE....................................Mr. JAMES KIRKWOOD
NICK, bartender at the "Polka"....................Mr. THOMAS J. McGRANE
THE SIDNEY DUCK, a faro dealer.....................Mr. HORACE JAMES
JIM LARKENS.......................................Mr. FRED. MAXWELL
"HAPPY" HALIDAY.................................Mr. RICHARD HOYER
"HANDSOME" CHARLIE............................Mr. CLIFFORD HIPPLE
DEPUTY SHERIFF.................................Mr. T. HAYES HUNTER
BILLY JACKRABBIT, an Indian.........................Mr. J. H. BENRIMO
ASHBY, Wells-Fargo agent..........................Mr. J. AL. SAWTELLE
JOSE CASTRO, ex-padrona of the bull-fights and horse-breaker.
now with Ramerrez's Band...................Mr. ROBERTO DESHON
RIDER OF THE PONY EXPRESS...................Mr. LOWELL SHERMAN
JAKE WALLACE, a traveling camp minstrel..............Mr. ED. A. TESTER
BUCKING BILLY, from Watson's........................Mr. A. M. BEATTIE
THE LOOKOUT......................................Mr. FRED. SIDNEY
A FARO DEALER..................................Mr. WILLIAM WILD
THE RIDGE BOY.......................................Mr. IRA M. FLICK
JOE..Mr. H. L. WILSON
CONCERTINA PLAYER..............................Mr. IGNAZIO BIONDI

Citizens of the Camp and Boys of the Ridge.

Time—During the days of the gold fever, 1849-50.
Place—Cloudy Mountain, California, a mining camp.

Programme continued on second page following

FIGURE 7
David Belasco (1853–1931), *The Girl of the Golden West* (1906), playbill. Private collection.

FIGURE 8

Belasco, *The Girl of the Golden West: Novelized from the Play* (New York: Grosset & Dunlap, 1911), cover illustration. Private collection.

FIGURE 9

Belasco, *The Girl of the Golden West: Novelized from the Play* (1911): undated reprint, title page, and movie still of actress Sylvia Breamer as "The Girl" in 1923 film directed by Edwin Carewe. Private collection.

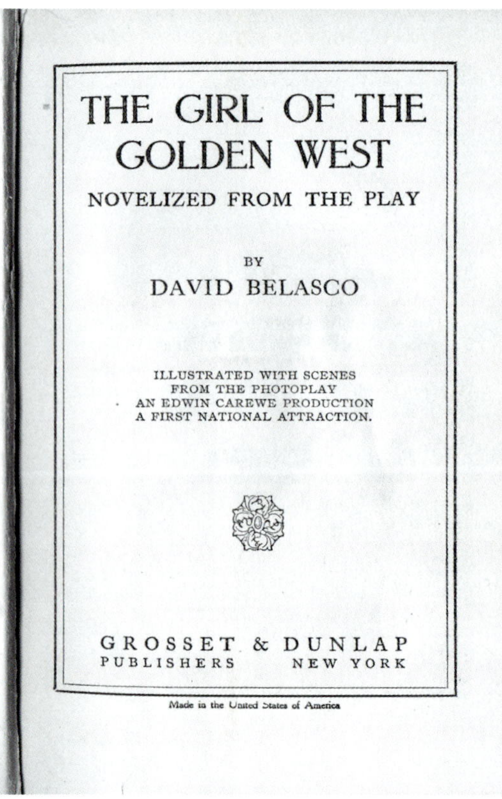
THE GIRL OF THE GOLDEN WEST

NOVELIZED FROM THE PLAY

BY

DAVID BELASCO

ILLUSTRATED WITH SCENES
FROM THE PHOTOPLAY
AN EDWIN CAREWE PRODUCTION
A FIRST NATIONAL ATTRACTION.

GROSSET & DUNLAP
PUBLISHERS NEW YORK

Made in the United States of America

FIGURE 10
John Francis Dillon (director), *The Girl of the Golden West* (1930), Vitaphone sound film by First National Pictures, movie herald. Private collection.

FIGURE 11
"The Girl of the Olden West," sheet music cover; lyrics by Haven Gillespie, music by Egbert van Alstyne and Charles L. Cooke (New York and Detroit: Jerome H. Remick, 1923). Private collection.

FIGURE 12
"Little Girl of the Golden West," sheet music cover; lyrics by Lester M. Stroube, music by Walter A. Stroube (Hammond, Ind.: Ultra Music Publishing Company, 1920). Private collection.

FIGURE 13
"Maid of the West," sheet music cover; lyrics by Roscoe Gilmore Stott, music by Clay Smith (Cleveland: Sam Fox Publishing Company, 1923). Private collection.

FIGURE 14
"A Girl from the Golden West," stereograph (1906), copyright by E. W. Kelley. Washington, D.C., Library of Congress, Prints and Photographs Division.

Golden West spawned an opera, a novel, pop tunes, songs and song recordings, and four films (five, if you count a 1943 Italian version). It gave its name to a country music duo, the Girls of the Golden West, Dolly and Millie Good, who achieved considerable fame in the 1930s. *The Girl of the Golden West* was also the subject of souvenir ephemera, including postcards and stereographs (fig. 14), souvenir-type paintings, cigarette-pack insert advertising (figs. 15 and 16), an inscribed ceramic vase in the shape of the Girl's bonneted head, and even a decorated metal fruit tin—objects that crop up from time to time on eBay. In brief—and this is my point—the subject touched something of a collective cultural nerve.

FIGURE 15

"Wills 's Cigarettes": cigarette-pack insert advertising for the 1930 film *The Girl of the Golden West* (front). Private collection.

FIGURE 16

"Wills's Cigarettes": cigarette-pack insert advertising for the 1930 film *The Girl of the Golden West* (back). Private collection.

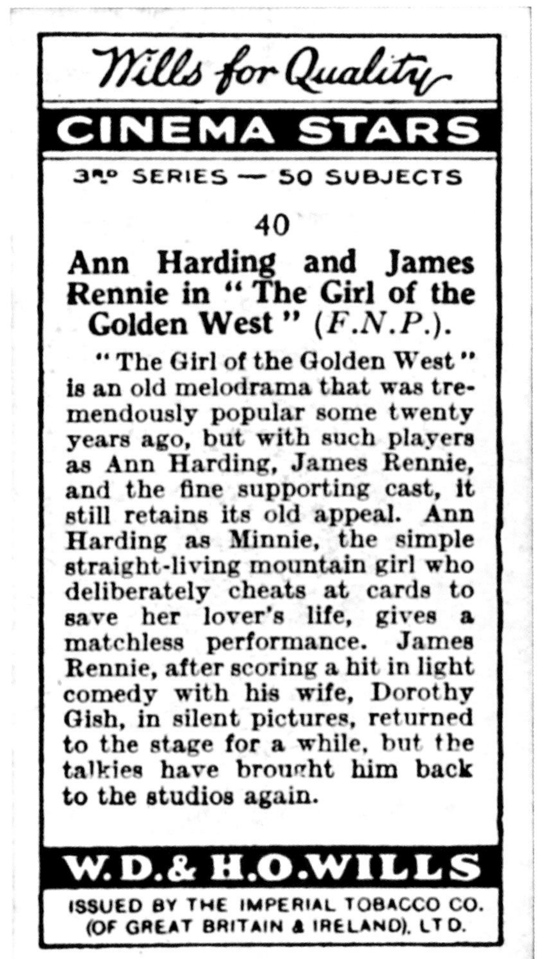

Wills for Quality

CINEMA STARS

3RD SERIES — 50 SUBJECTS

40

Ann Harding and James Rennie in " The Girl of the Golden West " (*F.N.P.*).

" The Girl of the Golden West " is an old melodrama that was tremendously popular some twenty years ago, but with such players as Ann Harding, James Rennie, and the fine supporting cast, it still retains its old appeal. Ann Harding as Minnie, the simple straight-living mountain girl who deliberately cheats at cards to save her lover's life, gives a matchless performance. James Rennie, after scoring a hit in light comedy with his wife, Dorothy Gish, in silent pictures, returned to the stage for a while, but the talkies have brought him back to the studios again.

W. D. & H. O. WILLS

ISSUED BY THE IMPERIAL TOBACCO CO. (OF GREAT BRITAIN & IRELAND), LTD.

BELASCO

David Belasco (1853–1931), born in San Francisco to immigrant parents, was involved in the theater throughout his childhood in the West. By the time he moved to New York in 1884, he was already widely experienced as an actor, prompter, and stage manager. In New York, where he remained until his death, he made his reputation as a producer, director, and playwright.[24]

First and foremost, Belasco specialized in a form of melodrama that emphasized naturalism. Indeed, every theatrical resource at his disposal was put to use in an effort to capture what he regarded as the essence of whatever place and time his plays represented. His often hoary plays, now notable for the strikingly old-fashioned tropes conventional to melodrama, were staged and acted out with the precision afforded by the most modern of stage technology, itself infected with an acute awareness of photographic and cinematic indexicality. Indeed, his special effects (and there were many) were as good as, or better than, those in period movies. His painted backdrops were sometime put in motion, not very different from what audiences experienced with the painted scenery of early cinema. Belasco's wind devices replicated blizzards, produced howls, and blew window curtains. He used lighting to effect fire that was indistinguishable from the real thing—indeed, so threatening that authorities were once called to investigate.[25] He even attended to the olfactory. In one play set in a forest he sprinkled pine needles on the stage so that when the actors moved about, crushing the needles, the scent wafted into the auditorium.[26]

The printed scene descriptions for each act of *The Girl of the Golden West* run to as many as five pages. The play's electrical plot occupies eight pages of precise settings and cues. The list of properties requires seventeen pages in all, enumerated in nearly exasperating detail.[27] The devices and materials for the second-act snowstorm, requiring a full page of instructions, provide the flavor of his concern for naturalism. The list includes wind machines, an air tank used to produce a "large shriek of wind," another with whistle attachments "for canyon effect of wind," and a "cluster of whistles attached to pipe and running to bellows under [the] stage." To further effect howling wind, he calls for an electric fan to blow both the curtains of the bed canopy and some tissue paper stored under the bed. He lists rock salt to simulate sleet, to be used with "two snow effect appliances," the salt to be blown against the cabin windows so that it can be both seen and heard. The instructions call for two offstage piles of snow, presumably flour, to be set in front of two fans and blown into the crevices between the cabin's log walls. Other snow reservoirs are placed elsewhere. When Sheriff Rance brushes snow off his overcoat, some of it landing in the fireplace, a hissing sound is to be made. And so on. These and other storm effects in the second act required thirty-two stagehands to activate, all of it coordinated by a conductor who could be seen by the each member of the stage crew.

Music was integral to Belasco productions. "If the play has a musical accompaniment," he wrote, "I read it to the composer I have engaged, indicating its moods and feelings. He must interpret every scene and speech as if he were writing the score for a song."[28] Belasco incorporated a great deal of music into *The Girl of the Golden West,* a combination of on- and offstage singing of thirteen old songs (including "Camptown Races," "O Susannah," "The Days of 49," "Sonora Slim," "Echoes of Home," "Clementine of '49," and "Ole Dan Tucker"),[29] employing two tenors, a baritone, and a bass, sometimes in costume on stage and at other times in the pit. An orchestra played a prelude (171 bars) at the start and also provided accompaniment to the male quartet between acts. Accompaniments were provided by the string orchestra, as well as by banjo and guitar, either solo or with orchestra. There are parts for other instruments as well—flute, clarinet, cornet, trombone, mandolin, accordion, piano, and drums—though their use was more restricted. Numerous brief musical cues occur throughout. The play's original music was composed by William Wallace Furst (1852–1917), who also arranged orchestral versions of some of the old tunes.[30] Between acts, song medleys were performed.

The Girl of the Golden West, in four acts, tells the story of a California mining camp during the gold rush. Called Cloudy Mountain, the settlement is populated solely by men, apart from one young woman, who until well into the play is referred to only as the Girl. Her name is Minnie and she runs the Polka saloon, the setting for the first act. Minnie is undereducated, virginal, and either soft or hard, as her situation requires. She has a heart of gold, and a ready trigger finger. Everyone loves her, and several of the boys are in love with her. The Girl, while saddled with the clichés of the domesticized professional virgin, is in other respects very much of the New Woman mold: self-reliant, fearless, and readily adaptable to changing situations. The local law, in the person of the sheriff, Jack Rance, intends to have her as his wife. He is the play's heavy. The Girl's (eventual) love interest is the road agent Ramerrez, a bad guy with his own heart of gold, who introduces himself to Minnie as Dick Johnson in act one, immediately sparking her libido. He first comes off as something of a dandy; he drinks his whiskey with water, which marks him as unmanly in the eyes of the miners, who take their drink neat. His half Mexican parentage renders him an Other. Belasco nonetheless represents him as a man of moral integrity, despite his profession and his ethnic heritage, which counted for little at the turn of the century.[31] Minnie, played by the famous actress Blanche Bates (fig. 17), whom Belasco especially favored, mothers the men and guards their gold.

Act one, which occurs at night, establishes Minnie's role in the camp. Johnson, intending to rob the gold, cases the joint, but sees Minnie and decides to ply for different treasure. They dance together (fig. 18); they fall in love.

Act two opens in the mountains, in the Girl's log cabin at one o'clock that same night. Dick comes courting. A storm ensues, the full force hitting just as the pair kiss for the first time. Soon thereafter, Rance and his posse arrive looking for Ramerrez, having learned of Johnson's real identity and suspecting him to be with the Girl. Minnie gambles at poker for Johnson's life (fig. 19). If she loses, the sheriff gets Johnson for a hanging and Minnie for his wife. The Girl wins, but only by cheating.

FIGURE 17
Blanche Bates (1873–1941) as Minnie in David Belasco's *The Girl of the Golden West* (1905–6). Billy Rose Theatre Division, The New York Public Library for the Performing Arts, Astor, Lenox, and Tilden Foundations.

FIGURE 18
Belasco, *The Girl of the Golden West* (1905–6), act one. Billy Rose Theatre Division, The New York Public Library for the Performing Arts, Astor, Lenox, and Tilden Foundations.

FIGURE 19
Belasco, *The Girl of the Golden West,* act two. Billy Rose Theatre Division, The New York Public Library for the Performing Arts, Astor, Lenox, and Tilden Foundations.

Act three, set in the saloon's adjacent dance hall a few days later, involves the recapture of Ramerrez and the passing of sentence for his execution by hanging. Minnie, coming in on the scene moments before Dick is to be killed, pleads for his life and wins over the miners.

Act four, about a week later, is set on "the boundless prairies of the West." Little more than a tableau, the scene lasts only a couple of minutes, during which the reunited lovers bid final farewell to the Sierra Nevada and California as they head east for their uncertain future.

The Girl of the Golden West opened at the new Belasco Theatre in Pittsburgh on October 3, 1905, and in New York at the Belasco on November 14 the same year; it played for 224 performances. It was mounted again on Broadway during the 1906–7 season, with Bates still in the title role. It was this staging that Puccini witnessed. Thereafter, for three years, the play was extensively toured in the United States in dozens of towns and cities from the East Coast to the Midwest.[32] It was also performed internationally, as far afield as Tasmania in 1909.

The remarks that follow are largely confined to two brief episodes from the play: its wordless opening, accompanied only by music, and its close, also with music, in the brief act four epilogue. What interests me is Belasco's evocation of nature, which I will connect to my larger concern with time and space relations.

PICTURE PERFECT

The representation of nature, which literally bookends the play, is constituted as an allegorical sublime within and against which the characters measure their existence. The play opens with house lights up during an upbeat musical prelude provided by the pit orchestra. The stage is hung with a painted curtain, illuminated by footlights, representing a scene with large evergreens in the foreground and mountains at the back (fig. 20). A brilliant sunset shows just above a ridge of mountain peaks, its impact heightened by a spotlight. Near the end of the prelude, four bars into the last section, marked *cantabile* (a 3/4 moderato, serving as the Girl's motive), the house goes dark and the prelude draws to a close, segueing to music in a quite different mood, an *andante misterioso* played by muted strings. After four bars, the curtain is raised in darkness, in preparation for what Belasco called the "First Picture." The music continues until the play proper begins.

The First Picture moves from day to night; the sunburst is gone, replaced by a moon transparency and soon followed by the ascent of an exactingly described panorama. Here, in excerpt, is how Belasco outlines it (unfortunately, no photographs exist, although the production was otherwise extensively documented):

> In the far distance a wild range of the Sierras peaks. . . . Near R., on a mountain, a cabin is seen, a winding trail coming up to it. We see that it is cloudy about the mountain. The mountains behind this cabin continue to a great height. . . . It is night and the moon hangs low over the mountain peaks. The scene is flooded with moonlight, contrasting oddly with the cavernous shadows. . . . The sky is very blue and cold. The snow gleams white on the highest peaks. Here and there pines, firs, and manzineta *[sic]* bushes show green. All is wild, savage, ominous. In certain places the mountains are very jagged—one deep sheer ravine is suggested, the purple mists rising up from the bottom. There is a faint light twinkling in the cabin of the GIRL. As this first impression gradually moves up out of view of the audience:
>
> SECOND PICTURE: The exterior of the "Polka" saloon . . .[33]

Belasco's two "pictures" are, of course, moving painted panoramas. Panoramas had already been used in the U.S. theater for decades, but the canvas rolls were conventionally at the back of the stage, not at the front, and the movement was normally lateral. Belasco's panorama moves upward, rising slowly and just behind the stage apron, revealing the described scene little by little, and in precise coordination with lighting cues, such as the light showing from inside the little cabin. The effect, which in cinematic terms would be a tilt down, was striking. That is, we first see the mountainous peaks, after which the view slowly descends to the valley in which the Cloudy Mountain camp is located.[34]

The act curtain and subsequent panorama are critically important to the allegory that organizes the play's narrative. What will become apparent by the end of the play is that

FIGURE 20
Belasco, *The Girl of the Golden West,* act curtain. Billy Rose Theatre Division, The New York Public Library for the Performing Arts, Astor, Lenox, and Tilden Foundations.

the sun marks several interlocking tropes. Fundamentally, Belasco's use of sunlight works to reverse time: it rolls history backward. The stage is first seen with a metaphorical setting sun (the act curtain), which registers an ending and the uncertainty of what will follow, followed by the moonlight represented in the panorama. The sunset and moon glow, however inadvertently, mirror Frederick Jackson Turner's then-recent proclamations about the closing of the American frontier. Darkness dominates in *The Girl of the Golden West;* indeed, the play's first two acts occur on the same night. Act three, while set in the morning and brightly lighted, is metaphorically dark, the mood brightening only near the end when the hanging is averted; and this in turn leads to the epilogue, where Belasco's handling of light matters far more than the short scene's very few words.

Act four occurs at sunrise, completing the reversal of time while alluding to new life and a hoped-for better future. But this ending nonetheless reiterates a profound uncertainty. To be sure, the lovers face the sunrise, but they are moving against the tide of American history as laid out by Turner: they are heading east, away from the new and toward the old.[35] More about this presently.

The opening panorama compresses time, just as it constitutes a journey. It begins, so to speak, in the clouds and drops to the mountain peaks; only gradually does it admit a human being, indirectly via the Girl's cabin, and all she represents. It eventually "arrives" by leaving the sublime for something of the ridiculous, a mining camp in societal gender disorder, a perverse family: one Girl and her odd all-male brood.[36]

Belasco invokes loss, history, and remembering before the curtain opens by means of a text that he quotes in the play's program and again as his novel's epigraph. The modernity of his subject lies less in its account of a localized version of manifest destiny and more in its insistence on society's nonentities, people who perhaps were not so much forgotten as never remembered, people, as it were, "known only to God": "In those strange days, people coming from God knows where, joined forces in that far Western land, and, according to the rude custom of the camp, their very names were soon lost and unrecorded, and here they struggled, laughed, gambled, cursed, killed, loved and worked out their strange destinies in a manner incredible to us to-day. Of one thing only are we sure—they lived!"[37]

Thus, before the curtain goes up, Belasco evoked a kind of freeze-frame in a look back on the young nation's still-younger days. His epigraph acknowledged loss (this is conventional to melodramas) and posited the West in 1905 as a site of enormous distance, but one less in miles than in time, hence history. Time consciousness, that is, girds the primeval nature that will shortly unfold to a troubled modernity defined by human anonymity, greed, and violence, which together seem to trump the allusions to pleasures and happiness. In brief, time and nature are in conflict. What the panorama and the epigraph together reinforce is a sense of loss, which the epigraph especially overdetermines. The gold rush, a mere fifty years in the past at the time of the play, presents itself as lost in the mists of legend. It can now only be imagined. Although by 1905 the West was well familiar to most Americans, Belasco's invocation pushes it back into a territory of the unfamiliar, as though it were a foreign geography. In brief, Belasco sought first to estrange the now-familiar, then to allegorize it, and thereafter to render it precise via a material naturalism, only in the end once more to throw all of it back into uncertainty, in a kind of *misterioso* complaint against the very modernity that he otherwise technologically fetishized.[38]

LIGHTING OUT

Belasco's act four two-minute epilogue marks the departure of the lovers onto what Belasco describes as "the boundless prairies of the West. On the way East, at the dawn of a day about a week later."[39] Act four is a looking back at paradise following the couple's self-imposed expulsion. The setting carried heavy weight for Belasco, despite its brevity and brief text, apparent not least in the number of photographs he had shot of it, proportionally much larger than those taken of the other, far longer acts.

The dialogue is little more than an afterthought, giving excuse for the scenery, the accompanying music, and, above all, the lighting. The music is a reprise of the tune "Old Dog Tray," first heard at the play's start and one that Puccini will make good use of as well, at least so far as the text is concerned, though he chose a different melody. It is a song about the loss of home. In act one, it is the home back east that has been left; at the end, it is the West—which is to suggest that there is no home.

The principal "character" of act four is light, on which Belasco lavished a great deal of attention, not to mention money.[40] He understood light as a kind of hermeneutic medium marking the passage of time, through which changes are enacted—changes in his characters and changes in the nature that surrounds and shapes them. He employed light with great subtlety as regards both intensities and colors, which he conventionally carefully blended. Belasco's light is never static. In order to effect nuanced change, he used extreme care in both the placement and types of lighting. The result resonates with Bierstadt; for Belasco and Bierstadt alike, light is at once expressive, dramatic, and apparently symbolic, however vaguely, an abstract entity that serves to define a kind of spiritual essence of both men's sense of the western landscape.

As dawn breaks, the Girl tells her lover that the foothills are growing fainter, that soon they will be invisible. "That," she says, "was the Promised Land." Dick, rather less convincingly, assures her that "the promised land is always ahead," a remark that is coordinated with the first glimmer of the rising sun seen on the foothills' foliage. All the while, from first curtain of the act and then via a series of four gauze scrims rising one after another, the scene very gradually lightens, the sky blues, clouds roll slowly across the sky (projected from a stereopticon cloud machine), and shadows begin to form. The final, fourth gauze remains in place, keeping the scene in a kind of soft haze. Nowhere else in the play does Belasco call for this effect. By employing it here, the naturalism so consistently employed to this point throughout the play is retired; in its place, allegory is visually referenced as both time and space begin to be distanced. History retreats as we are reminded less of the past and more of loss, even as a new day dawns. The scrim emphasizes the allegorical function of the scene's lighting, a modern expulsion from the promised land intermixed with the American myth of dynamic striving, but tinged more with regret than any convincing sign of conventional optimism about lighting out for the territory. As the first rays break above the hills, the Girl acknowledges the new day: "The dawn is breaking in the East—far away—fair and clear," she intones. The lovers in turn acknowledge "a new life!" And then the Girl speaks her last lines as she moves to embrace Johnson one final time as the curtain falls: "Oh, my mountains—I'm leaving you—Oh, my California, I'm leaving you—Oh, my lovely West—my Sierras!—I'm leaving you! [Then turning to her lover, she closes] O, my—my home."[41] Minnie, dramatically gesturing (well captured in the act four

FIGURE 21
Belasco, *The Girl of the Golden West,* act four (epilogue). Billy Rose Theatre Division, The New York Public Library for the Performing Arts, Astor, Lenox, and Tilden Foundations.

FIGURE 22
Belasco, *The Girl of the Golden West,* act four (epilogue): postcard published by the Rotograph Company, New York. Private collection.

photographs; figs. 21 and 22), looks toward the distant mountains one last time, sadly acknowledging what she has surrendered.[42]

The ambiguity of the play's ending is made clearer in Belasco's novel. Acknowledging the personal paradise of the couple's mutual love, in the same breath Belasco describes their location "at the edge of the merciless desert, stretching away like a world without end."[43] He then elaborates: "The Girl had ever been a lover of nature. All her life the mystery and silences of the high mountains had appealed to her soul; but never until now had she

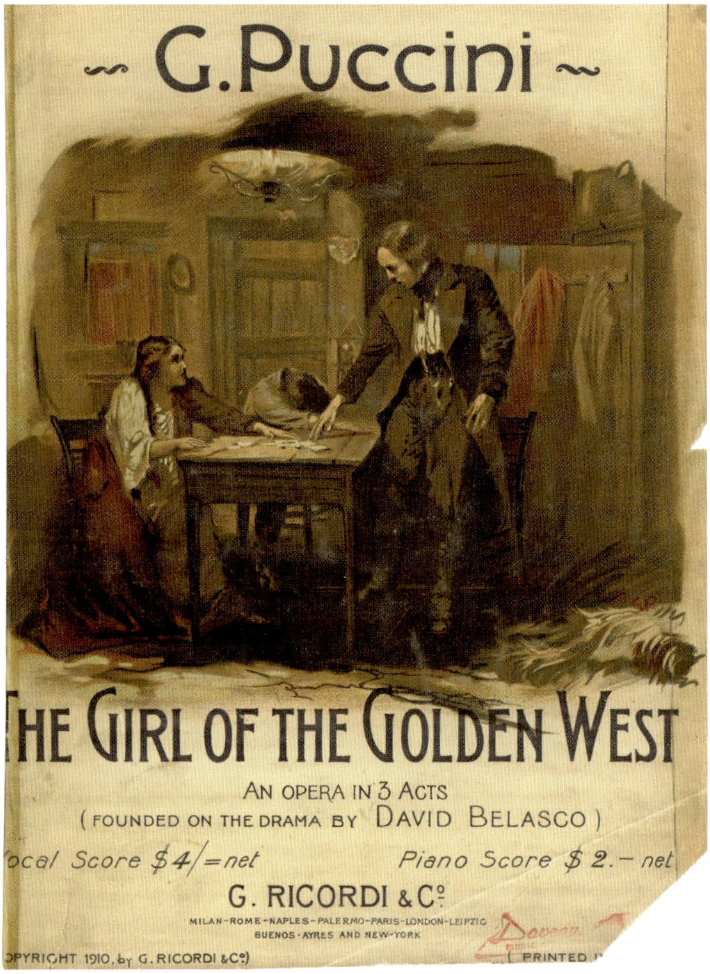

FIGURE 23
Giacomo Puccini (1858–1924), *The Girl of the Golden West* (Milan: G. Ricordi, 1910), piano-vocal score, cover illustration. Private collection.

realized the marvelous beauty and glory of the great plains. And yet, though her eyes shone with the wonder of it all, there was an unmistakably sad and reminiscent note in [her] voice."[44]

As she looks back on the faded view of the distant mountains, and as she acknowledges the need to look ahead, not back, her tone is one of "resignation." She thinks of all she has left, the people and the place, and thinks of them, as she puts it, "like shadows movin' in a dream—like shadows I've dreamt of."[45] Her words account for Belasco's use of the final scrim, keeping things hazy to the play's end.

PUCCINI'S ACOUSTIC WEST

La fanciulla del West (fig. 23) was the first world première in the history of the Metropolitan Opera, with music by the foremost living Italian composer. The stakes were high for all concerned; accordingly, no stone was left unturned to assure both notice and success.

Once the opera was secured for the Met (it was not a commission), the company's publicity apparatus was set in high gear, beginning already in May 1910, nearly nine months before the December 10 opening, the result being stories in many of the New York dailies.[46] The lengthy review of the first performance published in *Musical America* labors to reproduce an elevated sense of general anticipation. It opens as follows:

> New York, Saturday, Dec. 10, 1910—7 p.m.—In hundreds of homes of society people, singers, musicians, artists, authors, bankers, lawyers, doctors, business men, men-about-town, they are getting ready for an event. Fine gowns are being laid out, exquisite toilettes are being prepared, the finest jewels are brought forth from safety deposit vaults. Florists are rushing off orders. Not alone the musical and social world, but the great world of business, the world where men think of millions, has been moved to the core. Even cold-blooded "society" has determined to be in the opening and to forget for once the unwritten law which makes it "bad form" to appear in the "horseshoe" [of the Met's auditorium] before 9 p.m. [thereby staging a fashionably late entrance].[47]

The account of the evening makes clear that seemingly everyone of importance was present. By 8:15 P.M., the following:

> It is a most extraordinary and cosmopolitan audience! Sailing down the aisle with an immense diamond tiara is Mrs. Clarence Mackay, and not far from her is Andreas Dippel's beautiful wife. On another aisle you will see Louise Homer, the great singer, and her husband, the equally great composer.
>
> Presently as you look round again you will make up your mind that everybody who is anybody is here. Look up and you will see J. Pierpont Morgan in a box in the horseshoe. There sits Josef Hofmann, quite subdued, with his studious face; Mme. Gadski and her husband. Over there is Humperdinck, whose new opera, like Puccini's, will be produced for the first time in this very auditorium before many nights are over. In another place you see Blanche Bates, who created the original role of *Minnie* in the play. [And on it goes.][48]

The first performances, with Emmy Destinn (fig. 24), Caruso (fig. 25), and Pasquale Amato in the principal roles and Toscanini conducting, were a stunning success, with dozens of curtain calls for the cast and conductor, as well as for Puccini and Belasco, who had coached the acting of the principals and chorus.[49]

La fanciulla del West is an instantiation of the West of the imagination, though not with regard to a sonoric invocation of natural sounds but instead addressing nature's abstract temporal-spatial dimension in a state of crisis. The natural space—indeed, the natural paradise—of Puccini's West, like Belasco's, is mediated by the rawest form of cultural modernity registered in class distinction, ethnic and racial tension, economic destitution, jealousy, hatred, loneliness, greed, violence, and injustice. That is, in this opera the eternal sameness of a would-be perfect nature is confronted by modern history.

FIGURE 24
Emmy Destinn (1878–1930) as Minnie in *La fanciulla del West,* New York, Metropolitan Opera House (1910). Photo credit: The Metropolitan Opera Archives.

FIGURE 25
Enrico Caruso (1873–1921) as Dick Johnson in *La fanciulla del West,* New York, Metropolitan Opera House (1910). Photo credit: Washington, D.C., Library of Congress, Prints and Photographs Division.

The limitless *space* of nature meets modern *time*. This is the opera's modernity and of course its challenge to address.

Music has long played an important role in myriad practices associated with cultural and ethical assessments of time and its use or abuse. Music itself functions as a timing device, either to work with or against the clock time that in modernity so completely controls people's lives. Experienced *in* time and, in essence, *of* time, music invites a heightened experience of, but also an engagement with, temporality. Adorno once suggested that music has time as its problem and that its responsibility is to "act upon time, not lose itself to it."[50] In *La fanciulla del West* Puccini addresses time's impact on the civilizing process. The lengthy "Preliminary Note" appended to both the libretto and score describes the opera as "a drama of love and of moral redemption against a dark and vast background of primitive characters and untrammeled nature."[51] The opera, that is, works toward a reconciliation, but one, as it turns out, with a considerable price to pay.

Modernity emerged through the conjunction of space and time recognized as interrelated parameters for development—dynamism supplanting stasis. Since music is by definition both a temporal and spatial art, it is hardly surprising that it was early and often called upon to represent modernity—often to cheer modernity onward but sometimes to engage it critically. One response, often in protest, was the valorization of nature, increasingly placed in binary opposition to culture; this was especially evident in the music of the nineteenth century—the music, that is, that accompanied the industrial revolution and the hegemony of industrial capitalism.

Puccini noted that he intended his music as an evocation of the California primeval forest dominated by giant sequoias, in a mountain range that includes the highest peak on the continent outside of Alaska—none of which he had ever seen (he knew the Sierra Nevada from pictures; indeed, for the third act he provided his librettist with a postcard and photographs of the gigantic trees).[52] For Puccini, the West was experienced only at the greatest geographical and psychic distance, which itself may well have helped to provoke his fascination for it, alongside the challenge to invoke in sound a sense of its vastness as well as its seeming untamed essence—as it were, space remaining in the State of Nature.

In *La fanciulla del West,* Puccini had to deal with the seeming boundlessness of pristine western nature for the better part of two and a half hours, since everything that happens in the opera in one way or another is determined by this overwhelming setting; indeed, the characters themselves are transformed by the locale, which is largely foreign to them—until, at the end, the setting metaphorically morphs into the homeland that the lovers must leave, and very much against their will.

La fanciulla del West is different from Puccini's other mature works in that it begins with a one-minute prelude of thirty-four bars. Within that time frame Puccini introduces several tropes that govern the whole, foremost among which is an evocation less of nature than of nature's force, specifically in relation to human beings. The prelude constitutes a musical struggle, which in the end instantiates resolution but only in the final triumphant chord, introduced with an abruptness that does not fully convince.

EXAMPLE 1. Giacomo Puccini, *The Girl of the Golden West (La fanciulla del West)* (Milan: G. Ricordi, 1911), piano-vocal score, mm. 1–7, opening of prelude.

EXAMPLE 2. Puccini, *The Girl of the Golden West,* rehearsal no. 1, mm. 18–23, conclusion of prelude.

Marked *allegro non troppo, con fuoco,* the prelude begins almost brutally, a *fortissimo* with upward sweeping arpeggios, wind- and stormlike, climaxing on augmented chords held with fermatas, then falling back, only to repeat, in quick succession—all of it very un-Puccini-like, a kind of sonic calling card telling his auditors that what they are going to hear is not Puccini as usual. The prelude alternates among three musical ideas, the second, a whole-tone motif, associated with the lover's first kiss (act two, rehearsal no. 27 m. 3 and thereafter),[53] and it is this motif that gyrates in competition with the opening chords (ex. 1). The third motif, whose entrance is somewhat jarring, in syncopated cakewalk rhythm, is heard only three measures prior to the final chord; later it sounds again with the first appearance of Dick Johnson (ex. 2). The first two motifs unite nature with the Girl, less in competition and more to show what is immanent to both: strength, uncertainty, changeability, and forces that cannot be contained.[54] Into this alliance comes the man, rhythmically swaggering, a smart-ass know-it-all who, in a confrontation with both nature and the Girl, will himself be remade, be redeemed.

Everything about the prelude projects multiple acoustic instabilities—of nature, character, experience, and emotion.[55] The *tutti* ending, marked *violento,* ends on a C-major chord with considerable finality, which turns out to be ironic. No such musical triumph ends the opera. The final chord of act three, a barely audible E-major triad, played only by the first and second violins and bass, proclaims nothing and evokes only uncertainty. (In like fashion, the opera's first act concludes on a C-major chord, with the addition of the second and seventh scale degrees; in three bars the final chord diminishes from *fortississimo* to virtually inaudible, in apt reflection of all that remains unresolved.)[56]

La fanciulla del West, more than any other opera Puccini had previously written, is filled with dissonance, often with delayed resolutions or simply without resolution. Major and minor seconds and ninths are common, as are tritones. Vocal lines have wide tessituras (Minnie's is more than two octaves), and the vocal writing, especially for the Girl, is peppered with wide intervallic leaps. Vocal outbursts at high dynamic levels are common as well, more so with Minnie than with her lover, though he too is assigned passages of great drama. All of this carries over into the orchestra, Puccini's largest prior to *Turandot.*

The orchestra essentially serves as another character, something like a Greek chorus, whose musical metaphors are registered in the score with a striking range of markings, and especially ones that indicate force, violence, and brutality, as Mosco Carner has duly noted: *allegro incisivo, allegro brutale, allegro feroce, come gridi* (like shouts), *con strazio* (tearing), *robusto, strepitoso* (noisy, boisterous), *staccatissimo, martellato* (hammerlike), *marcatissimo,* and so on.[57] In like fashion, tempos change frequently, and the shifts deliver a jolt.

In brief, *La fanciulla del West* is an opera whose modernity is marked by instability and rapid change; accordingly, there are relatively few moments where action stops for the commentary typical of arias. Indeed, the lack of conventional arias was a regular complaint in the opera's early reception: Puccini did not sound like Puccini was supposed to, evident in the fact that very few of the opera's "numbers," apart from "Ch'ella mi creda," have been individually recorded.[58]

Puccini unquestionably understood tonality as a kind of sonic geography, a historical map tracing modern subjectivity and desire. But in *La fanciulla del West* he exploited tonal instabilities, laying bare his self-consciousness about the limits of conventionalized musical practice to represent the modern world. Sonically speaking, he recognized tonality's closing frontier and elected to head west, however tentatively, toward the outer boundary of the familiar, seeking the energy available at the margins of acoustic modernity.

The time was apparently ripe for this quest. Just a few years earlier, in 1905, Richard Strauss had done much the same thing in *Salome,* in which, however, the margins are sexual rather than geographical. As Lawrence Kramer has suggested, modernity is the subtext of the exotic distance of *Salome,* which places the opera at "modernity's cutting edge."[59] *La fanciulla del West* places a bet on modernity (and modernism) as well, although its investment in shock hardly achieves Strauss's level (no striptease, no severed head).

DISTANCE AND DISTANCING

Time, critical to the cultural discourse of *La fanciulla del West,* is compressed. Whereas Belasco's play involved the passage of a week, Puccini's opera unfolds in twenty-four hours, but it is not a day in the Aristotelian sense of dramatic unities. Puccini's time compression is one manifesting the urgencies of what Benjamin later coined as *Jetztzeit,* a Now-Time that exceeds what is contained in the concept of *Gegenwart.*[60] The opera's time compression, in sync with the rapidity of change in modernity, is neither celebratory nor historicist.

Among the musical devices that define the opera's allegory, one in particular stands out. Puccini made the decision to evoke the vast California wilderness by producing for his audience a sense of distance, and by that means to articulate not only space but also—and crucially—time and memory. Puccini's West, above all, evokes time through space; it is this relation that controls his understanding of the West's essence—as would be the case a generation later in the films of John Ford, albeit by means of the backdrop of Utah and Arizona's Monument Valley rather than the Sierra Nevada.

The opera's characters enter as if in a never-never land: when they arrive, they bring history with them; when they leave, history exits as well. What remains is a natural paradise, yet it is a paradise only so long as it is unpeopled: when it is only imagined or remembered. Puccini marks the phenomenological spatial excess that defines everything important about the opera by means of what I will call the fade-in and fade-out. Repeatedly, his characters are heard acousmatically well before they are seen on stage, and the voices are invariably on the move, as though making their way through the deep forest. Indeed, the opera's first voices come from offstage, what Puccini describes as *voci lontane,* distant voices, and to achieve this effect he sometimes altered what Belasco called for in the play and later described in his novel.[61] Thus at the opera's start, and at a distance, the miners returning to camp late at night boisterously greet each other with hellos, and then one of them quotes a tuneful lament, also about distance—and loss: "Là lontano, là lontan, quanto piangerà! . . . " (roughly: "Back home, far away, she'll cry for me"). This same trope is soon thereafter repeated, and amplified, in one of the opera's few real arias, "Che faranno i vecchi miei."[62] Choosing an aria form, one whose character is strikingly simple and folklike, in an opera that otherwise virtually abandons conventional arias, marks a past, a history—here musical—that the opera itself musically supersedes. The aria is the most strikingly old-fashioned music in the entire opera, a nostalgic sonic look-back. It is sung, *andante tranquillo,* by the camp minstrel, one Jake Wallace, a character based on a camp singer whom Belasco knew from his youth in California.[63] In the play, Jake Wallace is inside the Polka saloon when he sings his song.[64] In the opera, by contrast, Jake starts the song as he approaches slowly from offstage. He is physically distant from the homely saloon, and what he sings immediately marks *lontano,* in a slow-moving and sorrowful lament about faraway home, sad parents, and a faithful dog that might no longer recognize him. Before long, the rest of the men echo the lament in chorus, the previous hard-edged boisterousness turned soft (act one, rehearsal nos. 20–22). The loss, that is, is general, just as the distance is

EXAMPLE 3. Puccini, *The Girl of the Golden West,* act two, "Un baccio, un baccio almen!," rehearsal no. 26, mm. 10–19.

overwhelming, to the point that one of the miners, young Larkens, breaks down crying. The song's sentiment, its *lontano,* its distance, marks a general condition. What begins the opera, as it turns out, will be precisely what will end it as well.[65]

TURNING IN CIRCLES

By the opera's end, Minnie is a woman, no longer the child of nature who in act two tells Dick about her innocent life in the mountains, galloping her pony among the flowers—flora that do not in fact grow in the Sierra Nevada (Belasco gets the plants right; Puccini's librettist cluelessly substitutes jonquils and carnations and, for good measure, adds jasmine and vanilla).[66] Minnie's morph, however, begins much earlier. In the first act, she and Dick come together physically for the first time in a dance, a ritual metaphor of love and lovemaking, in essence establishing a bond that will make a new home—later, if temporarily, staged in the second act where the relationship is sealed with a fateful kiss, one duly and dramatically marked in the orchestra and by Minnie's high-C reaction (ex. 3). In the play, Minnie declines a waltz, saying she doesn't know how. Instead she polkas, or as she puts it, "polkys."[67] William Furst, Belasco's composer, initiates a waltz tune at first mention of that dance, only to break it off for the livelier and rather less romantic polka. Puccini dispenses altogether with the polka, writes a waltz, and alters the story further by having the Girl apologize that she has never once previously danced

EXAMPLE 4. Puccini, *The Girl of the Golden West,* act one, waltz (second iteration), rehearsal no. 86, mm. 1–6.

at all. She is nonetheless game, and, to the accompaniment of the men singing along softly and clapping the rhythm, the pair comes together. The tune as first sounded, to which Minnie and Dick dance, is folksy and disarmingly simple—to a fault. As the miners chime along, even lightly tapping their feet as they sing and clap, the orchestra softly evokes the rhythms associated with the gliding and whirling movements common to the dance. Dick and Minnie literally turn in circles, the uncertain outcome of their "progress" thus duly marked, even though they cannot take their eyes off each other.

The waltz marks a future and potential. The simple tune, like the budding relationship between the man and the woman, can become much more than it currently is, and the tune can be the acoustic vehicle for both producing and reflecting the change. The cultural associations between love and the waltz are soon thereafter exploited, as soon as the lovers-to-be are alone for the first time near the end of the act. Here the melody immediately gains the character necessary for advancing the relationship. It's first heard in the orchestra, with a sweet edge provided by seconds in quarter-note suspension. The waltz has become lovely and, in a word, poignant (ex. 4, mm. 5–6). Soon thereafter, in a one-minute arietta, Dick sings the entire melody to Minnie, with a text that speaks of dancing, hearts, trembling, and strange joy. In essence, taking the lead in the ritual dance of love, he acknowledges the thrill of sensing her trembling during their embrace. The tune, first heard in E major for the dancing, migrates to A major for the second iteration, and finally to G-flat as the arietta (ex. 5). In Belasco's play, at the moment when the Girl sets eyes on Dick, her first utterance is an inarticulate "H'mp!," followed quickly by a single word: "Utopia!"[68] Puccini's waltz accomplishes the same effect, but rather more gradually.

AMBIGUITY

Distance is evoked throughout the opera, and to its very conclusion. Thus, near the end, Minnie, at first singing offstage as if from some distance, rides into the scene astride a

EXAMPLE 5. Puccini, *The Girl of the Golden West,* act one, waltz melody as arietta, "Quello che tacete me," rehearsal no. 104, mm. 1–6.

horse, accompanied in the orchestra by a repeated staccato rhythm meant to resonate with the sounds of the galloping animal.[69] Her voice, audible well before she herself is visible, dramatically excites the miners (act three, rehearsal no. 29 m. 1 to 31 m. 8). Sheriff Rance, sensing an impending rescue, repeatedly demands that Johnson be hanged immediately.

The rescue comes, of course, and that triggers a final *lontano,* but in this last instance, what has been near will now become far; accordingly, sound will little by little fade away to nothing. In other words, the opera is book-ended by two forms of distance and distanc*ing*. At the start, action and history, so to speak, come onstage for us to experience; sounds get louder, becoming increasingly audible. At the end, distance increases and action ceases into a staged stasis once the lovers depart, their voices trailing off into the haze of history.

In each of the three acts, offstage voices reach our consciousness as if from nowhere, from great distances, slowly—ever so slowly—approaching the acoustic proscenium separating opera from audience. In one sense, the obvious one, they approach camp from working their staked claims, but in another sense, they approach as if being recalled from a faded memory of a time long past—spatial and temporal nostalgia in the heart of bustling 1910 Midtown, the epicenter of industrialized modernity in its prewar self-satisfied self-confidence.[70] The gap between the New York setting of the world premiere and the scene onstage, in the first really major opera about America, carries a significant ideological burden. The vastness of the opera's natural setting holds out the promise of an American paradise: eternal, without boundaries, a utopia of striking visual splendor—and this despite the fact that the old-growth forests of the Sierra Nevada had already long since been savaged (figs. 26–28). In other words, Puccini's West of the imagination, aesthetically speaking, provides modernity's rapaciousness with the deniability it ethically craved.[71]

The voices in the wilderness and from the past make their appearances, speak their peace—and then vocally fade away. Puccini's repeated use of motifs from "Echoes of Home" more or less constitutes the opera's defining leitmotif, the citation marking a perfect coincidence of time, space, and place, on the one hand, and memory in relation to loss, separation, and alienation, on the other.[72]

FIGURE 26

"Cutting down the big trees—a group of ax-men sitting in the undercut—Converse Basin, California" (c. 1902), published by Underwood & Underwood, New York. Washington, D.C., Library of Congress, Prints and Photographs Division.

FIGURE 27

"A Giant Sequoia Log" (undated), Generals Highway, Three Rivers, Tulare County, California. Washington, D.C., Library of Congress, Prints and Photographs Division.

FIGURE 28
"Ending a life of centuries, a giant tree falling, logging among the big trees, Converse Basin, California" (1902), stereograph, published by Underwood & Underwood, New York. Robert N. Dennis Collection of Stereoscopic Views, Miriam and Ira D. Wallach Division of Arts, Prints and Photographs, The New York Public Library, Astor, Lenox, and Tilden Foundations.

The third act of the play is set in the dance hall attached to the Polka saloon. Puccini set his final act in a forested wilderness. (Roughly speaking, Puccini collapsed Belasco's third and fourth acts, eliminating much of the third.) But in this instance nature matters so much that an overdetermined invocation is essential. As he put it to Giulio Ricordi: "I have a grand scenario in mind, a clearing in the great Californian forest, with colossal trees" (fig. 29).[73]

The opera's ending, a departure, is, perforce, "happy." The scene occurs at dawn with the sunrise, thus reversing the sunset with which the opera opened.[74] Minnie, whom we hear well before we see her, rides in, vocalizing her desperation and fury, Valkerie-like—in essence so as to ride off forever with her lover. (As every operagoer knows all too well, Puccini conventionally killed off his sopranos, whereas no one actually dies in *La fanciulla del West,* odd for a western.) Sonora, one of the miners, helps to convince his mates that the lovers are deserving; he hands off Dick to Minnie, fittingly to fragmentary strains in the orchestra from the act one waltz music (act three, rehearsal no. 44 mm.1–5). The lovers astride their horses slowly depart, their voices only very gradually fading as the dawn breaks. In short, the lovers move forward into time and history—but not necessarily with a sense of new beginnings. The audience is left less with a climax and more with the dynamic decay and inevitable disappearance of music itself. With the music's fading, as the miners lament Minnie's loss via a fragment of tune from Jake Wallace's act one "Old Dog Tray," the opera's own time fades into the timelessness of the vast forest that swallows up the departed lovers, who themselves head off into uncertainty, and in duet:

FIGURE 29
Giacomo Puccini, *La fanciulla del West,* New York, Metropolitan Opera House (1910), act three. Photo credit: The Metropolitan Opera Archives.

Addio, mia dolce terra!
Addio, mia California!
Bei monti della Sierra, nevi, addio!

The distinctive and often dissonant rhythmic percussiveness that marks much of the opera, and which delineates the real time experienced by the characters—modernity's freneticism, or something like that—fades into a virtually rhythmless drone in the orchestra's strings, as the lovers' voices trail off above this line. They fade, like time and like memory; next to nature, they are nothing. Nonetheless, as they voice their goodbyes to their beloved California, what is striking is less the happy reunion of the young lovers—that fact seems rather an afterthought—and far more the sense that their mutual terrestrial salvation comes at a high price: their expulsion from a natural paradise that they had experienced in a perpetual state of paradox, if not dialectical contradiction.[75] All that's left are the ageless trees, timeless like the mountains.[76]

The grand allegory that Puccini alleges represents the civilizing process, which is notably akin to what some years later Horkheimer and Adorno articulated as the defining moment of Western consciousness of what it is to be human. To be human, they suggested—that is, to be civilized—had been worked out at considerable cost. As they put it:

> At the moment when human beings cut themselves off from the consciousness of themselves as nature, all the purposes for which they keep themselves alive—social progress, the heightening of material and intellectual forces, indeed, consciousness itself—become void, and the enthronement of the means as the end, which in late capitalism is taking on the character of overt madness, is already detectable in the earliest history of subjectivity. The human being's mastery of itself, on which the self is founded, practically always involves the annihilation of the subject in whose service that mastery is maintained.[77]

Puccini's opera, and for that matter Belasco's play, acknowledge the reality that the civilizing process is not a guarantee of progress. Puccini's Sierra Nevada itself reflects a wish rather than a reality. The forests of his imagination have not already been clear-cut, as was in fact the case; the landscape has not been mined for all it could give up in favor of the closing of the frontier. In one sense, of course, both Puccini and Belasco acknowledge this reality, if indirectly. They make their characters leave the promised land, thereby preserving the dialectic: Nature-Culture, barbaric-civilized, binaries whose collapse can be imagined but whose realization remains at best not more than a distant probability, perhaps ever out of reach.

2

OPERA, AESTHETIC VIOLENCE, AND THE IMPOSITION OF MODERNITY

Fitzcarraldo

I consider opera a universe all its own . . . a complete world, a cosmos transformed into music.

WERNER HERZOG, *HERZOG ON HERZOG*

The operatic world is, whatever else, a world of magic invocations.

SIEGFRIED KRACAUER, *THEORY OF FILM: THE REDEMPTION OF PHYSICAL REALITY*

Werner Herzog's *Fitzcarraldo* (1982), set in the Peruvian Amazon sometime near the turn of the last century, tells the story of an Irishman of uncertain class standing, a passionate lover of opera who wants to build an opera house in the frontier town of Iquitos—a theater to rival the opera house in Manaus, the product of European rubber-baron largesse.[1] Fitzcarraldo intends for Caruso to inaugurate his theater. First, however, he's got to make some money. In the remote jungle, far from Iquitos, there lies a heretofore inaccessible and vast tract of land rich in rubber trees. One impediment stands in his way of reaching it, the wickedly impassable Pongo das Mortes rapids, deep in a gorge of the Ucayali River, an Amazon tributary. Fitzcarraldo hopes to overcome this challenge by first traveling upstream on the Pachitea River, another Amazon tributary that closely parallels the Ucayali; indeed, at one point the two rivers virtually meet, save for a steep hill separating them. Fitzcarraldo will pull his riverboat up this hill and down the other side, thereby reaching the Ucayali. By this means, having bypassed the rapids, he will then steam downstream to his rubber-tree tract and its awaiting fortune. The engineering challenge of moving a 350-ton riverboat overland is surpassed only by the challenge of pacifying a dangerously hostile indigenous population.[2] The raison d'être of the endeavor is opera, and the means to this end is opera as well; not only does opera provide the inspiration to meet the engineering challenge, but it also, and more importantly, will be the means by which the Indians are (temporarily) subdued.

MUSICS AND SOUND

The film employs four kinds of music, two of which are used nondiegetically and two diegetically, with virtually no overlap between the pairs. The principal nondiegetic music is provided by a purpose-composed score by Florian Fricke and his ensemble, Popol Vuh, a band that is also responsible for the music in several of Herzog's other films, including *Aguirre, der Zorn Gottes* (1972) and *Nosferatu—Phantom der Nacht* (1979). Popol Vuh's music comes off as a kind of ambient wall of sound whose acoustic vastness is matched by the vagueness of its cultural sources. The rampantly hybrid (not to say pastiche) quality of the music, something like New Age meets Orff, has an air of the ritualistic tempered with an off-the-shelf mysteriousness that is at once worldly and not. The music effects timelessness, if only on account of the mix of sounds that cancel out historical and cultural specificity. Throughout the film Herzog uses Popol Vuh's music as a discursive accompaniment to nature, nearly always represented in dire opposition to culture.

The only other nondiegetic music in the film is heard fleetingly. When the riverboat heads upriver for its fateful encounter with "nature"—setting out for, and later departing from, the last European settlement, a missionary outpost—brief excerpts from Richard Strauss's *Tod und Verklärung* play softly as background accompaniment.[3] The choice is apt, to the extent that Fitzcarraldo has now entered into the lived space of the Indians. As Fitzcarraldo proceeds, the threat of physical *Tod* becomes increasingly real; but the actual *Tod* will be that of Fitzcarraldo's dream, which becomes the inadvertent vehicle for the *Verklärung* of the Indians' dream, one entirely different from his. As the riverboat leaves the mission outpost, hence approaches the last remnant of "civilization," Strauss's music is accompanied by a thunderstorm and lightning as the sky darkens and the sun sets. In short, the trope announced by the composition's title is both aurally and visually overdetermined.

Throughout the film, Fricke's nondiegetic score is often abruptly intercut with the diegetic music principally provided by Italian opera. These two sound masses, radically different from one another, establish an acoustic binary that in turn underscores the design of the film's nature/culture narrative. Herzog also uses small bits of indigenous and pseudo-indigenous music, but it's opera that matters most. Opera determines the narrative, defines the antiheroic hero, and, not least, provides a commentary to the story of which it is a determinant. Opera is staged, "live" (in scare quotes), at the beginning and end of the film. At six other points opera is referenced, almost exclusively as part of the narrative action, via a wind-up, lotus-horn gramophone. (In only one instance does the diegetic use of the gramophone briefly morph toward the nondiegetic, and in only one instance, also brief, is operatic music used nondiegetically.) For the purposes of this chapter, although I will comment on Herzog's use of nativelike music, I will say nothing more about Popol Vuh's music (despite there being a good deal to be said). Most of what I have to say will concern Herzog's use of opera in *Fitzcarraldo,* concerning which I'll restrict the discussion to the live-action staged scenes that open and close the film, and to three of the six episodes where the gramophone is employed.

FIGURE 30
Werner Herog (director), *Fitzcarraldo* (1982), title, with Teatro Amazonas Opera House, Manaus, Brazil (1:15).

Herzog's story for *Fitzcarraldo* connects the Peruvian Amazon to an incomplete, timeless space seemingly caught in the ahistoric moment of its creation. The film's first visual is a static distance shot of the jungle, darkly green, functioning like a curtain that is about to be raised on the epic stage of the Amazon Basin, where a romantic parable will be played out in quasi-documentary style. The first "event" is acoustic—audible but invisible: thunder, in sonic allusion to trouble and change. The electrical discharge has no visual referent; we can hear what we cannot see, a hint that the film is literally about acoustic realities. Visual stasis is succeeded by a slow pan of the jungle shrouded in fog; the curtain, as it were, becomes a scrim. We see enough to know that we're not seeing what is there to be seen. The camera moves from the pan to a slow zoom into the "face" of the jungle, only to confirm its visual impenetrability,[4] an effect that overdetermines the sense of the invisibility that plagues seeing.[5] Herzog then cuts to the façade of the Manaus opera house, shot from below from the bottom of a long stairway. The opera house sits high like a gigantic altar, a site of art worship, whereupon the sacrifice of nature to culture will be celebrated (fig. 30).

POSSIBLE IMPOSSIBILITY

The logical "impossibility" that lies at the heart of opera organizes the film's logic. Opera is the film's form and its content. Opera as both an institution and sonic manifestation defines the film's narrative structure, particularly its overtly exaggerated situations, as

FIGURE 31
Sarah Bernhardt (1844–1923). Photo credit: Washington, D.C., Library of Congress, Prints and Photographs Division.

well as the character of its principal protagonist. Fitzcarraldo himself is operatically larger than life, and a man obsessed to hear life sung; every narrative element in the film revolves around this urgent need. As Fitzcarraldo puts it, "Opera gives expression to our greatest feelings."[6] Indeed, the function of spoken language in the film is wholly instrumental: its purpose is to lead to song.[7]

As the action begins, Fitzcarraldo, together with his lover, Molly, is furiously paddling his small boat into Manaus, after traveling 1,200 miles on the river, including two days at the end with a broken-down motor. They reach the opera house and Fitzcarraldo begs their way in just in time to see the performance conclude. It's *Ernani*. Caruso is performing the title role, and it's Caruso whom Fitzcarraldo came to hear, for the first time in his life. It's obviously a special performance, all the more so because the role of Elvira is performed by none other than Sarah Bernhardt (fig. 31), who mimes her part.[8] (The "soprano" whose voice Bernhardt lip-syncs is visible, in concert attire, well off to the side, though she too attracts some attention with her gesturing.)[9]

This scene was staged for Herzog by Werner Schroeter, who besides being a filmmaker already had experience directing opera, unlike Herzog at the time. Schroeter created a surreal, multiply overdetermined dream world on a stage illuminated in luridly saturated colors and peopled by actors who perform with intense emotion the ridiculous text Verdi has assigned them.

Ernani (1844) is early Verdi, his fifth opera, premiered five years after his first. Herzog's original plan had called for *Un ballo in maschera* (1859), a mature work whose plot—itself fairly ridiculous—is nonetheless positively Shakespearean by comparison with the abundantly ludicrous goings-on in *Ernani*. For that matter, the plot of Bellini's *I puritani*, used for the film's final scene, is equally absurd.[10] Indeed, epic-quality improbability constitutes the film's cultural logic, a point Herzog is keen to establish from the very start.[11] Although *Ernani's* tragic story is a triumph of nearly cosmic risibility, its score is often stunningly beautiful and a perfect vehicle for a great singer—here, Caruso—but one whose acting abilities are limited to stock gestures signaling the intensity of his passions. The now-ancient nonsinging Bernhardt, who not coincidentally lip-syncs atrociously (hinting that she barely knows her part), does everything within her powers of pantomime to draw attention to herself and away from Caruso.[12] She grandiosely performs the part of a Elvira, a would-be bride, decades after any amount of careful lighting and cosmetics could provide her credibility. Her heavy makeup, ghostly and ghastly, makes her visually arresting and commanding of attention, but in a haggish way, like an aged Salomé in a fright-wig.[13] Bernhardt, in life rail thin and just over five feet tall, here physically dominates the short Caruso. In sum, Schroeter represents her as a consummate ham, more a character fit for the music hall than a star of the legitimate stage.[14]

The mute actor playing the aged Bernhardt is a cross-dressed male,[15] poorly disguised—and that's exactly the point (fig. 32). Bernhardt essentially proclaims her transvestism, as it were, as the open secret of the surface foundation of opera's dream world.[16] Opera, especially as staged here, drives home the point that what we see (real fakery) claims little authority over what we can hear (the centrality of song). Thus the performance of *Ernani* is live, but all of it is *obviously* in playback. Bernhardt's mouth doesn't come close to fitting the text she purportedly sings (this is part of the diegesis); but then neither does the mouth of Caruso or that of the "real soprano" performing Elvira's role offstage (fig. 33). (The ventriloquism of Caruso and the off-stage soprano is plainly visible and hence discursive.) To complete the point, an actor plays Caruso playing Ernani; the actor's voice is neither Caruso's nor his own, but that of another singer whose performance he mimes.

We have our first look at the performance, in media res, as the aged Bernhardt, portraying one half of a romantic couple, missing her cue, enters the scene too soon at the top of a very long curved staircase; she checks herself, backs out of sight momentarily, and then reappears, but with arms outstretched as though she were confusing Elvira with Lucia and about to do a mad scene for the benefit of its heightened dramatic impact. Bernhardt's right leg was amputated in 1914, a biographical fact that Schroeter exploits vigorously. On the way down the stairs she moves haltingly, nearly stumbling, troubled by her prosthesis, but averting disaster, if barely. Her exaggerated clumsiness visually

FIGURE 32
Herzog, *Fitzcarraldo:* cross-dressed "Sarah Bernhardt" miming Elvira, together with Caruso, in *Ernani* (7:04).

FIGURE 33
Herzog, *Fitzcarraldo:* soprano in the orchestra pit singing the part of Elvira for Sarah Bernhardt, who mimes the role onstage (8:43).

degrades to near slapstick the overwrought drama of the approach to her lover, where, shortly thereafter, she will enact her own death. Verdi gives Elvira a faint at the end of *Ernani,* but Bernhardt, not to be upstaged by Caruso's text-authorized death scene, seizes his exceedingly large dagger after he stabs himself and impales herself in his footsteps, in a free adaptation that serves better her purposes. Bernhardt is played as a renowned actress who cannot bear to be upstaged by someone who laid claim to being the world's then-greatest voice. Indeed, she even tries to upstage him during the curtain calls—to Caruso's obvious irritation, as Schroeter is careful to represent.

Managing to gain admittance to *Ernani* just before its conclusion, Fitzcarraldo and Molly witness the operatic hero's self-inflicted death, a matter of profoundly misplaced homosocial, hypermasculine honor. On his wedding day, with a masked ball in progress and at the last possible moment, rival Silva sounds the hunting horn that signals to Ernani that he must kill himself to keep a promise made in the second act for reasons too foolish to require detailing here. Suffice to say that Silva blows the horn, and Ernani, true to his word, kills himself, as his bride-to-be stands helplessly by (though not, of course, silently).[17]

When Ernani/Caruso dies, he reaches out his hand toward the audience, a stock gesture that Fitzcarraldo and Molly both misread as Caruso personally passing opera's torch to the dream-beguiled Irishman. From that point forward, Fitzcarraldo recognizes no worldly impediment to his goal of bringing Caruso to his own personal part of the jungle.

Fitzcarraldo is a man in the middle. He hates the established bourgeois colonizers, whom he regards as vulgar. They're interested in rubber for money; he wants rubber for opera—just as he wants opera for the "natives," and the children especially. To bring opera to the Indians, he will colonize them, as it were for their own good. He'll become a rubber baron for art's sake. Fitzcarraldo's quest, driven by opera, is no less absurd than the heroics of *Ernani,* and no less credible than the sonorous passion of the hapless lovers singing their hearts out. It's all mad, *and* it's all perfectly congruent with that which it defines and simultaneously aestheticizes: atavistic romanticism in deep denial of what its own denials of rapacious modernity in turn help to authorize, stabilize, and reproduce. The very Indians who will benefit from Caruso in the wilderness are the ones he sarcastically calls "bare asses," picking up the lingo of the colonial Europeans he otherwise despises. The Indians are the laborers who will build his aesthetic pyramid—one constructed on what, to all *appearances* at least, is a foundation of cultural kitsch.[18] That is, Schroeter's staging of *Ernani* fundamentally comes off as a good deal less than the high art Fitzcarraldo himself considers it. In Schroeter's account, it's on a par with the music hall: overwrought and borderline camp, but at the same time utterly sincere in its multiple levels of exaggeration. The point, obviously enough, is that Schroeter and Herzog stage opera as a carnival-mirror reflection of modernity whose truth lies precisely in distortion.[19] Thus, the apparent *lack* of synchronous sound (a purposeful device Schroeter has vigorously exploited in a number of his own films), here produced by the consistently bad lip-syncing by everyone purporting to sing, produces a yawning gap between image and soundtrack. Any discursive semiotic overdetermination that might emerge from the synchronicity of sound and vision is denied, and obviously so.[20]

Herzog kept a journal throughout the advance preparation and filming of *Fitzcarraldo.* On April 14, 1981, he scribbled the following: "I was reading the translation of Piave's libretto of *Ernani,* published in Zurich in 1952, and in the foreword I came upon the breathtakingly idiotic comment that the most blatantly unbelievable passages had been deleted—when in fact it is precisely the incredible elements that account for the beauty of the story, or rather of opera as a genre, because those elements that cannot be accounted for even by the most exotic probability calculations appear in opera as the most natural, thanks to the powerful transformations of an entire world into music."[21]

OPERA AND TECHNOLOGY

The role of technology, as a fundamental constituent of modernity, helps to organize the film's narrative; technology, as a component part of the story, accounts in part for the documentary look of *Fitzcarraldo.* Herzog lavishes visual and sonoric attention on equipment and how, by means of equipment, things get done, in particular, of course, the lifting of the boat over the hill, a conceit that becomes literally real, since Herzog eschewed special effects in making this happen. (Herzog has stated that the scene was intended to have the quality of farce, specifically *despite* its actuality. He has also referred to the scene as "having the quality of Italian Opera.")[22] However crucial engineering know-how is to the success of Fitzcarraldo's endeavor, the technology of sound recording is, if anything, still greater.

As the riverboat, christened *Molly Aïda,* steams deeper into country seldom visited by Europeans, the signs of acute danger from hostile Indians increase, culminating in the sounds of mass chanting and drumming (though in fact it's African drumming, not lowland Peruvian, that Herzog employs).[23] Fitzcarraldo refuses to answer with the boat's cannon, the usual acoustic certificate of authority and overwhelming power, to silence the unseen Indians' drums and voices. Instead, he sets up a gramophone on the roof of the pilothouse. Herzog briefly shoots the gramophone in a close-up, stationary and secure against the shifting green backdrop of the passing jungle. "Now," Fitzcarraldo says, "it's Caruso's turn"—and the turntable is put in motion. The music insistently wafts across the water, a reflective natural amplifier permitting Caruso's voice to penetrate the jungle, spiritlike, and reach the ears of the Indians who, though they can be plainly heard, cannot be seen. The acoustic claim of the Indians is thus answered by "Il sogno" from Massenet's *Manon,* the second-act aria in which des Grieux relates to Manon a dream he's had of happiness in the country.[24] In his dream he is surrounded by beautiful nature, but his happiness is nonetheless incomplete because Manon herself is absent.

The aria fits the scene. Caruso, as Fitzcarraldo's alter ego, calls out to a Euro-feminized Nature, the Woman of the forest and the Indians, which he is prepared to make his own. For a few moments, the two musics compete, while Fitzcarraldo stands next to his gramophone, shot from behind as he looks into the green curtain of the jungle. Gradually, however, the sounds of chanting and drumming cease.[25] The mood of Fitzcarraldo, standing next to the revolving turntable, shifts from anxiety to confidence; he puts his hands on his hips in a kind of self-satisfied gloat while Caruso reaches melodic, and authoritative, climax. Thus the gramophone, built for and suited to the domestic parlor, merges into the public realm of Eden, with a voice that "speaks" with the authority of the Word made musical. The claim of music—of the Western variety—as the universal "language" plays out here, if only in Fitzcarraldo's lunatic dream, as acoustic conquistador (fig. 34). During the filming, Herzog noted in his journal that "the Grand Emotions in opera, often dismissed as over the top, strike me on the contrary as the most concentrated pure archetypes of emotion, whose essence is incapable of being condensed any further. They are axioms of emotions. That is what opera and the jungle have in common."[26]

Melody and harmony conquer rhythm. Culture, serviced by technology, trumps nature—or so Fitzcarraldo thinks. Caruso silences the Indians and then pulls them into visibility, out of the jungle and onto the river in their dugouts, a kind of watery Pied Piper. (In this regard, Fitzcarraldo's gramophone shares a functional relation with the stereo

FIGURE 34
Herzog, *Fitzcarraldo:* Caruso on the gramophone "silences" the Indian drumming (1:17:18).

system onboard Kilgore's attack helicopter in *Apocalypse Now,* except that Caruso attracts, whereas the acoustic blasts of *Die Walküre* repel and terrify.) The impact of Caruso is driven by technology and, indeed, would be impossible in technology's absence: in modernity, the voice is invariably mediated; it is never "natural"—not even when "live" in the opera house, as I have already suggested. In *Fitzcarraldo,* the social agency of opera is dialectically twinned with the social agency of technology.

There is a short scene early in the film involving Fitzcarraldo, in his hut by the river in Iquitos, relaxing on a bed and watched by a group of children, boys and girls, hovering near him. He smiles at them, reaches over and sets his gramophone spinning, and places the needle onto a Caruso record ("Vesti la giubba," from *Pagliacci*).[27] As Caruso's voice is first heard in recitative leading to the aria, Fitzcarraldo pulls himself to the bed's edge and looks down at the floor; the camera has pulled in tight, so we can't see what he's looking at as he begins to speak: "When I build my opera house, I'll see to it you have your own box and a velvet armchair." The camera then tilts down to show us that he is speaking to and stroking the snout of his pet pig, which grunts in apparent delight.

The children stare intently at the gramophone, though what most fascinates them—whether the apparatus itself or Caruso's voice—is unclear (fig. 35). Fitzcarraldo smiles as he watches the children's reactions, clearly assuming it is the aria that mesmerizes them. Above all, however, the most striking, deeply ironic impact of the scene is the conflation established in Fitzcarraldo's psyche between his opera-loving pig and the innocent but "uncivilized" children he has managed to draw near to him, virtually as though they too were pets, though metaphorically they remain "bare-asses."[28] Direct allusion to this scene returns near the end of the film, almost as though it were a kind of framing device. Planning his first and final staging of opera, *I puritani* aboard the *Molly Aïda,* he orders Paul, the boat's pilot, to go to Manaus and take from the opera house an armchair "with red velvet upholstery," explaining that "I made a promise to a pig that loves Caruso very much." That armchair, though not the pig, is well featured in the final scenes, Fitzcarraldo standing next to it as the performance plays out and the film ends.

FIGURE 35
Herzog, *Fitzcarraldo:* Indian children hear Caruso on Fitzcarraldo's gramophone (18:47).

Throughout the narrative, Fitzcarraldo evokes only Caruso's name, despite the fact that the music he plays on his gramophone is for the most part Caruso in ensemble—as is the case in the staged opera scenes that begin and end the film. The other ensemble voice parts are prominently those of women. They don't seem to matter much to Fitzcarraldo; he never once refers to them, though he does of course name his boat after an ancient operatic princess, as well as after Molly, a brothel keeper. When all is said and done, he hears only Caruso. Indeed, the women's vocal presence marks the absence of women in the film generally (Molly's rather small supporting role notwithstanding), except to the extent that embodied women serve as iterations of the feminine-nature trope—that is, as the foil that Fitzcarraldo both figuratively and literally penetrates.[29] In short, the feminine is displaced as nature, but as well the feminine is imagined *in* music and *as* music. It is the feminine "voice" of music, on which Fitzcarraldo focuses his most urgent desires (the desires he has for Molly, on the other hand, are barely bothered with). The real point is that music, which long played the role of Eternal Feminine in European consciousness, makes itself heard through the gender-colonized agency of a man's voice. The singing women are there to fill in the harmonies or, perhaps better stated, to make things harmonious.

Caruso's voice competes with the background noise common to shellac disks, the effect of which is to remind us of the modern technology upon which latter-day art worship rests, a worship that for Fitzcarraldo otherwise functions as a profound critique of that very modernity for which Caruso acts as antidote. In particular, the singer's muffled voice, the tinny-sounding small orchestra accompanying him, and the disk noise, not to mention the riverboat's engine (alternately subdued or heightened via Foley sound, as demanded by the context), together emphasize the technological authority brought to bear against mere nature, including the "natural" folk of the jungle. For Fitzcarraldo, that is, Caruso on shellac is His Master's Voice to the Irishman's Nipper; and what's good enough for Nipper will do fine for anyone else within earshot.[30] Whatever Fitzcarraldo introjects will in turn be shared by an uncompromising projection/transference, as it were, on waves of music.

FIGURE 36
Herzog, *Fitzcarraldo:* the *Molly Aïda* pulled up the hill (2:08.12).

This is to suggest that the cultural hegemony claimed by Caruso on the gramophone in the "wilderness" is overdetermined (if, in the end, oversubscribed by Fitzcarraldo himself). The Indians hear a voice from somewhere, but it's from nowhere they can recognize; the singing voice makes strange claims as it bares its soul in order to colonize theirs. Caruso's singing foretells, with the authority of an untranslated secular scripture, the Indians' future, and whether or not they recognize it matters only insofar as it concerns Fitzcarraldo's immediate instrumental need for their giving him safe passage and, subsequently, their labor to pull the boat over the hill (fig. 36).

Herzog lavishly documents this engineering feat, but these pictures, worth their thousand words, fail in the end. We're made believers in order to later recognize that the established (pictorial) facts are meaningless. Looks lie. The real story is told in the conflicts of sound: panpipes, drums, chants, birds, rushing water, even the anthropomorphically pained protests of the groaning riverboat as it's pulled uphill, in violation of its "nature"—and, of course, opera.[31]

BEAUTIFUL DISASTER

After the *Molly Aïda* is safely back in the water on the other side of the hill, and following a long night's drunken celebration by crew and Indians alike, the Indians cut the mooring lines: they have their own dream—namely, the sacrifice of the riverboat to the gods of the rapids. The boat tumbles helplessly toward disaster, careening through the rock-strewn gorge, while the hungover Fitzcarraldo and the few of his diminished crew on board are thrown about sufficiently to awaken from their stupor, but much too late to do anything besides hold on for dear life (fig. 37). In the midst of all this, so we're given to believe, the boat's uncontrolled movement (violently listing, crashing into rocks, etc.) somehow sets the gramophone into motion, shown in close-up (fig. 38); it gives us Caruso in the sextet from *Lucia,* with its various commentaries on love and its myriad complications, disillusionments, betrayals, and failures, made gloriously ironic by the interweav-

FIGURE 37
Herzog, *Fitzcarraldo:* the *Molly Aïda* lost to the rapids (2:21:16).

FIGURE 38
Herzog, *Fitzcarraldo:* the *Lucia* sextet plays on the gramophone aboard the *Molly Aïda* as the boat crashes against the walls of the gorge (2:22:36).

ing of voices that produce a rampant degree of melodiousness underwritten by the harmonic envelope in which the tunes are wrapped.[32] Even if one knows the language, it's impossible to follow the script, and here in the jungle no one knows Italian, or likely even the opera's plot, which narrates not only disaster but also the end of dreams. The unexpected entrance of Edgardo, triggering the sextet, mirrors the cutting of the mooring lines. Nothing will be the same thereafter. A mad scene, and deaths, will follow. Musically, however, the *Lucia* sextet *celebrates* disaster in its immensely pleasurable sonorities. Better said, the sextet "speaks" in its own way of hopeless hope—not through its dystopian text, but in its music: all those splendid thirds, sixths, unisons, and octaves. It is catastrophe aestheticized.

As the boat careens through the rapids, Caruso and his confederates serenade, the needle never skipping. The logically impossible diegetic incongruity—the diegesis confirmed at least at the start by means of a quick close-up of the spinning turntable—sets two sounds in dire conjunction: an operatic ensemble and a riverboat crashing into rocks in a raging rapids, the boat, like the shellac disks, turning in circles, a favorite visual effect found in Herzog films. Our eyes inform us of disaster and the violent triumph of nature; the soundtrack, however, describes the triumph of culture by means of the harmonies of intertwined voices, never mind the crisis that brought these voices together in song. As if to make the matter clear, Herzog gradually eliminates all sound except that of the sextet. The now-silenced diegesis, visually dramatic, demands sound, but hardly opera, except of course in the illusory reality of a film about dreams.[33] The beauty of Donizetti's acoustic wave, undisturbed by the chaos and turbulence surrounding it, is in fact matched by the sublime visual drama of the riverboat rebounding helplessly from one side to the other of the roaring river. The violence of the putatively "real" event, by being completely silenced, reverts to the conventional aesthetics of romanticized nature.

Caruso's arias give Fitzcarraldo's ears what his eyes deny him. If the gaze, filmic and otherwise, is intended to penetrate, throughout the film Fitzcarraldo's eyes hit a wall of impenetrable green that acts on him in a way analogous to a blue screen, in front of which he acts out his dream, with the keen assistance of a crucial prop that helps suture him into a narrative that he's trying desperately to write. The narrative is informed by psychic introjection via acoustic displacement. Metaphorically, if hardly literally, the ethereality of music—its ethereality underscored by the reproductive apparatus from which it emanates—drowns out the visually noisy but acoustically "silenced" enemy: nature and the "bare-ass" culture Fitzcarraldo includes under the term. All this notwithstanding, Fitzcarraldo acknowledges nature's agency, but as an amorphous fiend. Caruso, ever at his beck and call, provides him—and not just us—with what Adorno and Eisler claimed generally for film music, namely, that it corresponded to the "whistling or singing child in the dark."[34] In short, that is to say, the film's music addresses fear, and is its antidote. Put differently, the sublime visuality of the riverboat in the rapids demands the acoustic hermeneutics of opera for sense to be made of it.

Fitzcarraldo names his boat after two women, Molly, obvious enough, and Aida. Aida marks what matters about opera to Herzog. The singing voice makes sensible the utopian desire of perfect expressibility. Opera, as it were, finds the way to name the Name, the imaginary Absolute, the hoped-for Spirit. Aida voluntarily entombs herself so that she can sing to the end (or maybe forever) with her lover. If opera is "about" singing—understood as "saying" what speaking desperately seeks to convey but can't—then being entombed and ending life in a love duet is not the worst way to go. Indeed, it's possibly the ultimate form of peace (and *Pace* is the word that Amneris intones repeatedly in her blessing from outside the sealed chamber). What I'm suggesting is that *Aida* is about its ending, its *sense* of an ending. To die in love is good; to die in love and in song is to accomplish in death that for which life is lived—namely, once and for all time to be able to express love absolutely, exceeding the hopeless inadequacy of mere language.

Aida plays out its final scene in the metaphorical total darkness of a smothering tomb. The eyes can no longer see. Only sound conveys what must be said and before it's too late; those words must be sung—and, to be sure, sung in harmony, a sonoric oneness for all time. *Aida* ends in a dream world; its last scene, in effect if not in staged practice,

FIGURE 39
Herzog, *Fitzcarraldo:* saluting the "emperor" of opera (2:32:53).

is a long blackout. All we have is music conveying utterly selfless love. It's there to be heard; seeing it is utterly irrelevant. And just as *Aida* ends, so also does Fitzcarraldo. Herzog closes his film with a sustained blackout. The visual sense is denied, while the auditory sense is offered the privilege of a cadence. And this brings me to my own conclusion, via the film's final scene.

TO DREAM

Earlier in the film, in a scene involving a conversation with missionaries living in the remote bush and ministering to the Indians, Fitzcarraldo hears the priest's complaint that "we can't seem to cure [the Indians] of the idea that everyday life is only an illusion behind which lies the reality of dreams." Fitzcarraldo replies, simply: "Actually, I'm very interested in these ideas. I specialize in opera myself."

Fitzcarraldo's scheme for a rubber plantation whose proceeds would fund an opera house in Iquitos fails, but in failing he manages a momentary triumph, by realizing a substitute dream in the form of live opera on water. He sells the damaged *Molly Aïda* and uses the proceeds to hire a small itinerant opera troupe. The absurdity of the mise-en-scène is extreme. Ten small boats pull alongside the riverboat, loaded down, variously, with singers in costume, orchestra musicians with instruments in hand and wearing full formal attire—never mind the midday heat and choking humidity—and paltry scenery rather badly representing a castle atop a cliff and a cutaway of battlements. The musicians disembark on the shore, welcomed by Fitzcarraldo, and shortly thereafter take their places aboard the riverboat turned opera stage. During this disembarkation, the French horn players acknowledge Fitzcarraldo, however incongruously (and ironically), by playing the horn motif from the opening movement of Beethoven's *Emperor* Concerto (first heard at mm. 48–52).[35] Fitzcarraldo, so it seems, is king for a day, as sonically confirmed by the king of all the music that really matters (fig. 39).

FIGURE 40
Herzog, *Fitzcarraldo:* the *I puritani* love duet aboard the *Molly Aïda* (2:35:54).

Shortly thereafter, the boat approaches Iquitos for the last time, making a grand entrance with a staged scene from *I puritani* (1835) in progress on its top deck and pilothouse roof.[36] The scene is part of act one, scene three (beginning with Arturo's aria "A te, o cara, amor talora"), and involves the love duet between Arturo and Elvira, with the chorus performed by mestizo musicians.[37] The Puritan costumes worn by brown-skinned people is perhaps visually jarring to our eyes, but no such discomfort is evident among the singers or orchestra. Like opera itself, the hybridization is for them naturalized, indeed comfortable. And all of them seem uncannily happy. Herzog edits the scene to show, alternately, distance and close-up shots of Fitzcarraldo, who, despite the economic ruin facing him, is in a splendid mood. Proud as punch, and smoking what he describes as "the biggest cigar in the world," he happily takes it all in.

The operatic lovers express their delight and passion with the usual stock moves (fig. 40). But their happiness is ventriloquized: they lip-sync badly to the playback. The fakery is as obvious as the castle scenery is low budget. Nothing much is what it seems, apart from the sublime happiness registered on the faces of the large crowd onshore hearing opera for the first time. The *Puritani* lovers recall old torments, now convinced—mistakenly—that joy is at hand (though after subsequent trials and tribulations the opera eventually does have a happy ending). Fitzcarraldo, distinctly if only momentarily happy himself, smiling broadly, gestures to his audience onshore, inviting everyone to acknowledge opera's *promesse du bonheur* (fig. 41), and then the screen goes black. The music continues for a few seconds, after which the volume is cut quickly to silence at a cadence. We're at full stop, but not at closure. We have the sense, however momentary, of an ending—indeed, an insistence on it, since the film is literally over at this point, for which reason Herzog placed the credits at the beginning. The reality of the dream meets the alternate reality of the film's end: the house lights return us to the here and now. The dream is kept going only so long as music, which exceeds reality, plays against the perverted rationalities embedded in the film's visual narrative. Herzog sets music in striking dialectical tension with the seemingly "objective" character of the film image itself, which Herzog constantly

FIGURE 41
Herzog, *Fitzcarraldo:* Fitzcarraldo gestures his final triumph aboard the *Molly Aïda* (2:36:39).

inflects with both the resonance and actuality of a documentary. Yet what is documented is at once both more and less than the "reality" available to the eyes. For that matter, the aria and ensemble texts themselves relate *only* fictions. The truth, so to speak, is there nonetheless, but in the sonorous notes, in the evanescent reality of music.

Western music in *Fitzcarraldo* is constituted as a kind of storage mechanism for cultural time, a specific temporality that sounds in direct opposition less to the supposedly timelessness of nature itself than to the apparent timelessness of the "natural" beings, the indigenous peoples of the Peruvian Amazon—again, the "bare-asses." For Fitzcarraldo, their timelessness is an affront to time, which will be brought to them, like it or not, in two forms. The first, Caruso on gramophone, transported by a noisy steam packet whose clanking engine's sounds at key moments are subdued—indeed, made virtually silent—in favor of arias and ensembles broadcast across the water. This, obviously enough, is time aestheticized. The second temporality involves the organization of the indigenous labor force engaged in rubber harvesting, directly shown, documentary-style, in one brief scene early in the film. "Civilization" comes with a bill attached.

The film repeatedly marks movement as a central metaphor: close-ups of map routes; the boat on the river, on land, crashing into the rapids, steaming "home"; noisy close-ups of the boat's engine; close-ups of the winch and pulley system as the boat ascends the hill; repeated shots of the gramophone spinning (replicated in the circles turned by the *Molly Aïda* caught in the rapids). Movement signals change, insistently marking history and bringing into sharp relief the fact that culture is processural. The process-nature of culture in *Fitzcarraldo* takes on the strange character of a dialectical pairing: it is at once immaterial and spiritual, but its romanticized spirituality is underwritten in the most material (and usually materialistic) forms.

The utopian charge of opera in *Fitzcarraldo* is anchored in the insistence to hear life sung—and notwithstanding the myriad instrumentalities of opera's own material-institutional foundations. This much is acknowledged in repeated shots throughout the film of the gramophone and the shellac disks, which, taken together, visually concentrate the institutionality of opera in the commodity-form associated with mechanical sound reproduction.[38] In *Fitzcarraldo,* music gives life to sight. Life musically determined, however, includes nothing of the mundane; recitative is barred. What matters is life heightened in aria form: the acoustic sublime. The reality of Fitzcarraldo's dream-life is defined by assorted operatic fragments torn from their narrative context. What he chooses to hear, in other words, is a phonograph album of sonic snapshots. His utopian acoustic is constituted from fragile bits of treasured musical detritus inscribed on brittle shellac, which with every playing is damaged by the heavy tone arm tipped by a steel needle. Every hearing takes away from what he desires most, bringing closer to the foreground the static of the worn and damaged disk, technology's calling card, the noisy sign of the modernity that Fitzcarraldo at once depends upon and abhors. Each audition of Caruso promises Caruso's ultimate silence. The disk will be destroyed by the love of the writing on its surface.

Fitzcarraldo uses music from a long bygone era and of a sort—opera—that relatively few people today know or care much about. The musical quotations are likely unrecognizable to most viewers; figuring them out is a game of sorts, since none of the Caruso recordings is identified in the credits. Moreover, the staged opera scenes are made to play off distinctly exaggerated popular clichés about opera, the most characteristically overwrought of all modern art forms. Opera, in short, is now largely strange and estranged. For Herzog, I think, this strangeness constitutes its saving grace in late modernity, for which cinema commonly serves as an aesthetic proponent. In one sense, in other words, in *Fitzcarraldo* Herzog has made a film that functions in acute dialectical tension with the medium through which he speaks. In a film so visually dependent upon turning, and turning in circles, the "visual turn" of modern culture is called into question by the aural, not as supplement of the image, but as the foundation for the insight by which to critique it.

For Herzog, opera foregrounds the ever-widening gap between the mundane, perversely hyper-rationalized, and duly fetishized love affair with facts as the sole legitimate measure of the real, on the one hand, and the reality of the unreal, on the other. Whatever Herzog's own sharply dialectical relation to nature and to the Others without whom his film would have been impossible, he clearly valorizes the principle of otherness, just as he recognizes the refusal embedded in what Attali, paraphrasing Adorno, called "residual irrationality," which for both men was a form of principled alternative to *Mitmachen,* or going with the flow.[39] The old operas, as employed in this film, in spite of everything about them that is otherwise objectionable, still have a truth to tell about the social struggle embedded in the changing hierarchy of human sensing. But to get at this truth we have to look and to hear backwards, so to speak. The film begins with an ending (*Ernani* and death), and it ends with a mirthful beginning (the act one scene from *I puritani*) that, against the odds, celebrates another ending (the collapse of Fitzcarraldo's dream). Herzog thus sets the linearity of narrative historicism akimbo; the usual truths, here of narrative closure and pictorial objectivity, fail in the confusion.

Rilke once wrote that music is "the untrammeled superabundance of God, who has not exhausted himself in phenomena," adding that "artists take up this challenge in a vague urge to complete the world in the same spirit in which this power, continuing to create, would have acted, and to set up images of those realities that would have proceeded from the power."[40] Rilke's claim fundamentally defines *Fitzcarraldo* and the film's namesake alike, the latter a man who throughout virtually all of the film is dressed in one costume, a white suit, increasingly soiled, that visually evokes both Pagliacci and the eternally hapless Pedrolino/Pierrot of the *commedia dell'arte.* For his last hurrah aboard the *Molly Aïda,* he's borrowed a clean black tailcoat. Despite the diverting costume, he remains the clown.

Herzog's point, in a way, is to mark the fallibility of seeing in order to make audible the truths of hearing: hearing music. The advantage of opera is that it accomplishes both tasks at once.[41] All of its fallibilities and, indeed, its absurdities do not overwhelm the truths of the singing voice, the simple fact that people literally *need* to sing. One might say, I suppose, that it's precisely opera's lie through which its truth is revealed: that truth is at once acoustic, sublime, and in part utopian. Herzog's film, in tension with its own visually determined documentary excess, points to this alternative—and it's there for the hearing.

PART II

VOICING SUBJECTIVITY

EXCURSUS

OPERA, MONUMENTALITY, AND LOOKING AT LOOKING

By the seventeenth century, theaters for staging operas enjoyed considerable social status among a larger host of architectural statements of agency and prestige, whether on behalf of a court or, as time went by, a public (part actual, part imagined). By the nineteenth century major urban centers throughout Europe and the Americas had put up opera houses on grand scale befitting the cultural, ideological, political, economic, and institutional protocols dominant in their place and time. Indeed, "opera house" eventually served as a key component in civic narratives of civilizational status; in the American hinterlands, for example—perhaps known now principally from movie westerns—small towns commonly erected an "opera house," though the term, by then entirely generic, meant something like "gathering place" for local public needs, as well as a site for occasional visiting entertainments. The opera house "proper," however, was something else, far more like a secular temple for staging, at the farthest extreme, ambitious visual-musical fantasies (operatic in every sense of that multipurpose word) for which claims to aesthetic importance were vigorously asserted.

KNOWLEDGEABLE SPACE

The opera house belongs to the "effective knowledge" of lived experience. Inside and out, it articulates space. The theater auditorium, my concern, is what Lefebvre terms a "representational space," understood as an *intervention* that "occurs by way of construction—in other words, by way of architecture, conceived of not [simply or merely] as the building

FIGURE 42
Opera House of the Margraves (1744–48), Bayreuth, Germany, view toward the stage. Interior design by Giuseppe Galli-Bibiena (1696–1757) and Carlo Galli-Bibiena (1728–87). Photo credit: Erich Lessing/Art Resource, New York.

of a particular structure, palace or monument, but rather as a project embedded in a spatial context and a texture which calls for 'representations' that will not vanish into the symbolic or imaginary realms." As Lefebvre insists, "representational space is alive: it speaks. . . . It is essentially qualitative, fluid and dynamic."[1] The opera auditorium was as spectacular as the mis-en-scène of the staged productions. It was at once concrete and abstract, real and beyond real, a social-psychological fantasy projection on a scale that matched the ambitions of emerging modernity—and not least globalization—all of it put into the time-suspension of a world otherwise locked into the linear temporalities that define the concept and experience of being Now. The European opera theater was unlike any other sort of spatial enclosure either previously imagined or constructed. It was an enveloping space of appearance and appearances, its auditorium a spatial void framed in multiple elevations by decorative extravagance: baroque combinations of the real and the virtual, variously fashioned from stone, wood, stucco, bronze, marble, fabrics, glass, mirrors, paint, gilt, and crystal (fig. 42).[2] By the nineteenth century, when the adjective *grand* was attached to opera, grandness extended itself in nearly every imaginable direction

FIGURE 43
Jean-Louis Charles Garnier (1825–98), Paris, Opéra Garnier (1862–75), Grand Staircase. Photo credit: Bridgeman-Giraudon/Art Resource, New York.

of aesthetic comportment. Monumentality became the byword as a phenomenon gathering to itself, in Lefebvre's words, "the perceived, the conceived, and the lived" (figs. 43 and 44).[3]

Paris's Opéra Garnier, situated at the end of the Avenue de l'Opéra and sited to serve as a monument to an imagined France Now—distinct from the city's assorted monuments to the various heroic dead—stops the eye abruptly like a visual exclamation point. It *concludes* the larger space surrounding and framing it, just as it serves as the hub of major streets and boulevards flanking its sides and back. The Opéra defines the city surrounding it as part of Baron Haussmann's grand Second Empire restaging of Paris under the reign of Emperor Napoléon III (though site clearing began in 1862, the building was completed only in 1875, five years after the fall of the Second Empire and the emperor's exile to England).[4] Never mind that the hall was multiply purposed from the start; above all it was a temple to Grand Opera (and ballet) assertively marked as the past, present,

FIGURE 44
Opéra Garnier, Grand Foyer. Photo credit: Erich Lessing/Art Resource, New York.

and future of France's claim, and that of its capital city, as the heart of Western civilization. Lefebvre's general commentary on monumentality is apt: "Of this [monumental] social space . . . everyone partook, and partook fully—albeit, naturally, under the conditions of a generally accepted Power and a generally accepted Wisdom. The monument thus effected a 'consensus,' and in this strongest sense of the term, rendering it practical and concrete. The element of repression in it and the element of exaltation could scarcely be disentangled; or perhaps it would be more accurate to say that the repressive element was metamorphosed into exaltation."[5]

Every part mattered, but the interior mattered most. The auditorium proper required worthy surroundings as a preparatory experience, duly grand for what was still grander once the music started. No less important, the opera house announced itself as a site worthy of those worthies who sat in the best seats. Put differently, if the house mattered, the right audience mattered more. In this regard, at the Opéra Garnier, like others of its kind, a grand staircase and elegant foyer functioned as rationalized spaces for secular

FIGURE 45
Jean Béraud (1849–1936), *The Subscribers (An Elegant Couple Entering a Box at the Paris Opéra)* (1907), oil on canvas. Paris, Bibliothèque Nationale de l'Opéra. Photo credit: Erich Lessing/Art Resource, New York.

processionals enacting the mutuality of social power shared (unequally) by the upper bourgeoisie and aristocracy.

SOCIAL SCENERY

Jean Béraud's 1907 painting *The Subscribers,* subtitled *An Elegant Couple Entering a Box at the Paris Opera* (fig. 45), records the role that opera played in the articulation of social prestige. The hallways of the opera prior to performances were crowded with arrivals and intermingling; that fact notwithstanding, Béraud presents his couple as if entering late, after nearly everyone else is seated. The golden, highly reflective floor and ceiling situates them and a similar couple in the distant background as occupants of a kind of tabernacle. As subscribers, seasonal "owners" of their seats, they move toward a doorway to which they have sanctioned access. Only they matter as metaphoric stand-ins for the social register.[6]

The woman's fashionable, obviously expensive gown and outer wrap drag along the

FIGURE 46
Opera fan (1797). London, British Museum, Department of Prints and Drawings. © Trustees of the British Museum.

FIGURE 47
Opera fan (1797), detail.

floor, sweeping up whatever people's shoes have tracked in. This is not a problem; indeed, quite the opposite. The rampant impracticality of her costume is a characteristic marker for the wealth and power she possesses, if only as the decorative counterpart to her partner, stiffly upright at her side, his cane something like a gentleman's scepter. Someone else will clean up the dress; in any event, it's easily replaced, and next season's performances will require something new—planned obsolescence long predates the manufacturing and marketing practices of the twentieth century. (A late-modern analogue is the "trash the dress" practice in recent wedding photography, involving begowned brides wading into the ocean or running through mud, the presumed point being that the dress, no matter the cost, is only worn once.)[7]

FIGURE 48
Louis-Léopold Boilly (1761–1845), *Poor Box at the Opera* (1830), oil on canvas. Private collection. Photo credit: © Arthur Ackermann Ltd., London/Bridgeman Images.

Béraud's point is clear: Being seen at the opera was fundamental to the cultural purpose of the house itself and the musical art staged within. Thus the lady's opera fan, such as the one from 1797 shown in figures 46 and 47, printed on paper and sometimes on silk and revised each season, provided the elite audience participants with a spatial diagram of the social register. Who was who depended upon where one sat, and knowing that order was crucial to the rhetorical function of claiming one's identity within the circle of theatrical spectacle: "In *spatial practice*," Lefebvre points out, "the reproduction of social relations is predominant."[8] Critical to the experience of the opera was the sight of the social order enacted within the architectural, sonoric, and aestheticized frame that the setting as a whole provided. The spatial order immanent to the printed seating chart possessed as well a temporal dimension that added to the total power of the experience the audience at once witnessed and helped to realize. The social order was not a matter of the moment; it repeated itself night after night, reiterating the imaginary of a social status quo. In this respect, the opera fan's seating chart confirms the theater's purpose. Emptied of people, it's a shell of little consequence; filled to capacity, it serves as a second stage on which a narrative plays out—part real, part fiction—of the social and cultural order, in particular a site within which to host and elevate a restricted community, and never mind the plebs sitting (or standing) high in the topmost levels, people whose presence in fact helped to mark the significance of what occurred below them in the auditorium (fig. 48). That is, the opera house specifies and certifies a social order by both inclusion (those who gain admission) and exclusion (those who remain outside or relegated to the cheap seats), just as it establishes the differential hierarchal social register among the privileged.

FIGURE 49
"May I die if there isn't Sir George!—charming man!! as I live he's looking this way. O! the dear fellow!!" (1817), London, Victoria and Albert Museum. Photo credit: V&A Images, London/Art Resource, New York.

The social practice of attending the opera so as to be seen, a matter of considerable social seriousness, was in fact not taken seriously by everyone. Social satirists regularly had their way with audience pretensions by way of travesty scopophilia (fig. 49). Along these lines, Béraud, a trenchant if light-touch satirist of the Belle Époque, gives attention to men looking at women, or to be more precise, at women's backsides, as in figure 50 where the woman's exaggerated dress bustle fills the center of the image; to emphasize the point, Béraud adds a second man in the background, top-hatted, standing and holding opera glasses to his eyes to get his own look at her.

Contrast for a moment the distinction between Béraud's elegant couple (fig. 45) and the caricature of sitters occupying the so-named poor box (fig. 48), who together constitute something close to an unruly mob of grotesques, the most vulgar among them a woman picking her nose in the lower left. The comic parody registers disgust at the disordered lives of the lowly and, by implication, their musical insensitivity (ignoring the fact that they choose to attend the opera, the apex of the cultural food chain), a trope with a lengthy pedigree in western European representational history.

FIGURE 50
Jean Béraud, *The Box by the Stalls* (c. 1883), oil on canvas. Paris, Musée de la Ville de Paris, Musée Carnavalet. Photo credit: Bridgeman Images.

Culture represents itself through regimes of order acknowledging instantiations—in fact, systems—of disorder whose elimination or at least repression it seeks. The rationalized seating system outlined on the lady's opera fan replicated the preferred narrative for designating that part of the social spectrum commonly referred to as "The Quality" in England during the eighteenth century. That said, its putative story was both incomplete

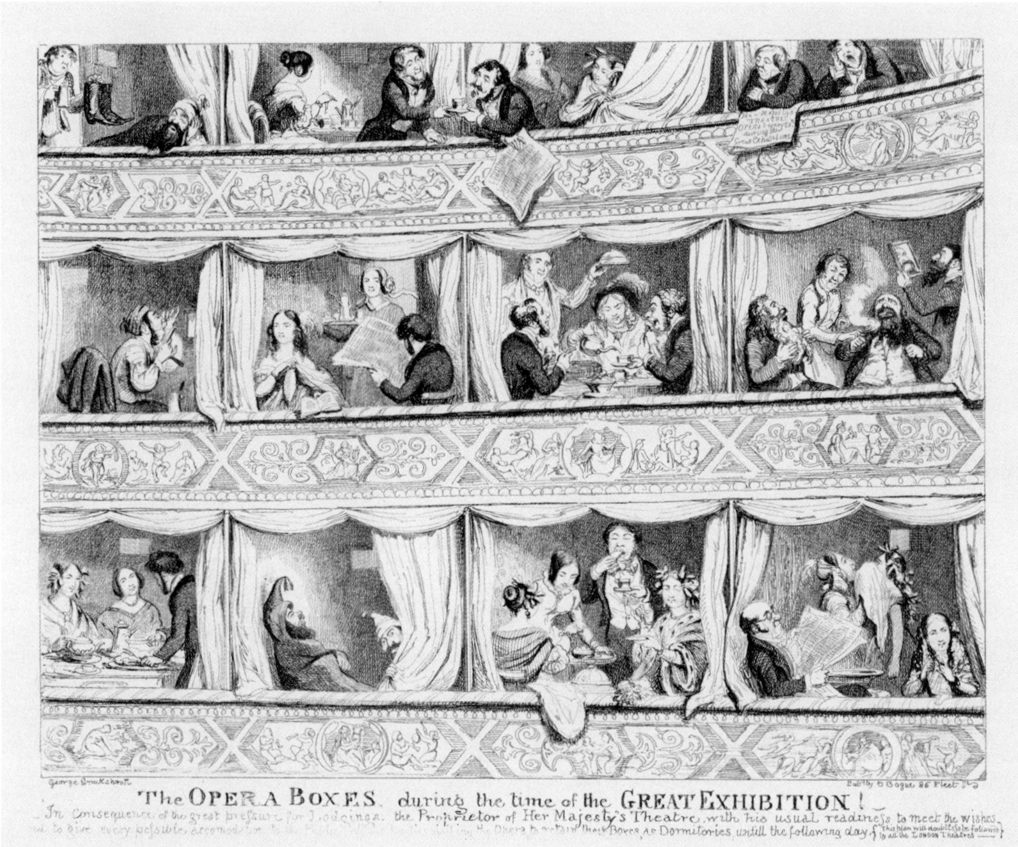

FIGURE 51

George Cruikshank (1792–1878), *The Opera Boxes during the Time of the Great Exhibition* (1851), etching. London, Science Museum. Photo credit: Bridgeman Images.

and highly subject to alternate, opposing accounts told by visual satirists, among whom George Cruikshank was perhaps the most accomplished—though he was hardly alone—in providing a glimpse of the unraveling of social propriety at the opera (fig. 51).

The social coding of theater design evident in the seating chart, reflected also in the scale of ticket prices and subscriptions, structured principles of behavioral decorum[9]—probably more idealized than ever realized—that could be undone by the affective impact of experiencing music. Visual satirists had something of a field day poking fun at those among the bourgeoisie who lost control of themselves, men in particular, at musical events. Gustave Doré's acid caricatures (figs. 52 and 53) register the decentering impact of music and overwrought musical enthusiasms; affective listening is transformed into pathologically obsessive looking. Each man's loss of self-control and ultimate emotional collapse is staged as a metaphorical self-castration, an unmanning feminization by

FIGURE 52
Gustave Doré (1832–1883), *Those Who Are Carried Away,* from *Grotesques* (1849). Private collection.

FIGURE 53
Doré, *Overcome,* from *Grotesques.* Private collection.

sonority (music's immaterial nothingness), utterly unlike the brave new world of industrializing economies and business, where materiality and manhood properly went hand in hand.

Disorder has several faces in the opera house. Some may be more or less unintended consequences of listening—being "carried away," for example. Other enthusiasms are manufactured, as with claques, laying bare—cynically—one means among many by which systems of social order were enacted as part of the aggregate disposition constituting the whole of the performance situation. By hiring a claque, singers hoped to encourage a general positive assessment of their skills, a bit like "live audience" (is there any other kind?) applause signs that illuminate at key points during television program tapings. *The Claque in Action* (fig. 54) articulates the fakery by emphasizing the physical appearance of the claque members, equipping each of them with grotesque profiles commonly associated in contemporaneous physiognomy treatises with the lowest ranks of the social order, men and women saddled with facial appearances as much animal as human,[10] and assigning them outsized, nearly monstrous hands. Simply put, the claque

FIGURE 54
French School, 19th century, *The Claque in Action* (c. 1830–40), lithograph. Paris, Bibliothèque des Arts Decoratifs. Photo credit: Archives Charmet/Bridgeman Images.

gives the lie to the putative natural order of the proceedings. That said, the obvious nature of their not properly belonging underscores the distinction from those who do, and to that extent the satirical image through its very dissonance helps to anchor the presumed prevailing status quo, however unstable its foundations.

The stability of the social order, perhaps especially at its apex, at best tentative, was smartly captured by Béraud in *Altercation in the Corridor of the Opera* (fig. 55), depicting the same hallway previously described (see fig. 45), now crowded prior to a performance, and involving one well-dressed gentleman slapping another as a woman attempts to intervene. The presumed decorum required by the setting—more fragile than the nearly fortresslike architecture of the Opéra Garnier might suggest—is exposed for what lies close to the surface of the social interactions of the patrons parading about. Decorum is an act easily superseded by ragged competition. The men surrounding the fight have largely abandoned their wives or mistresses to witness the momentary violence, while

FIGURE 55
Jean Béraud, *Altercation in the Corridor of the Opera (The Slap)* (1889), oil on canvas. Paris, Musée de la Ville de Paris, Musée Carnavalet. Photo credit: Erich Lessing/Art Resource, New York.

two women, bent at the waist, are caught in the thrall of the moment. The totality of disruption extends to a vignette at the far left, a man taking indecorous sexual liberties with a woman whose back is to us. Béraud overdetermines his point: a single slap almost completely upsets the apparent but fictional order of the whole. Adorno signals this dialectic: "If the theatre is a cabinet clock on which the hand of fate measures the progress of the world, evening after evening, then the foyer is the face with the second hand which duplicates in miniature the image of the world at large, as if an infinite system of mirrors were to be set up in which the world would gradually disappear. In the foyer the spectators are the players, presented to an imaginary public."[11]

SERIOUS LOOKING

Throughout the eighteenth and nineteenth centuries visual artists produced enormous numbers of images of opera houses, many representing general views of auditorium interiors, usually during a performance, and others, in close-up, of audience members, women especially, characteristically shown looking intently, typically in profile, commonly holding or looking through a lorgnette, though looking at what is generally

FIGURE 56
Mary Stevenson Cassatt (1844–1926), *In the Loge* (1879), oil on canvas. Boston, Museum of Fine Arts, The Hayden Collection, Charles Henry Hayden Fund. Photo credit: © Christie's Images/ Bridgeman Images.

unspecified (figs. 56 and 57). Represented in profile, the women lose some of their identity; indeed, they are usually intended as character types. What matters as much as themselves, and perhaps more, is their fixed gaze in a space where there is so much to look at, by no means all of it on stage. As Lefebvre points out, "Monumental space offered each member of a society an image of that membership, an image of his or her social visage. It thus constituted a collective mirror more faithful than any personal one."[12] The metaphor of the mirror is apt; wherever those people who truly belong at the opera look, they see themselves. Looking—foundational to the experience of opera—is what matters, far more than looking at anything in particular. Everything looked at mirrors back. The wealth of nineteenth-century, especially French, images representing operagoers looking drives home the significance that looking enjoyed as part of the cultural practice. But there's more to it. These images, many of them oil paintings (the most prestigious medium of visual representation), are *about* looking, as are all images; but images of people "simply" looking (without specific regard to what is being looked at) invites viewers to *look at looking*, a matter made more emphatic when the person looking within the

FIGURE 57
Cassatt, *In the Box* (c. 1879), oil on canvas. Private collection. Photo credit: © Christie's Images/ Bridgeman Images.

painting employs an optical device as a supplement to her eyes. Further, viewers looking at looking at the opera raises the stakes of the specific site where scopophilia is stimulated and maybe also sated. Opera as an experience of hearing marks just half of the equation. This is a longer story to which I'll return at the end of this book.

Eighteenth- and nineteenth-century representations of opera house interiors characteristically emphasize and even exaggerate the dimensions of the spatial enclosure and the numbers of people who could be accommodated (figs. 58 and 59). Closely related, set design emphasized the illusion of deep space effected by dramatic foreshortening and vanishing-point perspective, sometimes realized in ways that more or less seamlessly blended the theater's three-dimensional architecture and the two-dimensional architectural stage flats and backdrops (fig. 60). Set design morphed well beyond deep-space architectural fantasy in the course of the nineteenth century, culminating in clouds (fig. 61) and even the cosmos (fig. 62). In the theater, no matter where one's eyes focused, the opportunities for affective seeing were nearly infinite. In sum, whatever the aural impact of the music itself, looking was tantamount to the experience.

Adorno describes the disadvantageous seating (upper circle, first row, middle) at the opera. "At best," he says, "you get a good view of the audience and can look individual

FIGURE 58
Catteo da Stefano (dates unknown), *View of the Interior of the Teatro di San Carlo, Naples* (n.d.), oil. Paris, Bibliotheque Nationale de l'Opéra. Photo credit: Erich Lessing/Art Resource, New York.

FIGURE 59
Jean-Baptiste Arnout (1788–1865), *Imperial Academy of Music, Theater of the Opéra Garnier.* Color lithograph. Paris, Musée de la Ville de Paris, Musée Carnavalet. Photo: Bulloz. Photo credit: © RMN-Grand Palais/Art Resource, New York.

FIGURE 60
Pietro Domenico Olivero (c. 1652–1754), *Interior of the Teatro Regio during the Night of Its Inauguration.* Turin, Museo Civico. Photo credit: Scala/Art Resource, New York.

spectators in the eye. But the stage appears all too small down there below and is seen from the worst possible angle from the point of view of opera." He then, perhaps surprisingly, suggests the advantage of simply listening to opera: "Was it not the very purpose of the musical theatre to compensate those who would rather listen than see?"[13] That most operagoers preferred to look is beyond question, but this protocol gradually moderated—though a new cultural pedagogy was needed for the change to take place, the subject of the next chapter concerning the advent of phonography.

FIGURE 61

Carlo Ferrario (1833–1907), *Sketch for the World Premiere of Arrigo Boito's "Mefistofele" at La Scala in 1868*, watercolor. Photo: Alfredo Dagli Orti. Photo credit: Bildarchiv Preussischer Kulturbesitz/Art Resource, New York.

FIGURE 62

Karl Friedrich Schinkel (1781–1841), *The Starlit Hall of the Queen of the Night. Design for Mozart's "The Magic Flute"* (1815). Berlin: Kupferstichkabinett, Staatliche Museen zu Berlin. Photo credit: Bildarchiv Preussischer Kulturbesitz, Berlin/Art Resource, New York.

I have suggested that opera participates in a larger scopic regime for asserting and experiencing cultural claims on behalf of the Western social imaginary in modernity prior to the twentieth century. My intention next is to consider what happens when the dimension of sight is removed from the equation of experiencing opera (or music more generally) coterminous with the advent of sound recording. Phonography, in brief, required a recalibration of the sight/sound relation; as it happened, and surprisingly so, a substantial component of that recalculation employed opera recordings as the means by which to rethink and promote a new world of sightless sound, and it did so in significant part by playing off established principles of elevated aesthetic taste associated with opera, never mind that the taste for popular musics vastly outweighed the interest in classical musics of any sort, alike at the earliest history of phonography as today. This fact notwithstanding, opera became the measure of the worth of sound recordings and of domestic ownership of the playback equipment. Indeed, opera recordings served as the linchpin of phonographic promotions articulating democratic principles of an imagined universal accessibility to the best of musical sound. The story is a multifaceted mix of would-be aesthetics, industrial competition, business acumen, advertising and marketing, education, technophilia, ideologically inflected pedagogy, and perhaps above all, capitalist economics. Absenting the possibility of looking at music performed live, but especially opera, where looking is fundamental to listening, demanded epistemic change concerning what counted as musical experience. Once the experience of music is, as it were, "reduced" to listening, allowances have to be made, and a new pedagogy of hearing enacted. To be sure, acousmatic hearing had a long history in live opera performance when offstage singing occurred, but the separation from the sight of the human sound source was typically temporary. With sound recording, acousmatic listening was de rigueur, and therein, precisely, lay the problem.[14]

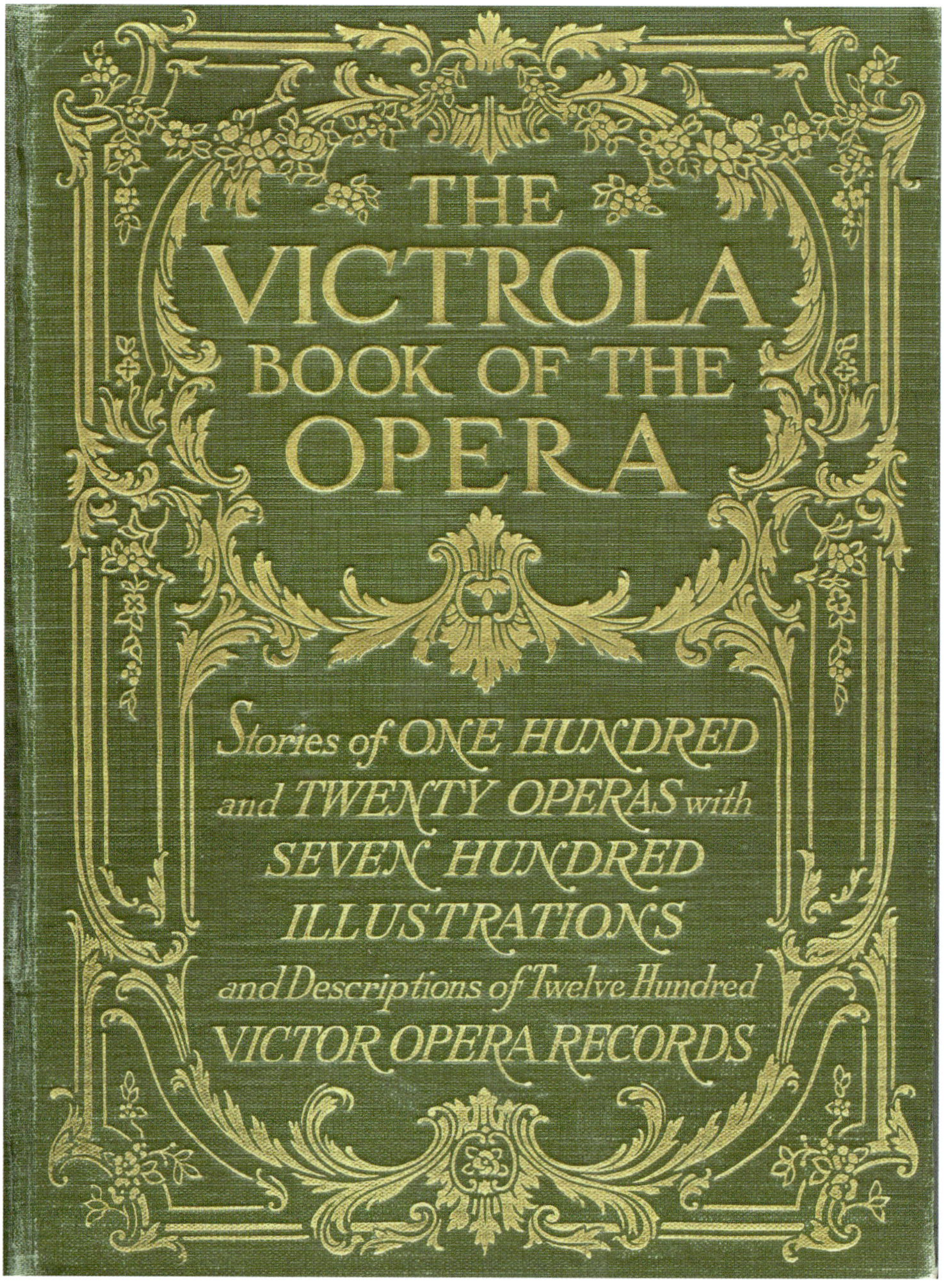

FIGURE 63
The Victrola Book of the Opera, 4th rev. ed. (Camden, N.J.: Victor Talking Machine Company, 1917). Private collection.

3

CARUSO, PHONOGRAPHY, AND OPERATIC FIDELITIES

Regimes of Musical Listening, 1904–1929

> The machine demands that we give bodies to the sounds emanating from it. For example, while playing an aria sung by a famous singer we see the stage he stands on, we see him dressed in an appropriate costume. The more it is linked to our memories, the stronger the record's effect will be. Nothing excites memory more strongly than the human voice, maybe because nothing is forgotten as quickly as a voice.
>
> RUDOLPH LOTHAR, *DIE SPRECHMASCHINE: EIN TECHNISCH-ÄSTHETISCHER VERSUCH* (1924)

In what follows, I hope to suggest some epistemological repercussions—social, cultural, and musical—that accompanied the technological advent of phonography, hence the move from live performance experienced in theatrical settings, particularly as regards opera, to the quasi-privatized listening made possible by the domestic gramophone. For the most part, the music of my concern will be operatic arias and small vocal ensembles whose total length could be contained on the single side of a shellac disk,[1] around four and a half minutes' duration. I'll be considering two American companies, Victor and Edison, to the exclusion of others except in passing reference.

PICTURING OPERA

The Victor Talking Machine Company,[2] inaugurated in 1901, in 1912 published a glossy hardback book titled *The Victor Book of the Opera*, subtitled *Stories of Seventy Grand Operas with Three Hundred Illustrations & Descriptions of Seven Hundred Victor Opera Records.*[3] Three editions were printed during the inaugural year. In 1917 a fourth edition appeared (fig. 63), the title altered to *The Victrola Book of the Opera* and the text this time credited to Samuel Holland Rous, editor of the Victor sales catalogue. Whereas the 1912 editions

FIGURE 64
Interior of Metropolitan Opera House, New York, in *The Victor Book of the Opera,* 3rd ed. (Camden, N.J.: Victor Talking Machine Company, 1912), 8. Private collection.

ran to 375 pages, the fourth had been expanded to 553 pages and the number of operas augmented to 120, accompanied by 700 illustrations and now listing 1,200 Victor opera recordings, a tally that does not appear to have increased in later editions up to the eighth in 1929, the most recent I have found, though additions and deletions of operas occur from one edition to another. Many of the operas (and operettas) included are today obscure. (The preface to the eighth edition indicates that more than three hundred thousand copies of the book had been sold.)[4]

Imagery in the 1912 third edition opens with photo spreads of European and American opera house exteriors, followed by one of New York's Metropolitan Opera House auditorium, sans audience (fig. 64). Victor advertising replicated similar photo spreads (fig. 65), part of its ambitious effort to suture home listening to the experience of live opera performed in the world's prestigious venues, for most people an experience only imagined.

The 1917 fourth edition's initial illustration is a composite photograph of twenty-six costumed singers (fig. 66), all exclusively Victor recording artists, among whom Enrico Caruso (1873–1921) held first rank, a singer whom Victor avidly promoted, on account of which his international celebrity was quickly secured.[5] It's clear that Victor's marketing department understood the stakes of star culture to a degree that its competitors, Edison

FIGURE 65
Victor advertisement: "The greatest opera house of all—the *Victor*," in *The World's Work Advertiser* 23 or 25 (March 1912 or 1913), inside front cover.

FIGURE 66
"The Great Singers of the World All of Whom Make Records Exclusively for the Victor," in *The Victrola Book of the Opera,* 4th rev. ed. (1917), 4.

in particular, did not (on which more below).[6] Victor's no-competition contract with Caruso served as a marketing ploy virtually from the moment he signed with the company in 1904, already apparent in a fashionably up-to-date *art nouveau*–styled advertisement from that same year (fig. 67).

Victor marketed opera for its cultural prestige value, a desideratum by then established by various democratizing general education movements.[7] The promotion of operatic high culture (as it was marketed) was intended to rub off on Victor's own image; its opera catalogue provided a cultural foundation for more or less any sort of music it sold. Put differently, classical music, but opera especially, supplied cultural merit, just as the company's other recordings provided popular entertainment promoted for its innocent pleasures.

The "Foreward" *[sic]* to the 1912 third edition of *The Victor Book of the Opera* lays claim to a relationship between, on the one hand, the volume's photographic reproductions of opera houses, gigantic and stately, duly grand for the grand opera referred to in the book's subtitle, and on the other hand, phonography as a medium. The text leads the reader beyond the limits of live opera in America, what it refers to as "merely the pastime of the well-to-do in New York City and vicinity," while crediting the proliferation of opera

FIGURE 67
Victor advertisement: "Victor: The New Caruso Records," in *Ladies' Home Journal* 21 (June 1904): 37.

performance ("hundreds") in other North American cities to the impact of "hundreds of thousands of grand opera records" sold under the Victor label.[8]

Victor records were available, as the text continues "at widely varying prices—from the double-faced records by well-known Italian and French artists of Europe, at 371/2 cents per selection, to the great concerted numbers by famous singers at $6.00 and $7.00."[9] The *Lucia* sextet, one of Victor's most popular opera recordings, sold at this very high price.

The lower price of $0.371/2 in 1913 (the first year available for American Consumer Price Index Inflation Calculator) would run to around $9 in 2014, while a record costing

$7 would be slightly under $166. Caruso, recording for Victor's Red Seal label exclusively, commanded top scale, though prices came down over time. His duet with Antonio Scotti, "Amore o grillo" from *Madama Butterfly,* costing $4 in 1912, was reduced to $2 in 1919—still a considerable sum for a few minutes of music.[10]

The cultural capital of opera recordings functioned as signs of economic privilege, however varied and relative, residing in ownership of a phonograph and a record collection. Media historian Lisa Gitelman suggests that "phonographs and phonograph records had rich symbolic careers, that they acquired and possessed meanings in the circumstances of their apprehension and use, and that those meanings, many and changeable, arose in relation to the social lives of people and of tangible things."[11] In this regard, David Suisman points out that the artificially high prices of Victor's Red Seal catalogue amplified prestige value "by placing a premium, both monetary and symbolic, on opera and European classical music."[12] Sales of opera arias and other sorts of classical music were dwarfed by the vast numbers of popular music recordings, to say nothing of recorded recitations, comedy sketches, and other forms of spoken word entertainment. Edison and Victor alike spent enormous sums of money advertising their classical catalogues, opera especially, and also linking their recordings to pitches for their upscale phonographs, a topic I will take up later.[13]

Victor's sales narrative emphasized that recordings provided consumers unlimited home access to the voice of opera stars, very much tied to an unfolding pedagogy of domestic aesthetic consumerism: "Do you think Caruso the greatest of tenors? Then do not be satisfied with an occasional hearing of his glorious voice at the opera, but let him sing for you and your friends."[14]

The obvious fact that only a small segment of the population ever heard Caruso live is ignored in most Victor promotions. Indeed, the company's ads, carefully selected for specific readership (by social class, and by gender to some degree), consistently positioned readers as avid operagoers. That said, Victor and its competitors were hardly appealing only to an established audience. Caruso, so to speak, was a singer for everyone; opera was his medium, to which Victor would be the guide. In no small part, due to Victor, Caruso became a textual-visual advertising code for singing itself and all that vocal music could "do" for its auditors in pursuit of democratically available self-improvement—provided one had the funds to buy the expensive disks.

Recordings expanded space: "Do you regret that Melba is in Australia? There is consolation in the thought that her voice is here in all its loveliness, incredibly impressed on Victor disks";[15] and recordings expanded time, permanently incorporating the past: "Have you memories of Tamagno when he was at his best? The Victor will revive these memories for you by bringing the voice of this singer back from the grave."[16] If a potential buyer wasn't quite ready to hand over the cash, Victor, like Edison, instructed its retailers to play listening samples as a sonic come-on.[17]

Victor insisted that its recordings were an "excellent substitute" for live performance, and with the considerable added advantage that any aria could be heard at home as often as one desired (but please change the needle after every hearing). To be sure, the scenery and costuming are missing, but at-home opera, unlike live opera, has no season; at-home opera is always. As *The Victor Book of the Opera* puts it, "The absence of these accessories will now be atoned for in some measure by the graphic descriptions and numerous illustrations in this catalogue."[18] A tone of apology and regret for what is "missing" is readily apparent.

The book's seventh edition (1924) includes a short essay, "What Is an Opera?," principally intended to accommodate a potential American audience in need of convincing and familiarization. The text describes what opera is (a language of emotion) and is not (the movies or "a photoplay" with the advantage of close-ups, action, and so on). "To the average American, unaccustomed to the conventions of opera, there is in this, perhaps, naturally something very strange." In opera, melody is paramount, but there isn't much of it, as the text puts it, that "can be readily whistled"; worse, melody is intermittent or, in the case of contemporary opera, hardly present (unquestionably the principal reason that Victor recorded very little opera that could be heard as modernist): "Those who go to a modern opera expecting a 'Celeste Aida' every other minute, are doomed to disappointment." Further, "If there is any 'melody' at all (and ultra-modern opera composers may seem to avoid giving us any!) it is reserved for the great moments, coming only once or twice in an evening," the text duly noting "the combinations and permutations of feelings, suggested by the interplay of strange harmonies, fragmentary melodies, and the voicing of strings, woodwind and brass."[19]

Foreign language presents still another challenge. Why isn't opera sung in English? Several explanations are provided, but the matter ends as follows: "Moreover, the opera with us is a luxury, supported by the wealthier class, many of whom keep a 'working acquaintance' with one or more European languages. They much prefer to hear operas unmarred by translation." That said, Victor offers opera both ways, in the original languages and, "as far as possible, by having records sung in English by acknowledged masters of the art, as well as records sung by foreign artists in their own tongue."[20] In other words, the worthiest of opera fans are not the unschooled masses, though by acquiring a taste for opera the previously inexperienced (or simply ignorant) can emulate the cultural trappings of their social superiors. Opera, in short, has snob appeal, and Victor sells snobbery.[21]

The first opera presented in the five editions of the Victor opera book available to me is Meyerbeer's *L'Africaine;* the initial photograph illustrating this opera is Caruso, Victor's star recording artist, as Vasco di Gama *(sic)* (fig. 68). The second is *Aida* (fig. 69); like many of the by-then standard repertory works, it is given a highly detailed (in this case, eleven-page) narrative incorporating fifteen images—some photographed, others drawn—featuring scenes as well as both top-tier Victor artists who had recorded arias and ensembles from the opera (Pasquale Amato, Caruso, Giovanni Martinelli, Leo Slezak; Emmy Destinn, Johanna Gadski, and Louise Homer) and numerous other singers now all but forgotten.[22] Illustrations of sets and photographs of in-progress

FIGURE 68
"Caruso as Vasco di Gama," in *The Victor Book of the Opera*, 3rd ed. (1912), 10.

(Italian)

AIDA

(*Ah-ee'-dah*)

OPERA IN FOUR ACTS

Text translated from the French of Locle by Antonio Ghislanzoni. Music by Giuseppe Verdi. First produced in Cairo, December 24, 1871; at La Scala, Milan, February 8, 1872; in Paris, April 22, 1876; at Covent Garden, June 22, 1876. First performance in America at the Academy of Music, New York, November 26, 1873, the cast including Torriani, Cary, Campanini and Maurel.

Characters of the Drama

AIDA, an Ethiopian slave .... Soprano
THE KING OF EGYPT .... Bass
AMNERIS, (*Am-nare'-iss*) his daughter .... Mezzo-Soprano
RHADAMES, (*Rahd'-ah-maze*) Captain of the Guard .... Tenor
AMONASRO, (*Am-oh-nahz'-roh*) King of Ethiopia .... Baritone
RAMFIS, (*Rahm'-fiss*) High Priest .... Bass
A MESSENGER .... Tenor

Priests, Priestesses, Ministers, Captains, Soldiers, Officials, Ethiopian Slaves and Prisoners, Egyptians, etc.

The scene is laid in Memphis and Thebes, in Pharaoh's time.

This opera was written by request of the Viceroy of Egypt, who wished to celebrate the opening of his new Opera House at Cairo by the production of a work upon an Egyptian subject from the pen of the most popular composer of the time. The story originated with Marietta Bey, the famous Egyptologist, and seems to have inspired Verdi to unusual efforts.

BERT, PARIS

CARUSO AS RHADAMES

Aida, daughter of *Amonasro*, King of Ethiopia, has been captured by the Egyptians and is a slave at the Court of Memphis, where she and the young soldier *Rhadames* have fallen in love with each other. *Rhadames* goes to the Egyptian war, and during his absence the *King's* daughter, *Amneris*, discovers his attachment and is furious, as she herself loves *Rhadames*.

Rhadames returns, covered with glory and bringing many prisoners, among them *Amonasro*, *Aida's* father. The *King* releases all the prisoners except *Amonasro*, and bestows his daughter on the unwilling *Rhadames*.

In the next scene *Amonasro* forces his daughter to persuade *Rhadames* to become a traitor. The latter's love for *Aida* and his distaste for the approaching union with *Amneris* lead him to consent. *Amneris*, however, has overheard the plot, and after vainly trying to induce *Rhadames* to abandon *Aida*, she denounces him as a traitor, and he is condemned to be buried alive. When the vault is sealed he discovers *Aida*, who had concealed herself there that she might die with him; and the lovers slowly suffocate in each other's arms.

ACT I

SCENE I—*A Hall in the Palace. Through the grand gate at the back may be seen the Pyramids and the Temples of Memphis*

The opera has no overture. The curtain rises, showing a hall in the palace of the King of Memphis, where *Rhadames* and the High Priest, *Ramfis*, are discussing the coming

15

FIGURE 69
"Aida," in *The Victor Book of the Opera*, 3rd ed. (1912), 15.

performances (fig. 70), scattered throughout all editions of the book, attempt to supply what sound alone could not.

Victor's opera book could not remain current. Indeed, the company was releasing so many records of every sort that it took to issuing monthly updates of its entire line, classical and popular. Opera figured prominently in these publications. Pedagogical advertising is characteristic, as in figure 71, featuring a Red Seal one-side disk with a photo of the singer, Caruso, and a paragraph about the work in question, and ending with

FIGURE 70
"The Return of Rhadames—Act II" (performance photograph), in *The Victor Book of the Opera,* 3rd ed. (1912), 18.

an invocation of what's absent, except in "the imagination."[23] The text, in other words, is intended to substitute for the missing sight of the musical sound: "As the great tenor sings it the imagination is carried to the interior of some large cathedral, whose dimlit spaces and lofty pillars echo and re-echo to the sonorous phrases. Almost one can see the great candles burning through a mist of incense while the white-clad priests kneel in prayer and the sinner pleads for mercy in an agony of repentance—'Have pity, O Lord.'"[24] In essence, such description provides the visual "memory pictures" analogous to, and serving the same function as, audience sound tests (about which more below).

The *Aida* entry, like others in the third edition, provides basic history of the opera: composer, librettist, first performance, first performance in America; characters and vocal type; and a brief synopsis. Thereafter follows a highly detailed plot narrative (fig. 72) in which each aria, duet, or ensemble is explained, sometimes with a short melodic incipit; text in English is provided; and always incorporating the Victor recordings available of the musical piece in question, together with the recording inventory number, artist, and cost. Thus "Celeste Aida" runs $3 for Caruso, but only $1 for Leo Slezak.

New Victor Records for March 1919

These records are the latest additions to the great Library of Music which is listed in the Victor Record Catalogue. A new Supplement is issued on the First of every month, the records being available on and after that date

Victor Talking Machine Company. Camden, New Jersey, U.S.A.

RED SEAL RECORDS

CARUSO, ENRICO

88599 Pietà, Signore! Attributed to Stradella 12-in. list price $3.00
(Lord, Have Mercy!)

Of all the legends of music none is more strange than that of Stradella, the almost mythical eighteenth century Italian composer. He is said to have been a man of singular gifts, not handsome but beautifully proportioned, an accomplished singer, violinist, organist and poet. Having gained the enmity of an Italian nobleman he was attacked, so runs the legend, by assassins sent by the man he betrayed. Such was the beauty of his voice, however, that the murderers relented upon hearing him sing. Ultimately, the vengeful Venetian is said to have accomplished his ends and Stradella was killed. The historians doubt the story, but can neither affirm nor deny it. As for the famous "Aria di Chiesa," or "Church aria," which Caruso has recorded, "Pietà, Signore!" some historians are inclined to credit it not to Stradella, as tradition asserts, but to Rossini. He sings of course in Italian. As the great tenor sings it the imagination is carried to the interior of some large cathedral, whose dimlit spaces and lofty pillars echo and re-echo to the sonorous phrases. Almost one can see the great candles burning through a mist of incense while the white-clad priests kneel in prayer and the sinner pleads for mercy in an agony of repentance—"Have pity, O Lord!"

Caruso
doffs his hat for the photographer

3

FIGURE 71
New Victor Records, March 1919 [Victor Talking Machine Company monthly catalogue], 3. Private collection.

Sales commentary regularly interrupts the plot walk-through, some of it making bizarre comparison between live performance and recordings: "[Celeste Aida] is seldom enjoyed at the opera, especially in America, as it occurs almost immediately after the rise of the curtain, and is invariably marred by the noise made by the late comers. With the Victor, however, it may be heard in all its beauty and the fine renditions by Caruso and Slezak fully appreciated."[25] Others simply praise a particular Victor release, as in a pitch for a Caruso disk with Rodolfo's act one aria from *La bohème:* "Caruso has never done anything more perfect in its way than his superb delivery of this number. It is one of his great scenes in the opera, and always arouses the audience to a high pitch of enthusiasm. He has sung it here with a fervor and splendor of voice which holds one spellbound. The tender sympathy of the opening . . . the bold avowal . . . the glorious beauty of the love

VICTOR BOOK OF THE OPERA—VERDI'S AIDA

invasion of Ethiopia; and *Ramfis* hints that some young and brave warrior may be chosen to command the expedition. *Rhadames,* left alone, hopes that he himself may gain the coveted honor, and promises to lay his triumphs at the feet of his *Aida.*

Celeste Aida (Heavenly Aida)

By Enrico Caruso, Tenor (*In Italian*) 88127 12-inch, $3.00

By Leo Slezak, Tenor (*In German*) 64113 10-inch, 1.00

Then occurs the splendid gem of Act I, the *Celeste Aida,* beginning

in which *Rhadames* chants the praises of the peerless *Aida.* It is seldom enjoyed at the opera, especially in America, as it occurs almost immediately after the rise of the curtain, and is invariably marred by the noise made by late comers. With the Victor, however, it may be heard in all its beauty and the fine renditions by Caruso and Slezak fully appreciated.

COPY'T MISHKIN

SLEZAK AS RHADAMES

RHADAMES:
Heavenly Aida, beauty resplendent,
Radiant flower, blooming and bright;
Queenly thou reignest o'er me transcendent,
Bathing my spirit in beauty's light.
Would that thy bright skies once more beholding,
Breathing the soft airs of thy native land,
Round thy fair brow a diadem folding,
Thine were a throne next the sun to stand!

A fine trio, expressing the emotions of the characters in the scene, then follows.

Ohimé! di guerra fremere (Alas! the Cry of War I Hear)

By Elena Ruszcowska, Soprano; Bianca Lavin de Casas, Mezzo-Soprano; Egidio Cunego, Tenor (*In Italian*) 88261 12-inch, $3.00

The *King's* daughter, *Amneris,* enters, and seeing the young warrior's glowing enthusiasm, delicately hints of her secret affection for him, saying:

AMNERIS:
What unwonted fire in thy glance!
With what noble pride glows thy face!
Worthy of envy—oh, how much—
Would be the woman whose beloved aspect
Should awaken in thee this light of joy!

Rhadames begins to explain his hope of securing the command of the expedition, when *Aida* enters, and the young soldier's expressive glance reveals to *Amneris* his love for the Egyptian slave.

The *King* and his guards enter and receive a messenger, who reports that Egypt has been invaded by the Ethiopian army, under the command of *Amonasro.* ("My father!" exclaims *Aida* aside.) Amid great excitement *Rhadames* is appointed leader of the army, and is presented with a banner by *Amneris.*

The *King* begins another trio, urging the Egyptian forces to guard with their lives the sacred Nile.

COPY'T DOVER ST STUDIOS

MARTIN AS RHADAMES

16

FIGURE 72

"Aida," in *The Victor Book of the Opera,* 3rd ed. (1912), 16–17.

motive at the end—all are given with characteristic richness and warmth of style by this admired singer, while the final high note is brilliantly taken." All this for $3. But there's also John McCormack's rendition, which will set you back just half as much: "An entirely different interpretation, though also a very fine one"—and three others besides, one in English, "to complete a list in which every lover of this beautiful air can find a record to suit his taste and purse."[26]

VICTOR BOOK OF THE OPERA—VERDI'S AIDA

Su! del Nilo (Nilus' Sacred Shores!)

COPY'T DUPONT

GADSKI AS AIDA

By Elena Ruszcowska, Soprano; Maria Cappiello, Mezzo-Soprano; Tapergi and Davi (*In Italian*) 88266 12-inch, $3.00

Following the trio comes a grand chorus:

To battle! We'll hunt the invader down.
On! Rhadames, thy brow may laurels crown!

All depart to prepare for the expedition, while *Aida*, left alone, gives way to her grief and sings the beautiful *Ritorna vincitor*, expressing her conflicting emotions.

Ritorna vincitor (Return Victorious!)

By Johanna Gadski, Soprano (*In Italian*) 88137 12-inch, $3.00

AIDA:
Return victorious! And from my lips
Went forth the impious word! Conqueror
Of my father—of him who takes arms
For me—to give me again
A country; a kingdom; and the illustrious name
Which here I am forced to conceal!
The insane word forget, O gods;
Return the daughter
To the bosom of her father;
Destroy the squadrons of our oppressors!. . .
What am I saying? And my love,
Can I ever forget
This fervid love which oppresses and enslaves,
As the sun's ray which now blesses me?
Shall I call death on Rhadames—
On him whom I love so much?
Ah! Never on earth was heart torn by more cruel agonies!

She gives way to her emotion for a brief moment, then sings the lovely and appealing

I sacri nomi (The Sacred Names)

By Celestina Boninsegna, Soprano 88223 (*In Italian*) 12-inch, $3.00

Rousing herself, she calls on her gods for aid and goes slowly out as the curtain falls.

SCENE II—*The Temple of Vulcan—in the centre an altar, illuminated by a mysterious light from above*

Ramfis, the High Priest, and the priests and priestesses have assembled to bless the expedition. The chant in praise of *Ptah* is heard from an invisible choir. *Rhadames* enters and receives the consecrated veil.

RAMFIS:
Mortal, beloved of the gods, to thee
Is confided the fate of Egypt. Let the holy sword
Tempered by the gods, in thy hand become
To the enemy, terror—a thunderbolt-death!

RHADAMES:
God, who art leader and arbiter
Of every human war,
Protect thou and defend
The sacred soil of Egypt!

Nume, custode e vindice (God, Guardian and Avenger)

By Antonio Paoli, Tenor; Perello de Segurola, Bass; and Chorus (*In Italian*) 88268 12-inch, $3.00

COPY'T DUPONT

EAMES AS AIDA

17

Complete opera recordings were released gradually, the first of which was *Ernani*, a 1903 "His Master's Voice" (HMV) set on forty single-sided disks.[27] By 1929 Victor was advertising a complete recording of *Aida* on nineteen two-sided disks, issued in two volumes, in the "Musical Masterpieces" series for $28.50 (around $391 in 2014 dollars); that same year, Columbia advertised seven complete recordings of standard-repertory operas, including one of *Tristan und Isolde*, twenty disks in three separately priced

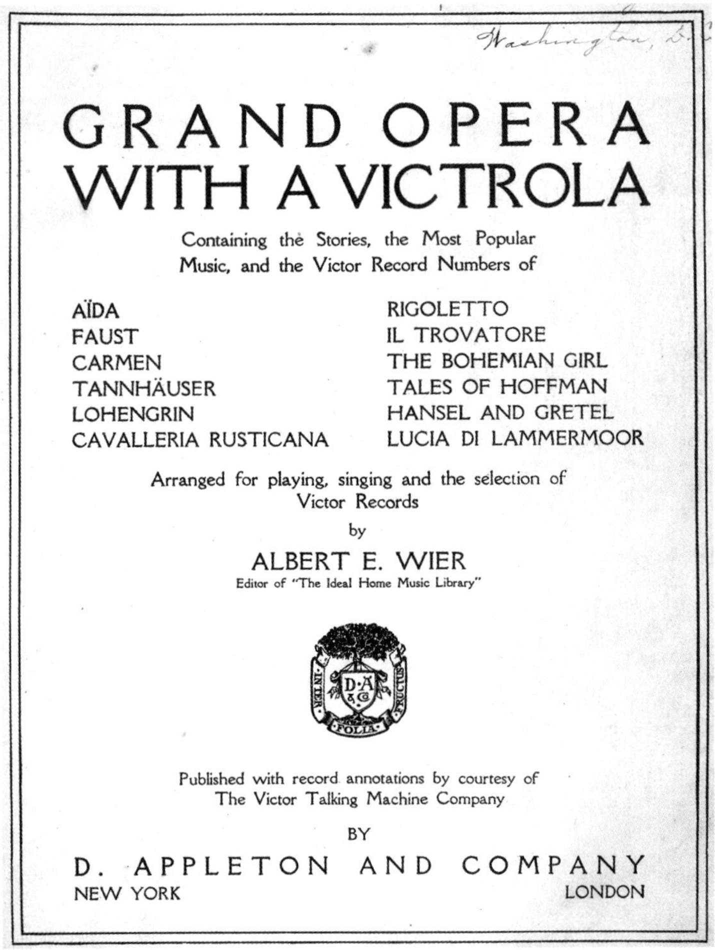

Washington, D.C.

GRAND OPERA
WITH A VICTROLA

Containing the Stories, the Most Popular Music, and the Victor Record Numbers of

AÏDA	RIGOLETTO
FAUST	IL TROVATORE
CARMEN	THE BOHEMIAN GIRL
TANNHÄUSER	TALES OF HOFFMAN
LOHENGRIN	HANSEL AND GRETEL
CAVALLERIA RUSTICANA	LUCIA DI LAMMERMOOR

Arranged for playing, singing and the selection of Victor Records

by

ALBERT E. WIER

Editor of "The Ideal Home Music Library"

Published with record annotations by courtesy of The Victor Talking Machine Company

BY

D. APPLETON AND COMPANY

NEW YORK LONDON

FIGURE 73

Grand Opera with a Victrola, arranged by Albert E. Wier, published with record annotations courtesy of The Victor Talking Machine Company (New York: D. Appleton, 1915–16), title page. Private collection.

volumes.[28] Instrumental arrangements of opera music—opera without words—were also marketed.

As an alternative to imagining a performance while listening to the Victrola—the sight of it in the mind's eye, so to speak—one might play and sing on one's own the operatic numbers available in publications like *Grand Opera with a Victrola* (fig. 73), an anthology of arias from twelve operas in the standard repertory, as the title page puts it, "arranged for playing, singing and the selection of Victor records."[29] Each opera is provided a brief plot summary interspersed with various numbers organized act by act, a dozen or so arias, ensembles, choruses, and orchestral interludes for each, and all vocal texts in English only. Each number is linked to a Victor recording. An instructional page, "To the Victrola Enthusiast" (fig. 74), explains several ways the collection will enhance one's knowledge and enjoyment of the Victrola recordings available for purchase, ending

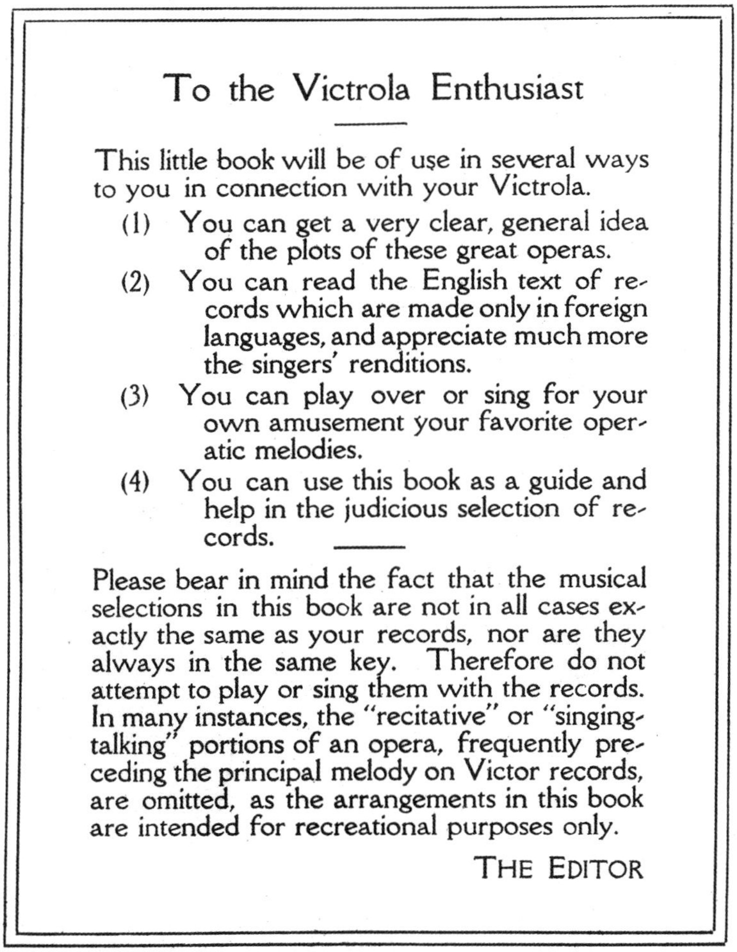
To the Victrola Enthusiast

This little book will be of use in several ways to you in connection with your Victrola.

(1) You can get a very clear, general idea of the plots of these great operas.

(2) You can read the English text of records which are made only in foreign languages, and appreciate much more the singers' renditions.

(3) You can play over or sing for your own amusement your favorite operatic melodies.

(4) You can use this book as a guide and help in the judicious selection of records.

Please bear in mind the fact that the musical selections in this book are not in all cases exactly the same as your records, nor are they always in the same key. Therefore do not attempt to play or sing them with the records. In many instances, the "recitative" or "singing-talking" portions of an opera, frequently preceding the principal melody on Victor records, are omitted, as the arrangements in this book are intended for recreational purposes only.

THE EDITOR

FIGURE 74
"To the Victrola Enthusiast," in *Grand Opera with a Victrola*, 3.

with a weird disclaimer on the absence of recitatives, stating that "the arrangements in this book are intended for recreational purposes only."

The middle pages of the twenty-four-page monthly Victor catalogue update from March 1919 (fig. 75) are devoted to a primer, "How Artists Study Operatic Roles." Its opening approaches the subject in words that evoke a somewhat fay perception of opera's domestic audience familiar to readers of Wayne Koestenbaum's book *The Queen's Throat*:[30] "Those who flit with butterfly lightness from one Victor opera record to another have little conception of the hours, days, weeks of love and labor, of nerve-wracking effort and heart-anguish that such records represent." There follows a step-by-step account of learning a role, performing it in public, and ultimately recording it for Victor, leading to this:

> For the artist's personality no less than his voice is registered by the needle, and the aria he sings contains within itself all the subjective thought and effort he has put into the role.

FIGURE 75
New Victor Records, March 1919, title page.

> When an artist stands before the Victor recording instrument, he is shorn of all the trappings of opera. . . . All his attention is concentrated on the singing . . . so that, as you listen, you can enter into the spirit of the music. . . . It is a veritable soul revelation through the voice.[31]

The appeal is to the release of refined affect, to sensibility and sensitivity; it's as though—as will become apparent in what follows concerning Victor advertising campaigns—Caruso is singing for you alone in your home. Perhaps more to the point, Victor suggests that home listening offers a *better* experience than attending a performance, since in the recording studio performers attend solely to their singing. Live opera gives you Caruso's *body;* Victor gives you his *soul.* The move downgrades the materiality of embodied performance on behalf of the secularized spirituality of the disembodied voice captured in the material substance of the disk.[32]

The catalogue ends with a chatty bit called "By the Way," a series of brief comments, all directly (if by some circuitous routing) to music and Victor. The eight short disconnected paragraphs narrate a gamut of politics, exercise, audience appeal, staging a home recital with recordings, and the like, all of it pedagogical.

> [Politics:] A hundred and eighty million Russians in revolt, but so far not a single "Marseillaise." They do these things better in France.
>
> [Exercise:] If you are one of those strenuous people who must exercise every morning, do your calisthenics to a Sousa March on the Victrola. Keys you up quicker than anything.
>
> [Audience appeal:] There are some people to whom music is merely a hobby—a little more than photography, a little less than golf; and some to whom music is all in all. The Victrola has something to offer to everybody between those two extremes.
>
> [Home recital:] A hint to those who give home music recitals with the Victrola: A strong first number; a strong middle number, and a big finale at the end. Run a few lighter pieces in between. About seven numbers are sufficient. A good recital, like a good meal, leaves one just a little hungry for more.[33]

Victor produced annual comprehensive catalogues of their recordings starting in 1912. The layout, as exemplified in the 1923 edition (fig. 76), begins with some basics—how to use the catalogue, how to play a record, and how to get best results (for example, "don't use a steel needle more than once"), followed by four pages of recommendations for assembling a basic collection, opera listed first, followed by standard songs, sacred songs, band and orchestra records, instrumentals of various sorts, comic monologues, recitations ("Casey at the Bat"), and the like, and ending with dance numbers. Several hundred pages list every Victor recording available, given in one multipurpose alphabet: by title, artist, musical type ("Accordion Solos"), and so on; all by serial number, disk size (10″ or 12″), and list price. Occasional illustrations are included of artists (classical and popular), composers, opera sets, etc. The catalogue also advertises for *The Victrola Book of the Opera*.

At the back, printed on pink paper, there follows a separate catalogue of the Red Seal recordings (fig. 77)—sixty-eight pages, of which Caruso requires four (fig. 78); the principal emphasis is on opera, and the title page employs the "His Master's Voice" logo. Victor kept current the backlist of its most prestigious singers well after their passing; indeed, prominent deaths were highly fungible. Caruso's passing on August 2, 1921, generated heavy newspaper coverage throughout Europe and the Americas, which amounted to free advertising, well supplemented by Victor in a flurry of ads with banner headlines such as "My Victor Records shall be my biography" (fig. 79), indicating that there are "many records to be issued" beyond the 178 Caruso recordings already available.[34] Repeatedly stressing the immortalization of its star singer, Victor declared that it had "bridged the oblivion into which both singer and musician passed" (fig. 80). Victor's monthly catalogue for October 1922 featured a photographic portrait of the singer in profile ("The Late Enrico Caruso") and directed the reader to the inside front cover announcing the first new Caruso recording since his death fifteen months earlier, the

1923 CATALOGUE
OF
VICTOR RECORDS
WITH
Biographical Sketches
Opera Plots, New Portraits
& Special Red Seal
Section

VICTOR
TALKING MACHINE COMPANY
Camden, New Jersey
U. S. A.

Copyright 1912, 1913, 1914, 1915, 1916, 1917, 1918, 1919, 1920, 1921, 1922
By the Victor Talking Machine Company

FIGURE 76
1923 Catalogue of Victor Records (Camden, N.J.: Victor Talking Machine Company, 1923), title page. Private collection.

aria "Mia piccirella" from the now-obscure opera *Salvator Rosa* by the Brazilian composer Antônio Carlos Gomes (1836–96). Promoting the recorded performance, the narrative concludes, "Living, not dead, it is the man himself."[35]

In 1932, after the introduction of electrical recording and following the 1929 sale of Victor to the Radio Corporation of America, RCA stripped away—as best they could, however imperfectly—the original accompaniments to Caruso's acoustic recordings, leaving the voice intact, and overdubbed new electrically recorded orchestral accompaniment,[36] by means of what RCA called "the Bi-Acoustic principle": "Caruso sings again. Caruso lives anew! A thing that cannot be—but is!" (fig. 81). As Jason Stanyek and Benjamin Piekut nicely put it, music "has been a particularly fertile growth market for dead talent."[37] In point of fact, Caruso was one of the first recording artists subject to what today is termed necro-marketing, a practice of sufficient profit that *Forbes* magazine since 2001 has published an annual accounting of "Top-Earning Dead Celebrities."[38]

FIGURE 77
"Victor Red Seal Records: A Library of Famous Voices," in *1923 Catalogue of Victor Records,* unpaginated.

FIGURE 78
Caruso recordings in the Red Seal portion of the *1923 Catalogue of Victor Records,* unpaginated.

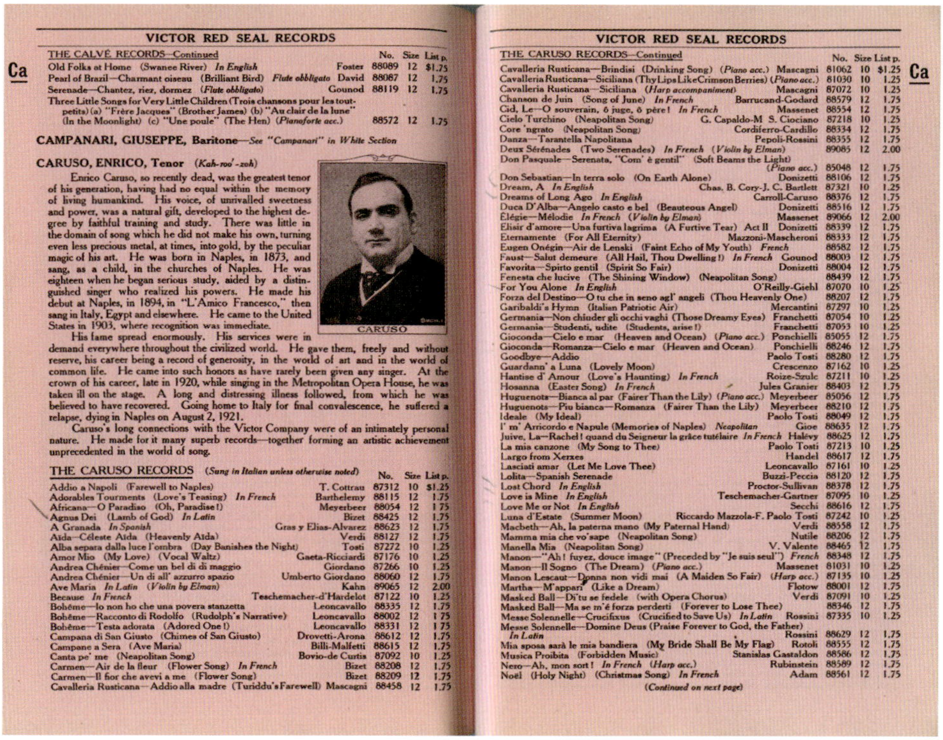

VICTOR RED SEAL RECORDS

Ca

THE CALVÉ RECORDS—Continued

		No.	Size	List p.
Old Folks at Home (Swanee River) *In English*	Foster	88089	12	$1.75
Pearl of Brazil—Charmant oiseau (Brilliant Bird) *Flute obbligato*	David	88087	12	1.75
Serenade—Chantez, riez, dormez (*Flute obbligato*)	Gounod	88119	12	1.75
Three Little Songs for Very Little Children (Trois chansons pour les tout-petits) (a) "Frère Jacques" (Brother James) (b) "Au clair de la lune" (In the Moonlight) (c) "Une poule" (The Hen) (*Pianoforte acc.*)		88572	12	1.75

CAMPANARI, GIUSEPPE, Baritone—*See "Campanari" in White Section*

CARUSO, ENRICO, Tenor (*Kah-roo'-zoh*)

CARUSO

Enrico Caruso, so recently dead, was the greatest tenor of his generation, having had no equal within the memory of living humankind. His voice, of unrivalled sweetness and power, was a natural gift, developed to the highest degree by faithful training and study. There was little in the domain of song which he did not make his own, turning even less precious metal, at times, into gold, by the peculiar magic of his art. He was born in Naples, in 1873, and sang, as a child, in the churches of Naples. He was eighteen when he began serious study, aided by a distinguished singer who realized his powers. He made his debut at Naples, in 1894, in "L'Amico Francesco," then sang in Italy, Egypt and elsewhere. He came to the United States in 1903, where recognition was immediate.

His fame spread enormously. His services were in demand everywhere throughout the civilized world. He gave them, freely and without reserve, his career being a record of generosity, in the world of art and in the world of common life. He came into such honors as have rarely been given any singer. At the crown of his career, late in 1920, while singing in the Metropolitan Opera House, he was taken ill on the stage. A long and distressing illness followed, from which he was believed to have recovered. Going home to Italy for final convalescence, he suffered a relapse, dying in Naples on August 2, 1921.

Caruso's long connections with the Victor Company were of an intimately personal nature. He made for it many superb records—together forming an artistic achievement unprecedented in the world of song.

THE CARUSO RECORDS (*Sung in Italian unless otherwise noted*)

		No.	Size	List p.
Addio a Napoli (Farewell to Naples)	T. Cottrau	87312	10	$1.25
Adorables Tourments (Love's Teasing) *In French*	Barthelemy	88115	12	1.75
Africana—O Paradiso (Oh, Paradise!)	Meyerbeer	88054	12	1.75
Agnus Dei (Lamb of God) *In Latin*	Bizet	88425	12	1.75
A Granada *In Spanish*	Gras y Elias-Alvarez	88623	12	1.75
Aïda—Céleste Aïda (Heavenly Aïda)	Verdi	88127	12	1.75
Alba separa dalla luce l'ombra (Day Banishes the Night)	Tosti	87272	10	1.25
Amor Mio (My Love) (Vocal Waltz)	Gaeta-Ricciardi	87176	10	1.25
Andrea Chénier—Come un bel di di maggio	Giordano	87266	10	1.25
Andrea Chénier—Un di all' azzurro spazio	Umberto Giordano	88060	12	1.75
Ave Maria *In Latin* (*Violin by Elman*)	Kahn	89065	12	2.00
Because *In French*	Teschemacher-d'Hardelot	87122	10	1.25
Bohême—Io non ho che una povera stanzetta	Leoncavallo	88335	12	1.75
Bohême—Racconto di Rodolfo (Rudolph's Narrative)	Leoncavallo	88002	12	1.75
Bohême—Testa adorata (Adored One!)	Leoncavallo	88331	12	1.75
Campana di San Giusto (Chimes of San Giusto)	Drovetti-Arona	88612	12	1.75
Campane a Sera (Ave Maria)	Billi-Malfetti	88615	12	1.75
Canta pe' me (Neapolitan Song)	Bovio-de Curtis	87092	10	1.25
Carmen—Air de la fleur (Flower Song) *In French*	Bizet	88208	12	1.75
Carmen—Il fior che avevi a me (Flower Song)	Bizet	88209	12	1.75
Cavalleria Rusticana—Addio alla madre (Turiddu's Farewell)	Mascagni	88458	12	1.75

VICTOR RED SEAL RECORDS

Ca

THE CARUSO RECORDS—Continued

		No.	Size	List p.
Cavalleria Rusticana—Brindisi (Drinking Song) (*Piano acc.*)	Mascagni	81062	10	$1.25
Cavalleria Rusticana—Siciliana (Thy Lips Like Crimson Berries) (*Piano acc.*)		81030	10	1.25
Cavalleria Rusticana—Siciliana (*Harp accompaniment*)	Mascagni	87072	10	1.25
Chanson de Juin (Song of June) *In French*	Barrucand-Godard	88579	12	1.75
Cid, Le—O souverain, ô juge, ô père! *In French*	Massenet	88554	12	1.75
Cielo Turchino (Neapolitan Song)	G. Capaldo-M S. Ciociano	87218	10	1.25
Core 'ngrato (Neapolitan Song)	Cordiferro-Cardillo	88334	12	1.75
Danza—Tarantella Napolitana	Pepoli-Rossini	88355	12	1.75
Deux Sérénades (Two Serenades) *In French* (*Violin by Elman*)		89085	12	2.00
Don Pasquale—Serenata, "Com' è gentil" (Soft Beams the Light) (*Piano acc.*)		85048	12	1.75
Don Sebastian—In terra solo (On Earth Alone)	Donizetti	88106	12	1.75
Dream, A *In English*	Chas. B. Cory-J. C. Bartlett	87321	10	1.25
Dreams of Long Ago *In English*	Carroll-Caruso	88376	12	1.75
Duca D'Alba—Angelo casto e bel (Beauteous Angel)	Donizetti	88516	12	1.75
Élégie—Mélodie *In French* (*Violin by Elman*)	Massenet	89066	12	2.00
Elisir d'amore—Una furtiva lagrima (A Furtive Tear) Act II	Donizetti	88339	12	1.75
Eternamente (For All Eternity)	Mazzoni-Mascheroni	88333	12	1.75
Eugen Onégin—Air de Lenski (Faint Echo of My Youth) *French*		88582	12	1.75
Faust—Salut demeure (All Hail, Thou Dwelling!) *In French*	Gounod	88003	12	1.75
Favorita—Spirto gentil (Spirit So Fair)	Donizetti	88004	12	1.75
Fenesta che lucive (The Shining Window) (Neapolitan Song)		88439	12	1.75
For You Alone *In English*	O'Reilly-Giehl	87070	10	1.25
Forza del Destino—O tu che in seno agl' angeli (Thou Heavenly One)		88207	12	1.75
Garibaldi's Hymn (Italian Patriotic Air)	Mercantini	87297	10	1.25
Germania—Non chiuder gli occhi vaghi (Those Dreamy Eyes)	Franchetti	87054	10	1.25
Germania—Studenti, udite (Students, arise!)	Franchetti	87053	10	1.25
Gioconda—Cielo e mar (Heaven and Ocean) (*Piano acc.*)	Ponchielli	85055	12	1.75
Gioconda—Romanza—Cielo e mar (Heaven and Ocean)	Ponchielli	88246	12	1.75
Goodbye—Addio	Paolo Tosti	88280	12	1.75
Guardann' a Luna (Lovely Moon)	Crescenzo	87162	10	1.25
Hantise d' Amour (Love's Haunting) *In French*	Roize-Szulc	87211	10	1.25
Hosanna (Easter Song) *In French*	Jules Granier	88403	12	1.75
Huguenots—Bianca al par (Fairer Than the Lily) (*Piano acc.*)	Meyerbeer	85056	12	1.75
Huguenots—Piu bianca—Romanza (Fairer Than the Lily)	Meyerbeer	88210	12	1.75
Ideale (My Ideal)	Paolo Tosti	88049	12	1.75
I' m' Arricordo e Napule (Memories of Naples) *Neapolitan*	Gioe	88635	12	1.75
Juive, La—Rachel! quand du Seigneur la grâce tutélaire *In French*	Halévy	88625	12	1.75
La mia canzone (My Song to Thee)	Paolo Tosti	87213	10	1.25
Largo from Xerxes	Handel	88617	12	1.75
Lasciati amar (Let Me Love Thee)	Leoncavallo	87161	10	1.25
Lolita—Spanish Serenade	Buzzi-Peccia	88120	12	1.75
Lost Chord *In English*	Proctor-Sullivan	88378	12	1.75
Love is Mine *In English*	Teschemacher-Gartner	87095	10	1.25
Love Me or Not *In English*	Secchi	88616	12	1.75
Luna d'Estate (Summer Moon)	Riccardo Mazzola-F. Paolo Tosti	87242	10	1.25
Macbeth—Ah, la paterna mano (My Paternal Hand)	Verdi	88558	12	1.75
Mamma mia che vo'sape (Neapolitan Song)	Nutile	88206	12	1.75
Manella Mia (Neapolitan Song)	V. Valente	88465	12	1.75
Manon—"Ah! fuyez, douce image" (Preceded by "Je suis seul") *French*		88348	12	1.75
Manon—Il Sogno (The Dream) (*Piano acc.*)	Massenet	81031	10	1.25
Manon Lescaut—Donna non vidi mai (A Maiden So Fair) (*Harp acc.*)		87135	10	1.25
Martha—M'appari (Like a Dream)	Flotow	88001	12	1.75
Masked Ball—Di'tu se fedele (with Opera Chorus)	Verdi	87091	10	1.25
Masked Ball—Ma se m'é forza perderti (Forever to Lose Thee)		88346	12	1.75
Messe Solennelle—Crucifixus (Crucified to Save Us) *In Latin*	Rossini	87335	10	1.25
Messe Solennelle—Domine Deus (Praise Forever to God, the Father) *In Latin*	Rossini	88629	12	1.75
Mia sposa sarà le mia bandiera (My Bride Shall Be My Flag)	Rotoli	88555	12	1.75
Musica Proibita (Forbidden Music)	Stanislas Gastaldon	88586	12	1.75
Nero—Ah, mon sort! *In French* (*Harp acc.*)	Rubinstein	88589	12	1.75
Noël (Holy Night) (Christmas Song) *In French*	Adam	88561	12	1.75

(*Continued on next page*)

FIGURE 79

Victor advertisement: "My Victor Records shall be my biography," in *National Geographic* 41, no. 3 (March 1922).

FIGURE 80
Victor advertisement: "Caruso immortalized," in *National Geographic* 39, no. 2 (February 1921).

FIGURE 81

Victor advertisement: "Caruso sings again," in *National Geographic* 62, no. 4 (October 1932).

During the first decades of the century both Victor and Edison manufactured phonographs in staggering numbers of models, to say nothing of the phonographs sold by many other companies (e.g., Columbia and Brunswick). Edison's first recordings were released on cylinders, with disks following in 1912;[39] Victor's recordings were only released on disk. The cost of disk-playing phonographs varied widely. The cheapest could be had for about the same price as a few Caruso recordings; the most expensive, designed as fine furniture and with the turntable mechanism and acoustic horn concealed in the cabinet, were listed for extraordinarily high prices, for example a 1913 Victrola "XVI" in Circassian walnut for $250, or a 1917 Victor "Period" model in a fancy Louis XV cabinet for $750. Victor ran ads for "special designs"—in effect, for cabinets made to order "as quickly as the requirements of the highest–class workmanship will permit" (fig. 82). For its part, Edison aggressively competed with Victor for the high-end market. By 1917, thirty Edison models priced between $1,000 and $2,000 had been bought.[40] In 1919, Edison published a thirty-page phonograph sales catalogue titled *Edison and Music* filled with prose promoting sound quality, the result of $3 million in research and development costs, and incorporating the inventor's presentation of his personal ideals concerning "good music," manifested by what he decided to record (Edison himself kept tight control of his catalogue for decades on end).[41] The catalogue includes sketches of seventeen strikingly expensive cabinets, ranging in price from $120 to a staggering $5,500 ($74,641 in 2014 currency), the so-named Art Models, the most expensive of which were built to order, in very small numbers and clearly intended for the carriage trade (fig. 83).[42] Edison's cabinet styles favored copies of eighteenth-century designs, mostly English (Chippendale, Sheraton, Hepplewhite), but also French and Italian, as well as one cheaper (but hardly cheap) small model, the "Moderne" ($120). Further regarding phonograph cabinetry, in 1912 Edison designed and marketed both cylinder and disk models made from concrete, intended for the low-end working-class market, this in ongoing efforts to capitalize on his concrete business. Few were sold; as noted in press criticism, the cabinets were both heavy and fragile and commonly broke apart in shipping.[43]

Company claims on behalf of recorded sound linked the permanence afforded by the new technology, on the one hand, with the preservation of cultural treasures, classical music and opera especially, on the other. From the earliest history of music recording, the importance of preservation was a foundational principle whose worth was multiply articulated and indeed fetishized.

Mary Ann Doane suggests that the photograph is a "trace and hence corroboration of an existence," adding: "it is not coincidental that the privileged form of the index has been associated with death."[44] The same holds true for sound recording. Time as a defining principle of modernity involved time at the mercy of nowness. In Now Time the past remained present in ways heretofore unimaginable but fondly wished. Early sound recording met head on the issue of terrestrial eternity, heavily promoting itself on these

FIGURE 82
Victor advertisement: Victor Art-Shop Phonograph Cabinet (1934). Private collection.

grounds. For the price of a recording, anyone who had the wherewithal to be a customer could possess and consume at will time frozen in its own moment, encapsulated on shellac disks. Victor's advertising for Caruso recordings following his death reflects perfectly the abiding insistence to retain the past in the present, recognizing above all the fungibility common to both, alike then as now. That said, the postmortem Caruso reissue redubs acknowledge the uncertainties of newness, at the same time as they promote a "new" existence to what is recognized, precisely, as the inadequacy of the past inscribed on the surfaces of the original. Time, in short, remains a problem.

In *Cinema 2: The Time-Image,* Deleuze, reflecting on Bergson, addresses the conundrum of the simultaneous contradictory experience of modern temporality: "Since the past is constituted not after the present that it was but at the same time, time has to split itself in two at each moment as present and past, which differ from each other in nature. . . . Time has to split at the same time as it sets itself out or unrolls itself: it splits

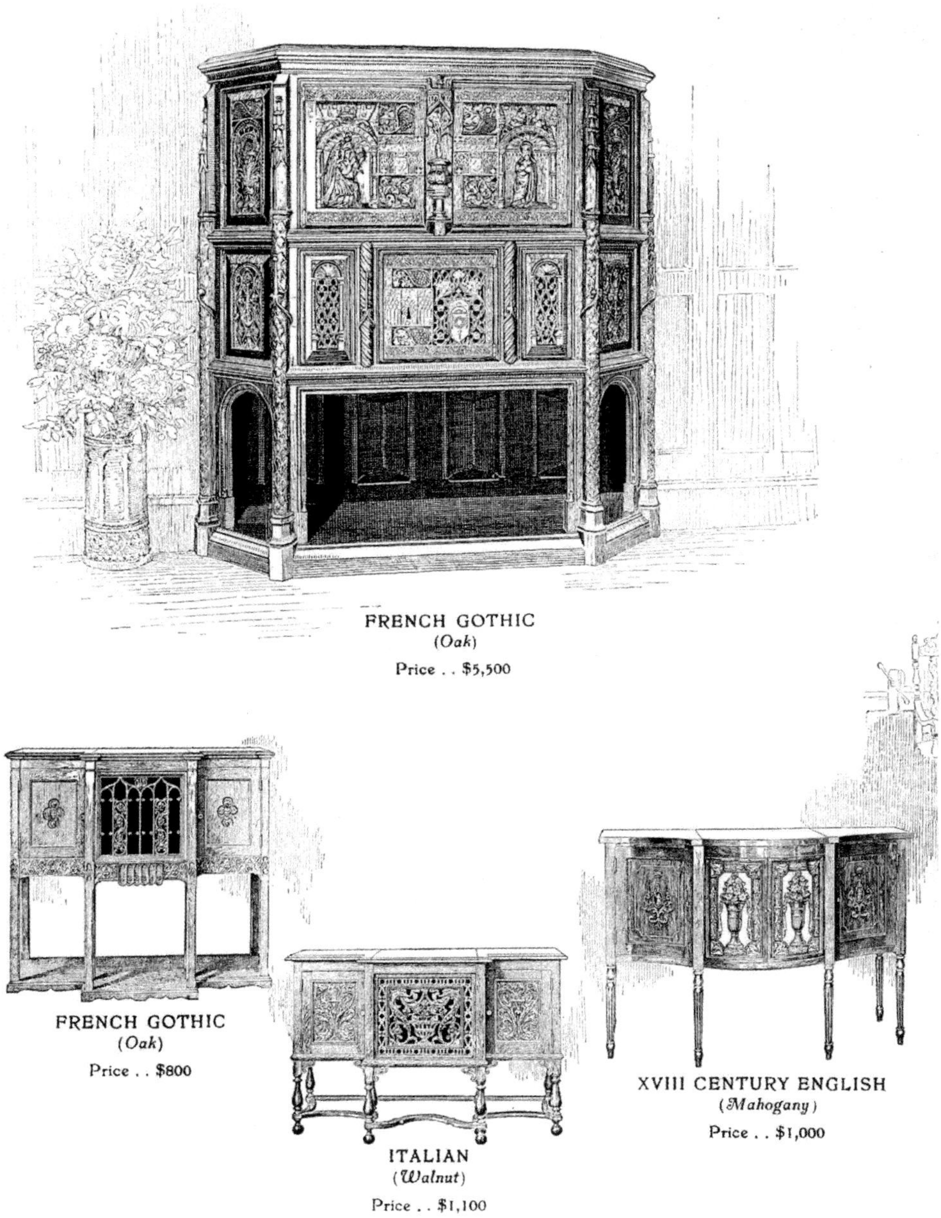

FIGURE 83
High-End, Made-to-Order Phonograph Cabinets, in *Edison and Music* (Orange, N.J.: Thomas A. Edison, 1919), 16.

in two dissymmetrical jets, one of which makes all the present pass on, while the other preserves all of the past. Time consists of this split."[45]

Classical music recording, constituted on the foundation of prevailing ideologies of aesthetic greatness and permanent worth, responded to the actuality of a brave new world of stark impermanence, appropriately embedded in the worthlessness of yesterday's newspaper and last season's fashion, and never mind that the bulk of what the recording industry released—popular music—was, precisely, ephemeral, its attractiveness in fact constructed on the principle of its *temporary* nowness.

Not the least irony as to the permanence of recorded sound was its actual common impermanence, whether by being rendered useless by worn-out needles or careless handling of the brittle disks, both leading to myriad complaints from consumers. These issues notwithstanding, recordings froze moments of sound like photographs froze a sight. In both instances, different temporalities collide: the time recorded, the momentary time of playback (repeatable at different times), and the lived time through which everything passes (linear time). Recordings allowed auditors to control recorded time—use it, archive it, discard it—at will. At a moment when temporality fundamentally defined life as never before (linear time being one of the most rudimentary components of modernity and responsible for its many anxieties: clock time, be on time, time is money, etc.), the home phonograph provided auditors with a kind of tacit control over a piece of temporality associated with pleasure aggressively promoted on precisely this ground. In the apt words of Jonathan Sterne, "The technology of sound reproduction fits oddly into this description of modernity as a form of at once hypertemporalized and detemporalized social consciousness. In bourgeois modernity sound recording becomes a way to deal with time."[46]

FIDELITY AND TRUTH

A perennial concern with sound recording, as real in 1900 as today, was fidelity in reproduction; the ultimate goal for the technology was transparency, the closure of any gap between the recorded live performance and its playback, the experiential erasure of a mechanical interface. Both Victor and Edison addressed the issue in their marketing of recordings and phonographs. Both companies claimed high levels of achievement in this regard, alongside increased dynamics as well.[47] The companies' very expensive advertising campaigns consistently engage sound fidelity, starting with the claim that objective listeners could not tell the difference between live performance and a recording—pitches analogous to the "Is it live or is it Memorex?" cassette tape commercials of the early 1970s.[48]

Between 1915 and 1925, Victor frequently held public "Tone Tests." An onstage performer alternated with her own (or even another person's) recorded performance of the same piece in an effort to prove there was no audible difference between the two. (In the instance where the onstage singer was not the same individual who was recorded,

FIGURE 84
Victor advertisement: "Which is which?" in *McClure's Magazine [The Marketplace of the World]* (1908). Private collection.

the live performer imitated the recorded voice as closely as possible—hardly an easy feat—though different vocal timbres would not necessarily have been obvious given the sonic limitations of acoustic recording technology.)[49] The recording played throughout the test; the live performer in turn was sometimes silent and at other times sang along with the record.[50] The larger point to glean from this exercise has less to do with the actuality of the supposed equivalence of the voices (live or recorded) than with the company's audacity in putting its claim on the line. What matters, in the end, is that the Tone Test provided a pedagogical framework for listeners to be *convinced* of the equivalence.[51] Victor's promotion of the sound fidelity of its recordings, only to be realized fully on Victrola phonographs and with Victor needles, focused on singing, opera, and (usually, if not always) Caruso, under auspices of the company's "Which is which?" and similar advertising campaigns (figs. 84–86).[52]

FIGURE 85
Victor advertisement: "Both are Caruso," in *Ladies' Home Journal* 30 (October 1913): 102.

Victor Tone Tests were matched by similar demonstrations on the part of rival Edison (usually referred to as "Realism Tests"), staged as pedagogical exercises for proper listening but also intended to put the listener in a mood receptive to the advertising claims for sound fidelity and at the same time to address concerns that recordings lacked the sight of live performance. Edison tests followed a precise protocol, specified in the company's directive "The Tone-Test and Its Stage Setting," calling for a "small Davenport or settee, mahogany, upholstered" with "chairs to match Davenport," along with "the best framed picture of Mr. Edison you can produce" and a "picture suitable to 'balance' [Mr. Edison's] (May be a landscape)," as well as potted palms, ferns, and so on.[53] Edison sponsored more than four thousand such tests between 1915 and 1920,[54] with the largest audiences

FIGURE 86
Victor advertisement: "No other combination accomplishes the same result," in *Saturday Evening Post* 193, no. 41 (April 9, 1921): 56–57.

numbering in the thousands (figs. 87 and 88), though demonstrations of this size were restricted to major cities.

An advertisement for the Christmas market in 1919 appearing in the *Ladies' Home Journal,* spread over two full pages, illustrated a variation on the live-performance-or-recording trope, this one with two photographs of soprano Frieda Hempel standing next to a phonograph in front of five well-dressed men, vaguely described as "Edison's musical experts," who are seated and blindfolded. In the first photograph, she sings; in the second, she is silent while her recording plays. "The blindfold test is the most severe of all musical tests," notes the accompanying text; "shutting off a person's sight greatly increases his acuteness of hearing." Nonetheless, the men are fooled: they detect no difference between Hempel's singing and her recorded voice.[55]

Edison offered advice to listeners for conjuring access to the otherwise absented sight of sound while listening to its records—promising virtual operatic images as real as reality itself, and never mind that relatively few record enthusiasts had experienced opera *except* via disk. Record companies' concern developed in part from a perceived need to overcome the problem of acousmatic listening.

Steven Connor suggests, "Human beings in many different cultural settings find the experience of a sourceless sound uncomfortable, and the experience of a sourceless voice

FIGURE 87
Edison Company advertisement: "All Pittsburgh Was Amazed!" in *Ladies' Home Journal* 37 (February 1920): 88–89.

intolerable."[56] The issue of concern is a voice in the absence of the body. In the early history of phonography, the lack was sometimes acutely felt, and extreme measures might be taken to address the problem—as in the case of a British listener who constructed miniature stages to look at while listening to opera recordings.[57] The Victrola opera books, richly illustrated, worked toward the same end. To be sure, the human voice issuing from the horn of a phonograph has an apparent source; it does not, however, have a visible body. The soma has to be imagined, in Connor's words, as "a surrogate or secondary body, a projection of a new way of having or being a body, formed and sustained out of the autonomous operations of the voice."[58]

Brian Kane points out that "the acousmatic reduction disorients and redirects listening by *reducing sounds to the field of hearing alone,*" in other words to the substance or content of hearing; as Kane later adds, the sensorium is split "to separate the ear from the eye, and intensify the act of listening."[59]

The Edison Company sought to address the problem of the split sensorium while at the same time promoting the advantages of what Pierre Schaeffer refers to as "pure

FIGURE 88

Edison Company advertisement: "4000 heads get together," in *Collier's: The National Weekly* 67 (April 16, 1921): 23.

listening."[60] The customer was advised to go to her local Edison retail shop, where the necessary materials were waiting. Once there, pick out a record; face away from the phonograph; look through the scrapbook provided by the dealer and read one random clipping relating to the type of voice or instrument the customer will shortly hear. All of this is the set-up. At this point, she is instructed to conjure a memory picture of the most recent live performance she has experienced, after which she informs the demonstrator that she's ready to hear the recording.

The instructions thereafter concern her mind's eye, and would seem to require a timekeeper with a stopwatch. At the start, for forty-five seconds, she is to keep her eyes open, staying "in the moment"; thereafter, for a minute or more, close them. Then open the eyes for fifteen seconds, "but do not gaze at your surroundings" (whatever that means); thereafter she should close her eyes until the recording ends.

The point of the demonstration is to produce the mood necessary to create what Edison called the identical "re-action" experienced by a theatergoer at a live performance in the past. If the exercise fails, it's your problem, and you need to fix it by repeating the protocol. In other words, the result is guaranteed—unless it's not. The instructions end with the following cautionary note: "If you do not obtain this re-action at the first test, it is due to the fact that you have not wholly shaken off the influence of your surroundings. In that case you should repeat the test until you are no longer influenced by your surroundings."[61]

Efforts by both companies to minimize listeners' awareness of any distinction between a live performance and its recording systematically ignored two factors contributing to the challenge that both Victor and Edison had to face regarding their claims about sound fidelity: surface noise and tinny-sounding instrumental accompaniments.[62] Surface noise or, more accurately, acoustic interference has bedeviled recording since its inception, but the problem for early phonography was particularly acute,[63] though Edison's Diamond Disk recordings, released along with the first Diamond Disk phonographs in 1912—an ultimately unsuccessful effort to compete with Victor's market domination—represented, as Emily Thompson has noted, "the pinnacle of the technology of acoustical recording and sounded far better than anything that had preceded them."[64]

So long as records sounded scratchy, hoped-for transparency (erasure of the mechanical medium) was unachievable. Surface noise guaranteed resistance between the obvious materiality of the medium (records, phonographs) and the immaterial soulfulness and spirituality insistently claimed for the high-toned music at the apex of arguments for the very existence of records. Surface noise, in short, was *noise,* the uncompromised opposite of musical sound.

Mary Ann Doane points out that we "tend to think of a medium as a material or technical means of aesthetic expression . . . which harbors both constraints and possibilities, the second arguably emerging as a consequence of the first"; she then adds the corollary that material resistance is nonetheless "an *enabling impediment.*" In short, surface noise, or for that matter tinny-sounding orchestral accompaniment endemic to opera aria disks, sonically affirms indexical possibility as well as the actuality of the medium's falling short of the very illusion it defines as the marker of its worth. Though Doane's concern is cinema, she concludes by citing a point made by art historian E. H. Gombrich to the effect that "there must be some sort of gap, absence, or lack to enable the most important spectatorial [here: listening] activity, which [Gombrich] labels 'projection.' Far from being 'taken in' by the illusion, the viewer actively participates in the construction of an impression of the real and is led by experience and expectation to 'project,'"[65] precisely a function of tone tests and realism tests. Further, the very ubiquity of surface noise over time likely more or less erased itself to some degree from listeners' consciousness, similar to the experience of not consciously hearing cassette tape hiss.

SHOW/HIDE

The success of a domestic market for sound recording ultimately hinged on how the sound reproducer actually *looked* in the home setting. The home-as-sanctuary, the private sphere, was conceived and promoted not least as a refuge from the brave new world of modernity and its technological, mechanical-industrial foundations. The first phonographs proudly displayed their workings, making pointedly visible the technological achievement of the new medium. Most visually insistent was the horn, from which sound emerged as from a gigantic open mouth. The domestic sphere, the locus of purported traditional values of the human and the humane, did not long welcome the phonograph on such terms. The phonograph as *furniture* was much preferred. The horn especially seemed visually dissonant in the parlor, and it was easily bumped.

Hence, the horn was soon hidden once the domestic market for phonographs established itself. Victrola first offered phonographs with a concealed horn in 1906; other companies soon adopted the redesign.[66] Lisa Gitelman points out that "to emphasize the changing visuality of music, phonograph advertisements from the 1890s to the 1920s picture listeners watching the machine. Listeners stare vacantly at unseen . . . performers, as if by some collective premonition, keeping their gaze steady for radio and then television."[67] Once cabinetry concealed the mechanism, the voice, its source further disguised, now emerging from the interior of a decorative enclosure, was made the more acousmatic.

Now marketing sound reproduction equipment as furniture, Edison upped the ante by promoting its concealed-horn Diamond Disk phonograph as a *musical instrument.*[68] In fact, Edison and Victor advertising commonly associated the phonograph with bourgeois habits of domestic music-making, never mind that the instrument played by itself; it's likely that Edison's "musical instrument" promotion borrowed from already well-established similar advertising for player pianos. Edison pressed the issue by instructing its dealers to refer to the phonograph demonstrations as "recitals," thereby virtually anthropomorphizing the device.

Victor likewise advertised the design and cabinet construction of its phonographs using descriptions appropriate to the acoustic features of musical instruments, with texts

FIGURE 89
Victor advertisement: "Tone," in *McClure's Magazine* 44, no. 4 (February 1915): 122–23.

that speak of "concealed sounding boards and amplifying compartment of wood"—essentially three thin panels set in a compartment behind which the acoustic horn was located—and "Modifying Doors" that could be left closed for a muffled sound or opened to increase volume (fig. 89). Not to be outdone in this regard, one of Columbia's Grafonola models, its "Grand" (fig. 90), priced at $500, adopted the approximate shape of a grand piano, the advertising for which stressed both tradition (an upper-class, virtually *ancien régime* setting) and innovation (the electric motor-driven turntable). In place of a keyboard, louvers open to emit sound, made visible in the advertisement by musical notation floating in waves from the invisible horn.

In 1919, Edison published a full-page advertisement in the *Ladies' Home Journal* illustrating a Chippendale cabinet model set in an elegant, indeed aristocratic domestic interior and reproducing a letter excerpt from Lady Randolph Churchill, mother of Winston, praising her new phonograph. "Instead of the usual dentist-like looking cabinets, [Edison's] designers have succeeded in putting the character and feeling of the best periods into his phonograph cases"; in brief, she finds the new Edison "an attractive piece of furniture." Edison corrects Lady Churchill's assessment: she was misled by the look "so

FIGURE 90

Columbia Gramophone Company advertisement: "Just two ways of hearing all the Music of all the World," in *Country Life in America* 23 (March 1913): 115.

artistically conceived, so exquisitely made" that she mistakenly thinks Edison phonographs of this sort are only for "the fortunate few."[69]

Lady Churchill was not alone passing judgment. "With its movable horn and its solid spring housing, the gramophone's social position is that of a border marker between two periods of musical practice," wrote the twenty-four-year-old Theodor Adorno in 1927, duly acknowledging the sociocultural change encompassed within the history of the phonograph. His concern starts with its *look:* "The fate of the gramophone horns marks [the development of the phonograph as bourgeois furniture] in a striking manner. In their brassness, they initially projected the mechanical being of the machines onto the surface. In better social circles, however, they were quickly muffled into colored masses or wood chalices. . . . In the functional salon, the gramophone stands innocuously as a little mahogany cabinet on little rococo legs. Its cover provides a space for the artistic photograph of the divorced wife with the baby. Through discrete cracks comes the singing . . ."[70]

Adorno had a good deal more to say about the phonograph; more on that presently.

PUSHBACK

Company promises of sound fidelity, realism, or "tone" (or, for that matter, tone's absence)—take your pick from the promotional narratives—indirectly, but importantly, react to the dominant actuality that music until very recently could only be experienced in live performance. Sound recording providing an interface—some would say interference—between performance and audition engendered criticism in some quarters.[71] The best known, appearing within a decade of the advent of commercial recording, was voiced by John Philip Sousa (1854–1932), one of the most famous American musicians of his time and very much a public figure. In an oft-quoted essay, "The Menace of Mechanical Music," published in 1906, he makes sarcastic reference to the phonograph and its "canned music." Canned: dead, if preserved; and in this regard transposing onto recorded music one of Edison's initial claims on behalf of his new invention, namely, the preservation of the voices of the dead. As Sousa puts it, there comes now onto the American scene a "mechanical device to sing for us a song or play for us a piano, in substitute for human skill, intelligence, and soul."[72] Sousa laments the sound; he regrets as well the passivity promoted by the device. The (bourgeois) home, long a locus of amateur music-making, would now surely devolve into a site for audition only.

The half-life of Sousa's metaphor extended at least to 1943 in comments made by Virgil Thomson. Speaking about radio, made possible by the microphone technology that transformed sound recording in the 1920s, Thomson preserves Sousa's complaint, but principally on account of dissatisfaction with sound quality: "This music is never wholly realistic. The electro-mechanical devices by which music is preserved or transmitted all give it a slight flavor as of canned food. The preserved stuff, however, is nourishing and incredibly abundant; and one could neither wish nor imagine its abolishment. . . . This does not mean that processed music is completely interchangeable with fresh. It will sustain life, of course, at least for brief periods; and some of it has a special charm of its own, like canned peaches, boxed sardines, and filets of anchovy."[73]

Adorno, by contrast, came at the issue from a different angle, equally critical. In a note to himself in 1956, posthumously published in *Towards a Theory of Musical Reproduction*, he objects, precisely, to the *loss* of the acoustic interference readily discernible in acoustic recordings but now strikingly diminished following the advent of electrical recording and the appearance of the long-playing record. Adorno, in other words, laments the near achievement of sonic transparency—the erasure or elimination of audible evidence of its machineness at the point of interface between the original performance and its reproduction: "Concerning the problem of mechanical reproduction. The old, relatively primitive gramophones are preferable to the pseudo-perfected modern record players, as they do not create the *illusion* of an original, rather appearing as its shadow." Looking back in time, in other words, Adorno isn't buying into fidelity and realism claims for acoustic recordings. He continues: "But the closer that mechanical duplication strives to come to the living, the more its untruth—not least as the 'magnified,' bloated and therefore unclear sound—becomes apparent. The threshold is most likely marked by electrical recording techniques. Of course [and here Benjamin comes into play in Adorno's thinking], the quantity can transform itself into quality, i.e., the imitation can be perfected to such a degree that the category of the original loses its vitality."[74]

Adorno thus ends his note on a point of ambivalence. Writing nearly thirty years earlier, in the years immediately following the demise of acoustic horn recording in favor of the microphone, he is more direct in his critique; his concern (still informing his thinking three decades later) is less recorded sound as such and more a panoply of interlocked—for him dystopian—social realities of which sound recording is but a microcosm: business interest, fungibility, privilege, and privatization, all of which not coincidentally are as embedded in the history of early-century acoustic recordings as in today's fetishization of high-end audiophile equipment. The passage is worth quoting in full:

> The moment one attempts to improve these early technologies through an emphasis on concrete fidelity, the exactness one has ascribed to them is exposed as an illusion by the very technology itself. The positive tendency of consolidated technology to present objects themselves in as unadorned [i.e., *transparent*] a fashion as possible is, however, traversed by the ideological need of the ruling society which demands subjective reconciliation with these objects—with the reproduced voice as such, for example. In the aesthetic form of technological reproduction, these objects no longer possess their traditional reality. . . . The gramophone belongs to the pregnant stillness of individuals.[75]

Adorno was well aware that the classical music available on record throughout—and well beyond—the period of acoustic recording was almost entirely standard repertory. Some of it was relatively new music, to be sure, but just about none of it was the New Music (avant-garde) that he principally cared about. For Adorno, very much a modernist, it was

New Music that engaged, even embraced, modern technological culture itself, hence distinct from the prevailing circumstance where the modern technological apparatus serves merely as the medium promoting the fungibility of musical product (old classics, new hits). In sarcastic passing reference, Adorno notes the fetishistic appeal of the apparatus itself, whose operation may attract more attention than the music played on it. He offers two extremes: the consumer who simply pays the piper and takes what he can get ("just drops in his dime") and the expert who "examines all the needles and chooses the best one."[76]

Ever the dialectician, Adorno revisited sound recording a few years later, in 1934, at the momentous juncture of political crisis. Whatever his abiding concerns over the "canning" of music and the real (or at least to some degree imagined) loss of self-performance of music, part and parcel of German upper-bourgeois *Gemütlichkeit,* the phonograph record now has a critical role to play as a kind of message in a bottle for a future that might not happen. "The Form of the Phonograph Record," as his essay title suggests, considers the disk rather than the machine. Adorno here quite radically detours from the path taken in the previous essay, particularly regarding the question of the phonograph record as archive. He begins almost poetically with a physical description of the disk itself, in order to build toward a particular image: the disk "covered with curves, a delicately scribbled, utterly illegible writing."[77] Allusion to writing provides Adorno with the opportunity to liken the disk to a plate, or tablet, and thus eventually to the metaphor of archaic knowledge preserved for a later time, in this instance a future beyond modernity. The recording preserves the trace of intersubjectivity in its momentary capture of the past. His point is that the phonograph recording in the context of dystopian modernity may perform a kind of salvage anthropology for what will otherwise be lost. The phonograph, he suggests, while petrifying music, "absorbs into itself . . . the very life that would otherwise vanish. The dead art rescues the ephemeral and perishing art as the only one alive. Therein may lie the phonograph record's most profound justification, which cannot be impugned by an aesthetic objection to its reification."[78] In other words, his thinking at this juncture reverts to Edison's first instrumental insight as to the phonograph's social utility: an archive for the voices of the dead.

All the objections to the "canning" of music notwithstanding, beginning with Sousa, counterarguments came to its rescue. Writing in *Collier's* in 1921, for example, musician and writer (poetry, criticism, books on composers) Robert Haven Schauffler (1879–1964) sang the praises of the player piano and its music as an agent of democracy: "Within the last generation canned music has come—the greatest spiritual boon of modern time—to make the art democratic. . . . Most of the critics have already discovered . . . the superiority of the musical food served from the new, germ-proof can over that served from the open tin pan of the average pianist."[79]

Writing in the same magazine a month later, Schauffler again stressed the link between music and democracy, in this instance via the "canned" music provided by the phonograph. His argument is pinned on the phonograph's potential for putting high culture into the ears of the masses:

FIGURE 91
"Some enthusiastic fans give phonograph concerts to their friends, maintaining rigid discipline against talking," cartoon illustration by M. L. Blumenthal, in Robert Haven Schauffler, "Canned Music—The Phonograph Fan," in *Collier's: The National Weekly* 67 (April 23, 1921): 11.

> Be it ever so humble, there's nothing like a little culture for giving a man an agreeable sense of superiority over his fellows. Though two out of every three people would not recognize culture if they met it on the street, and would shy at its very name, everybody likes to get it and to show it off.
>
> The word has a bad sound, but its bark is worse than its bite. For culture simply means getting acquainted with the best that has been known and said and sung in the world.

He continues: "The phonograph, by opening up culture to everyone, has made music democratic. The balance of musical power has now passed from the professional to the amateur, from the performer to the listener, and from the concert stage to John Jones's parlor, which is now the musical center of the world."[80]

Schauffler later emphasizes the seriousness of purpose that presumably newly-created classical music "fans" adopt as their domestic listening habits, replete with a quasi-comic cartoon illustration to emphasize the point (fig. 91). Not coincidentally, Schauffler replicates the parameters of domestic musical experience repeatedly promised in Victor's opera recording advertising: "Some superlatively enthusiastic fans go the length of giving phonograph concerts to their friends, maintaining as rigid a discipline against talking during the music as if Caruso or Rachmaninoff were there in person. In extreme cases they even go the length of handing around printed programs."[81]

Schauffler explains the degree of cultural maturation that results from home listening to classical music, a version of cultural maturity understood as a gain in privatized self-satisfaction, hence precisely replicating Adorno's criticisms but in this instance as an "achievement" to be wished. "Grown out of his early crude wonder—that an imitative voice could come of a machine—[the listener makes himself] into a genuine connoisseur of music who collects records with the same intelligent type of gloating with which others collect coins or paintings."[82]

PROMOTIONAL EXCESS

Victor's efforts to achieve the domestication of opera were aggressively public, the quintessential example of which was the company's gigantic, thousand-bulb illuminated sign mounted over New York's Herald Square—near to the Metropolitan Opera, Caruso's home venue, at 39th Street and Broadway. The sign reproduced Victor's "His Master's Voice" logo (the voice-besotted terrier itself was twenty-five feet high), below which in huge letters ran the words "The Opera at Home."[83] The company's principal efforts, however, were carried out through extensive print-media advertising, much of it in color, appearing in the nation's largest mass-circulation early-century weekly and monthly magazines.[84] Edison vigorously competed with Victor for the same audience, both nationally and internationally. Victor and Edison alike promoted their products for their contribution to the advancement of musical taste. Victor's advertising in particular, early on and into the 1920s, repeatedly stresses the homology between classical music and the cultural uplift of its recordings. On the aesthetics front, leaving little to chance, Victor maintained an active presence in general education schemes in the nation's schools, organized through the company's Education Department.[85]

The domestic market for the phonograph depended to a large degree on appeals to women, the sex principally assigned responsibility for the wholesomeness of the domestic sphere, the raising of children, and the holdover Victorian (and earlier) ideology according to which the wife provided the moral anchor for the family.[86] Women were often the purchasers of phonographs, their taste whetted by the many advertisements run in magazines like the *Ladies' Home Journal, McCall's,* and *Women's Home Companion,* especially in time for the Christmas market and often printed in eye-catching color.[87] Victor's "Will there be a Victrola in your home this Christmas?" campaign was probably the most important of these appeals (figs. 92 and 93). The promotion ran from 1912 to around 1924; in 1925, in time for the Christmas market, Victor first advertised its combination phonograph-radio, supplanting the phonograph-only as the ultimate Christmas gift.[88] Although the ad texts often reference popular musical entertainment—Victor has it all—the imagery usually implies a narrow band of musical taste. Costumed singers, opera stars all, crowd

FIGURE 92
Victor advertisement: "Will there be a Victrola in your home this Christmas?" *National Geographic* 42, no. 6 (December 1922).

into the entry hall, the front door open to the winter cold; they look around, strike attitudes, and in some cases take a look at the family whom they are meeting for the first time. Caruso, virtually as important to Victor as Nipper, is nearly always dressed as Radames; he strikes a haughty pose while stationed next to the new Victrola at the right.

An earlier ad of similar sort (fig. 94), appearing in a variety of magazines for several years running, emphasizes the exclusivity of "Victor talent," proclaiming Victor artists as "the best friends you can have," even if, as in this instance, the retinue—operatic and otherwise—appears to have disembarked from Lilliput.[89] The home they've entered is grand, and to judge from the books, paintings, and grand piano, its occupants are already appropriately cultivated. The Victor machine, fine furniture itself, fits the locale. Husband and wife, formally dressed, face the phonograph, its mouth-door open, presumably

FIGURE 93
Victor advertisement: "Christmas morning—and in come the greatest artists!" in *Ladies' Home Journal* 37 (December 1920): 197.

"singing" to them—and only to them—although in this instance the retinue includes a marching band (next to the Victrola), a solo violinist (standing atop the phonograph), and part of an orchestra (at the back), as well as a comedy act (a man, presumably in blackface, and a clown next to the homeowner's chair). One way or another, so the text insists, referring solely to the "great masters" of musical art, your heart strings will be touched and provide you with "a wellspring of inspiration."

The evening goes still better if there is someone from outside the family to notice the cultural privilege and *arrivisme* certified by the addition of the fine phonograph. "What a coincidence! That Caruso record you just played on the Victrola was the same aria we heard him sing at the opera tonight!" (fig. 95). Still more, the text notes, you can "have as many encores as you desire." In effect, buy the record and you will own Caruso and can use him just as you wish. The "gift" of a recording is its repeatability matched to mythologies of personal choice and control.

No less important than the value ascribed to repeatability (encores!), record advertising assigned cultural value to collecting records, that is, to ownership, a phenomenon with a longer history in printed music and the by-then well established popularity of

FIGURE 94
Victor advertisement: "Victor Exclusive Talent," in *Women's Home Companion* 43, no. 1 (January 1916): 56 (back cover).

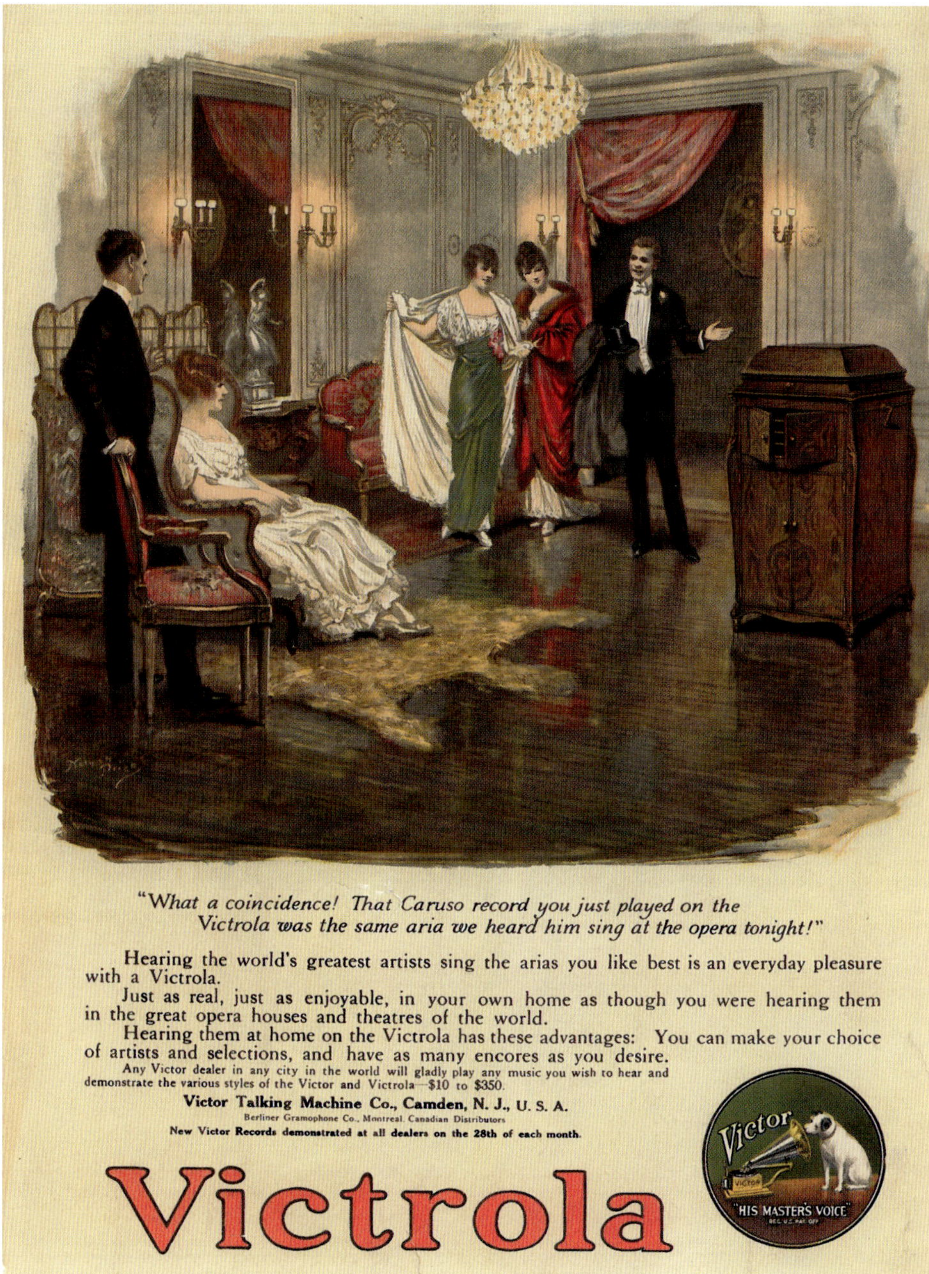

FIGURE 95

Victor advertisement: "What a coincidence! That Caruso record you just played on the Victrola was the same aria we heard him sing at the opera tonight!" (1915). Private collection.

piano rolls.[90] As Adorno once wryly put it, "Most of the time records are virtual photographs of their owners, flattering photographs—ideologies."[91] The home furnishings in these ads harken back to aristocratic lineage, whatever the modern fancy dress worn by the homeowners. Further to the point, Victor tended to place its snootiest ads in magazines where the presumed audience would be of appropriate class rank, while at the same time sometimes aiming the same or similar ads to a less well heeled audience, presumably one with some cash on hand and aspirations of cultural "improvement." The "What a coincidence!" advertisement, for example, ran in at least three magazines of somewhat different readership, all in 1915: *Collier's*, *Country Life in America*, and *Theatre Magazine*.[92]

In the end, these promotions, of which there were very many and of considerable variety, betray a certain anxiety on the part of Victor, located in the challenge to move its audience from the relative familiarity and expectations associated with live performance to private listening at home. Indeed, early in the history of the phonograph, companies sometimes staged "performances" of their machines in public theatrical venues, de facto promoting such events as though they were concerts or recitals. High-end phonographs in particular, their cost a marker of social cachet, offered a cultural supplement to the established practice of attending the opera and there experiencing—being part of—the social register in the flesh, the looking and the being looked at. Presumably, that sort of *frisson* could be imitated in home surroundings, especially if guests were invited. A sure sign of cultural achievement was one's demonstrable gain in sensibility, already a literary trope in the eighteenth century and amplified by the romantics. Victor asks, regarding the *Rigoletto* quartet, "Could you tell this story?," supplying the catalogue inventory numbers for five different renditions (fig. 96). Victor's appeal is distinctly personalized. The music may "portray some spiritual struggle that you yourself have experienced." The payoff promised, however, is less spiritual than mundane: once you've committed to the music properly, you can show off "satisfaction to yourself and to your hearers."

"The best friend of a hostess is the Victrola," so reads a 1913 advertisement from *McCall's Magazine* prominently placed on the magazine's inside front cover (fig. 97). The elegant, operatically attired special guests, led by Caruso, enter one by one, to be introduced by the lady of the house, her audience appropriately dressed as for opening night of the new season. The phonograph has been moved to the center of the room, the audience surrounding it as if attracted by its magnetic force. In this regard, Victor's promotions established the phonograph—many models equipped with record storage space—as a kind of tabernacle for musical art treasure, preserving performances as though they were relics, retrievable at will.

For Edison, the *sound* of the voice of the deceased subjectively mattered more than the words actually spoken, which after all could more easily be preserved in writing. Edison's insight is anchored in the phatic semiotics of speech, that is, in the emotional import of language in excess of words' meanings. It is precisely here that the recorded operatic voice takes on importance in the history of early recording. Heightened emotion, richly

FIGURE 96
Victor advertisement: "Could you tell this story?" in *Cosmopolitan Magazine* 74 (January 1, 1923): 1.

apparent in opera singing, as well as the cultural value ascribed to opera, was marketed by Victor for the thrall promised by the experience. "To appease the hunger for beauty which lies deep in every one of us—that is the mission of the Victrola. . . . Can *you* afford to miss the daily pleasure, the heart's-ease, that the Victrola so abundantly gives, and which is always yours to command in your personal hour of need?"[93] Simply stated, records fill a spiritual lack.

Caruso recorded the sextet from the second act of *Lucia di Lammermoor* three times for Victor, with varied ensemble of other singers.[94] An advertisement from 1908 promotes the first of these, recorded February 7 of that year, describing the music as "noted for its extreme beauty and powerful dramatic qualities" (fig. 98). In this instance, the scene in question is illustrated, the actors adopting dramatic body, arm, and facial gestures that underscore the scene. Whereas *The Victrola Book of the Opera* supplies

FIGURE 97
Victor advertisement: "The best friend of a hostess is the Victrola," in *McCall's Magazine* 41 (October 1913), front cover verso.

FIGURE 98
Victor advertisement: "Victor: The great Sextet from 'Lucia,'" in *Country Life in America* 15, no. 1 (November 1908): back cover.

English-language text translations and narrative summaries, what is promised has little if anything to do with either the specifics of language or plot situation. What matters is the human voice that sings beautifully. Individual arias in romantic (and other) operas have love as a subject second to none. Ensembles, such as the *Lucia* sextet, constitute a collection of conflicted emotions quite impossible to make sense of in the muddle of words. What matters instead is the phatic quotient of the whole that sonically ravishes the listener. What's here, Victor promises, is "great," "grand," "dramatic," and above all—and simply—beautiful. Opera ensembles (the ad alludes to several others) voice individual melodic lines and vocal harmonies, upping the affective ante by means of unisons, octaves, thirds and sixths. What the vocalists are actually singing about is a lesser matter. Beauty for its own sake, and beauty's impact on the listener, are the selling points, precisely because beauty *as such* enjoys cultural value. Victor delivered world-class singers singing their hearts out to music promoted as the highest expression of subjectivity in a culture where human worth was measured in part by the ability to *feel,* a trope traceable from *The Sorrows of Young Werther* (1774) to the closing moments of *La bohème* (1896).

In 1912, Victor published a full-page ad in *Country Life in America* titled "The greatest musical center in the world" (fig. 99). Its verbose text concerns itself almost exclusively with opera. Here's the opening, with commentary interspersed:

> Greater than the Metropolitan Opera House [rhetorical import: *America's temple of operatic art, equal to all others*]; greater than Covent Garden, where the royalty of England is entertained [*art/high society*]; greater than La Scala at Milan, the Grand Opera House of Paris, and the Royal Opera of Berlin [*international art form*]; greater in fact than all the opera houses and places of entertainment in the world, is the seventh floor of Building No. 5 [*just one among twenty-one numbered buildings*]—the center of a city in itself [*more than merely a factory*] formed by the modern structures of steel and concrete [*industrial power in the service of art*] that house the giant industry of the Victor and Victor-Victrola [*a unified, vertically organized, self-enclosed entity unlike any other*].
>
> To this building in the city of Camden, just across the historic Delaware River from the city of Philadelphia [*Founding Fathers, quintessentially American*], comes a never-ending procession of the greatest artists in the whole world [*see the accompanying parade of stars, classical at the top, Marine Band at the bottom, in characteristic hierarchy of cultural value, but fully democratic: a sound-world just for you*]. Today it may be Caruso or Amato, and tomorrow it may be Farrar, Gadski, or Melba, Sembrich, or Tetrazzini, . . . or it may be several of them assembling to unite in making a masterpiece like the "Sextette from Lucia." . . . But whoever it is or whatever the organization, rest assured that within the four walls of this building is heard, day in and day out, year in and year out, music in all its forms such as no other place in the world has ever heard [*time/space relation in perfect accord, both seemingly infinite*].
>
> And unlike music that is heard in any other place, which is only a momentary pleasure ending with its rendition, Victor music [*ours alone*] lives forever. From its beginning in Building No. 5 [*creation*], it goes through the various processes necessary for its perpetuation [*euphemism for massive industrial replication*] and eventually leaves the shipping department . . . to be heard again and again in hundreds of thousands of homes [*democratic domesticity*], just as it is heard in the sacred precincts of the recording room [*site of the music's "creation," art religion*] on the seventh floor of Building No. 5.

The advertisement reproduces in dim shadow the busts of ten composers, but hardly in the hierarchical order typical to the established musicological canon: Verdi is positioned at the top, Beethoven at the bottom. Six of the ten composed operas (besides Verdi and Beethoven, Handel, Rossini, Wagner, and Gounod).[95] The single most eye-catching aspect of the imagery is a bright red curving line that connects the first text ("The greatest musical center in the whole world") to an eye-shaped black oval whose pupil is the Arabic numeral 5, identifying the location of the "sacred precinct." The red line traces a

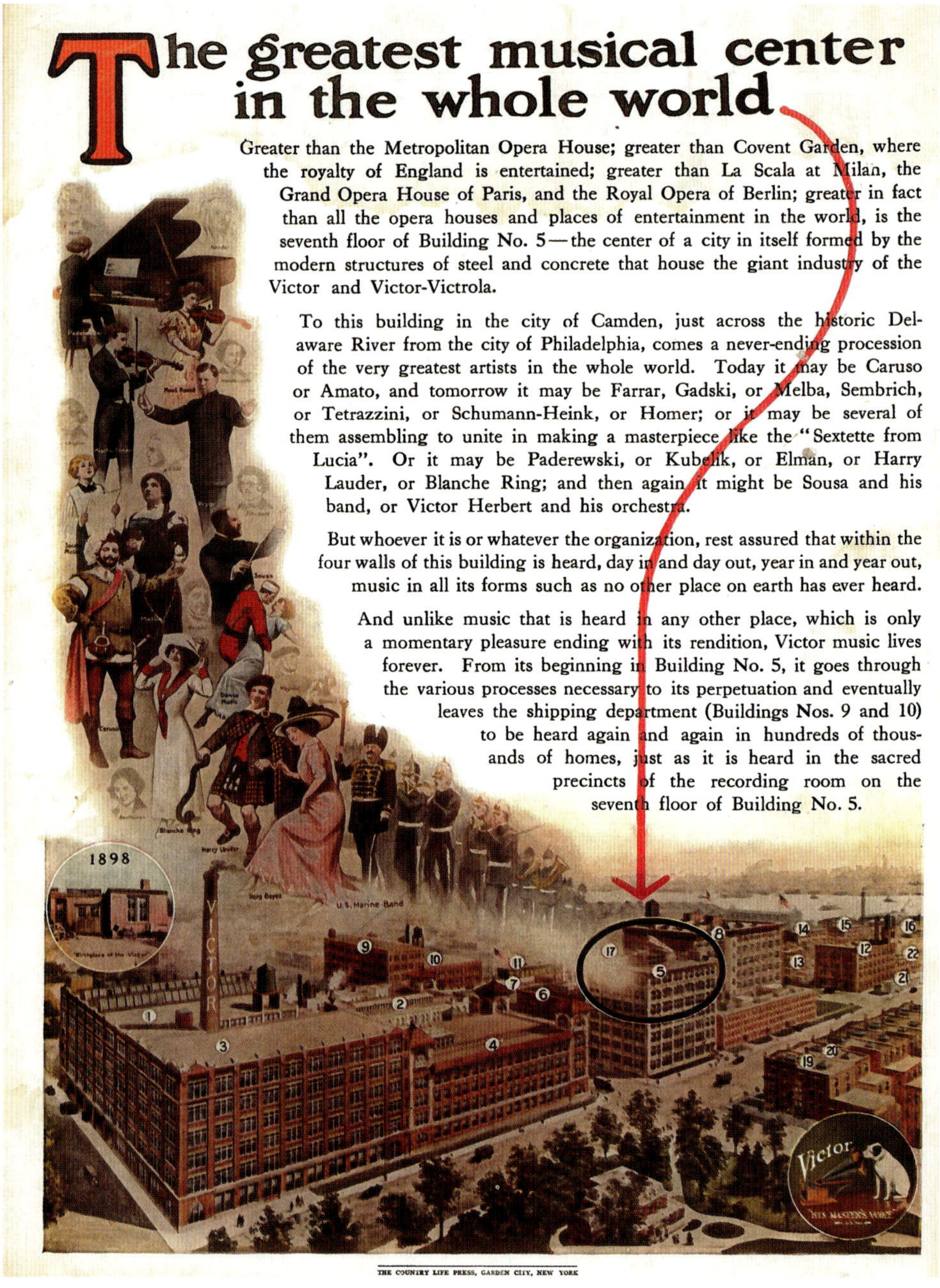

FIGURE 99

Victor advertisement: "The greatest musical center in the whole world," in *Country Life in America* 22 (July 1, 1912): back cover.

question mark, pointing to the building in question; the ad's lengthy text provides a gloss to answer the question whose urgency is registered by the red that sharply directs the eye to the site that exists for the benefit of the world's listening collective, *the* site for all the sounds that matter.[96]

SETTING THE MOOD

Edison, long trailing Victor in record sales, initiated a new advertising scheme in 1920, promising a "remarkable and enjoyable sensation" (fig. 100). Victor's promotion of its Building No. 5, located in the company's sprawling factory complex and distribution center in Camden, New Jersey, was now matched by Edison's campaign invoking the more fashionable address of its retail shop on New York's Fifth Avenue, upping the ante to Victor's "sacred precinct" metaphor. Edison's Midtown store was a "temple of music," worthy to house the company's anthropomorphized "Phonograph with a Soul."[97] Edison's promotional narrative, appearing in one of the foremost women's magazines, is ripe with the language of religious experience befitting a nineteenth-century opera libretto:

> The great rear hall, semi-visible through half-open doors, was steeped in a profound hush. A voice drifted to my ears from within—a voice lovely and full with a depth of feeling. . . . The exquisite beauty of the music instinctively drew my eyes through the doors—that I might gaze upon the singer. Instead, I beheld three men seated before the stately Chippendale cabinet. Their heads were bowed. The magic spell of the beautiful song [a "beloved ballad" in this instance] was full upon them.
>
> . . . . . . The music died away. The three men sat on in silence. They were lost in reverie.[98]

The music's beauty magnetically attracts the speaker; what his ears hear, his eyes long to behold, expressed in language too akin to Scripture to be ignored ("that I might gaze upon . . . I beheld"); the men sit, heads bowed, as if in prayer. Abruptly, however, the reverential mood is interrupted by an intrusive reference explaining what all the fuss is about, namely, a "stately Chippendale cabinet" and what issues from it. As if to underscore the mystical experience, the advertising copy signals the passage of time, even the loss of an awareness of time, by inserting a double ellipsis at the head of a new paragraph as a way to mark that, in the end, "the music died away," the putative service therefore concluding. The three heads-bowed auditors remain silent until "finally one found his voice." The ad's accompanying image, based on an "actual photograph," shows the reverential-appearing men looking down at pieces of paper in their hands (which turns out to be the Edison Realism Test protocol). Somberly dressed for the occasion, each puts on a serious face appropriate for a prayer service. Each in turn remarks on the realism of the singing voice and the effect it had on them. One is carried back to a summer during his youth; a second man simply notes the "free and unrestrained" voice, the "presence of a living singer" that affects him; the last assesses what matters most, in keeping with the

Noted Psychologists try the Realism Test

From actual photograph taken in the Edison Shop, Fifth Ave., New York, when Messrs. Bingham, Farnsworth and Follett came in and asked to hear the Realism Test.

Get remarkable and enjoyable sensation from Mr. Edison's unique musical experiment

IT was in that temple of music—the Edison Shop on Fifth Avenue, New York. The great rear hall, semi-visible through half-open doors, was steeped in a profound hush. A voice drifted to my ears from within—a voice lovely and full, vibrant with a depth of feeling. I recognized the first, appealing notes of a beloved ballad.

The exquisite beauty of the music instinctively drew my eyes through the doors—that I might gaze upon the singer. Instead, I beheld three men seated before a stately Chippendale cabinet. Their heads were bowed. The magic spell of the beautiful song was full upon them.

...... The music died away. The three men sat on in silence. They were lost in reverie.

Finally one found his voice: "I could have sworn there was a living singer behind me. It was marvelous. Carried me back to a certain summer I spent in my youth."

The second stirred himself: "I felt the presence of a living singer. She was singing—free and unrestrained. The accompaniment seemed by a separate instrument."

The third spoke up: "The music filled my mind with thoughts of peace and beauty."

The Realism Test

IT was Mr. Edison's unique Realism Test—given specially for three men of international renown in art and science. The man who first spoke was Dr. W. V. Bingham, Director of the Department of Applied Psychology, Carnegie Institute of Technology. His two colleagues were Prof. C. H. Farnsworth, Director of the Department of Music, Teachers College, Columbia University, and Wilson Follett, Esq., distinguished author and music critic.

Perhaps no other three men could be found in America, who have delved so deeply into that fascinating subject of research: *How does music exert its strange power on our minds and emotions?*

Perhaps no similar group of men could combine, to an equal degree, the viewpoint of scientist, musician, and music-lover.

The test was to determine scientifically the emotional re-actions produced by the realism of Mr. Edison's new phonograph.

The reactions of these highly critical minds demonstrated that Mr. Edison has succeeded in devising a new and fascinating way for you to judge the New Edison. It brings into play your whole temperament and your fullest capacity to feel the finer emotions.

Would you like to try the same test?

THE Edison dealer in your city is equipped to give you the Realism Test. Look for his announcement, or if you do not know who he is, write us for his name.

Send for the fascinating book, "Edison and Music." It is a story, written by one of Edison's right-hand men, that helps you understand the marvelous art of Music's RE-CREATION which Edison developed at a cost of 3 million dollars.

THOMAS A. EDISON, Inc.
Orange, N. J.

The NEW EDISON
"The Phonograph with a Soul"

FIGURE 100
Edison advertisement: "Noted Psychologists try the Realism Test," in *Ladies' Home Journal* 37 (May 1920): 87.

phonograph's "soul": spirituality. "The music [not further identified] filled my mind with thoughts of peace and beauty." The depth of the music's impact ratchets up with each successive commentary, and concludes with a kind of aesthetic reconciliation with the world.

The three men "of international renown in art and science" are identified; the first matters most, Dr. W. V. Bingham, Director of the Department of Applied Psychology, Carnegie Institute of Technology.[99] Bingham brings science to the discussion. The advertisement's headline reads, "Noted Psychologists try the Realism Test" (in fact, only Bingham is identified as a psychologist). Bingham and his colleagues were charged with a task that exceeded the mere certification of the Edison phonograph's sound fidelity. More, they are credited with having "delved so deeply into that fascinating subject of research: *How does music exert its strange power on our minds and emotions?*" (original emphasis). The listening test, so the narrative explains, "was to determine scientifically the emotional re-actions produced by the realism of Mr. Edison's new phonograph." Scientific proof trumps self-interested company claims. The commercial gets personal: The Edison soulful phonograph "brings into play your whole temperament and your fullest capacity to feel finer emotions." In short, the Edison phonograph will make you more human, and these guys have proven that this is so.

Six months later, Edison (himself famously deaf)[100] ramped up his campaign to advance the cause of emotional uplift. In February, the company ran a full-page, text-laden advertisement in a number of magazines, including *the American Magazine, Collier's, Cosmopolitan,* and the *Saturday Evening Post,* inviting readers to participate in an extraordinary national "Experiment" (fig. 101). After the universality of music's uplift is mentioned, we learn from Confucius that music is coterminous with "the sacred tongue of God"; from Martin Luther that it is "the only art that can calm the agitations of the soul"; and, in an unmodulated shift of emphasis, from Napoleon that "music is the art to which law makers ought to give the greatest encouragement." Animating Edison's promotion is his latest phonograph, now marketed as "The NEW EDISON," the aforementioned "Phonograph with a Soul." This machine does not reproduce music; it re-creates it, or, as the narrative puts it, the phonograph produced "such perfect realism that its Re-Creation of music cannot be distinguished from the original music."

The major recording labels promoted classical music, opera especially, by replicating discourse inaugurated in nineteenth-century cultural aesthetics combined with popular principles about self-improvement. Classical music offered sound culture for sale in a world increasingly acoustically fecund and often foreboding: urban sounds, machine sounds, traffic, industry, and the like. Music tended to the soul, reordering the sound world through an appeal to a purported need to experience beauty. Classical music provided an alternative acoustic to the mundane and *noisy* world—in particular, the world beyond the precincts of the home. That said, the form of listening offered up was part and parcel of the same world to which it presumably provided an alternative: the sped-up world of money and rank materialism, all of it experienced in an unending temporal dash. Time was (already) money, and time was precious. Concerts were long, while records played well under five minutes. Musical listening was leisure activity, with leisure restricted to after-hours, after life necessities were completed. Aesthetic spirituality, relief for the soul, so to speak, was available in short doses, however repeatable. Music was short-form; opera came in snippets. In advance of the long-playing record in 1948, many (even most) complete works of classical music required multiple disks. Even with mechanical disk-changer phonographs, music could only be experienced with interruptions and needle noise at both the start and end of each disk. Musical experience, in other words, was necessarily atomistic, except with regard to popular forms of musical entertainment, as with self-contained songs that early records could comfortably accommodate—like many arias—but with the difference that the songs were complete in themselves, not excerpts from larger works.

Realism Tests by 1921 were not news, but the published promotional "results" were, structured around mood enhancement and mood change. Affective listening, in brief, was now about *you*. To sort out the relation between listening and mood, Edison called on social science, though he initiated the investigation with a private cop (fig. 101). The reader is shown a reproduction of an "actual photograph" (objective truth) of one William J. Burns, former Secret Service agent, now head of the international detective agency bearing his name; he also served as director of the Bureau of Investigation (precursor of the FBI) from 1921 until 1924, when he was forced to resign for his involvement in the Teapot Dome scandal during the Harding administration, following which he devoted himself to writing detective and mystery stories until his death in 1932. Edison invited Burns to take the very first test, selecting him because as a detective he would be "the least susceptible to emotion," thus putatively a difficult subject for music to impact. The very same Mood Change Chart that Detective Burns holds in his hand is reproduced in large size at the right for the reader to peruse.[101] Hearing Schumann's "Träumerei" (*Kinderszenen,* op. 15, no. 7, for piano solo) changed his mood to serious, though changed from what isn't clear, since Burns notes that he had arrived "from a very serious conference." The second number, "Alice's Blue Gown," from the 1919 Broadway musical *Irene,* made him "gay."[102]

There are several parts to the survey card, in addition to the date and place where the test occurred: time of day (morning, afternoon, evening), weather (dull or bright, cold or warm), the kind of music you felt like hearing (tender, solemn, martial, simple, joyous, weird, gay, or sad), the mood you were in immediately preceding the test (serious or gay, depressed or exhilarated, fatigued or unfatigued, worried or carefree, nervous or composed, sad or joyful, discouraged or optimistic), and the mood change that occurred. No explanation is provided as regards the supposed worth of most of this data; it is not interpreted. Having taken the test, the listener notes the mood change that each piece produced and "comment[s] on manner in which mood changes occurred." At the bottom, space is provided for the auditor's signature and address.

Edison's invited the public to participate. If the reader already owned the New Edison, her local dealer would provide the test sheet; if she could gather some friends, she could

From actual photograph taken at Edison Shop, New York City

The First Man to Fill Out The Mood Change Chart

William J. Burns

Head of The Wm. J. Burns International Detective Agency

WHEN the Mood Change Chart was printed, Mr. Edison said "Who is the most sophisticated man in New York? That man will be an ideal subject for the Mood Change Test because he will be the least susceptible to emotion."

Mr. Edison selected William J. Burns, the great detective, as the most sophisticated man. Mr. Burns' chart is reproduced. Mr. Edison needs thousands of charts because his research work must be conducted on the law of averages.

MOOD CHANGE CHART

An Analysis of Your Mental Reactions to Music, as RE-CREATED by the New Edison, "the Phonograph with a Soul."

Date of Test Nov 15th '20

1. *Place* Edison Shop
(Home or Where)

2. *Time* (Mark X in square)
Morning ☐ Afternoon ☒ Evening ☐

3. *Weather* (Mark X in square)
Dull ☐ Cold ☒ Bright ☐ Warm ☐

4. *What kind of music did you feel like hearing?* (Mark all words which describe such music with X in square).
Tender ☐ Vivacious ☐ Joyous ☐
Solemn ☐ Majestic ☐ Weird ☐
Soothing ☒
Martial ☐ Exciting ☐ Gay ☐
Simple ☐ Dreamy ☐ Sad ☐

5. *What was your mood immediately preceding test?* (Mark X in square)
Serious or ☒ Worried or ☐
Gay ☐ Carefree ☐
Depressed or ☐ Nervous or ☐
Exhilarated ☐ Composed ☐
Fatigued or ☐ Sad or ☐
Unfatigued ☐ Joyful ☐
Discouraged ☐
or Optimistic ☐

6. *As a result of the test, what were your most noticeable mood changes?*
(Serious to gay, gay to serious, worried to carefree, nervous to composed, etc.)

MOOD CHANGE			RE-CREATION CAUSING SUCH CHANGE
Serious	to	Carefree	[illegible]
Carefree	to	Gay	Alice Blue Gown
	to		

7. *Please comment on manner in which mood changes occurred:*
I came from a very serious conference and noted the fact that listening to the music produced on the Edison my (over)

Please fill in, sign and hand to Edison dealer.

MUSIC RESEARCH DEPARTMENT
EDISON LABORATORIES
ORANGE, N. J.

Signed Wm. J. Burns

Address

Will You Join Mr. Edison in an Experiment?

2400 years ago, Confucius called music "The sacred tongue of God." 400 years ago, Martin Luther said: "Music is the only art that can calm the agitations of the soul." 116 years ago, Napoleon said: "Music is the art to which law makers ought to give the greatest encouragement."

Mr. Edison has recently produced a new phonograph of such perfect realism that its RE-CREATION of music cannot be distinguished from the original music. As a result of this wonderful new invention, every home can now enjoy the full benefits of the world's best music.

For many centuries, the power of music has been appreciated—but never has it been fully understood. For the purpose of ascertaining and classifying the effects of music on the minds and moods of mankind, Mr. Edison has associated with himself world-famed psychologists. Much research work has already been done. Will you assist by analyzing your own mental reactions to music, and those of as many friends, as you can interest in the work? Your co-operation will be appreciated by Mr. Edison and his associates.

Please examine the chart that is reproduced above. The Edison dealer in your locality will furnish you as many of these charts as you require.

If you do not own a New Edison, the Edison dealer in your locality will welcome your making the test in his store. Should you like to call in some of your friends, the Edison dealer will probably be willing to loan you an instrument and the necessary RE-CREATIONS, so that you can make the test in your own home. Watch for his announcement in your local newspaper. THOMAS A. EDISON, Inc., Orange, N. J.

The NEW EDISON

"The Phonograph with a Soul"

FIGURE 101

Edison advertisement: "Will You Join Mr. Edison in an Experiment?" in *American Magazine* 91 (February 1921): 57.

have as many sheets as needed. If she didn't own the New Edison, the dealer would administer the test, or if she could put together some friends, the dealer "will probably be willing to loan you an instrument and the necessary Re-Creations [distinct from mere records], so that you can make the test in your home." Edison's use of the term *re-creation,* as opposed to mere recording or reproduction, was trademarked in 1916.[103]

In 1921, the Edison Company published the "results" of the national experiment in a thirty-two-page booklet called *Mood Music,* its contents established with the assistance of "a corps of noted American associates," their work "based on Psychological experiments conducted under the direction of Dr. W. V. Bingham."[104] In brief, *Mood Music* was a kind of abbreviated record catalogue, "a compilation of 112 Edison Re-Creations according to 'what they will do for you.'"[105]

Characteristic of Edison himself, the booklet's narrative reaches beyond music's pleasures to its "practical" applications. That is, Victor's promotion of its products' cultural uplift competes against Edison's promise of the consumer's immediate return on investment: affective agency instrumentalized. "Has it occurred to you that music might be made to bring more than pleasure?—that its mysterious compelling power might be utilized to do you much practical good?" Music ought to be consumed regularly, like vitamins, for the promised benefits of the sonic relief: "Therefore, why not 'take' music every day, for our mental well-being, just as we take food for our physical well-being?" If that fails to convince, "Think of the millions of men who have been worried with business cares, worn out by work, kept at nervous tension by the struggle for a living. Music might have banished their worries, supplied renewed vigor, brought back the contented frame of mind."[106] This and other like bromides are illustrated by character types whose lives can be immediately improved simply by listening (figs. 102–107): in addition to the man of business, there are the equally put-upon stock watcher, the upper-crust woman exhausted from shopping, the tired farmer (though well off to judge from his domestic furnishings), the young lovelorn woman, and the exhausted homemaker. Members of the urban working class are absent.

Each supporting vignette registers a life problem and its solution. Problems dominate the picture space; each is unbounded without a surrounding frame. In rhetorical terms, the illustrated character types are decentered, lost in the empty space surrounding them. By contrast, each person benefiting from musical relief is precisely framed; the space each inhabits is compositionally rationalized, the better to reflect the emotional well-being that music brought them.

The *Mood Music* text explains that the experiment began with 589 Edison Re-Creations, classical, opera, jazz, vocal, and instrumental, of which in the end 135 were chosen, because the mood-effect that these pieces produced was shared by the most auditors (though the title page lists 112, not 135). The Edison catalogue number, along with current price, for each recording is listed. In all, the booklet provides music to stimulate twelve "moods," the numbers in parentheses indicating the number of recordings available for each category:

FIGURE 102
"The tense strain of business / Music's pleasant relief," in *Mood Music* (Orange, NJ: Thomas A. Edison, Inc., 1921), 4.

FIGURE 103
"Nervous and exhausted from shopping / Soothed and refreshed by music," in *Mood Music*, 12.

FIGURE 104
"A bad jolt / Steadied by music," in *Mood Music*, 15.

FIGURE 105
"Too tired to eat / Refreshed by music," in *Mood Music,* 18.

FIGURE 106
"Comforted by music / Lonesome," in *Mood Music,* 23.

FIGURE 107
"Too tired to get dinner / Music brings back the 'pep,'" in *Mood Music,* 27.

1. To Stimulate and Enrich Your Imagination (15)
2. To Bring You Peace of Mind (14)
3. To Make You Joyous (10)
4. In Moods of Wistfulness (8)
5. Jolly Moods and Good Fellowship (10)
6. For More Energy! (9)
7. Love and Its Moods (11)
8. Moods of Dignity and Grandeur (10)
9. The Mood for Tender Memory (12)
10. Devotion Is Also a Mood (13)
11. Stirring (9)
12. For the Children (16)

The list is somewhat inconsistent as to purpose, to the extent that some categories (as explained by the accompanying text) seem intended to elevate a mood already in place. Roughly along the same lines, the function of "For the Children" is more or less simply to get them moving ("prance and dance . . . catch the childish fancy and make it merry with glee"). Each mood category is preceded by the diagnosis of a mental or physical anomaly, followed by its musical antidote. "Then there's the day when everything goes wrong. Your face lengthens out to twice its normal appearance. Your mouth droops down at the corners. The world seems a pretty dismal place to live in—and nobody loves you. At such a time, play some of these selections. They are full of joy. They change the gloomy mood into one of cheerfulness."[107]

Many recordings listed are of popular songs of the time, together with some older ballads (e.g., Stephen Foster). Dance music shows up (favoring upbeat foxtrots), as do short-form mid-cult light orchestral classics and ballet bits; opera, however, is all but absent. With the exception of Bach, Handel, and Mozart, the classical or quasi-classical composers represented date from the second half of the nineteenth century. Very few performers have current name recognition. The choice of musical selections for any particular mood category, especially those that readers today might still recognize—classical pieces especially—is often difficult to fathom. Why, for example, would the overture to *La forza del destino,* with its varied tempi, juxtaposed and sharply delineated mix of lyrical and martial sections, highly varied orchestration, and often foreboding character, lead to energizing an exhausted person, whose brain, as the textual gloss suggests, "refuses to function"?[108]

Mood Music concludes with an essay by Bingham, "Research on Moods and Music," promoting social-scientific research truth claims.[109] As Bingham explains, the first part of the process was to employ three human subjects, two women and a man, "experts in introspection," all three trained psychologists, two of whom were musicians. To judge from Bingham's account, *only* these three individuals were employed to sort out both the mood categories and the music appropriate to each. (The text elsewhere refers to "numerous different normal [!] listeners," perhaps a reference to the fact that in May 1921 the test was administered to twenty-six Yale University students in the psychology department as part of a music program consisting of five numbers for band, orchestra, violin, and soprano.)[110] No mention whatever is made of the company's national advertising campaign inviting the general public to participate in the research project, despite the fact that the booklet reproduces the very Mood Change Chart filled out by Detective Burns that we saw earlier (fig. 108). A gloss to the chart oddly refocuses attention away from the scientific research described in the advertising to a function something akin to a party prop: The chart "has proved so interesting an experiment . . . that hostesses have requested supplies of charts for Mood Change Parties, and families have used them for evening entertainment." They're free for the asking.[111] Short-lived, the mood-music campaign was dropped by Edison in 1923, six years before the company gave up altogether on the recording business.[112]

By the advent of the electric era in the mid-1920s, the terms defining the reception of sound recording had evolved. Opera retained a substantial but nonetheless diminished hold on advertising budgets. Advertising for nonvocal classical recordings gradually increased, alongside popular dance music and other sorts of popular entertainment. Over time, the "missing" sight of opera performance became a lesser concern, readily apparent in later editions of *The Victrola Book of the Opera*. Compare the *Aida* sections of the 4th (1917) and 8th editions (1929, for the first time published by Victor's successor company, RCA Victor). The earlier *Aida* entry, fourteen pages, included English translations of major arias, a musical incipit for "Celeste Aida," and nineteen photographs of costumed singers, stage sets, and performances. The *Aida* section of the 1929 edition, in slightly larger trim size, is eleven pages and included only eight photographs, fewer scene and set shots, a few abbreviated aria texts, and no aria incipit.

Victor's early-century foray into an ambitious program of opera recording—its records numbering in the thousands—was underwritten by a data-rich array of advertising come-ons and de facto instructional manuals about what to listen for and how to listen. Not leaving matters to chance, Victor widely promoted its opera book in national magazines, in single-page black-and-white copy and two-page color as well. Victor and opera were inseparable, distinctly more so than Edison, no small intended consequence of the Victor's general marketing strategy.

The acousmatic panic—if panic isn't too strong a word—I have marked as a phenomenon accompanying early phonography was variously marked: serious, focused response by Victor; low comedy in other circles (fig. 109). Edison's instrumentalized narratives about mood change, offering "practical" solutions to various forms of mundane stress and anxiety characteristic of modern life, were matched by other forms of recorded advice for getting ahead in the world, some at once ironically cynical and comic (fig. 110). But to end the matter with farce, whatever the pleasures, sells short a trope with a history that harkens back to the dawn of modernity. It's worth a look.

The Mood Change Chart

Would you like to observe music's effects on yourself?—its effects on your friends?—how potent it is in changing your mood?

These questions are answered by the Mood Change Experiment, outlined on the Mood Change Chart. This chart was originally used for gathering data in Mr. Edison's music research. It has proved so interesting an experiment, however, that hostesses have requested supplies of charts for Mood Change Parties, and families have used them for evening entertainment. If you wish copies, apply to any Edison dealer or to Thos. A. Edison, Inc., Orange, N. J. They are free.

MOOD CHANGE CHART

An Analysis of Your Mental Reactions to Music, as RE-CREATED by the New Edison, "the Phonograph with a Soul."

Date of Test Nov 15th '20

1. *Place* Edison Shop
(*Home or Where*)

2. *Time* (*Mark X in square*)
Morning ☐ Afternoon ☒
Evening ☐

3. *Weather* (*Mark X in square*)
Dull ☐ Cold ☒
Bright ☐ Warm ☐

4. *What kind of music did you feel like hearing?* (*Mark all words which describe such music with X in square*).
Tender ☐ Vivacious ☐ Joyous ☐
Solemn ☐ Majestic ☐ Weird ☐
Soothing ☒
Martial ☐ Exciting ☐ Gay ☐
Simple ☐ Dreamy ☐ Sad ☐

5. *What was your mood immediately preceding test?*
(*Mark X in square*)

Serious or ☒ Worried or ☐
Gay ☐ Carefree ☐

Depressed or ☐ Nervous or ☐
Exhilarated ☐ Composed ☐

Fatigued or ☐ Sad or ☐
Unfatigued ☐ Joyful ☐

Discouraged ☐
or Optimistic ☐

6. *As a result of the test, what were your most noticeable mood changes?*
(Serious to gay, gay to serious, worried to carefree, nervous to composed, etc.)

MOOD CHANGE	RE-CREATION CAUSING SUCH CHANGE
Serious *to* Carefree	Traumerei
Carefree *to* Gay	Alice Blue Gown
to	

7. *Please comment on manner in which mood changes occurred:*
I came from a very serious conference and noted the fact that listening to the music produced on The Edison my (over)

Please fill in, sign and hand to Edison dealer.
MUSIC RESEARCH DEPARTMENT
EDISON LABORATORIES
ORANGE, N. J.

Signed Wm. J. Burns

Address

FORM 4644 (SEE INSTRUCTIONS ON REVERSE SIDE)

FIGURE 108
"The Mood Change Chart," in *Mood Music,* 32.

FIGURE 109
English (20th century), "I want to see the place where the noise comes from" (c. 1905–10), color lithograph. Private collection. Photo credit: © Look and Learn/ Elgar Collection/Bridgeman Images.

FIGURE 110
"Advice to Girls about to Marry—get used to this language when you tell him that you want a new hat" (c. 1905–10). New York, The Museum of the City of New York. Photo credit: Art Resource, New York.

HEARING AND THE ACOUSTIC SENSORIUM

In the Low Countries during the early decades of the seventeenth century, a very large number of artists churned out paintings, sometimes on a nearly industrial scale, making allusion to music, whether in the guise of musical instruments (piled up in still-life paintings, for example), more or less real or more or less imaginary musical performances (alike among the social upper crust and the socially outcast), and music both secular and sacred. Musical subject matter in visual art ran the gamut from the everyday to the special occasion (music at home, in church, at court, in the pub, at weddings, at country fairs, in ritualistic celebratory parades, and what have you, together forming a list of subjects of considerable length). Among all of these subjects, perhaps the most culturally significant, as well as unusual, was the topos of the Five Senses, sometimes represented together within the frame of a single painting, sometimes separated into five separate paintings. Representations of Hearing gave pride of place to what was judged most hearing-worthy: music, most of it secular in apt reflection of the changing epistemic order of humanism. Five Senses paintings are allegories with roots in ecclesiastical narratives about the sacred truths of existence but now put under severe pressure by the gradual movement toward free thought—Enlightenment reason, if you will, if somewhat prior to its full emergence.[113] Exceptions noted, modern Hearing is resolutely secular.

The painting shown in figure 111, part of a series of five, each articulating a single, isolated sense, is noteworthy on several counts. Its appeal is firmly materialistic, organized around heaps of well-wrought luxurious *objets,* each of which in one way or another is not only good to look at but also, and more to the point, capable of making sound. The painting's semiotic charge is driven in part by the way it controls our time: we're made to commit to it. Brueghel smartly gets us to look, and to look hard, by giving us so much to look *at,* inviting—almost requiring—us to shift our eyes back and forth, up and down, as if by so doing we could make sense of what is in fact a scene devoid of logic except by the terms of a critical absent presence: the cacophony of sound that we might vaguely be able to imagine but which we absolutely cannot hear. We're offered a sight of sound in a sonic vacuum of comprehensive silence. We may take pleasure in what is denied us, our potential frustration perhaps diverted by the attendant scopophilia directed toward the centrally placed female nude, no doubt a secular muse—Euterpe, we might reasonably suppose—certainly neither angel nor saint, nicely articulating an alternate form of pleasure often accompanying sensuality: "If music be the food of love . . . "

In several mutually reinforcing ways, Brueghel's painting interpellates us into privilege, its impossible elegance, the visual summation of an earthly utopia—and literally a no-place except in the realm of wish and its more potent cousin, desire. The painting gives us what we are *not* and *may not have,* except in the vividness of our imagination.

The pleasures immanent to Brueghel's picture are produced by the degree to which the accumulated objects make no functional sense, except as a kind of archive of related

FIGURE III
Jan Brueghel the Younger (1601–78) and Jan van Kessel the Elder (1626–79), attr., *Hearing,* oil on wood. Whereabouts and date unknown. Photo credit: IRPA-KIK-Brussels.

objects. An archive: like recordings. Here: recorded eye-sound. As an inventory, Brueghel's sound-making collection pleases by its function*less* excess. The visual logic, so to speak, lies in the apparent lack of logic, the degree to which the inventory seems impossible, a mere fantasy, except for the fact that nearly all the objects in the room not only are painted with notable precision but also are objects of contemporaneous use: the visual fantasy has its feet planted in a recognizable reality.

The musical instrument horde occupies a space out of time, at the same time as the instruments are, as it were, at once time bound and entirely timely. Like recordings. We might fairly compare Brueghel's musical instrument inventory to the Edison and Victor product catalogues. The ever-past inhabits every present, fleeting moment. Time collapses, as does space. Brueghel's fauna include the utterly ordinary and the notably exotic—the local and the foreign. (The small stag functions, obviously enough, as a kind of internal label that identifies the painting's organizational principle to be that of Hearing.) Like time, space is radically concentrated. The painting brings us a sound *world* analogous to a collection of disks and the world of music inscribed in their grooves—commercial recording from its earliest moment was rampantly international, and soon global.

The epistemology underwriting Five Senses paintings is culturally related to early-modern scientific classificatory schemes in general; the images are distinctly modern, despite the fact that their organizing principle is allegory. Such images mark the pleasure of excess consumption, linking it directly to power/wealth. They situate physical, embodied pleasure in a quasi–medical-psychological discourse about the *mechanics* of pleasure. Pleasure becomes something not simply to be enjoyed but an experience to be isolated into its component parts, and then appealed to, one sense at a time. More, Five Senses representations evoke modernity's troubling conflation of work and play (or perhaps the erasure of play). That is, the pleasure of the seeing comes from the effort expended to make sense of the classification schemes organizing the painting's material contents. Complicit with this general and long line of thinking, Victor offered its would-be consumers advice on how to build their collections: how to amass sound commodities, acoustic cultural capital, by way of the company's aforementioned "Selected List from Which to Choose Your First Records,"[114] roughly 133 records all told and of various genres, and this merely a starter set.[115]

Five Senses paintings, unified by a philosophy of the hoard, are nonetheless underwritten by an anxiety about loss, in part driven by the fact that "having" in the two dimensions of a painting is not analogous to having in three dimensions the objects represented. Imagery stimulates desire precisely by frustrating it, except for those individuals who have both the paintings *and* what the paintings represent. But for other viewers, those who have only the sight of what is represented, such paintings mark the enormous gap separating the realm of "having" from the realm of "having (merely) a look."

Brueghel's painting invokes the pleasures of hearing, so far as music is concerned, principally by its absence, a lack made the more pertinent given the extraordinary possibilities for musical (and other) sonority visually evident. The pleasure of music resides in its possibility rather than actuality. Paintings are perforce silent, but their silence itself becomes a trope when so much potential music remains unrealized, with reference to the many instruments scattered carelessly in the foreground. Two background ensembles perform, as does a bell ringer, the muse-organist, a child piper, and the shawm-blowing primate. And this says nothing about the possible acoustic contributions of clocks chiming, a dog barking, and exotic birds screeching.

In sum, the painting invokes the possibilities accorded to hearing organized around the most privileged of sounds—there is not a single instrument associated with the peasantry. That said, the beauty of the *visual* music we might imagine exists in extreme tension with what is actually represented, namely, musical simultaneities that together produce noise: the price paid for too much of everything. Yet what matters most is not reality, but the invocation to a fantasy of accumulated pleasures whose foundation is structured from an immense degree of social power and accumulated wealth.

Let's pause for a moment to look away from this enchanted splendor to consider an alternate reality, at once comic, nasty, even brutal. If Brueghel offers us the "cooked" variety of some imagined actuality, there also exists a "raw" type, bearing more trace of lived experience for the 99 percent (fig. 112), though the purported actuality represented in David Teniers the Younger's *Musicians at a Tavern* is itself imagined through putative eyes that look down from atop the social pedestal. The point of view, in truth as skewed,

FIGURE 112
David Teniers the Younger (1610–90), *Musicians at a Tavern* [*The Five Senses*], oil on wood. Turin, Galleria Sabuda. Photo credit: Art Resource, New York.

as cooked, as distorted as Brueghel's, envisions a grimly homely (in both senses of the word) epistemology of seemingly happy survival, a society of anonymous underlings taking simple pleasure in simple surroundings. Unlike the saturated Technicolor world typical of the period painting *Hearing,* Teniers's painting is dimly lighted, a shadow world of overwhelmingly brown hues (the whole brightened only by a limited view through a window at the back and the white shirt and red cap of the main character): living with life wrung out of it. Beyond the narrow confines of shallow space—very different from the virtual infinity of the distant vanishing point in Brueghel, a world without apparent end—there is an economy of scarcity. Here, the pleasures are few, basic, and easily measurable; those in Brueghel establish a perimeter surrounding a cluttered acoustic sublime.

If the sound potential in Brueghel is fundamentally (if not entirely) what we would understand as musical, what's here by contrast consistently borders on noise, as Teniers takes care to emphasize. The fiddle player (Teniers used himself as the model) happily scrapes his bow while singing along with insouciant confidence, however ill founded and ill considered, for what is experienced is vulgar and crude. He stands for Hearing. The man directly behind him, playing the role of Smell, holds his nose with one prominently pointed finger. Rather than his actually smelling something, his gesture constitutes an aesthetic judgment on the music to which he subjects himself: it stinks, and so badly that even a peasant as uncouth as himself knows as much.

But it gets worse. The old codger next to him has a lute, an instrument that at the time was characteristically represented in elegant spaces, part and parcel of everything upper crust (though this was not invariably the case). By and large, the instrument was associated with what we would understand as the drawing room, not the pub. It is out of place here, and to be certain that we understand this fact, Teniers provides clarification: the old guy isn't playing the instrument; he's tuning it—or better, trying to. Teniers mocks the man's efforts. To supplement the fun poking, Teniers incorporates a violoncello, violin, and part books in a kind of heap at the front right, and cornett, shawm, and cittern on the wall at the back. Little of any of this instrumentarium makes any sense in such a setting; it's roughly the equivalent of placing a Bösendorfer grand in a cheesy strip club—precisely the point of his cynically cheap exercise.[116] The painting is intended as a joke rather more imbibed with sarcasm than irony.

At issue in these paintings are commentaries that envision a society of the present set against the consummate exaggerations of the high and the low and organized around the human sense of hearing but also (and more to the point) around a sound world, variously traced on the continuum of an aesthetics that humanizes and ennobles the sensing body of some, but hardly all.

In this early moment of a brave new modern world, the stakes were already well set for the musics and musical judgments of our own time and place. This is not to suggest that nothing has changed; indeed, it might be fairer to say that a great deal (if hardly everything) has since changed, especially in the decades close to our own moment, at least concerning the stakes of listening in relation both to what is available for the hearing and by what means and to the various forms of cultural prestige attached to each. One change is especially noteworthy. Market capitalism learned quickly that sounds of all sorts were fungible. Opera usefully served to promote acousmatic listening, hence record consumption, as a cultural practice worthy of general emulation. To be sure, record companies understood from the start that their bread was best buttered by popular sound culture—by entertainment, not art. Over time, the prestige value of opera as a marketing ploy gradually diminished, all the more with the advent of radio in the 1920s, though it never entirely disappeared from the companies' advertising.

SECOND LOOK/LISTEN

In the last year of his life, Adorno wrote once more about phonograph records, a few aphoristic pages he titled "Opera and the Long-playing Record."[117] Compared to his earlier forays concerning phonography, here he significantly changes his tune. His points are few but nonetheless significant, not least for the clarity with which he reimagines the progressive potential of what was, after all, a dominant commodity form. Adorno had long regarded opera as a fading anachronism (he doesn't alter that assessment), kept on life support in opera houses catering to a culture-vulture bourgeoisie by one of two means, both calling forth opera's visual appeal and perfect for the televisual age, though he doesn't explicitly make the connection: period-piece confections (his example is *Figaro* in a rococo staging), pretty and pretty tired, or else opera upgraded into the present-future (i.e., *Regieoper*), the characters—as he puts it—"dressed in sweat suits," the updating-as-shock begging the questions What's the point? and Why even bother putting it on stage? Adorno nevertheless valorizes opera's *music,* its "true object." Opera on long-playing record excises the visual distraction of lavishly enacting opera's obsolescence, in favor of what he names the text. "The LP makes its entrance as deus ex machina. Shorn of the phony hoopla, the LP simultaneously frees itself from the capriciousness of fake opera festivals. It allows for the optimal presentation of music, enabling it to recapture some of the force and intensity that had been worn threadbare in the opera houses."[118]

The long-playing record permits experience of an opera's temporal dimension without distraction (including those caused by record-change breaks of the 78-rpm era); it also permits reaudition of parts in order for the listener to focus on musical details. Adorno does not critique the private listening experience in this instance, largely, I suspect, because he finds the "ritual of performance" within the opera house still more regressive.

Adorno remembers phonography's acoustic past with little affection, his reasoning here quite unlike his earlier thinking: "Looking back, it now seems as if the short-playing records of yesteryear—acoustic daguerreotypes that are now already hard to play in a way that produces a satisfying sound due to the lack of proper apparatuses—unconsciously also corresponded to their epoch: the desire for highbrow diversion, the salon pieces, favorite arias, and the Neapolitan semihits whose image Proust attached in an unforgiveable manner to 'O sole mio.'"[119]

Adorno acknowledges the fetishization of possession that accrues to record collecting, but essentially writes it off as a fact of modern life: "There remains hardly any means other than possession, other than reification, through which one can get anything unmediated in this world—and in art as well."[120] While he seems to reimagine the private listener in essentially positive terms, he nonetheless laments the condition of (pervasive) loneliness. That is, whether privatization is the result of turning away or of being turned away, it prevails. Adorno's listener in this instance is alone and lonely, but his loneliness has been turned against loneliness through the trace of intersubjectivity inscribed in the record's grooves. In the case at hand, technology provides an opportunity for its force to act against the interests that it characteristically serves. Opera on the phonograph offers, for Adorno, the sound of hope.

4

AESTHETIC MEANDERINGS OF THE SONIC PSYCHE

Three Operas, Two Notes, and One Ending at the Boundary of the Great Divide

Opera . . . puts normality into question.

LAWRENCE KRAMER, "OPERA: TWO OR THREE THINGS I KNOW ABOUT HER"

AFFECT AND ABJECTION

It's fair to say that subjectivity needed opera; it's a good deal more certain that opera needed subjectivity—or, better, the anxieties associated with subjectivity—for opera to have taken on the cultural force it enjoyed, particularly by the time history puts Wagner into the equation. As a principal site where subjectivity could be staged, witnessed, and indeed celebrated both visually and aurally, opera was at the same time a discourse that, by the very nature of its social standing and interpellative agency, attracted serious philosophical attention—witness Schopenhauer, Kierkegaard, and Nietzsche. Opera was serious cultural business. Wagner in particular regarded opera as a form of cultural pedagogy, such being the ultimate function of Bayreuth, after all, in the composer's megalomaniacal urge for full and eternal control of his discourse and its social impact. The potential for entertainment as such had little purchase in Wagner's imaginary (and even without bothering about any of his endless musings on such matters, one gets that notion firmly established by nearly every thought that entered Cosima's head concerning her husband and duly confined to her diary). Bayreuth's hard-luck bench seating, not for nothing churchlike, somatically reinforced a form of listening deemed appropriate for the wished-for *Bildung* of the proper bourgeois, no matter Wagner's ambivalence toward his social class;[1] and like church, the music was to be experienced, to borrow a phrase from Peter Gay, in "worshipful silence," but certainly not without affect.[2]

As regards subjectivity, and to express matters with some hyperbole, what audiences saw and heard enacted in opera (Wagnerian or otherwise) was the unruliness of desires whose realization was characteristically self-suppressed or else experienced only at great cost. No cultural coincidence, in opera desires were made the more pleasurable, however perversely, precisely by *not* being fulfilled, and never more than when the death drive triumphed at the final cadence.

Opera, alike in sight and sound, played to the exotic, sensual, and dramatic fantasies of the audience, a musico-dramatic interpellation along the lines of what Jeremy Tambling, channeling and adapting Benjamin, has called the "aural unconscious," or what Kaja Silverman, addressing the female voice in film, terms the "acoustic mirror."[3] Opera, in short, is a form of sonic psychology. Paul Robinson, commenting on what he terms operatic music's "emotional eloquence," notes its ability "to address the great subjects of psychological life—desire and fulfillment, anxiety and relief, despair and ecstasy—with unparalleled immediacy. It thereby touches," as he puts it, "the core of sentiment informing different ideals of selfhood and personal relations."[4] In this regard, the opera house as a sonic enclosure serves as a kind of acoustic womb, wherein is made audible what Adorno, citing Stendhal's assessment of Rossini (no coincidence), called music's *promesse du bonheur.*[5]

Wayne Koestenbaum, in *The Queen's Throat,* has a related but distinctly more dystopian take. "Opera," he says, "has the power to warn you that you have wasted your life"[6]—a line presumably cribbed from Adorno writing on musical kitsch (a loaded word to be sure).[7] This insight Koestenbaum amplifies by way of what he calls a "rushing intimation of vacuity and loss" that reads as follows: "You haven't acted on your desires. You've suffered a stunted, vicarious existence. You've silenced your passions. The volume, height, depth, lushness, and excess of operatic utterance reveal, by contrast, how small your gestures have been until now, how impoverished your physicality; you have only used a fraction of your bodily endowment, and your throat is closed."[8]

What follows in this chapter concerns the problematics of articulating the social and personal actuality of wounded subjectivities and unfulfilled desires that interested Freud and found voice, an audible trace, onstage and for the delectation of the audience by way of sonically induced transference. The three operas I consider maintain gestural allegiance to a musico-Freudian language while traversing the border separating late Romanticism from modernism. My argument concerns what I take to be in the musical notes, a semiotic immanence, without necessary regard to any particular performance or production, whose values may either enhance or mitigate the meanings I ascribe. What follows is a kind of micrology of two singular gestures from two operas read within the specific contexts of their usage as sedimentations of the history of subjectivity, and especially under fraught circumstance. In brief, I will suggest what might be Freudian, so to speak, about a grace note and a high C. I'll conclude with a few related remarks about a late-modern musical rewriting of the ending of another opera seventy-five years (and a lot of history) after its premiere.

ORNAMENTAL SEMANTICS

NOTE ONE. *La bohème* (1896) was based on Henri Murger's *Scènes de la vie de bohème,* published as a collected whole in 1851 (but appearing initially between 1845 and 1849 as a series of stories) and as a theatrical adaptation by Théodore Barrière in 1849. The nearly half-century framing the literary models and the opera perfectly accommodates the operatic "pre" of my immediate interest as the set-up for the "post" that comes later with regard to the cultural-musical history of modernism. The specific micrological gesture of my concern is Puccini's assignment of grace notes to Rodolfo in act three. To be sure, grace notes are performed by all the opera's principals, but, except for Rodolfo and Mimì, they are unremarkable for what I'm after, though it's worth acknowledging that Musetta is provided more grace notes (nine) in her second-act aria than is the case in any other set piece in the whole of *La bohème,* hers consistently marking a deeply ironic stance toward the signification that Puccini encodes with this gesture in the music assigned to Rodolfo and Mimì.[9] For the opera's two lovers, Puccini typically employs grace notes as the aural expression of desire emergent in elocutions associated with love in its various forms, including in particular its manifestations encompassing states of abjection in act three (fig. 113).

Rodolfo and Mimì's grace notes, first by the numbers:[10]

	RODOLFO	MIMÌ
Act 1	6	2
Act 2	4	4
Act 3	**8**	**7**
Act 4	2	0

The act three grace notes are assigned a distinct, one might say heavy, function that simultaneously runs in two directions: profound regret and loss on the one hand, and on the other, a marked effort to vocalize these emotions in an effort to heal the wound through reconciliation with the estranged beloved. This function defines every one of Rodolfo's carefully placed eight grace notes.

In the overwrought emotional situation of a relationship on the rocks—never mind Mimì's terminal illness—efforts to put things right mark act three as the opera's dramatic climax. Everything heard previously leads to this scene; everything afterward is simply a working out, a move toward closure. (Act four doesn't possess the emotional power of act three, nor can it claim music anywhere near as affecting.) Act three concentrates on the abject mourning experienced by the lovers, concluding with a supposed, if temporary, resolution asserted by the *tutti* dominant-tonic close to the act. Sonically coming from nowhere, unprepared, the cadence loudly asserts what cannot otherwise be accepted, by either the lovers or the audience.[11] The half-life of the purported third-act reconciliation occurs in the future and out of earshot, in silence, during the break between acts; by the

FIGURE 113
Giacomo Puccini, *La bohème* (1896), act three scene design by Luigi Morgari (1857–1935), color lithograph. Milan, Civica Raccolta Stampe Bertarelli. Photo credit: Bridgeman Images.

start of act four it's well over. All that remains is the staging of a rather conventional Italian *Liebestod*.

The emotional agency of act three is concentrated in the lovers' exchange, ironically complemented by the quarreling of Marcello and Musetta. For Rodolfo and Mimì, this is a new love duet, one far more emotionally mature than the love-at-first-sight exchange that closed act one. Between then and now, too much life has intervened, life whose cruelties are made sonically more apparent by the fifteen grace notes (counting only the single-note ornaments).

Mimì employs grace notes first, in Rodolfo's absence, in her exchange with Marcello when for the third time in succession she calls out her lover's name, thereby emphasizing his power over her emotional well-being.[12] Moments later she sings double grace notes (or a turn or a mordent, take your terminological pick) on the first syllable of *fugge*, noting his apparent turning away from her, and repeats this gesture two measures later in reference to his destructive jealousy ("per gelosia") (ex. 6). Puccini in effect musically italicizes these key words, each of which encompasses the feelings of hopelessness that Mimì experiences. But to my larger point, he consistently employs grace notes for this purpose for both characters as a musical gesture that overdetermines the psychic damage each experiences. Beyond the words the lovers sing (fraught words to be sure), what matters most is the phatic impact of the grace notes' sound.

The grace notes assigned to Mimì, within the history of operatic gestures, are fundamentally the more conventional to the extent that open expression of emotion by soprano heroines runs in sync with nineteenth-century gender assignments. This is rather less so for men, which is to say that the masculinities on aural display in operas of the period tend to push back more forcefully against behavioral models of reserve and decorum

EXAMPLE 6. Puccini, *La bohème* (Mineola, NY: Dover, 2000), piano-vocal score, act three, rehearsal no. 9, mm. 11–16.

established as fundamental markers of bourgeois propriety. Rodolfo's third-act grace notes are semiotically out of bounds vis-à-vis the bourgeois male ideal of emotional self-control already well in place by the mid–nineteenth century.

La bohème casts Rodolfo as a poet, which is to say that, like the male piano virtuoso, his identity is culturally marked as liminal between the feminine and the masculine; his given "profession" provides him cultural license to express himself as he does, with far greater emotional instability in act three than would otherwise be appropriate. To be sure, opera was a principal cultural site for staging emotion *tout court,* including emotions associated with male heroics in testosterone-driven display (as in Manrico's "Di quella pira"). That said, the representation of male emotional vulnerability was culturally fraught terrain. It's one thing to display feeling; it's quite another to show abjection, to the extent that abjection signals weakness and loss of control. To keep the operatic representation of male emotion within acceptable boundaries of nineteenth-century (principally bourgeois) decorum was no small matter, in regard to which Puccini is in very good company, if at the end of the cultural line. Puccini, however, is open to violating this decorum to a degree that strikes me as unusual. What he accomplishes with the grace notes assigned to Rodolfo is very much part of a changing cultural terrain near the turn of the last century. This is more obvious if we take a brief look at an opera written at a moment when that terrain was at least *apparently* more certain, an opera that momentarily disrupts conventions of male self-control precisely so as to insistently reestablish these conventions soon thereafter. Consider the famous male-male (tenor-baritone) duet "Au fond du temple saint" from the opening act of Bizet's *Les pêcheurs de perles* (1863).

The scene involves two men, Nadir and Zurga, comparing notes about a magical night long ago during their shared youth when they caught sight of a beautiful woman, Leïla, and found themselves equally transfixed, love at first sight. Bizet's music is a melodious mix of unisons, octaves, thirds, and sixths, most of it in synchronized rhythm; the singing is lushly accompanied by the strings, with solo flute and solo harp prominent in the mix, exactly conventional for a boy-girl love duet (ex. 7). Following this distinctly atypical operatic representation of male-male affection, the men, now sensing the danger to their friendship that a competitive pursuit of Leïla would produce, agree to preserve their relationship by renouncing love. In brief, the male homosocial bond trumps heteronormative desire (and never mind that Leïla will shortly reappear and upset that agreement). Put differently, the tenor and baritone sing a kind of momentarily gender-bending routine that cannot culturally be sustained. Indeed, male-male opera duets almost always presage trouble—think of *La forza del destino* (1862; act three, scene two, "Solenne in quest'ora") or *Otello* (1887; act two, "Sì, pel ciel"), both of which likewise concern women and are followed by violent deaths: of the male rival in the former, the woman in the latter.

In *The Pearl Fishers,* gender order is soon reestablished. Forswearing what they call the temptation of *"ce fatal amour,"* the men revert to form (where boys will be boys), reenacting boyness musically. Briefly stated, Bizet writes a second male-male duet, but without any of the stretched-out, languid, smoothly flowing melodic lines of the first one; the second time around there's no lush accompaniment (the harp is banished—too girlie). This duet is up-tempo and a bit up-rhythm, and as it develops, it's increasingly exuberant. The strong beats are often punched; the dynamic level gradually increases, building to a climax of masculine vocal prowess. In short, Bizet writes some buddy music to reassert the supremacy of the phallus by means of the celebratory expulsion of the woman (ex. 8). But there's something else: in the second duet there remains more than a hint of mutual tenderness in the music they sing. That is, within the male homosocial bond, tenderness is not musically banished; indeed, the bond provides sanction for the affections of male comradeship, but within strict bounds. In looking at his friend, each man looks in the mirror and likes what he sees: himself unthreatened. A final explosive dominant-tonic cadence punctuating the close of the scene says as much and at the same time is usefully and dutifully aggressively masculine.[13]

By contrast, in *La bohème*'s third act, Rodolfo's grace notes decenter his character, penetrating his psychic invulnerability, putting it on display, and affecting both Mimì and the audience. Lawrence Kramer encapsulates in one sentence the cultural and psychic principle of manhood at work here but in this instance violated: first, and certainly foremost, he notes, "manhood is defined as a wholeness, an intactness, an integrity of self." Later Kramer states, in complementary fashion: "Masculine abjection . . . always debases; it disfigures; it castrates."[14] I suggest that the grace note is precisely a metaphorical cut, a mere flick of the vocal wrist, so to say, but with a sharp acoustic blade. It's a wound that,

EXAMPLE 7. Georges Bizet, *Les pêcheurs de perles* (Paris: Editions Choudans, 1975), piano-vocal score, act one, rehearsal no. 46 m. 1 to 47 m. 4.

EXAMPLE 8. Bizet, *Les pêcheurs de perles,* act one, rehearsal no. 51D m. 9 to 52H m. 5.

EXAMPLE 8 *(continued)*

EXAMPLE 9. Puccini, *La bohème,* act three, rehearsal no. 30, mm. 6–10.

EXAMPLE 10. Puccini, *La bohème,* act three, rehearsal no. 30, mm. 16–19.

when heard, may be at once abhorred and enjoyed for the pleasures of its sonic masochism.[15] Kramer elsewhere perfectly captures the point again, though here he has in mind operatic sopranos. Substituting Rodolfo for Mimì (my intention) does no harm to his insight: "Voice in extremis . . . presents itself as a mighty accumulation of emotional-libidinal capital expended (in a double-sense, both depleted and lavished, incurred as expense and proffered as expenditure) in acts of surplus expression";[16] or, as he remarks in a quite different context, expression occurs "at the moment of exception, the moment of turning or transport."[17]

Rodolfo's grace notes vocalize the instability of this foundational principle, or better, foundational fantasy and fiction, of masculinity. Rodolfo, attempting to reconcile, employs grace notes on key textual references to Mimì's smile ("sorriso") (ex. 9) and caresses ("con carezze") (ex. 10). Thereafter, nearly all the grace notes are assigned to both lovers in unison at the octave, the first of which marks the reference that to be alone in winter is death, followed four measures later by a double grace note (or turn) but now with reference to the new life associated with spring (ex. 11). To be sure, if the narrative situation, together with the music that precedes these gestures, were less fraught, in effect less overdetermining in advance of what the grace notes underscore, the piling up of the gesture in such concentrated fashion could hardly have been as effective.

EXAMPLE 11. Puccini, *La bohème,* act three, rehearsal no. 31, mm. 1–8.

Slavoj Žižek suggests that the "ultimate lesson" of psychoanalysis is that "humans are not simply alive but are possessed by the strange desire to enjoy life in excess, passionately attached to a surplus that derails the ordinary run of things."[18] In opera, as Catherine Clément puts it, "just like in psychoanalysis, everything counts; just like in an analysis, the important part of the signifier is said in passing, lightly, at the beginning, and nothing points to its being the crux of the drama."[19] Overdetermination is a trope that defines for opera the text-music relationship, especially the case when subjectivity is at stake. These grace notes—quickly passing and duly light of being—"say" something in excess of the words to which they are attached.

Opera signifies on account of its excesses, and none is more foundational than its own logical "impossibility"; its form and content alike don't so much suspend the rules of everyday expressive life as ignore them. Excess on multiple fronts of signification is especially the case when the expression of subjectivity is at stake. Opera reconstitutes life, and subjective life in particular, by speaking—rather, singing—the otherwise inexpressible. Michel Chion has noted, with reference to speech, that "the presence of a human voice structures the sonic space that contains it."[20] The *singing* voice significantly raises the stakes of Chion's insight. In act three of *La bohème,* there is a surplus (an excess) of grace notes, to say nothing of other ornamental turns that occur nowhere else in the opera with such abandon. The stakes are that high.

In this act Rodolfo sets the stage for reconciliation with the simplest of observations: "Addio, sogni d'amor!" (Goodbye to our dreams of love!),[21] after which the dream is described on the basis of the psychic imbrication of their once united bodies. Each character stages memory pictures for the other. Rodolfo's melancholia, what Freud termed "a profoundly painful depression,"[22] acknowledges what he now knows to have been experienced as imaginary: "Addio, sognante vita!" (Goodbye to life in a dream!).[23] Peter Brooks refers to the "extremity" of opera, its "impossible heightening of life where it takes on the form of dreams . . . , in a world where one can sing, over and over again, with all the possible embellishments 'I love you' or 'He betrayed me,'"[24] in the context of which grace notes are ornaments, but they are not ornamental.

Rodolfo's poignant grace notes resonate with the failure of *logos,* the loss of control, the perpetual male anxiety to stage masculinity properly. The voice, duly masculinized, hits each pitch precisely and holds onto it for whatever length the situation requires. Each sound is anticipated by the cultural expectation that gender be performed appropriately. The grace note deflection undercuts the assertion of masculinity, less to destabilize it (at heart always already unstable) than by all too adroitly to announced the fact of its fragility. The ripe emotion conveyed in this opera by grace notes for both sexes does so with a particular resonance for Rodolfo. It announces itself as the aesthetic version of a voice breaking, one of those embarrassing experiences for boys at puberty that gives an acoustic lie to the transition to manhood and along with it to the authority and agency claimed as the adult male's cultural inheritance.[25] Not coincidentally, Rodolfo's grace-note vocal break links culturally to what has been described as a "vocal tear" (in fact, a grace note) in the lament songs, notably those concerning despair over failed relationships, conventional to country music (Hank Williams and Patsy Cline, two of country music's canonical stars, commonly employed this gesture as a way to mark emotional vulnerability musically).[26]

Lawrence Kramer suggests that music "both *attracts* and *enacts* understanding"; he then aptly elaborates his point: "As an aesthetic medium it does so through sensory, bodily events; as an imaginary or symbolic medium it does so through cultural tropes and hermeneutic windows.[27] Stanley Cavell suggests that aria singing expresses "the sense of being pressed or stretched between worlds—one in which to be seen . . . and one from which to be heard, one to which one releases or abandons one's spirit"—what he later calls "this expression of the inexpressible . . . [that] requires understanding without meaning." Cavell perceives the "intuition of transcendence in operatic singing . . . as a realm of intervening . . . to be understood as an irrupting of a new perspective of the self to itself."[28]

SURROGATION OF HAPPINESS

The cultural necessity of opera is rooted in the degree to which it firmly establishes a narrative space for singing the unspeakable, and in particular a space for remarking civilization and its discontents—a space, in short, for *voicing* loss.[29] Adorno, something of a dreamer himself (see the Conclusion), eloquently speaks to this: "Music that has merely to begin in order to define itself as an exception to normalized life, as a more elevated extreme, places itself, by dint of its always already potentially perceptible and nowadays complete integration into the average normalcy of a false life, in contradiction to the claim that its mere sounding inevitably makes."[30]

In complementary fashion, by way of a Lacanian move, Michal Grover-Friedlander suggests that "the voice is nearer to the original state of union, belonging to a state prior to entry into language, a state retrospectively desired."[31] Clément amplifies this insight. "Musical patterns," she suggests, "act upon most listeners in ways that are not rationally explicable; it is as though one is connected to the subjectivity of another *without mediation*—as though still linked to the mother's body."[32] If this is the case, it is fair to say that the quest for *jouissance* functions alike for the stage characters and the audience, who in the case of *La bohème* can't get enough of it. The quasi-novel and the play upon which Puccini's opera is based are all but forgotten; the opera's popularity remains secure well more than a century since its premiere, no matter the wear and tear from too many performances, too many recordings, and its musical vocabulary otherwise imitated on Broadway or, as it were, *Rent*-ed out. Not the least of reasons for the opera's long half-life appends to Puccini's ability to give voice to ordinary human emotions, joy and sadness principal among them, and to hyperbolically make apparent the stakes of fraught subjectivities. He does so by musical gestures at scales both large and small. The micrological grace-note emotional articulations are not the least reason for his talents in this arena.

Freud poses for himself the question of "what men themselves show by their behaviour to be the purpose and intention of their lives." The answer is obvious and requires only a simple declarative sentence: "They want to become happy and to remain so," amplified by his explanation of life's purpose as "simply the programme of the pleasure principle."[33] Happiness and its pleasures are uncertain and elusive at best, as Freud immediately notes in a comment deeply tinged with the irony born of modernity: "One feels inclined to say that the intention that man should be 'happy' is not included in the plan of 'Creation.' What we call happiness in the strictest sense comes from the (preferably sudden) satisfaction of needs that have been dammed up to a high degree, and it is from its nature only possible as an episodic phenomenon."[34] In opera, the episodic satisfaction of needs typically arrives at moments that require action to stop in favor of a character's expressive engagement with the unfolding situation: moments that call for an aria. At moments when dammed-up need is mutually shared by two characters, a duet emerges, whether celebratory (*La bohème,* act one) or not (act three); if the need for satisfaction is still more general, an ensemble is required (Rodolfo-Mimì-Marcello-Musetta or, a better example, the sextet in *Lucia di Lammermoor*). To be sure, operatic "happiness" often has less to do with the characters—love duets in opera more often than not progress toward tragedy—than with the audience that takes pleasure in the beauty of the music which misery in particular inspires onstage.

Freud tends to voice his remarks about civilization in ontological ubiquity, but it's hardly difficult to extrapolate that the modern world is his informant, implicit in a comment that the "external world," as he puts it, "may rage against us with overwhelming and merciless forces of destruction."[35] Opera falling within the cultural milieu of *La bohème* functions simultaneously at purpose and cross-purpose to Freud's insight: at purpose to the extent that it provides satisfying dramatic catharsis as aesthetic protest against merciless actualities; at cross-purpose not least because the musico-aesthetic protest simultaneously celebrates merciless actuality by wrapping its miseries in sonic beauty—a dialectic that finally got its comeuppance around the time of Bartók and Berg (more on that to come).

Freud points to what he calls "the interesting case" in which "happiness in life is predominantly sought in the enjoyment of beauty, wherever beauty presents itself to our senses and our judgment," adding that "this aesthetic attitude to the goal of life offers little protection against the threat of suffering, but it can compensate for a great deal." Modernism early on confronted this problematic: think Lukács, think Brecht. "The enjoyment of beauty has a peculiar, mildly intoxicating quality of feeling," Freud suggests. In brief, beauty is compensatory, and for modernism, or at least a good deal of it, therein lies the problem (to say nothing about the limitations, and implications, of what Freud means by "beauty"). "Beauty," he writes, "has no obvious use; nor is there any clear cultural necessity for it. Yet civilization could not do without it." For Freud, if hardly for opera, aesthetics is an out and out failure.[36]

Late Romantic operas often resonate with dreams and daydreams, no matter their variable quotient of semi-gritty reality (*verismo*, most obviously), precisely because of the music's captivating beauty, experienced both as an acoustic sublime and, not coincidentally, as a momentary alternative to the mundane realities of instrumentalized late-modern life. The beauty of the music, in other words, accords poorly with what misery does to people, except as a fantasy-life imaginary. Opera's dream world underscores myriad actualities distinctly recognizable to the audience, and opera in part is effective on just this score. The whole is enveloped in an acoustic presence that not only permits but also specifically encourages auditors to enjoy the sufferings represented because they are made so sonically beautiful; the disharmony—social, personal, physical, psychic—of the staged lives is writ over by the musical harmonies incumbent on tonality, exploited to its rhetorical fullest. Opera's compensatory dream ends with the final cadence, the inevitable ending in the now glare of house lights that will banish us from the theater to rejoin our own realities, our *Jetztzeit*, fittingly enough following the mournful, desperate protests of Rodolfo as he embraces the corpse of his lover. His cries, staged so effectively by Puccini, momentarily—satisfyingly—become our own.

". . . THE SOUND OF BREAKING AND FALLING, CRASHING AND DESTRUCTION"

Fixing the date of epistemic change is risky business. It would be easy to choose an alternate chronology for the advent of musical modernism: *Salome*, say, or *Erwartung*. But for convenience I'll stick with Woolf's December 1910 time boundary and move on to the second of the two notes referenced at the start of the chapter.

NOTE TWO. This note, a high C, made its appearance shortly following Virginia Woolf's signal date, in Béla Bartók's *Bluebeard's Castle* (1911, rev. 1912, new ending 1917, premiered 1918).[37] I'll argue that this note constitutes itself as a micrological modernist rejection not only of the pleasure principle that opera had provided by means of tonal harmony but also, and more important, of the socio-cultural semiotics that tonality promoted. It's fair to say that by 1911 too much history had intervened to retain the old musical language intact in good conscience; in what follows, I suggest that Bartók addressed the issue directly and with distinctly dramatic impact.

Bluebeard's Castle has long been discussed in terms of its apparent concern with the psychological status of its two characters, Duke Bluebeard and his new wife, Judith. In the moments following the brief prologue, the groom first brings his bride into the large main hall of his castle with its seven sealed doors, which Judith in due course repeatedly insists that he open to her view. Bluebeard fiercely resists, but in each instance he eventually gives in to her demands. The doors are opened to reveal, in turn, Bluebeard's torture chamber, armory, and treasury; thereafter his garden, his entire kingdom, a pool of tears, and finally, disastrously for both Bluebeard and Judith, a room containing his three former wives, whom Judith will now be forced to join, leaving both her and Bluebeard bereft.

As most readings have it, Judith probes the psyche (or soul) of Bluebeard only in the end to learn too much;[38] at the same time, she exposes her own desperate need to deprive him of anything private to which she feels she has a claim.[39] Bartók and his librettist, Béla Balázs (1884–1949)—who a few years later turned to film, producing influential work in cinema theory[40]—give the audience access to an unfolding psychodrama that involves only the most minimal action, confined to a dark, indeed dismal physical space. Judith and Bluebeard barely move, except from door to door. When each door is opened, we don't see what Judith sees (at least, such is the case in typical productions); we have only her word for it, together with a considerable orchestral *supplément*. Bluebeard, for his part, has everything except love and happiness: he inhabits an unending nightmare. His one hope lies in Judith, who wants to know him, all of him. We are never given any indication whether she herself has any secrets; in any event, he doesn't ask. As Susan McClary puts it, Judith wants "the truth of his human rather than transcendental status" as authority and patriarch, in command of *logos*.[41]

At the moment Judith opens the fifth door, she is momentarily blinded by light (the stage direction is explicit on this account and instructs her to cover her eyes).[42] She experiences somatic shock and likely a stab of pain common to a sudden exposure to bright illumination in darkness, in reaction to which she sings a (perhaps agonized) high C, her highest pitch in the opera and one that she does not repeat (ex. 12).[43] When she removes her shielding hands from her eyes, she has an unimpeded view of Bluebeard's kingdom, which musically marks the opera's dramatic climax (fig. 114). Bluebeard immediately thereafter begins the first of three descriptive iterations of the glories and extent of his lands, the tangible domain of his power, anchored in language of an aesthetics of natural beauty: tranquil, perfect, endless. It's all hers, he says: "Here sun, moon, and stars have dwelling. They shall be thy deathless playmates." What she eventually notices, however, are not his lands, but the "blood-red shadows" cast by the clouds.[44]

EXAMPLE 12. Béla Bartók, *Herzog Blaubarts Burg* (Vienna: Universal-Edition, 1921), piano-vocal score, rehearsal no. 74 m. 11 to 78 m. 4.

EXAMPLE 12 *(continued)*

Not acknowledging Judith's cry—or perversely misreading its import—Bluebeard's proclamation enjoys the full support of a C-major chord played at deafening volume, densely orchestrated (more so than at any other place in the opera), and further supplemented by an organ doubling the harmonies as well as four trumpets and four trombones from offstage, these instruments employed nowhere else in the score, the extra brass supplementing already heavy brass scoring.[45] This stately, extraordinarily triumphant chord is followed by others, each pounded out in 4/4 quarter- and half-note martial beats moving in strict parallel motion through six measures that start and end on C-major chords, the volume opening *fff* and ending *ffff*. All seventeen chords are major (the movement is as follows: C-E-D-C-E-D-C-G-A-C-E-D-C-G-A-C-C), which is to say that the three triads built on D and E, and the two built on A, flavor the sequence as a tonal-modal

FIGURE 114
Thomas Moran (1837–1926), *Bluebeard's Castle* (1915), oil on canvas. Huntington, New York, The Heckscher Museum of Art, August Heckscher Collection. Photo credit: Bridgeman Images.

hybrid. The final chord is held for nine measures, accompanying Bluebeard as he completes his initial pronouncement, interpreting the vision for Judith.

Recovering her sight *and* her insight, Judith responds to Bluebeard's proclamation in a way that seems devastating (indeed, quasi-castrating), not in what she literally says but in how she says it. Judith waits through a full measure of total silence before reacting, then replies: "Fair and spacious is your country"—a remark, essentially recitative, that gives back to him just one measure of her emotional time. Without accompaniment, she offers up eight eighth-notes, in a *parlando* utterly absent of affect (the performance direction reads, "[Judith] stares fixedly out, distracted"; her singing is instructed to be *"senza espressione"*).[46] So Bluebeard tries again, his second pronouncement preceded by the same orchestral *tutti,* now opening with an F-major triad, the subsequent major chords proceeding, as before, in strict parallel motion.[47] His reiteration is again greeted with Judith's indifference and with the same text as before, the unaccompanied response sung a fifth higher, following another measure of silence that again breaks the spell of insistence in the orchestra (now ending on a G-major chord). Bluebeard, orchestra in tow, tries yet again, but this third time the martial energy of the repeated orchestral *tutti* motive, opening with an A-flat triad, quickly dissipates, along with the triadic harmonies, in favor of increased chromaticism and unstable, if not quite atonal, gestures that characterize the score as a whole—all this as Judith turns to the remaining doors, insisting that they be opened.[48]

Bluebeard's pronounced iterations about the brilliance and glories of his kingdom, ambitiously underwritten in the orchestra, claim more than they can deliver so far as

Judith is concerned, no matter his repeated efforts to make the assertions stick. The opera's one moment of blinding stage light is assigned the role of overriding the acute disappointment and disillusionment Judith experiences when she sees what lies behind the first four doors. Music is the backup to this task, one that it takes on in a state of some desperation. That is, the need for brightness to underscore semiotically the sonic impact of Bluebeard's claims is answered by major chords only, thereby hybridizing the harmonic effect—at once making it acoustically special, overreaching convention, but in the end setting up Bluebeard for the fall he will repeatedly take when Judith refuses to respond in kind. In brief, no music he can imagine will provide him the agency over Judith that he seeks. It's as if the urgency of the situation extends beyond what major-mode tonality is capable of. In its place, Bartók gives us a kind of tonality *in extremis,* no longer at home in its own sonic skin.

The sound and sight of this scene can serve as a metaphor of an allegorical enlightenment mirroring *the* Enlightenment, but in a state of ironic collapse concerning which the modernists were quite well aware by December 1910 and thereafter. Bluebeard's insistence that he is, in effect, the light of a secular world is not convincing. The historicist teleology culminating in turn-of-the-century modernity is recalled by Bartók in just the manner we might anticipate, with a single sustained (if hardly stable) sounding, one final time, of resonant sonorities on life support: pure consonance. We may take pleasure in them—their life as sonic commodities is after all well established, part of our acoustic lingua franca. We've been well schooled to consume accordingly. So Bartók invokes the sound in his own slightly twisted way and uses it against itself. Judith, for her part, reacts as though she just can't be bothered, though the more serious way to account for her reaction, fully complementary, is that she is already thinking *beyond* tonality—and right after her one and only high C atop the full orchestra's major-chord underscore. For her, the teleological pull of the harmonic rhythm, however modally inflected, has lost its magnetic force. She already gets what it's up to, and she's not impressed. In this regard, this extended moment in *Bluebeard's Castle* is as much about the history of music as it is an exploration of subjectivity and the psyche in existential crisis: music itself *lives* social crisis, sometimes in modes of consolation, sometimes, we might say, as engaged analyst.

HOW TO END?

And so to end, with an ending about two endings: *Turandot.* The story of Puccini's death prior to completing the opera is too well known to be repeated here except briefly in broad outline. At the time of his death, Puccini had completed, with the full orchestration, everything up to the point in act three where Liù commits suicide, thus leaving unfinished the crucial transformation of Turandot's hatred of men into love for Calaf—a matter that caused Puccini endless difficulties—and subsequent conclusion. The redemptive transformation was to occur with a kiss, presumably one carrying the same musico-dramatic weight as the meeting of the lovers' lips in the second act of *La fanciulla del West.* The challenge Puccini faced in particular—and of which he was keenly aware—was how to make the transformation convincing in the wake of the final aria and self-destruction of the servant girl, who loved Calaf more than life itself and whose suicide he had witnessed. How could one kiss successfully overcome the dramatic challenge produced by this situation?

Puccini's friend Franco Alfano was assigned the task, but with an aggressively attentive Arturo Toscanini looking over his shoulder. In the end, Alfano produced two endings; the one usually performed is the shorter of the two by about 25 per cent (102 measures), this thanks to Toscanini's objections to the first and longer version. Alfano had some, but not many, Puccini sketches to work with, the details of which have been carefully examined by Linda B. Fairtile and Marco Uvietta in two distinctively intelligent, insightful essays.[49]

The prevailing critical and scholarly assessments of Alfano's work have been anything but kind, starting from the year of the first performances, 1926.[50] The descriptors, at their worst, include "bombast" and "kitsch." Mladen Dolar, pushing the point perhaps further than necessary, summarizes Alfano's ending as "worthless stuff" and refers to it as a "failure." In what was intended as a particularly unkind (and rather snotty) cut, he likens it to the work of Andrew Lloyd Webber, a comparison that is all the more troubling to him because Turandot herself, as Dolar puts it, "belongs to the space of modernism." The opera, he concludes, "is already a postpsychological entity."[51] Alfano's ending—deeply satisfying if auditors like triumphant cadential *tutti*s with full brass, never mind the dramatic inadequacy—made for the grandest of grand operatic closures, duly martial, duly fitting for a *Star Wars* score or a royal wedding. Simply put, the opera's final scene, by itself, makes the whole a dish ripe for a Zeffirelli to design—or on a still grander, and more celebratory, scale, a production employing as backdrop the Forbidden City in Beijing (fig. 115).

Dolar summarizes his disgust by blaming Puccini and Alfano alike, attacking the opera's happy ending as lacking integrity. As he puts it, "The very obvious ridiculousness of the last scene signals that something else should have been there, something Puccini didn't dare to encroach upon but whose absence he was nonetheless honest enough to render palpable."[52]

One possibility of the "something else that should have been there" came about in 2002—the same year Žižek and Dolar published *Opera's Second Death*—with Luciano Berio's new ending for *Turandot.* Berio (1925–2003) addressed head-on the challenging dramatic chasm separating the moment of Liù's death from what was to follow. Her suicide cannot be swept aside, yet that's exactly what Alfano's ending did. As Berio adroitly put it, "Alfano just turns back to Calaf and his perpetual erection!" (that is, as if Liù never existed).[53] Berio's ending, in contrast, leads Puccini from the acoustic culture of late-nineteenth-century romanticism toward the stylistic modernism that he was clearly moving haltingly in the direction of, though in a distinctly back-and-forth manner: consider the sharp stylistic jostling among his operas written after the turn of the century: *Madama Butterfly* (1904) and *La rondine* (1917), both lushly romantic, between which falls *Fanciulla* (1910), and later there's the stylistic mash-up readily evident in *Il trittico* (1918), including the sometimes sharply discordant *Il tabarro.*

FIGURE 115
Puccini, *Turandot* (1924/26), act three, conclusion; staged in Beijing's Forbidden City (1998), production directed by Zhang Yimou.

Berio's ending attacks both certainty and musical historicism, taking advantage of cultural as well as musical history subsequent to 1924, a "final" moment read as the last gasp of opera writ large. Berio's ending, surrendering operatic spectacle to the actuality of blockbuster films and the technologies of special effects, produces instead a character study as the means to an ending culturally appropriate not only to now but also—and maybe more importantly—to 1924. What results bears resemblance to a reemergence of something like the bourgeois subject, but with a twist. That subject, in opera of the Grand Tradition, essentially can't keep its mouth shut. This holds for Calaf and Turandot as much as for Mimì and Rodolfo or Aida and Radames or Tristan and Isolde. Berio, by contrast, puts a gag over their mouths. He largely shuts them up and where it matters most. Berio "speaks" for them through the orchestra by means of an extended interlude (about three minutes' worth), giving voiceless access to Turandot's innermost subjectivity under virtually traumatic stress. Berio provides psycho-sonic access to her crucial transformation from Medusa to something maybe vaguely resembling a soft-hearted Pamina (admittedly to state the matter somewhat generously).

Alfano's *Turandot* transforms Turandot so as to insist, absolutely, that all is fine. Berio, as compositional analyst, puts her on the couch and through the orchestra gains access to what she is otherwise incapable of voicing—not least because of the loud, harmonically teleological, and triumphant orchestral veil cast by Alfano's cover-up. Uvietta's remarkable study of the new ending for *Turandot* accounts for Berio's accomplishment, which—to borrow from Adorno—adds up to its late-in-coming but fundamental

FIGURE 116
Puccini, *Turandot* (1924/2002), act three (final scene); Salzburger Festspiele production (2002), directed by David Pountney.

Wahrheitsgehalt. Berio's numerous quotations from Puccini, reworked from the composer's completed sections and the sketches alike, duly reconsider history subsequent to the moment when the opera was frozen in time upon Puccini's death. Berio's Turandot-transforming orchestral interlude, incorporating harmonies from Wagner and Mahler along with a sly quotation from Schoenberg's *Gurre-Lieder,* underscores what Uvietta aptly terms "opera in tonal crisis," reflecting Turandot's personal "crisis of subjectivity" as a stand-in for something larger than herself:[54] a disharmonized harmony, as it were, at war with itself (its past, present, and putative future), the whole of it destabilized, searching, radically uncertain. Berio writes a new normal that can no longer be suppressed in favor of whatever consolation the old way—Alfano's way, or Puccini's for that matter—sought to provide.

Turandot loves her man in the end—so, happy ending achieved? Well, hardly, and that's the point. Berio's ending is restrained. There is singing in the finale; even the chorus gets back into it, but *quietly.* The disarmingly simple decision to tone down the opera's concluding dynamics in itself transforms the cultural history of the Grand Tradition, and not just for opera. Any hint of the historicism one might imagine in the fantasy of the talking cure is absented. The ending drifts off into the fog of ambiguity, the psychic effect of riding into a metaphorical distance, not unlike Minnie and Dick Johnson astride horses that will lead them from the fantasy paradise of the Sierra Nevada back to realities less like the nature preserves now constituted by the western national parks and more like the rapacious economic inequalities of the last century's Gilded Age. In short, Berio buries cultural and—no less important—*musical* teleology. The opera's last word, several times

FIGURE 117
Puccini, *Turandot* (1924/2002), act three (final scene), conclusion.

voiced by the two lovers, is *Amor,* a redemptive word that semiotically resonates perfectly with the *Addio* that quietly concludes *La fanciulla del West.* Whether it will work out in the end, however, is a question that the music's major cadence manages to leave open.

As the opera approached its close, the 2002 Salzburg Festival production brought the chorus slowly back onstage, now in modern dress. The singers don't line up like a musical military formation to proclaim glory, typical in Alfano-ending productions. Instead, they mill about aimlessly, looking at Liù's body on the gurney, looking at Calaf and Turandot, or just . . . looking (fig. 116). They've come onstage to help stage an ending, but they don't seem to know how to go about it. Berio's music makes quite clear that their nearly aimless meandering is the only sensible movement available to them. Ultimately, they simply face forward to sing the notes of the Alfano/Puccini final fanfare, its impact now seriously undercut by the dynamics, subdued to a pianissimo, and also by Berio's cutting off the tune after only one brief iteration. The hints of the Puccini of old are now echoes of a historical claim that has musically, culturally, and indeed politically more than run its course. The opera ends with the embrace of Turandot and Calaf, this gesture repeated by the chorus whose members have also coupled up, though Berio's accompanying music falls short of underscoring any long-term guarantees (fig. 117). The old certainties were never certain, and nearly everyone knew as much, including Puccini, for whom love was an experience that rarely led to a happy end. The truth content of these uncertain certainties lies in wish, not reality: as dream. Berio had the good sense and honesty to insist on precisely that much and little more. This is no small thing, to be sure; it's also rather less than what we otherwise are well taught to experience in the institution that is opera.

PART III

MODERNITY, NATURE, AND DYSTOPIA

EXCURSUS

NATURAL BEAUTY / ART BEAUTY

> I used to be able to embrace all this and feel like a god in its abundance! How the magnificent creatures of this infinite world came to life in my soul! I was surrounded by titanic mountains, abysses lay at my feet, waterfalls tumbled down steep slopes, rivers flowed beneath me, and forest and mountain resounded with it all. . . . Something has been drawn away from my soul like a curtain and the panorama of eternal life has been transformed before my eyes into the abyss of an eternally open grave.
>
> JOHANN WOLFGANG VON GOETHE,
> *THE SORROWS OF YOUNG WERTHER* (1774)

NATURAL CONTRADICTION

In common parlance we locate nature beyond history; yet the concept of nature, culturally constructed, is necessarily historical.[1] Accordingly, as a concept, nature is located within the parameters of the very thing to which it stands in opposition: nature, in a dyadic relationship with culture, represents itself as a problem. In *Dialectic of Enlightenment,* Max Horkheimer and Theodor Adorno argued that our historical relation to nature is one of conflict. As they put it, "What human beings seek to learn from nature is how to use it to dominate wholly both it and human beings."[2] They argued that the fundamental forms of domination organizing modernity had their roots in the primordial efforts of humans to survive in a nature—primordial totality—that they feared. Ironically, fearing nature expressed not least a fear of the human, to the extent that people are not only *in* nature but also *of* nature; hence, the othering of nature othered the self from itself.

And yet human beings lament the very separation from nature upon which their identity (the sense of being human) is ultimately grounded. Thus, by the principle that Adorno and Horkheimer articulated, the designation of national parks, which first occurred during the heyday of the industrial revolution—signaling triumph over nature—directly responded to our fractured relation to nature. That is, the setting aside of small and as-yet "untamed" geographies signified less a nostalgic return to nature than a material acknowledgment of the permanence of the damage done to it. In the same way, contemporaneous salvage anthropology in essence picked among the graves and ruins to remember what "advanced man" had destroyed to become advanced.

At the end of his life, in *Aesthetic Theory,* Adorno staked out in detail his position on natural beauty, which he regarded as the defining issue of aesthetics and a good deal more besides. Our longing for nature—for example, ecological regard and wilderness preservation, but also and in particular art, in Adorno's argument—is a projection of a lack.[3] The concept of nature in essence protests its relationship to culture, or as Adorno put it, "The concept of natural beauty rubs on a wound."[4] Art is called upon to answer for natural beauty, in effect to substitute for it. Art—wholly artifactual, that is literally unnatural—perpetuates the attack on nature;[5] yet art does more, for it acknowledges the natural beauty that the human subject has otherwise degraded yet nonetheless desires in its nonextant "perfect" state. Art reflects on this fact. Art, Adorno says, "want[s] to keep nature's promise. . . . What nature strives for in vain, artworks fulfill."[6]

Adorno once commented, "Whenever nature was not actually mastered, the image of its untamed condition terrified." This, he said, "explains the strange predilection of earlier centuries for symmetrical arrangements of nature"[7]—think French landscape design with its severe topiary or, in England, the aesthetically contrived naturalism of Stourhead or Stowe, where "raw" nature was severely reorganized to appear, so to speak, more *suitably* natural. In other words, once human beings imagined they had mastered nature, it became their lost friend, only to be reimagined and sometimes fetishized.[8]

ORDER (ALIVE OR, PREFERABLY, DEAD)

Western art has long been taxed to visualize the cultural complexities of the human relationship to nature, response to which was characteristically riddled with contradiction. By the seventeenth century, hence at the dawn of modernity, representations of the domination and othering of nature were already legion, though the costs were aesthetically disguised. (The Romantics would later reconsider the matter in different light, as suggested by the epigraph above.) I want to pause here to consider several paintings from the Low Countries, each thematizing, indeed fetishizing, nature *tamed.* My choice of region is not accidental. The Low Countries (today's Holland and the northern parts of what is now Belgium) were centers of European world trade, one of the most important early manifestations of globalization and accompanying economic and cultural impact. The riches of the region stimulated an enormous appetite for visual representation on myriad secular subjects celebrating materialism (sometimes with hints of spiritual second thoughts, as in vanitas pictures), among which nature tropes, broadly conceived, were particularly common. Paintings, unquestionably the most prestigious form of imagery at the time, were churned out by the hundreds of thousands for decades on end by hundreds of highly trained, skilled artists, for a market both local and international; pictures were purchased not only by an aristocracy long practiced in art collecting but also by the newly emerging mercantile classes. In brief, the point of view concerning nature evident in this body of

FIGURE 118
School of Jan Brueghel the Elder (1568–1625), *Orpheus Charming the Animals,* oil. Rome, Galleria Borghese. Photo credit: Alinari/Art Resource, New York.

work (to be sure not wholly of a single mind, though what I will present is typical of a great deal of it) spread far and wide.

Perhaps the most seemingly benign conceptualizations of the nature-culture relation in early Western modernity, one that enjoyed significantly heightened interest, was the ancient trope of Orpheus charming the animals (fig. 118), in metaphorical reference to a would-be utopia made peaceful by Orpheus's musical agency to get the world to do his bidding. So powerfully affecting was his music that animals lay down at his feet in a harmony that suspended interspecies violence; so arresting was his music that even the trees bent toward him and rocks softened.[9] The beauty of many paintings on this trope is readily apparent. In the case of the Brueghel School example shown here, the rich *colors* concentrated within a relatively small space attract viewership, as does the subject itself, an apparent utopian world in perfect harmony, dependent upon the improbable (and literally impossible) incorporation of exotic and local species happily residing in close proximity. So apparently perfect is this moment in mythic history, and so beautiful is its rendering, that we are easily distracted from the fact that Orpheus's musical agency

FIGURE 119
Paul de Vos (1591/2 or 1595–1678), *The Birds' Concert,* oil. Bilbao, Museo de Bellas Artes de Bilbao. Photo credit: Alfredo Dagli Orti/Art Resource, New York.

enacts a new regime on the animal/natural world, a *denaturalization* of nature that, were it to last long, would produce annihilation of species on account of the starvation of carnivores, to state merely the most obvious impact, and a radical ecological imbalance. The musical "utopia" of enforced peacefulness, in other words, wholly imaginary to be sure, functions only so long as the tune lasts; were it to have a long half-life, hellish implications for the natural world are readily imaginable. Peace has been *imposed;* its supposed benefits for nature in the modern world are poorly thought out.

Another trope, likewise quite popular at the time, was the bird concert (fig. 119), a subject providing painters with the opportunity to display their talents at rendering feathered fauna of the most spectacular and distinctly colorful variety by means of a startling visual conceit that directly engages dialectics of time and space. The visual appeal of the painting shown here derives in part from the surreal suspension of reality demanded by the composition, which gathers together birds (as well as a bat) from the near and—mostly—far. The absurdity is plainly visible; indeed, it is made a point. At heart, the image is about ownership, built on a foundation of worldly dominion. Its apparent subject is birds; its real subject, people. The landscape is northern European, staffed by a peasant worker of sorts who gazes at the same sight that we look upon from outside the image. The conceit once again attracts through its strangeness. He looks; we look: the sight is startling.

And it's no accident, but the birds look as well. To be precise, and as the saying goes, they face the music—"ours," not theirs. They focus their attention on a small music book on which some notation is scribbled; they are all following the same script in order to produce (an impossible) heteronomy, that point emphasized by the contorted necks of some of the birds, as if straining to follow the acoustic-temporal orders, while grouped together like a feathered *schola cantorum,* performing in unison (that much is clear, though not much else, in the notation). The little music book, visually inconsequential as though little more than an afterthought, nonetheless possesses more than sufficient cultural authority to determine the entire composition. Around the two tiny sheets touched by flecks of black notation there swirls a phenomenal array of color—literally spectacular—like matter being pulled into a black hole—in this instance, the black hole of near-modernity. In brief, the birds have been *put into time;* they have been made historical. Culture trumps nature, and nature serves. (One absurd sign of the import of the conceit to the painting's semiotic charge is the decision to perch the swan in a tree.) The birds in this aviary have been selected for their beauty *in our eyes;* plain birds are of no interest (in this regard, the small bat—by comparison ugly and not a bird—serves as a small signal of antithesis within the composition); their "worth" (or worthiness) is determined by the degree to which they are nice to look at as eye candy.

Aesthetics is never passive, and music, the most abstract of art forms, is never devoid of meaning. The purported purposelessness of aesthetics and music here serves as both mask and sweetener for the shape of society and the human subjects within it. Ultimately, pleasure is never without consequences; it is a component of history and comes with a price to be paid. Music in this instance—on specifically human terms—determines birdsong, and music aestheticizes the domination of nature that establishes the functional protocol. Natural history is historicized; vast terrestrial space is colonized for its visual riches, here exotic fauna to be made to perform within an improbable aviary of human arrogance.

One more visual trope needs to be entered into this story, a subject vastly more popular than the two subjects referenced thus far. If the Orpheus tale and the bird concert aesthetically disguise the underlying cultural dialectics of nature in the service of humans, the gamepiece (or hunting) still life proclaims it openly as violent blood sport structured on class privilege.

The territories of Holland, from its wetlands and dunes to its forests and fields, supported a rich array of fauna—ducks, swans, pheasants, grouse, rabbits, deer. Migratory birds in large numbers passed through the territory. Virtually every species was fair game. Yet from the early years of the sixteenth century and long thereafter hunting was regulated by seasonal dates, time of day, device (long guns, bows, snares, nets, etc.), strict bag limits,

FIGURE 120
Jan Weenix (1640/41–1719), *Dead Swan* (1716), oil on canvas. Rotterdam, Museum Boijmans–van Beuningen. Photo credit: Museum Boijmans–van Beuningen.

and—most notably—social class. Hunting was a privilege granted to the nobility and a few others enjoying permission from the Forest Master. The hunt, especially for the most desired animal species, was a sport of the highest social prestige; it served as a sign of difference, and one well celebrated in still-life paintings of dead game. The Dutch gamepiece, despite its antecedents in the late sixteenth century, achieved extraordinary popularity in the second half of the seventeenth century when the vibrant Dutch economy led to the rapid expansion of a wealthy, if not necessarily aristocratic, upper class.[10]

With the work of the Amsterdam painter Jan Weenix, in the case of *Dead Swan* (fig. 120) a painting produced late in the story I'm relating, the beholder is witness to a visual ecstasy linking the (human-regulated) deaths of animals to the triumph of (some) men. Weenix is something of a special case: his paintings fed royal, not bourgeois, appetites, and he received direct commissions for monumental hunting trophies from aristocrats throughout Europe. The Dutch bourgeoisie, not allowed much hunting, typically bought ready-made gamepieces directly off the flourishing art market. The typical market-ready image was seldom a match for those by Weenix, a fact not lost on anyone buying gamepieces: Weenix's pictures are notably flamboyant and excessive; they raise death to the level of riveting spectacle. Accordingly, his paintings appropriately parallel the power of those who actually possessed the privilege to hunt. Indeed, such paintings' size by itself made them unsuitable for anything but the walls of monumental buildings, hence not those of Dutch burghers living in comparatively small houses, however richly furnished. (Among Weenix's most important commissions, for Johann Wilhelm, Elector of the Palatinate, were a dozen canvases in a series: "grand displays of booty and hunting scenes, often measuring up to 11 by 18 feet.")[11] These paintings' scale confirms difference—and size always matters; it is a rhetorical device, if among the most overstated and obvious.

Most immediately striking about this enormous picture (roughly 6 feet by 5 feet) is the swan, among the most prized of all game birds—so much so that the legal right to hunt it was extremely restricted. (It was a subject especially preferred by Weenix, who painted it many times over.) Indeed, the hunting regulations for swans were so restricted as to increase their value as highly prestigious trophies. Largest of all European waterfowl, the swan was noted for its beautiful plumage and its "regal," seemingly effortless, graceful, and dignified, movement on water. All of this mirrored the aristocracy's own idealized view of properly aristocratic physical grace, which was dutifully and obsessively taught (and most spectacularly realized in social dancing, the treatises and instructional manuals for which were legion throughout the period).[12]

The dead swan itself performs the metaphoric role of the vanquished enemy. This is no small matter to the proper functioning of the image. According to age-old warrior codes dating back to the Middle Ages (as for example in *The Song of Roland*), no personal prestige attaches to defeating any enemy lesser than oneself. To gain fame and to increase one's authority by killing, the opponent had to enjoy at least parallel stature. The trophy still life, in other words, functioned as a kind of aesthetic transliteration of then-popular battle pictures (scenes celebrating decisive military victories). The sport of hunting down rare and markedly beautiful game mirrors that of waging successful war. Painted representations of both types of event lay permanent visual claim to certifying the results. Such pictures possess documentary, as well as aesthetic, value. Whether the individual who commissioned the picture actually killed the swan is fundamentally irrelevant. In any event, the trophy bird that Weenix used as his model was almost certainly the result of taxidermy—a studio prop—but its unusual "pose" makes it appear to be a fresh and specific kill *for this image* (no small commentary on the painter's technical skills). Its wings and neck alike, remarkably painted, appear limp, as though brought into the studio while still bleeding.[13]

Taken as part of a quasi-narrative, Weenix's swan is not killed to be eaten but killed so as to become a spectacle confirming the identity of the privileged putative hunter. The animal is not valued for what it is so much as for what it purports regarding he who killed it. In this regard, hunting trophies commonly indicate vanquishing by situating dead game in the most unnatural poses, like enemies fallen on a battlefield, but in such a way as to appear heroic in death—an effect further charged by Weenix's use of theatrical lighting focused on the white bird set against everything else, which is relatively dark. Weenix's subtle modeling of the swan—his use of light and shadow—invites savoring the swan's "noble" form made pathetic in death. In sum, the image is principally about the death of

FIGURE 121
Jan Fyt (1611–61), *Still Life of Game* (1651), oil on canvas. Stockholm, Nationalmuseum. Photo credit: Erich Lessing/Art Resource, New York.

the Other and the resulting perpetual enshrinement of the self. And though the swan receives the painting's principal emphasis, Weenix provides enhancing flourishes via the subsidiary "small deaths" lying beside it, in a kind of visual aside, a parenthetical "not only . . . but also," as if to emphasize that the license to kill were unrestricted.

Indeed, "Not Only . . . but Also" might name a gamepiece by the Fleming Jan Fyt (fig. 121) where the principal victim is a stag, an animal whose prestige as hunting booty exceeded even that of the swan. As a manifestation of power and vanquishing, the painting is heavy-handed, rhetorically beyond the pale: it valorizes slaughter and more. The disemboweled stag is displayed so that its sexual parts are prominent and highlighted, a visual thumbing of the nose at its defeat, masculinity made impotent. The stag's pathos is charged by the visual effect of its limp and dangling hind leg, the failed source of its awesome ability to outlast pursuers. Fyt presents the animal in such a way as to hint at no less than a ritual execution. By adding drapery to the scene, an outdoors setting, conventional reference is made both to an aristocratic owner-perpetrator (such drapery was common to aristocratic portraiture) and to a theatrical event, namely the spectacle of contemporaneous and formally staged state executions, the final part of which was the public "humiliation" by mutilation of the criminal's body, which metaphorically restored full honor to the sovereign whose authority had been challenged by the crime committed.[14]

In sum, the gamepiece genre valorizes animal life for its service to human beings who themselves enjoy a life of privilege, evident not only in their wherewithal to possess such paintings but also in the choice of subject matter, intended to flatter (and perhaps exaggerate) their position within the social hierarchy. The fauna, simply stated, enjoy little value for what they are; their value emerges, rather, from their instrumental usefulness to human subjects. Our attraction to animals (the love of pets; in the seventeenth century, the urge to own menageries) itself seems natural; indeed, the beauty of fauna has been praised in written records from time immemorial. That said, the desire literally to own that beauty proves costly to the object of that love and desire.

DIGNITY

Adorno insisted that any theory of art required reflection on natural beauty but that such reflection, in modernity, had been repressed. "Natural beauty vanished from aesthetics as a result of the burgeoning domination of the concept of freedom and human dignity, which was inaugurated by Kant and then rigorously transplanted into aesthetics by Schiller and Hegel; in accord with this concept nothing in the world is worthy of attention except that for which the autonomous subject has itself to thank." The (autonomous human) subject is everything; all else is other. "In the experience of nature, dignity reveals itself as subjective usurpation that degrades what is not subordinate to the subject." And more, claims for dignity as perforce immanent to the subject are, for Adorno, ideology pure and simple. "Human beings are not equipped positively with dignity; rather, dignity would be exclusively what they have yet to achieve."[15]

Adorno suggests that as the suffering of modern subjects has increased in what he termed a "mangled and administered world"—that is, in a world precisely marked by the dedignification of human beings—the appreciation of, indeed longing for, natural beauty intensified.[16] This led to the increasingly common realization in late modernity that the condition of otherness is so complete than nothing escapes, especially not the human subject, whose special status is determined by not being othered. Art, for Adorno, is the site where the engagement with this contradiction—the otherness of the subject—occurs, the point being that artwork addressing this urgent task both confronts and, *in appearance* (though hardly in reality), allows at some level of imaginative experience the de-othering of our otherness: reconciliation, a closing of the gap between subjects and their others. Closing of the gap requires, for Adorno, a rethinking of the conjunction that joins natural beauty to art beauty, hints about which emerge in nineteenth-century Romanticism, as in the words of Lord Byron: "Are not the mountains, waves and skies,

FIGURE 122
"Tasayac, or the Half Dome, from Glacier Point, Yosemite Valley, Mariposa County, Cal.," stereograph, published by C. Watkins between 1871 and 1878. Washington, D.C., Library of Congress, Prints and Photographs Division.

a part / Of me and of my soul, as I of them?"[17] "Art is not nature," Adorno comments, "a belief that idealism hoped to inculcate, but art does want to keep nature's promise."[18]

The concept of natural beauty is historically unstable. For nature to be experienced as beautiful, it was first necessary for it to be dominated, however imperfectly. "Wherever nature was not actually mastered, the image of its untamed condition terrified,"[19] a fact that in no small part accounts for the rush, the thrill, the sense of the sublime (i.e., the immeasurability) of "genuinely" untamed (but precisely bounded) wilderness that could be (safely) experienced in the first national parks. The heart-pounding experience in the late nineteenth century of peering into the abyss beneath Yosemite's Half Dome, even if only imagined via a stereograph (fig. 122), was simultaneously made palpable by the realization that a rush was what we were *supposed* to experience: the thrill was *planned*. The "best" vistas were chosen, and trails to them were soon established—something quite different, say, from whatever members of the Donner party felt attempting to traverse the Sierra Nevada range. What is to be feared—and this is the real point—is not what is *in* the wilderness park but precisely what is outside of it, the space principally accorded for experiencing modern life.[20] Thus natural beauty's otherness becomes desirable, but it can be experienced only vicariously (in representations) or briefly, by passing through the boundary of its perimeters. Natural beauty nonetheless makes promises, which is precisely why we seek it out; indeed, its readily apparent difference from what it is not offers consolation (useful indeed for maintaining the status quo upon which the need for nature's otherness depends)—the key to its being marketed. That said, consolation is not necessarily antagonistic to the possibility of reconciliation.

Nature does not, indeed cannot, provide what society lacks. Nature is not a replacement for culture, or better, what culture might be or become. That said, nature is culture's victim. In this regard, and to take a quite ordinary example, in *Minima Moralia,* Adorno briefly confronted the vast American interior—in essence, the Great Plains of Terrence Malick's *Days of Heaven* (1978), the subject of the next chapter—in a single, aphoristic paragraph, which, not coincidentally, he titled "*Paysage,*" not the worst clue to the foreignness of what filled his visible horizon on what must have seemed like a very long trip from New York to the Pacific in 1941. Famous (or perhaps infamous) for paragraphs that commonly stretch pages on end, Adorno's account of the American plains merits only a couple dozen lines—and this from a man who was as sensitive to nature as Mahler, a composer whose works Adorno admired in large part for what he perceived as the aesthetic confrontation with humankind's fractured relation to nature, precisely the point of this landscape paragraph.

Adorno's account begins about as one might expect of a European intellectual with no prior experience of the vast North American interior: "The shortcoming of the American landscape," he wrote, "is not so much, as romantic illusion would have it, the absence of historical memories, as that it bears no traces of the human hand. This applies not only to the lack of arable land, the uncultivated woods often no higher than scrub, but above all to the roads."[21] And here, for Adorno, the road turns, and in a direction that sheds light on the more general, and indeed important, part of his exile experience.

Adorno is not in the least put off by the seeming emptiness of the interior but rather by what he perceives as the way that its human inhabitants relate to it, namely, with a degree of indifference that shocks him. He is reacting to the roads. "These," he says, "are always inserted directly in the landscape, and the more impressively smooth and broad they are, the more unrelated and violent their gleaming track appears against its wild, overgrown surroundings."

Adorno is almost certainly reacting to the transcontinental highways that systematically parallel the railroad tracks across the Great Plains. These roads, he laments, are "expressionless. Just as they know no marks of foot or wheel, no soft paths along their edges as a transition to the vegetation, no trails leading off into the valley, so they are without the mild, soothing, un-angular quality of things that have felt the touch of hands or their immediate implements." Adorno then provides a striking metaphor of the unreconciled separation of subject from object, of man from nature, his most persistent encapsulation of dystopian modernity: "It is," he says, "as if no-one had ever passed their hand over the landscape's hair. It is uncomforted and comfortless."[22]

Schopenhauer, in a lengthy discussion of the sublime, wholly imagined an American *paysage* in ways complementary to Adorno. "Let us transport ourselves into a most lonely region," he suggested, "with unlimited horizon, under utterly cloudless skies, trees and plants in entirely motionless air, no animals, no people, no moving waters, the deepest stillness." Such regions, for Schopenhauer, are "like a summons to seriousness, to contemplation, together with a tearing of oneself away from all willing and its neediness." This, he notes, "is the species of the sublime that is reputed to attach itself to a view of the endless prairies in the interior of North America."[23] It's not entirely clear what Schopenhauer has in mind, whether a kind of broad vista—a whole, as it were—or something more specific and indeed more typical to his time: a somehow bracketed landscape, defined in part by its strangeness and incommensurability, literally *sublime,* a concept deeply valorized within the broad philosophical terrain of early Romanticism. Along similar lines, and about a century later, Sergei Eisenstein, long interested in cinematic landscape, suggested estrangement of a related but different sort, here quoting D. H. Lawrence: "The American landscape has never been at one with the white man. Never. And white men have probably never felt so bitter anywhere, as here in America, where the very landscape in its very beauty, seems a bit devilish and grinning, opposed to us."[24]

Taken together, these three assessments, separated by a century, make room for Malick fittingly to make his entrance. His films are heavily invested in, and indeed in large part defined by, the problematic thus outlined, which is the subject of the next chapter. The nature/culture dyad engaged in all of his cinema unquestionably reflects the long history of American anxiety over, on the one hand, the notion of the New World as a place of, and opportunity for, reclaiming moral innocence, set against the mythologies and actualities of European decadence, and on the other, the endless succession of reminders from colonial times to the present of the myriad ways in which neither innocence nor moral superiority tracks well in the chronicle of American history. To American filmmakers working in the 1970s, near the end of the Vietnam War or in its immediate aftermath—a period of intense reconsideration of the so-named American Century—the promise of the New World and the hope structured into the mythology of an imagined westward expanse was more than merely frayed. In brief, by the 1970s who in their right mind could look at any of the five dozen or so paintings churned out by the nineteenth-century Quaker Edward Hicks on the popular, and clichéd, Peaceable Kingdom trope (fig. 123), pictures naive in look and substance, with anything short of deep-seated irony—and never mind the scriptural source (Isaiah 11:6–8 and 65:25): happiness everywhere, a nonviolent world, the natural world as if in the permanent thrall of Orpheus. That world never existed; expulsion from the promised land of such wish-making was long complete. Malick's films, from the 1970s to date, center on this problematic, in regard to which he began his film career in very good company, with Michael Cimino, Francis Ford Coppola, and Arthur Penn, among others, much of this cinema set on the final frontier of hopeless hope, the American West.[25]

Landscape, for Georg Simmel, is the result of a consciousness that marks difference, separateness. If what we intend by "nature" is "a representation and symbol of that wholeness of Being," by "landscape" we mark something different, characterized by detachment "from that indivisible unity of nature in which each piece serves as a transit-point for the totality of the forces of existence." In other words, landscape—commonly valorized, by definition—heralds precisely a lost wholeness, and at the same time offers consolation by

FIGURE 123
Edward Hicks (1780–1849), *Peaceable Kingdom* (c. 1830–32), oil on canvas. New York, Metropolitan Museum of Art, gift of Edgar William and Bernice Chrysler Garbisch, 1970 (1970.283.1). © The Metropolitan Museum of Art. Photo credit: Art Resource, New York.

aestheticizing the need we feel for that inclusiveness. The creation of landscape, in Simmel's words, "necessitated a tearing away from that unitary feeling of the whole of nature."[26] And yet, viewed dialectically, it is precisely the loss of the unity with nature that allows the contemplation both of the concept of nature itself and of what a reconciliation with it would make possible: happiness. It is through art, for Simmel and Adorno alike, that reconciliation can be imagined. On this score, Simmel is worth quoting at length, not least given the degree to which Malick's work so consistently enacts the insight offered here:

> An artist delineates one part within the chaotic stream and infiniteness of the immediately given world, and conceives of and forms it as a unitary phenomenon. This now derives its meaning from within itself, having severed all threads connecting it to the world around it and having retied them into its own centre. We follow the same procedure—only in a less developed, less fundamental degree, and in a fragmentary way unsure of its boundaries—as soon as we perceive a "landscape" in place of a meadow, a house, a brook and passing clouds. What this reveals is one of the most profound determinations of all mental and productive life.[27]

Reconciliation of the subject to the other, hence in part with the otherness of all nature beyond the self, cannot result from a reversion premised on the end of history. Resolution is not defined by a move "back to nature"; rather, the *concept* of nature itself critically marks the necessity of resolution. To experience natural beauty is to experience the remnant of a world without domination, even though, as Adorno notes, it's one that "probably never existed."[28] But left at that point, the inadequacy of natural beauty to the problem of reconciliation becomes undeniable: its wholeness, so to speak, is imagined and explicitly—*needfully*—an actuality desired but not real. After all, in simple terms, nature is violent; big fish eat little fish. But that's not the point. Freedom, so central to Western modernity's concept of the subject, is *not,* in a word, natural. Indeed, the principle of "natural law" upon which post-Enlightenment democracies depend is distinctly and exclusively cultural. It is not least the result of rational thought applied to the concept of nature. Nor is it by historical accident that so-named natural law marks for modernity the highest form of terrestrial moral authority—nature made sense of, made orderly. In short, there is no nature without culture, but culture is nonetheless inadequate to its own concepts of nature, the natural, and natural beauty.[29] The very otherness projected upon nature and natural beauty guarantees our inability to make full sense of it, and this in no small measure renders it the more desirable as that which is beyond human domination, a fact we both treasure and often abhor: consider the political battles waged whenever setting aside additional land as a national park is proposed (the land's fungibility thereby more tightly circumscribed, though nonetheless commodified as a travel destination and organized around the services provided by concessionaires who bid with the government for the exclusive, monopolistic profit-making within the confines of the park's protected spaces.)[30] Consciousness does justice to the experience of nature, Adorno insisted, "only when . . . it incorporates nature's wounds," which is to say that nature in sublated by what lies beyond its actuality: nature "is broadened by what is already no longer nature. Otherwise nature is degraded to a deceptive phantasm. . . . For in every particular aesthetic experience of nature the social whole is lodged."[31]

THE SOCIAL WHOLE OF NATURE

It is the social whole lodged within nature itself that Malick's films engage, even and indeed especially when he turns his camera, almost always fleetingly, on strikingly beautiful fauna, often in frame-filling close-up, a compositional practice that organizes a good deal of *Days of Heaven* and *The Thin Red Line,* as well as a significant number of his other more recent feature films. Adorno's expression of the dialectical tensions I'm considering are repeatedly engaged by Malick, for example his paratactical juxtaposition of natural beauty (landscape, flora, fauna) with longer scenes of war and other forms of inhuman brutality; Adorno: "In the face of beauty, analytical reflection reconstitutes the *temps durée* through its antithesis."[32] For Malick, the hyperbolic gap between the beautiful and the ugly is critical; it is the exaggeration that clarifies the price to be paid for the promulgation and ideological/political elevation of the principle of the subject-object dyad upon which modernity and the subject alike depend.

The beautiful in nature, for Adorno, "is what appears to be more than what is literally there."[33] That is, the art of the film does not lie in the beauty of flora and fauna, seascape and landscape, but in what those cinematic images, in this instance realized in an artwork, permit us to understand. Malick's point is not simply to provide momentary relief, however ironic, in the face of the injustices and degradations of which human beings are so culpable, but to remind us of the costs and to imagine an alternative, even when confronted by apparent hopelessness. Adorno understood art not as an imitation of natural beauty but as the faint promise of happiness that lies at the heart of nature's otherness vis-à-vis the subject: the trace "of the nonidentical in things under the spell of universal identity," the semblance of *what might be,* what we commonly refer to as utopia. In sum, for Adorno, "the dignity of nature is that of the not-yet-existing."[34]

RECONCILIATION AS ENDING *(LIEBESTOD)*

Adorno's concluding aphorism in *Minima Moralia* opens with a remark addressing philosophy, which he would unquestionably apply to art as well: "The only philosophy which can be responsibly practised in the face of despair is the attempt to contemplate all things as they would present themselves from the standpoint of redemption."[35] Adorno pointed out elsewhere that art "embodies something like freedom in the midst of unfreedom. The fact that through its very existence it stands outside the evil spell that prevails allies it to a promise of happiness, a promise it itself somehow expresses in its expression of despair."[36] His insistent invocation of hope, found throughout his writing, hinges on the ordinary insight that the world as it is didn't just happen; it was made to happen. Our future isn't written in the stars but is to be written on earth, a point repeatedly made in Malick's films as well, whose various acousmatic voices both directly and indirectly invoke precisely this point. In the end, we might say, it's ultimately up to "us," with the first step taken being one that leads to a change in consciousness: "The neon signs which hang over our cities and outshine the natural light of the night with their own are comets presaging the natural disaster of society, its frozen death. Yet they do not come from the sky. They are controlled from earth. It depends upon human beings themselves whether they will extinguish these lights and awake from a nightmare which only threatens to become actual as long as men believe in it."[37]

At the end of *The Mansion* (1959), the final volume of William Faulkner's Snopes family trilogy (the other volumes are *The Hamlet* and *The Town*), the aged, worn-out Mink Snopes, alone and exhausted, perceives his death as a return into the earth whence he came: "Because a man had to spend not just all his life but all the time of Man too guarding against it; even back when they said man lived in caves, he would raise up a bank of dirt to at least keep him that far off the ground while he slept, until he invented wood floors to protect him and at last beds too, raising the floors storey by storey until they would be laying a hundred and even a thousand feet up in the air to be safe from the earth."[38]

But Mink has had enough and decides to risk it, to give earth "a fair active chance just to show him, prove what it could do if it wanted to try." He lies down on the ground and soon, almost imperceptibly, feels himself "beginning to creep, seep, flow easy as sleeping . . . down and down into the ground already full of the folks that had the trouble but were free now." Finally, in death, there is reconciliation with the allness of the past as well as the future he will not experience. Faulkner allows Mink Snopes to imagine his reabsorption, a reconciliation of sorts not experienced *on* earth, but only in a return *into* earth. He won't live that reconciliation, but he can at least imagine it, and that much at least, or so Faulkner gives us to think about, is worth something.

> . . . so that it was just the ground and the dirt that had to bother and worry and anguish with the passions and hopes and skeers, the justice and the injustice and the griefs, leaving the folks themselves easy now, all mixed and jumbled up comfortable and easy so wouldn't nobody even know or even care who was which any more, himself among them, equal to any, good as any, brave as any, being inextricable from, anonymous with all of them: the beautiful, the splendid, the proud and the brave, right on up to the very top itself among the shining phantoms and dreams which are the milestones of the long human recording—Helen and the bishops, the kings and the unhomed angels, the scornful and graceless seraphim.

Lying on the ground, Mink Snopes feels the tug of the earth calling him back: "He could almost watch it, following all the little grass blades and tiny roots, the little holes the worm made, down and down into the ground already full of the folks that had the trouble but were free now."[39] The experience brings him peace.

Modernity from its first moments to its more recent end has articulated its relationship to nature (for Faulkner, concentrated, simply, in earth) in terms of love and hate, mirror-image emotions whose agency knows few bounds and whose impact on human experience remains profound, perhaps the only constant. The passage from *The Sorrows of Young Werther* (1774) providing the epigraph for this excursus, reflecting the morbid psychological state of the decent but narcissistic young romantic shortly before his suicide, ends as follows, the words of a man-boy whose pantheistic love for nature ("I am alone and glad to be alive in surroundings such as these, which were created for a soul like mine") has resolved itself into one of revulsion, a sad, hyperbolic reflection of an actuality well embedded in the social practices of modernity (if not necessarily in the imagination of its subjects): "My heart is undermined by the consuming power that lies hidden in the Allness of nature, which has created nothing, formed nothing, which has destroyed neither its neighbor nor itself. Surrounded by the heavens and the earth and the powerful web they weave between them, I reel with dread. I can see nothing but an eternally devouring, eternally regurgitating monster."[40]

5

SOUND, SUBJECTIVITY, AND DEATH

Days of Heaven (promesse du bonheur)

> With high woods the hills were crowned,
> With tufts the valleys and each fountain side,
> With borders long the rivers; that Earth now
> Seemed like to Heaven, a seat where gods might dwell,
> Or wander with delight, and love to haunt
> Her sacred shades.
>
> MILTON, *PARADISE LOST*

PLOT. *Days of Heaven* (1978). The story is set initially in Chicago and thereafter in the Texas Panhandle in 1916–17. The film is narrated in voiceover by Linda (Linda Manz), a girl of about twelve years of age, whose older brother, Bill (Richard Gere), is the lover of Abby (Brooke Adams). They are destitute. Bill works in a foundry; Abby salvages detritus from garbage heaps; Linda makes paper flowers. Bill, provoked at work by his foreman, attacks and perhaps kills him, and immediately runs. Soon thereafter the trio flee Chicago, heading west by hopping a freight train. Once in Texas, they go to work for a young, wealthy (unnamed) Farmer (Sam Shepard), having been hired as migrants to help with the harvest. Bill and Abby masquerade as brother and sister. The farmer develops an interest in Abby. Bill encourages the romance, having overheard that the Farmer is terminally ill. Bill plans for Abby to marry the Farmer and, after his predicted impending death, inherit his lands, after which Abby, Bill, and Linda will be fixed for life. Abby reluctantly agrees. The Farmer's foreman, who regards the younger man as a son, is deeply suspicious of Bill and Abby.

After the harvest and the departure of the other migrants, the three itinerants stay on, living with the Farmer in his Victorian house on the open prairie. Over time, Abby falls in love with the Farmer, triggering Bill's increasingly dangerous jealousy. The couple marry; Bill departs. The Farmer, Abby, and Linda live together in obvious contentment. Bill unexpectedly returns the following season, triggering the story's tragic ending. The

Farmer eventually discovers that Bill and Abby are not siblings but would-be lovers; he experiences anger toward Abby and outright rage toward Bill, all of which comes to a head during the harvest, which coincides with a plague of locusts that is rapidly destroying the crops. The Farmer orders the migrants to drive off the insects using smoke from a controlled fire set for this purpose. Soon thereafter the effort turns chaotic when the Farmer, furiously lashing out at Bill with a kerosene lantern tied to a long pole, inadvertently ignites the uncut grain, which soon burns out of control, destroying the unharvested field and the farm implements.

The next day, amidst the still-smoldering, blackened land, Bill—knowing the Abby loves the Farmer and not him—prepares to leave. He is confronted by the Farmer, who stalks towards him pointing a pistol; Bill, who is repairing his motorcycle and holding a long screwdriver, fends off the Farmer, stabbing him in the chest and killing him. Bill, Abby. and Linda flee, pursued by the distraught foreman and a posse, who eventually catch up. Bill is shot in the back, dying instantly.

At an unspecified later time, the final scenes show Linda in a small-town boarding school taking a dancing lesson. Abby, handsomely dressed—presumably she has inherited from the Farmer—bids Linda goodbye and leaves to catch a train. Linda shortly thereafter escapes from the school, meeting up with a young woman whom she befriended while on the farm; the two of them walk along the railroad tracks and into their unspecified future.

STILL PHOTOGRAPHY AND HISTORY: OPENING CREDITS

The title sequence of *Days of Heaven* is set against a series of twenty-four late-nineteenth/early-twentieth-century black-and-white photographs, most paced at about four to five seconds each, principally of urban laborers and the destitute, adults and children of both sexes, of the sort famously captured in the muckraking exposé *How the Other Half Lives* (1890).[1] The music underscore is the seventh section, "Aquarium," of Camille Saint-Saëns's *Le carnaval des animaux* (1886), of which more presently.

The first photograph serves as a kind of establishing shot, initially of the upper stories of buildings on an urban block, then tilting down to a teeming street scene, seen from above. The photograph fixes time: long past, essentially strange, silent, dead to us. The tilt-down has the effect of putting the image in motion, the better to focus and discern its unfamiliar contents. The second image is a street-scene close-up of a poorly dressed boy caught unexpectedly by the camera and looking back over his shoulder while lighting a cigarette, his demeanor suspicious and streetwise—the antithesis of late-Victorian bourgeois mythologies of childhood as the age of innocence.[2] The third photograph is of a much younger child in close-up staring without expression directly at the camera; here, as elsewhere among the facial stills, the camera moves in tight, so that her straight-on gaze dominates the frame. The fourth image breaks this sequence, introducing reference to recreation via the façade of a gigantic ice-block fortress, replete with crenellated walls

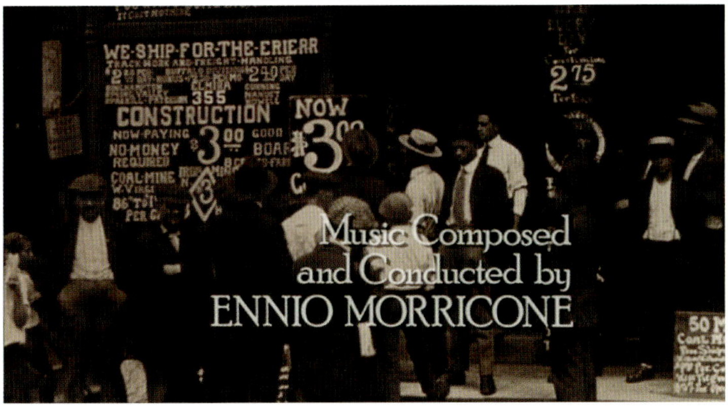

FIGURE 124
Terrence Malick (director), *Days of Heaven* (1978), title (1:19).

and towers. What follows thereafter, principally images of the down and out, suggests what was commonplace (misery) and what was not (relief, in the form of leisure activities, and then, to judge from the costuming, mostly for the better off or well-to-do). For the most part, the photographic collection documents poverty, street life, tenement living, and irregular labor. One photograph shows the exterior of a work center covered with large advertisements for day laborers and toward which peer a small crowd of presumably unemployed men and boys (fig. 124). The people are mostly immigrants, apparent from their dress. Few smile; they simply look back at us, as though we were strangers in their midst. Even the face of a young bride, briefly shown, is reserved, undecipherable. The scrapbook of urban images provides virtually no reference to the natural world, apart from the miseries brought on by harsh weather.

There are only three photographs of pleasures, apart from the ice castle: one of a nicely dressed young woman in white sitting on a rock in profile to the camera and staring out at the sea, and two by photographer H. H. Bennett shot at Wisconsin Dells. The first captures two working-class men in a canoe (c. 1890–95), and the second, well known and often reproduced, documents a young man, in fact Bennett's son, leaping in midair between tall rock outcroppings (1886).[3] These few images of simple exurban pleasures, set against the others forming the montage sequence, establish a troubled binary relation that constitutes the film's driving force, one fraught with tensions—social, ideological, political, and spiritual—and marked by the separation of the natural world from its historico-cultural other.[4] By and large, the people photographed belong to the nameless masses or, in the case of close-ups, are individuals whose unique faces matter only as types, part and parcel of a population of extras, such as the sweatshop workers in a garment-industry facility, the lot of them approximately as important as the acres of laundry hanging on lines suspended between tenements shown in one of the last photographs in the sequence. Life beyond the parameters of hard work and occasional leisure is referenced in a single image of President Woodrow Wilson standing together with five other men in long coats and doffing his top hat to an unseen crowd, an otherwise absent

FIGURE 125
Malick, *Days of Heaven*, title (final shot): Linda (2:17).

presence of wealth, position, and power—an image that helps to fix the specific temporality of the film.

The last photo is a full-body medium shot of a poor teenage girl sitting on the ground and looking at the camera. The image, modern but made to look like those that precede it, is of actress Linda Manz, who narrates the film's voiceover as Bill's younger sister, Linda. The camera moves in to frame her blank stare (fig. 125), then slowly dissolves, overlapping with a five-second exterior "live" shot of a grim iron foundry, set against an equally dull sky, the site where her brother Bill works.

Hereinafter, the film is in color and in motion, initially morphing to a ten-second shot of Bill's lover, Abby, sorting through a refuse pile with other women. As the "Aquarium" section of *Le carnaval des animaux* accompanying the title sequence concludes, the film's acoustic diegetic narrative is initiated, the music initially mixed with, and thereafter surrendering to, the sound of water draining from two vertical pipes into a sewage canal next to the garbage heap, the elevated dynamics overwhelming the music's final cadence. The two audio sources briefly juxtapose, after which the sounds (drains) and sights (garbage) of urban modernity pull the viewer from the black-and-white past, which by its obvious temporal separation from the viewer may seem remote, into a strikingly brown present, wherein the colors of the dump are undifferentiated from the filthy garments worn by the women searching for something useful among the detritus. Color, however dreary, and motion pull the historical referents in the title sequence into a here and now of sorts.

Malick opens his film as though we were flipping through an old photo album, to the accompaniment of the dreamlike Saint-Saëns score, constructed almost entirely on a repeated two-bar motive with filler (arpeggiated chords, 16th- and 32nd-notes, played on two pianos), the overall effect being one of stasis and sonic confinement (ex. 13). The sound-parameters of harmony, melody, rhythm, dynamics, and timbre together reinforce a narrow circularity in which very little "happens." Sonically, the music of "Aquarium" "swims" in its own small acoustic structural enclosure.[5] The whole of the miniature is a

EXAMPLE 13. Camille Saint-Saëns, "Aquarium" from *Le carnaval des animaux (Grande fantaisie zoologique)* (Paris: Editions Durand, 1922), mm. 1–2.

kind of variation on an established motivelike theme, subsequent iterations of which are interrupted by breaks of chromatic sixteenth-note passages on the pianos that serve as transitions, precisely, back to the beginning (ex. 14). "Aquarium" does not progress toward climax; instead, it repeats as if circling around itself. It doesn't so much conclude, as end.

The narrow compositional parameters imposed by Saint-Saëns serve well the music's function within *Days of Heaven,* on specific account of the avoidance of anything sonically reminiscent of development and teleological drive. In this regard, "Aquarium" is antihistoricist, and hence modern, no matter its otherwise conventional musical vocabulary; it duly puts into sound the endlessly repetitive miseries (and few pleasures) documented in the title-sequence photographs, for which it serves as accompaniment and sonic commentary.[6] That said, "Aquarium" nonetheless—and in a word—is *pretty,* and is thus an acoustic antithesis to what is captured in the still images. Perhaps its sounds accord well with something akin to the distanced poignancy that we experience when looking at very old photos; almost no matter the subject, they invoke the reality of what is beyond reach, an awareness of loss, unimpeachable distance, and the universality of death. And to be sure, old photos do constitute nostalgic forms of remembrance. But the prettiness of

EXAMPLE 14. Saint-Saëns, "Aquarium" from *Le carnaval des animaux,* mm. 9–12.

"Aquarium" is not quite so easy to subsume under the category of misremembering, and it is in this regard that the choice of the piece, especially for the film's opening, is distinctly appropriate, and not the least of reasons for the aptness of Ennio Morricone's prominent borrowing of motivic material from "Aquarium" for important cues throughout the film.

Both the photomontage and the "Aquarium" underscore are repetitive; image track and soundtrack together offer only minor respite from the consistency of sameness. Set that fact aside and one might judge the music inappropriate, given its blatant consonance, to the extent that its sound aestheticizes the ugliness and misery captured in the images. But perhaps the apparent sound-image gap makes sense for what follows in the film. Malick and Morricone have established a sound/sight dialectic. Late-nineteenth-century European art music widely, if hardly universally, established itself as the acoustic analogue to bourgeois triumphalism, profoundly teleological and historicist—thus fundamentally requiring the sound revolt by Schoenberg and those who followed in his footsteps at just about the time this film is set. In other words, the sound/sight dialectic of the title sequence establishes modernity as a problem.[7] To be sure, and whatever the sonic "attractiveness" of "Aquarium," the piece does not fit well the historicist paradigm; if anything, it ironicizes the cultural foundations upon which its musical procedures rest.

Days of Heaven engages the fraught culture/nature, subject/object relation as its central problematic. *Le carnaval des animaux* does so as well, if principally through humor and irony sometimes tinged with sarcasm. Subtitled *Grand fantaisie zoologique,* the piece mostly characterizes and caricatures wild animals in quasi-anthropomorphic terms, as in the opening, the royal entry of the lion, principal witness to the ensuing entertainments. Throughout the composition, Saint-Saëns attempts to capture an acoustic sense of animal motion, wherein the natural movements of fauna apparently exist for human pleasures and amusement. But in the case of "Aquarium," motion is sonically confined to a small enclosure as though for the best possible acoustic/visual "viewing," inviting us to put our sonic "eyes" right up to the glass. The point, obviously enough, is that the piece as a whole represents entertainment commonly associated with the zoo or—to be anachronistic—the animal theme parks of our own time. It is nature harnessed, made alternately cute or funny and often "performing"—though the inhabitants, metaphorically caged, also include *"personnages à longues oreilles"* (critics) and *"pianistes"* who labor endlessly on their technique, playing scales via Hanon studies. In sum, *Le carnaval des animaux,* whatever the composer's intentions, is representative of the regulation and domination of nature that lies at the foundation of modernity, much of which is intraspecies and involves human beings.

The underscore for the title sequence helps to mark the defining problematic of what unfolds in the film, and beginning only a few seconds into the in-motion narrative.[8] Consider the transition at the close of the title sequence as the story itself is initiated. Still images are replaced by movement; black and white by color of sorts. The physical activities of the garbage-hunting women are tightly confined within a small space. We look at them from a place they don't inhabit. The accompanying sound design transitions from orchestral aesthetics referencing motion in water to the sounds of water flowing from sewage pipes. The two sound masses are briefly sutured, establishing a shared connection. Art beauty hits hard against lived reality. Aestheticized animal captivity is one thing, human confinement another, but the two are not unrelated.

The *sound* of "Aquarium" has something uncanny about it, an effect principally produced by the interrelation between the music's circularity and repetitiveness on the one hand and its timbre on the other. The texture is crystalline, bright: strings, two pianos, flute, and—critically important—glass harmonica. (Most recordings replace the glass harmonica, with its distinctly eerie sound, with celeste or glockenspiel, which is a shame.) The glass harmonica plays in hocketlike alternation with the flute's quarter-note legato of the opening motive. Its eighth-notes, on the offbeat and an octave higher, softly but audibly punctuate or accentuate the motive. The glass harmonica helps to situate the sound mass in an unfamiliar acoustic frame; it contributes to the defamiliarization of the whole, in part otherwise achieved by the brittle sounds of the two pianos. Defamiliarization of the familiar is a hallmark of Malick's cinema and a gateway to his engagement with modernity and its troubles. The soundtrack at the film's opening accesses this trope.

DIALECTICS

Immediately following the brief glimpse of Abby and other women sorting through garbage, a jumpcut takes us to the foundry's interior and Bill shoveling coal into a furnace amid very high-decibel, Dolby-heightened (or "sweetened") noise that renders all but indecipherable the few angry words spoken between him and his foreman moments before Bill strikes the head of his boss with what looks like a sledgehammer (though he had previously held a shovel), knocking him onto the concrete floor, wounding or perhaps killing him, and thus providing the impetus for everything that follows: a flight from the literal and metaphoric hell of urban industrial life, humming with robotic, dehumanizing labor, and movement westward in pursuit of a new start in an imagined paradise that will be experienced all too briefly. The mind-numbing Foley sounds of the foundry emphatically erase any memory of the musical underscore of the opening in favor of noise and the chaos that the actions producing it enact on its victims, just as the unnatural darkness of the interior—as though natural light no longer existed—is moderated only by the hellish fires visible through the open doors of the furnaces.

As Bill turns to flee, his sister, Linda, begins her voiceover narration that will continue throughout the film.[9] She marks the story as a remembered past from a putative future that remains without specification or even certainty, and not least because, as narrator, her insights remain those of a child, at once guileless and knowing but by no means necessarily always insightful. Locating herself in the future, she remains the same child she was in the past. At the level of practicality, her voiceover helps to connect narrative events that would otherwise be unclear, in part because of Malick's preference for severely limiting the conventional role of dialogue. This is not to say, however, that Linda's voiceover functions simply as a device for rectifying ambiguities, since what Linda says often amplifies the film's purposeful open-endedness. (Michel Chion usefully points out that voiceovers "have a habit of opening quotation marks for a story but often 'forget' to close them.")[10] Malick's use of voiceover is but one of several temporal discontinuities within the film, of which more further on.[11]

In the midst of her commentary, the scene cuts from the foundry to Linda as a child laborer in a tenement room, busy fashioning yellow paper roses, the work accompanied by the sounds of an off-screen crying infant. She bends to her work in a dark, barely illuminated nighttime environment; her covered head and fingerless gloves suggest that the radiator directly behind her is cold. Abby, in the same room, lying under a blanket, is comforted by Bill, who sits beside her. The sounds of a train intrude; they live near the tracks, which shortly will serve their escape.

Malick provides this shot of Linda, only nine seconds long, to open the transition between two worlds. It is a move *toward* a return to nature, the desire for which is congealed in the bright-yellow artificial flower Linda labors over and, even more, in the ample bouquets she has already finished; the flowers mark the first bright color in the film, apart from the furnace fires in the foundry and the molten metals being poured into molds in the immediately previous scene. Treated dialectically, color makes its initial appearance in the browns of the garbage dump and immediately thereafter in the foundry as the bright fires of a manmade hell. Linda's artificial flowers mark a midpoint between the real and unreal, and death and life. Only in the natural "paradise" of the western plains will a more positive valence to color emerge, however imperfectly and temporarily.

This brief shot signals the aesthetic artifice of the film that follows, seen, as it will be, through the lens of Linda's memory. As the film's narrator, she constitutes the connective tissue (the interior hermeneutics) of the story that she narrates. It is through Linda's eyes that we know what happens, though at the same time we see clearly the limitations of her insights, child that she is—in a manner that precisely parallels (but is hardly identical with) the voiceover narration by Holly, a slightly older teenage girl, in Malick's *Badlands* (1973).[12]

The severe limitations on the aesthetics of flower-making are obvious from the assembly-line repetitiveness of her exercise, which not coincidentally parallels Bill's presumably endless shoveling of coal into the maw of the furnace, his physical movement confined to a tight circle. Also by no means coincidentally, he moves like a fish trapped in an aquarium. Still, the need (beyond money) to make flowers, or better, the presumed fact that other people somehow covet even artificial ones, points to the nature trope around which the film is constructed: a desire for a purposelessly purposive otherness that lies beyond ourselves. The flowers in this context point to something in excess of the profoundly limiting experience of the film's characters as established in the opening minute of the narrative. Like Linda fashioning flowers, Malick, as filmmaker, weaves his own artifice: the relation between making flowers and making a film, established in these few seconds of visual transition, marks a critical relation between art beauty and natural beauty, about which I will have more to say below.

As Linda makes a paper rose, the nondiegetic sounds of a twelve-string acoustic guitar sonically transition the scene, momentarily, to the rail yard as Bill, Abby, and Linda light out by hopping the rails, and thereafter to a long shot of a coal-fired steam engine pulling a train across a high trestle, filmed from below so that the frame is otherwise filled by a bright sky and puffy clouds. The folksy tune "Enderlin," written and performed by Leo Kottke, marks a distinct, dramatic acoustic difference from the preceding scenes. However "new" the composition, the tune registers in sonic memory as folk-authentic, and here for the first time in the film both sound and image seem to be in sync. The quick-paced fingerpicking, the major mode, the upbeat rhythm, and the repetitive theme together accord with the rhythmically reassuring clickety-clack of the wheels on the rails, a happy road trip trope, reinforced by the smiles and waves of the dozens of riders atop the freight and grain cars. By this point, the city has disappeared for good in the film; the setting almost instantly morphs to the Great Plains and the Texas Panhandle, where the narrative hereinafter unfolds.

To this point in the film, less than five minutes from the opening, the brevity of the scenes, complemented by the nearly constant movement of the camera, is readily apparent; indeed, scene-brevity and camera movement characterize the film as a whole, together with minimal dialogue. Ordinary relational connectives produced by speech are limited, which lends greater weight and urgency to both the film's nonspeech sounds and its music, diegetic and nondiegetic alike. But this is not to suggest that Malick assigns to sound effects and music the role of "saying" what dialogue does not. Quite the opposite. The lack he studiously imparts is functional; it alters the terms of viewership, bringing closer to the film's forefront what lurks within sound film: the silent cinema.[13]

In the same regard, the film's high degree of documentary naturalism, whether of the landscape, period set dressing, or costumes, is never the point. Nor is social realism as such. The allegorical import of the story, and, in fact, of cinema itself, seems of greater concern to Malick. In the words of Eric Repphun, "His films are at the same time dream-like and confrontational."[14] Malick's debt to Heidegger's philosophy of the ontology of Being, often cited, while considerable and indeed obvious in each of his films, informs only part of his concerns.[15] No matter the fictional character that pervades even his putatively "historical" films (*The Thin Red Line* and *The New World*), existential ontology persistently confronts, and is in turn confronted by, history, in every instance the troubled history of American experience, from the early colonization of the North American continent to the de facto present. The issues that concern him, notably so in the "earliest" history he examines (the Jamestown colony in the early seventeenth century), are undeniably the traumas associated with late modernity, whose foundations were established well before the first colonists set foot in the New World.[16]

Days of Heaven marks a fundamental dialectic between the natural world, timeless but threatened, and modernity, shown at its height of self-confidence in the immediate lead-up to World War I, defined by industrialization, mechanization, speed, restlessness, and freneticism, all of it driven by rampant social inequality. The train that takes sister, brother, and his lover west is the product of the very world they run from. The black plume belching from the engine's smokestack, photographed from various angles, is intrusive, inviting an awareness of the dystopian associations common to its color, a blot alike on the blue sky and the greens and harvest gold of the grasslands and crops on either side of the tracks, unfolding as far as the eye can see fig. 126). Atop the grain cars, Bill, Abby, and Linda ride with other migrants, crowded together and enjoying no protection from the coal smoke, as Linda's voiceover relates her story of meeting a man named Ding Dong (a name typically assigned to a fool, but a fool in the Shakespearean mold in this instance) who tells her that the whole world is going up in flames—biblical Armageddon in lay-terms vernacular; it is a story of Last Judgment, an unstable dyad of retribution and salvation. (Where there's smoke—and there is plenty of it in this escape scene—there will soon enough be fire, in a climactic, lengthy sequence toward the film's end, immediately preceded by a biblically resonant plague of locusts.)[17]

As Linda relates Ding Dong's parable, Kottke's bright music plays on, accompanying Bill and Abby in a long embrace, as smoke nearly envelops the background. As if to make the visual dissonance more insistent, the film cuts to show the train in long view, the black plume extending the full length of the attached cars and somewhat oddly taking on the appearance of storm clouds. The shot jumps to a momentary look at three pronghorn antelope—the first of many fauna to appear in the film—after which it cuts to the arrival

FIGURE 126
Malick, *Days of Heaven:* train trip (6:03).

FIGURE 127
Malick, *Days of Heaven:* farm gateway and farmhouse in distance (7:09).

scene in the Texas Panhandle and the prairie farm where most of the film's action will occur, the setting established by three large red grain elevators stationed along the tracks. Kottke's guitar fades out as the wealthy Farmer's foreman yells through his megaphone for day laborers.

Shortly after disembarking from the train, the workforce is transported from the rail siding to the farm, driven there by a combination of flatbed truck and horse-drawn wagon. They traverse through an elaborately designed wooden-arch entry gate (fig. 127), absurdly placed in the middle of a ripe wheat field, referencing a property boundary that is otherwise invisible, the fields stretching far into the distance.[18] The characters seem metaphorically to have been transported through the gates of a terrestrial heaven, an American Eden in which nature's bounty is man-directed and benevolent. Near the end of the film, Bill, Abby, and Linda will once more pass through the gate, now mostly destroyed by fire, as they flee following the Farmer's murder, experiencing their metaphorical expulsion from paradise (fig. 128).

The next scene, visually beautiful, makes explicit the breadth of the plains and their bounty, but the "nature" that Malick provides here, and repeatedly throughout most of

FIGURE 128
Malick, *Days of Heaven:* fleeing through the burned farm gateway (1:18:47).

the film, is not wilderness but one of labor-intensive bonanza farming typical of the early years of the last century, involving a transitional mix of technologically advanced machinery and premodern grunt labor. The point, then, is hardly to suggest that the characters have escaped to a natural paradise. On this score, Malick is not nostalgic; there is no "pure" nature manifest, except in the form of fauna, often shown as threatened and frightened, especially those fleeing from the fires set to kill off the swarms of locusts that are attacking the crops. Nearly the only natural "nature" is the sky, itself besmirched by the coal smoke of the train bringing the main characters to the realm where they will act out their few short "days of heaven."

Color at this juncture takes on particular force. Malick shows us a vast field ready for harvest and an even vaster blue sky, the hues of both softened by filming shortly after sunset—the time of day when much of the movie was shot, during the so-named "magic hour," which lasts until roughly twenty minutes after sunset.[19] For anyone raised in this part of the world (for Malick, it was West Texas), the term fits. The western plains during the height of day are unforgivably bright, even harsh. Colors bleach, and shadows are few, produced only by farm buildings and occasional trees (all of this is especially discernible in *Badlands*). But the end of the day, even more than around daybreak, is almost literally magical. Light softens, as does everything it illuminates, and the plains take on an uncanny loveliness, reinforced by the cool breezes that moderate a summer day's often intense heat.

NATURE, WIND AND CHANGE

The cinema [is] of its essence a dramaturgy of Nature.

ANDRÉ BAZIN, *WHAT IS CINEMA?*

The transport of the migrant laborers from the rail siding to the farm is accompanied by attentive sound design; indeed, a series of interrelated sounds are distinctly heightened so as to assert their presence and significance. The various sounds combine from several sources, each in its way invoking the unnatural in the nature setting—initially, the rhythmic rattle of the four-cylinder truck engines, soon thereafter mixed with the horses' hooves, wagon wheels, and a horse's neighing. As the first vehicles pass through the arched gate, a crane shot slowly reveals in the far distance the Farmer's Victorian house, roughly similar to the sort found in Hopper paintings (this no accident), amid a sea of grain still green but fully headed. At this point, in close succession, Malick contrasts two sounds: the late-summer chirping of crickets, which in fact occurs only in the evening hours, and the spinning wind generator (07:18) atop the Farmer's house, as though the two were in competition. The two sounds register the film's overriding concern with the fraught nature/culture relation.

Malick films a close-up of the house and a shot of the Farmer, well dressed in suit pants, suspenders, tie, and bright white shirt—kept clean by the washing machine directly behind him, a detail not left to chance, all the more in relation to the dull and often filthy clothes worn by the workers, immediately referenced in a jumpcut. The Farmer surveils the arrival of the migrants as he bites into an apple (underscored by an exaggerated Foley sound), thereby metaphorically anticipating the fall from grace and the loss of the imagined paradise with which the film concludes, an ending that echoes the story of the Last Judgment as related moments earlier in Linda's tale about Ding Dong.

The generator is set in motion by the winds that perpetually blow across the vast inland prairies of North America, serving both literally and metaphorically as the harbinger and agent of change. The wind charger's sonically sweetened acousmatic Foley-effect whirring (see table 1), heard while the camera is focused tight on the Farmer, defines the scene aurally, while the front end of a shiny-new car does so visually (07:40), referencing an unstable brave new world of money, class distinction, and power differential. (Note: The four tables referred to in this chapter, providing information concerning the film's sound and music design, including diegetic and nondiegetic music cues, may be found in the appendix, pp. 259–67.)

The next shot interrupts the narrative flow to provide a wordless commentary on the film's exploration of the dialectic of enlightenment. Filmed late in the day, Bill walks alone in a golden field of ripe wheat (07:58), the land softly undulating in a mix of hills and shallow valleys, the camera low so as to all but eliminate the horizon. Here the wind itself is audible for the first time—along with the chirping of crickets—whereas wind can only be assumed in the immediately prior shot of the wind charger atop the house (we don't hear the wind driving the charger). The wind sets the ripened wheat in beautifully rhythmic motion.

As Bill, slightly smiling, stares fixedly into the distance, Malick cuts to a small herd of bison (08:11); one imposing animal directly in the center of the frame stares at the camera as if at Bill as Malick cuts back to Bill (shot/reverse-shot), his own gaze fixed. The establishing-shot and point-of-view relation is unambiguous, but Bill's apparent seeing stands beyond the inner working of the plot's unfolding and is the more crucial precisely on that account. Put differently, his seeing (his gaze) is functional on account of its nonfunctionality. That is, the bison herd stands in a field of ripe grass, not in the vast wheat field that surrounds Bill (the animals would hardly have been tolerated to wander freely into an unharvested field). The animals' presence makes no literal sense, except as an attribute of the American prairie and, more generally, mythologies of the West for generations of children and adults alike, both in the time of the film and in ours. Once numbering in the millions, bison constitute an especially dramatic account of natural bounty, no matter that by the 1916–17 setting of the story the animals had already been all but exterminated, partly in an effort to deny any Plains Indians not yet settled on reservations access to their traditional food source. Accordingly, the brief shot of the herd might logically be little more than a fleeting presence in Linda's memory, but not without purpose. Béla Balázs, writing about landscape, refers to its possessing "a very definite, if also indefinable expression of feeling, with an evident, if also incomprehensible, meaning." He adds, "Nature's soul is not something given *a priori* that can 'simply' be photographed." For us, he says, "the soul of nature is always our own soul reflecting itself in nature."[20] His insight fits the semiotic functionality of the bison: "This process of reflection can occur, but only through art."[21] Bill seemingly stares at Nature in a setting vastly different from what he best knows; Nature, so to speak, meets his gaze, but offers him nothing in return. Malick does not anthropomorphize nature.

In a similar vein, in a later six-second shot, Linda and a young woman she has recently befriended frolic close to the bison (16:36). The scene, taken literally, is nonsensical; sane people would never play anywhere near an open-range herd of such powerful, unpredictable wild animals readily given to stampede. Both scenes more logically function as imagined memory traces of the mythic plains, whether drawn from the recesses of Linda's imagination or imposed into the narrative as part of the film's larger constellation of allegorical effects. Both shots—the second as if to underscore the first—are characteristic of the numerous discontinuities common to Malick's films, the impact of which is to mark nuanced constellations of social and cultural truths by straining the linear narrative flow, if not quite utterly disrupting it.[22] The sense of estrangement caused by the disruptions pushes against the film's visual and sonic beauty and by this means helps to clarify the underlying wounds that organize the reality inherited by the film's principal characters within which context their lives unfold.

Turning his gaze from the bison, Bill looks toward the call of a distant hawk, the first of a number of shots of low-flying lone birds. The camera tracks its low flight above the ripened wheat field, little more than a dot of dark against the dim, postsunset sky (08:19). These shots, anchored in Bill's gaze, fix his physical presence on the prairie, but as a lone figure in a vastness made more explicit by the low camera angles, a stranger to the nature of which he is a part. Malick provides a collision of signs, extraordinarily musical in its flow—and not coincidentally reminiscent of what Eisenstein termed "the music of landscape."[23] The moment is polemical but without so seeming, though exactly where its

FIGURE 129
Malick, *Days of Heaven:* scarecrow (9:59).

allegorical "argument" leads at this point is uncertain: the aggregate, though pedagogical, is reserved in what it seeks to claim.[24]

The next scene, also set in a wheat field and tightly framed, has Linda walking with her young woman friend. The hand-held Panaglide camera is at the level of the heads of the grain. The sound of the rustling straw caused by their walking is so heightened that the scene is as much a sonic event as a visual one (08:31), as if—to quote Chion on a different film—sound was *"seeking to leave its trace in the image."*[25] Malick frames the pair against the whitening sky at their backs, putting them almost in silhouette. Linda finds a locust—Malick shoots it in extreme close-up (09:20)—concerning which the woman remarks, "I don't think they like us," thus anticipating the horrendous swarms of the insects that, together with an out-of-control fire, will destroy the crops at the end of the following growing season.

In a shot soon thereafter, Malick cuts to a nearly dark postsunset sky, the last rays over the horizon illuminating Maxfield Parrish–like orange clouds. The landscape is entirely in deep shadow, all but black. Standing out, center frame, is a scarecrow whose arms move slightly in the wind (09:59; fig. 129). Again, the wind. The figure, as it were, looks west, the direction of the once-open "frontier," replete with the quotient of emancipation attached to that metaphor and articulated in the hopeful myths of American exceptionalism duly mirrored by the expansiveness of the open prairies. But farmers don't place scarecrows in wheat fields; the birds photographed by Malick are not a threat to small grains. Rather, the scarecrow's function in the narrative is allegorical. Staring blindly at the magnificent beauty of the sunset's afterglow and the distant infinity over the horizon, its arms helplessly flapping in the breeze, it dutifully awaits whatever greater nature sets in its path.

Weather is the soul of nature brought on with the wind, a spirit force of life as of death. On the prairie, everyone watches the sky as much as the land, and for good reason. Malick takes this actuality and increases the stakes, setting nature (its beauty, its unparalleled if indifferent omnipresence) in tension with the culture that at once insists on saying what nature is while commonly setting itself in opposition to what it has duly named. In these efforts, and by his decision to set his film in the vastness of the American grasslands, Malick realizes an insight of Eisenstein, that "landscape can serve as a concrete image of the embodiment of whole cosmic conceptions, whole philosophic systems."[26]

Malick cuts to workers waving large flags as they walk amid the ripened crop (the purpose of which is unclear). The Farmer, also in the field, picks a head of wheat, rubs it between his hands so as to separate the kernels from the chaff, blows away the chaff, and bites into a kernel, testing it for hardness (10:10). If harvested while soft, the moisture level is too high and the grain spoils in storage. All of the sounds—picking, rubbing the palms together, blowing away the chaff, biting down on the kernel—are sweetened, the effect of which is to call attention to the beginning of the harvest, the most visually dramatic labor on the Great Plains. The crop is ready. The farmer gives the signal to begin. The scene cuts to an in-field prayer service, a blessing of the harvest, which coincides with the first music cue of Ennio Morricone's score constructed on the opening motive of "Aquarium" (table 4, cue 3). Immediately following the prayers the harvest operation is initiated with the cutting and bundling of the crop (despite close-ups of heads of ripened wheat that are intercut in this scene, the crop is oats). As the horse-drawn cutter-binders move in tandem across the field, Malick intercuts extreme close-ups of small animals either hiding or running from the machinery: rabbit, skunk, and pheasant.[27]

The sound of the binders' cutting sickles is uncannily similar to that of the wind charger—conspicuously so, for the sound is heightened to the point that all other sounds function only as sonic background; complementarily, the reels of the binders, pulling the standing grain toward the cutting bar, replicate the motion of the whirling blades of the wind charger. In this scene, and in a number of others that follow, the visual-aural impact of motion, whether the effect of wind or machine, is striking; indeed, Malick clearly attached significance to these phenomena as governing tropes. The visual focus on turning devices (propeller-driven wind charger, the reels of the grain cutter-binders), together with the sound of wind, presage the interconnectedness of turns of season and the endless repetition of natural cycles, coupled with the uncertainties of what the wind will bring and the uncertainties of human efforts to control nature. What is constant is the certainty of the uncertainty and the dialectical tensions that emerge from the relationship between constancy and change.

Without any preparation in the narrative flow, Malick follows the initial scenes of grain cutting with a dramatic change in early fall weather. After a warm evening's recreation and play there comes a sudden snow, which Malick establishes in four successive shots: Bill and Abby, shivering and miserable, huddle in a straw pile (detritus from the threshing machines), their overcoats covered with snow (19:22); five adults, bundled in blankets against the wind, trudge across the prairie, in a scene of misery reminiscent of Goya's *The Snowstorm* (1786/87) (19:33);[28] Abby's face is shown in close-up, followed by a final shot of the snow-bedecked horses. The sound of wind increases as these shots unfold. The horses neigh, skittering, and the screen goes black (19:57). Malick next

FIGURE 130
Malick, *Days of Heaven:* accountant and Farmer (22:16).

focuses on a close-up of standing, ripe wheat, covered with dew. Warm weather has returned. The grain gently sways in the breeze, and crickets chirp. Late-summer "normal" restored with the appearance of so-named Indian summer, the threshing moves ahead in earnest and with urgency, the migrants being ordered to speed up—all of this commented upon in Linda's voiceover.[29]

The natural beauty surrounding the film's characters bears no necessary relation to their quotidian concerns or comforts. The days of heaven in their stunningly beautiful setting, utterly different from the miseries of urban degradation, are in fundamental ways more or less wholly imagined. Nature might offer the appearance (and to some extent the reality) of providing for what is otherwise missing in their lives, but this is not to say that nature anthropologically somehow has their interests at heart.[30]

Precisely this point is apparent in a scene proximate those just described, involving the Farmer's accountant adding up the presumed take from the harvest. The scene is set outdoors, apparently in the same field of oats shown in the immediately previous scene. The Farmer's relation to the outdoors is profoundly, and improbably, at a remove from those of his laborers. While his accountant works at the additions, the Farmer reclines on a sofa brought from the house, his feet in the air; dressed in a suit, he is playing with his fedora and enjoying the shade of a large umbrella whose outer edges flap in the breeze (21:51). The immediate impression is of comfort, class distinction, and control. In the same vein, the well-dressed accountant's worktable includes ledgers, strongbox, and—illogically—a fancy microscope. A telescope on a tripod stands next to the table, soon to be used by the farmer to espy Abby (fig. 130). The microscope and telescope are, of course, objects for surveillance of what is near and far, large and small. They are devices for measuring the world and, as regards the Farmer's looking at Abby, for taking charge of others. (The relation between the telescope and the riflescope in this regard is apt.)[31] Indeed, when the farmer looks through the telescope (22:19), Malick employs a masked point-of-view shot, the effect of which is to emphasize his possessive gaze. As for ownership, the accountant, finishing his projections, informs the farmer that "you're talking over six figures, . . . which should make you the richest man in the Panhandle," adding that he should get out "when you're this far ahead." The Farmer's relation to the land, as to the migrants, in other words, is understood to be wholly instrumental, accurately representing the logic underlying early-century bonanza farming practice.

Two elements of the sound design are noteworthy in this scene: the constant blowing of the wind, an acoustic evocation of unencumbered nature, and the noise of the manually operated adding machine, evoking the instrumentalization of nature by a culture organized around the principle of universal fungibility. As if to underline this point, the shot that immediately follows that of the Farmer gazing at Abby through the telescope is a close-up of straw being shot from the long pipe (a match cut replicating the shape of the telescope) extending from the threshing machine; the two images dissolve, one into the other, the better to establish the relation. The noteworthy difference, duly emphasized, lies in the contrast between the sounds of the gentler prairie winds and the high-decibel force with which the straw is blown (22:24), a visual-acoustic marker for the wealth piling up in the Farmer's coffers, already discernible in his dramatically outsized house, whose Hopperesque, distinctly solitary, lonely profile dominates the natural landscape.

Malick then cuts to the open door of a steam-tractor's firebox (22:30), framed in black, precisely like the shot through the telescope and likewise replicating the open door of the furnace into which Bill shoveled coal at the film's start.[32] Here too the sound is sweetened so that we hear an acoustic close-up of the fire itself, the effect of which comes off as a sort of contained inferno. Malick concludes the series of close-ups with a tight shot of the centrifugal governor atop the tractor, its fast-spinning motion reminiscent of the generator-propeller on the farmer's house. These visual-acoustic vignettes together emphasize the urgency of the harvest, the effort to beat the fall rains or, for that matter, the insects. They likewise help to anchor the sharp distinctions of the dialectical tensions between modern culture and the natural world: the necessary, urgent efforts to beat the punch of nature that comes with the change of seasons.

For the most part, visual and/or acoustic reference to wind relates to the main adult characters, and for this purpose the wind charger is especially relevant (fig. 131; table 1). For example, immediately following the tractors' steam whistles collectively announcing the shutdown at the end of threshing, Malick provides a view, shot from below, of the Farmer's house, interior lights shining into the night (27:20). As if to emphasize the detail's significance, Bill, walking behind Abby, stares back at the building in a long take; the only sounds are the couple's footsteps in the dry grass and the whirling of the propeller, both acoustically exaggerated.

Indeed, among the numerous visual and sonic references to the prairie winds, none carries more weight throughout the film than that of the wind generator that charges the storage batteries powering the house lights—lights that provide the only competition for the natural illumination from the moon and stars, as Malick takes care to show.

This mechanical device invites several associations. As a sound and sight it complements Chion's insight—in reference to the sound of a movie projector—that the "'whirring

FIGURE 131
Malick, *Days of Heaven:* wind charger (44:38).

FIGURE 132
Malick, *Days of Heaven:* Farmer at wind charger watching Abby and Bill (1:06:26).

of the machine' is, of course, the first noise of cinema," and one that would "persist, concretely or symbolically, into the sound film." He gives the sound a name: "fundamental noise."[33] The generator's sight and sound, whether "present" separately or together, more or less whirrs throughout the film, but, as I will discuss further in what follows, its sound presence is made insistent at fraught moments in the narrative, instances of what Chion aptly calls "emergence," when something occurs in the film that strongly solicits the viewer's consciousness (fig. 132).[34] The spinning propeller, like the slowly turning reels of film stock, reminds us of our outsidedness (or, perhaps better, as rapt viewers, inside/outside status) to what unfolds on the screen and is emitted from the loudspeakers. But the function of the audio-visuality of the wind charger hardly ends there.

The well-established association of light to enlightenment and, via the Enlightenment, to modernity informs the engagement of the culture/nature dialectic that so troubles *Days of Heaven* to its innermost core. In this regard, the wind generator helps to underscore the film's allegorical drive. Malick's repeatedly records the spinning propeller (it is never photographed not moving) in both visual and sonic close-up, the effect of which is to render its function semiotic, a propos of which is Rick Altman's insight that "every sound initiates an event" and "every hearing concretizes the story of that event."[35] Indeed, the charger provides *meaningful* background to the main events throughout the film, from the moment when Bill, Abby, and Linda first set eyes on the house (7:19) to the point immediately prior to the Farmer's final confrontation with Bill (1:16:11). It functions as a kind of mechanized Greek chorus to the unfolding narrative, and usually in relation to tense developments then happening or soon to occur. The propeller spins through the characters' time in their relative paradise, sitting above them as if in surveillance; its presence is repeatedly emphasized to the viewer but never once commented upon by the characters in the narrative. Malick repeatedly anchors the whirring propeller's allegorical *charge* (the pun is intended), not least by his frequent use of jumpcut references to the device edited jarringly into the narrative flow; in every such reference, the sound of the device matters as much, and sometimes more, than its sight (table 1).

Just as the camera frames an image, the microphone frames a sound. Sound, like image, is *composed.* Sounds recorded are sounds in representation: they are "written"; they mean. Malick's manipulation of sounds, especially by denaturalizing their "naturalness," by making them hyperbolic, pulls them into the range of audition that makes them thought-worthy, functioning in auditory excess beyond the merely indexical or informational. Sound in *Days of Heaven,* distinct from dialogue, is employed as a category of the philosophical; the sounds that matter the most at once help to articulate and engage the nature/culture relation.[36]

The use of the wind generator motif as a fundamental part of the film's aesthetic and semiotic structure is particularly dependent on montage, to which Malick is extraordinarily attentive. Having devoted two years to the editing *Days of Heaven,* he left little if anything about the final cut to accident or mere convenience. Eisenstein suggests that "sound, treated as a new montage element (as a factor divorced from the visual image), will inevitably introduce new means of enormous power to the expression and solution of the most complicated tasks that now oppress us with the impossibility of overcoming them by means of an imperfect film method, working only with visual images." In this regard, the film achieves part of its formal unity by means of what Eisenstein termed "orchestral counterpoint," a specifically nonsynchronous relation between the visual and the aural, in *Days of Heaven* usually, but not always, realized in his references to the wind charger but also in numerous other direct references to wind itself (table 2).[37] In sum, and in the words of Béla Balázs, "The vocation of the sound film is to redeem us from the chaos of shapeless noise by accepting it as expression, as significance, as meaning."[38]

Malick's use of wind and the wind generator in the film's unfolding (tables 1 and 2) is constellational;[39] in Adornian terms, both are part of a force field *(Kraftfeld),* a dynamic interplay of tensions, oppositions, and contradictions.[40] The insistent acoustic presence of wind throughout the film, far more than a supplement to its visual phenomenology, not only transmits a sonic insistence on temporality, change, and the impermanence of everything except change, but at the same time functions as an aural demarcator of the space of the prairie and the significance of spatiality in the larger sense. Sound, as Malick employs it, has sign value in excess of its ties to the logic of unfolding narrative. As a force field, sound in *Days of Heaven* at key moments stops the narrative in its tracks, not least on account of Malick's paratactical jumpcut close-ups of the whirling, noisy generator. The wind itself, semiotically loaded—again, *charged*—remains invisible. Its presence is marked only in what it does: drive the generator's propeller, usually at such high speed that the entire device vibrates on its stand. Wind, as a stand-in for nature, is a force that moves everything, human subjects most notably.

Malick's formal references to the semiotics of wind are many. For example, following their marriage, the Farmer gradually senses a distance growing between himself and Abby, but without understanding its cause. Speaking to her in their bedroom as Abby undresses, he plaintively asks, "Why are you so uneasy with me?," then adding, "It seems like I don't know you." Malick abruptly cuts to a crane shot of a small pond whose surface is disturbed by the evening wind blowing across its surface, the wind's sound significantly enhanced, and he holds the shot for a long fourteen seconds. He then sharply shifts the tale, again by another jumpcut to a close-up of the *Amarillo Dispatch,* October 7, 1916, whose headline announces the visit of President Wilson. In other words, he juxtaposes his juxtaposition: bedroom–pond–newspaper headline. Throughout the film, events that string together the characters' lives announce themselves as fragments of a whole that is unavailable either to them or to us, precisely because holistic narrative, fully explainable, would undercut and even destroy the nuance upon which the film depends for its engagement with the dialectical forces that underwrite its otherwise quite simple putative plot.

Along the same lines, when Bill and Abby run off into the night (he having awakened her as she slept next to her husband), we hear the augmented sound of the wind charger as they leave the house and Abby asks, "What's the matter with you?" (45:04). Malick then cuts to the gazebo (45:08), where earlier that day the Farmer, Abby, Bill, Linda, and some visiting circus performers had entertained themselves. The empty structure is now silhouetted against the night sky, its diaphanous curtains flapping in the wind. He cuts again (45:12) to Abby's umbrella, seen earlier (42:02) during the couple's honeymoon, now lying open in the grass and rolling back and forth in the breeze. Finally, he cuts again and holds for three seconds a shot of the scarecrow (45:14), this time filmed from below, looking into its face—here seen for the first time. Set against a cloudy night sky, the figure has the look of an Old Testament prophet of the sort found in Romanesque church sculpture (almond eyes, flowing beard), gazing back in a blank stare that seems judgmental.

Earlier in the film, Linda, alone and lying on the ground, wonders about her future. Playing with a clod of dirt, she remarks, "I could be a mud doctor, checking out the earth underneath"; she then puts her ear to the soil. The connection established between the girl and the earth is obvious, and not least because the brief episode serves no logical point in the story, except to the extent that it draws upon and helps to amplify the film's allegory on the nature/culture relation. As if to drive home the point, however obliquely, Malick immediately cuts to a lone frog, croaking, sitting among some glacial-deposit rocks, and then to three grazing mule deer, as thunder echoes offscreen. It is as though the fauna await her mud-doctor diagnosis. Malick then cuts to a static image of a distant approaching storm (33:51) that all but blots out the surrounding sky and plainly shows both the characteristic dark color of rain mixed with the white streaks typical of hail falling from the roiling clouds. Rain usually spells life on the prairie; hail presages destruction. The approach of such storms can be seen from many miles away and hours in advance of their arrival, leaving long uncertain whether to expect saving rain or sudden catastrophe. Malick holds this image for ten long seconds, during which the low-register rumbling of thunder is constant—the only time in the film when this sound is heard—as though in an acoustic commentary that Linda, unwittingly, evokes.

The film's recurring tropes addressing the culture/nature dialectic are not easily explained, not least because Malick insistently renders radically ambiguous just what nature itself is. The significance of nature to human subjects in late modernity may lie partly in the uncertainty of the line between "it" and us, on the one hand, and in our inability to make sense of nature's "it-ness," on the other. We are *of* it, and the characters in *Days of Heaven* are *in* it, but it is not us. But its *it-ness* remains almost infinitely desirable—even though we may only fleetingly reflect on this fact—in this film, not least on account of the stunningly beautiful cinematography of the natural world, much of it caught in the fading light of the early evening. It is a beauty, in other words, that is nearly out of reach.

In a number of scenes, many constructed as a series of brief shots only a few seconds long, the principal characters seem to confront nature's *it-ness* in ways that suggest an awareness of the gap between nature and themselves that this reflexivity momentarily narrows. Bill (even if only in Linda's imagination as she tells the story) walks in the field of golden-ripe wheat, a scene of striking beauty, and suddenly looks directly into the gaze of a bison, as if imaging closure between himself and the other. Linda and her young woman friend walk in the standing wheat as it rhythmically moves in waves caused by a gentle breeze. The tall crop nearly swallows them; the straw, as if speaking, crackles with their every step. (Ripened wheat, even in a slight breeze, makes sound, partly the result of countless strands of the dry straw bumping together, the airspace of hollow stems helping to amplify the effect, a kind of background to a quite different acoustic effect produced by the long brittle beards of the wheat scraping together. The old wheat varieties, prior to the development of short-straw, short-beard genetically altered hybrids, characteristically were tall—durum wheat in particular could reach four or even five feet—and the seed head had a long beard.) Linda and her companion acknowledge the pleasure of being there, after which, characteristically for the film as a whole, the mood is soon broken when they find the first locust.

In a shot of this sort, Malick makes full use of the acoustically rich and intensified semiotic potential of multi-track Dolby stereo optical soundtrack, drawing our listening attention to what we might otherwise hardly notice. That is, the Dolby stereo sound in *Days of Heaven* could be experienced in the theater—and this must have been especially the case when Dolby was new to audiences—as semiotically fecund. In the properly equipped theater, Dolby surround sound envelops the viewer, who, like it or not, becomes—is *made*—a *listener,* hence more than someone who merely *hears.* Linda and her friend, happy in momentary release from labor, enjoy their literal brush with nature, and nature, in turn, seems *audibly* to respond. Nature makes them happy—though it's not that simple. The two women are not walking on the virgin land; the prairie grass has been burned and the sod plowed in preparation for the seeding of domestic grains, of which wheat was the principal cash crop. Once the land is exhausted by the lack of crop rotation (an effort to wring the greatest profit from the soil in as concentrated manner as possible), the bonanza farming will move on to virgin land and repeat the process, precisely what the Farmer's accountant had advised.

Dolby sound in *Days of Heaven* takes on characteristics of both materiality and spatiality, what Christian Metz has described as the quality of an "aural object."[41] Michel Chion, pointing out that *Days of Heaven* was one of the first films to "make the subtle sounds of nature audible through the successful use of Dolby," moves to a larger point in part reflecting the impact of Malick's sound design.[42] Chion calls *Days of Heaven* "a very curious, haunting work, which places the audience in an unstable position while simultaneously enchanting them."[43]

Instability is critical to the film's aesthetic potential to the extent that the truths about modernity reside in its immanent contradictions. The film renders the dialectics at once visible *and* audible within the matrix of its allegory. That said, Malick's "sense of an ending" is not aesthetically to solve a late-modern social-cultural—and political—aporia but instead to make perceivable the costs assessed against humanity and nature alike.

If cinema can render sound malleable, it can do the same for the visible world. Whatever is large or small need not remain so on the screen. Malick continually shifts his kino-eye from, on the one hand, a size narrative that is fundamentally experienced as unremarkable (a camera that seems to see as we see), to one experienced as sharply "abnormal," on the other, such as a locust that fills the entire screen (fig. 133). A full-frame close-up of an insect by itself is hardly shocking, except to the extent that the monster-size bug momentarily takes hold of the narrative and insists on its significance. Chion notes that "in Terrence Malick's cinema, the animal living its animal life, the landscape and the sun, human beings, their questions, their preoccupations and their machines are all placed on the same scale. The film uses its own means (framing, editing, sound, light) to illuminate the strange cohabitation of human beings with animals and with the world, in the same 'moving box.'"[44]

To which he adds: "Human, plant or animal, we all live in the same world. But that's all we can say. It is in the image of this world of superimposition and juxtaposition, this world of parataxis, where ties of cause and effect and relationships between cohabitants are problematic, that Malick's cinema is built. In it, the 'door' opened to an

FIGURE 133
Malick, *Days of Heaven:* locust (1:09:31).

understanding of our animality and our humanity by the Darwinian theory of evolution seems to have closed."[45]

MUSIC

Malick *visually* references what might be called the "aquarium condition" at the point when Bill and Abby, having run off in the night and now wading in the river shallows, drink wine from glasses pilfered from the house. (The unlikelihood that furtive lovers would run onto the prairie carrying delicate glassware is overridden by the role the wineglasses play within Malick's allegory.) Bill drops his glass and briefly looks for it; Abby tells him to leave it be. Malick will return to the dropped glass, but he first cuts to a close-up of the adulterous lovers now lying in the prairie grass. As they snuggle, Malick moves to a medium shot of a moonlit pond framed by trees in the background; audible wind causes ripples across the surface, a bird calls out, and a musical "Aquarium" reference begins (table 4, cue 14).

To this point in the film, various citations and adaptations of Saint-Saëns's "Aquarium" have been heard five times, invariably at moments that have a high quotient for visual and narrative significance. However, the music employed in this, the sixth, cue is distinctly different from those heard previously. Morricone's borrowing of the two-measure, six-note motive that opens "Aquarium," and which provides the principal melodic substance for Saint-Saëns's piece as whole, is in this unique instance *not* immediately apparent in that the cue opens with a chordal drone. The telltale motive is delayed until Malick cuts to a shot of the nearly full moon shining through a light haze, at which moment it is played in very slow motion that produces an aural sense of uncertainty, instability, and perhaps even entrapment.[46] The drone radically slows down a key moment in the film as if to provide the film's lovers as well as the film's viewers with a longer moment to take in the import of the moment, the fraught nature of which is articulated by the semiotic conventions associated with bass sounds of this sort, drone or otherwise, throughout the history of film sound—think *Jaws* (1975).

In acoustic terms, the drone is aquarium-like. And here, as if to underline this point, Malick cuts to an extreme close-up of the intact wineglass that Bill dropped, now resting in the river shallows like a piece of fish tank décor, artfully leaning against a small rock and with a small fish swimming by. Malick prepared us for this detail earlier in the film at the point where Bill walks through the farmhouse parlor staring at its furnishings while the Farmer and Abby are on their honeymoon; adopting Bill's point of view, the camera focuses on a decanter and the two wineglasses that will later be pilfered, now resting atop a small table, and holds the shot for nearly four seconds (41:46–41:50). We later look at the wineglass in the river as though our noses were metaphorically pressed against an aquarium's glass. (At the end of the film, Malick again momentarily references the act of looking into an aquarium when Bill, just shot, falls face down into the river shallows and the camera looks up at him from below [1:25:14–1:25:15]; in fact, the detail was photographed using a fish tank.) Subsequent to the shot of the wineglass in the river shallows, Malick cuts to the lovers running back to the house, Abby to fabricate an explanation to the Farmer, while the "Aquarium" citation very slowly continues. At the start of this shot, Morricone returns to the drone effect by suspending movement, then repeating the original motive, after which the music immediately segues to a very slow version of the "Days of Heaven" theme (table 4, cue 14, second part—of which more later), its minor-mode harmonies underscoring the fragile temporality of what is promised by the film's title.[47] The "Days of Heaven" music, heard previously as up-tempo and celebratory, is now nonteleological and distinctly elegiac; appropriately, it continues through to a brief scene showing the Farmer, alone, in a bathrobe and on his bed writhing in pain, presumably related to his unidentified terminal illness but metaphorically, to be sure, in anticipatory reflection of the psychic agony that he will soon endure. The music of "Days of Heaven" continues in this vein through brief succeeding shots involving the main characters, mostly without dialogue, all of it adding up to the emerging conflict between Abby and her two lovers. It concludes, in a fade, as the Farmer and his aged foreman have a confrontation over Bill and Abby. The old man senses what is going on; the Farmer is in denial.

The final "Aquarium" cue, a verbatim replay of mm. 1–20 of Saint-Saëns's original score, comes near the film's end (table 4, cue 26).[48] Linda makes her escape from the girls' academy in a scene reminiscent of a silent movie comedy, via a second-story window from which she slides to the ground on sheets knotted together, soon to reconnect with the young woman she befriended near the story's beginning. The comedy is ironic, to the extent that what Linda escapes to is entirely uncertain: at the film's ending, we see Linda and her friend hiking together down the railroad right of way, as if borrowing from the happy, if ambiguous, close of Chaplin's 1936 movie *Modern Times* (figs. 134 and 135). The music that accompanies this final scene is Morricone's set piece "Days of Heaven," now distinctly upbeat, whether fittingly or not (never mind the minor mode), underscoring the

FIGURE 134
Malick, *Days of Heaven:* Linda and friend on the tracks (end) (1:30:30).

FIGURE 135
Charlie Chaplin (director), *Modern Times* (1936), end.

hopeful outlook of the young women walking into their futures. The piece continues after the fade to the credits.

The minimal six-note, two-bar thematic material of "Aquarium" is heard in the strings and flute, accompanied by arpeggiated harmonies moving in contrary motion, played by two pianos, one starting high and descending, the other starting low and ascending, one in 32nd-notes and the other in 16th-notes (mm. 1–8, 13–20, and 25–29, of 39 measures overall). Interspersed between the thematic repetitions are two brief transitions that lead back to repetitions of the thematic motive (mm. 9–12 [see ex. 14] and 21–24). The extended close of "Aquarium" (mm. 29–39), in part constructed on fragments of the already fragmentary opening motive, is at once the most extended "section" of the piece and literally the only part that bears any resemblance to development. The eleven-bar gesture toward closure, more than a third of the length of "Aquarium," only hints at musical development that is fundamentally absent in a composition that otherwise essentially repeats itself.

"Aquarium" provides acoustic commentary on the cultural logic of all things zoological in the ordinary understanding of the term: nature and the natural captured, confined, and controlled. It does so in part by eschewing any hint of the teleological impetus that characterizes (and drives) so much nineteenth-century orchestral music. The opening motive of "Aquarium" forms the foundation for much of the film's subsequent music, a great deal of which seems to function as a sonic metaphor of enclosure that at nearly every key moment in the film confronts the dream of happiness with its alternate reality, if not literally present in the narrative then nonetheless haunting it, no matter the psychic projections of the main characters.

The ironic humor of *Le carnaval des animaux,* captured alike in its title and parenthetical subtitle, *Grand fantaisie zoologique,* can reasonably be read as possessing a degree of insight as to just who is in the zoo: not only hens and roosters (section 2, *Poules et coqs*), farmyard fauna and wild asses (3, *Hémoines*), tortoises (4, *Tortues*), or birds (individually: 9, *Le Coucou au fond des bois,* and 13, *Le Cygne;* or collectively: 10, *Volière,* Aviary), nor even the more genuinely exotic (1, *Marche royale du lion;* 5, *L'Eléphant;* 6, *Kangourous*). Saint-Saëns's zoo also houses the long dead (12, *Fossiles,* a comical musical *danse macabre* that, by means of fragmentary quotations from nursery tunes, among other things, reinforces the bromide that all things die). But more, and this is my larger point, the piece is also about *us,* if by means of quite specific human referents: *Pianistes* (section 11, doing nothing more interesting than running scales) and *Personnages à longues oreilles* (8, Long-eared characters)—human asses (critics as it were), with little useful to say and saying it by means of two violins that echo one another, one and two notes at a time, over a grand total of twenty-six measures, far longer than necessary for what each has to "say." The effect, well known, is the braying of asses, but since Saint-Saëns has already given us asses—wild ones at that (section 3), which, if nothing else, at least have enormous energy (sixteenth-notes in breathless *presto furioso* from start to finish)—in the later section he is clearly after asses of the two-legged variety. In other words, *we* are part of the zoo, and in musical terms just about the least interesting of the acoustic exhibits.

Whether the viewer-listener recognizes Saint-Saëns's composition (and thus the title's semiotic potential within the film) matters less than what is otherwise readily apparent to the ears, namely, its notably restrained musical resources. What one hears in the first two bars is just about all there "is" for the remaining thirty-seven bars. Whatever its surface attractiveness, the constipation of the structural framework is hard to miss, not least after repeated hearings at various points in the film where the soundtrack "reads" the severe personal and societal constraints playing out in the narrative, usually via Morricone's adaptation. (The general importance of music in the film is underscored by its use, diegetically and especially nondiegetically, in slightly more than 40 percent of the running time.)

EXAMPLE 15. Ennio Morricone, "Days of Heaven" (love) theme from *Days of Heaven* (1978), mm. 1–8.

The title soundtrack set-piece "Days of Heaven" occurs four times, though it is heard in its entirety only during the final credits (table 4, cue 27, 3:14 in length), an allegretto played at about 96 bpm, in B minor, most prominently strings, acoustic guitar, flutes, oboe, bassoon, and celeste (the score calls as well for piano, synthesizer, organ, and vibraphone, but these are not apparent in the final sound mix). The diatonic melodic material (ex. 15), principally given to the flutes, is also passed to the oboe and is often doubled on celeste. The piece is semiotically ambiguous. On the one hand, the tempo is upbeat, and the orchestration lush, warm, and enveloping. On the other hand, the composition's minor mode pushes against what might otherwise be heard as unambiguously celebratory, and this in full keeping with the film's emphasis on the aporia marking the nature/culture dialectic—concerning which Malick provides a final audio reference as the music to "Days of Heaven" concludes.[49] It's the sound of the chirping mating call of crickets, produced by males rubbing together the rasplike edges of their wings. It is this sound alone that remains when everything else is finished, an echo, whether accidental or intentional, to Voltaire's well-known assertion that human beings are little more than "insects of a summer's day," a bitter critique of human arrogance amid the optimism of the Enlightenment that established the philosophical and ideological foundations of modernity.[50]

Crickets can be heard everywhere on the prairies in late summer and fall prior to killing frosts. Their call acoustically enlivens the night and commonly produces a conflicted human response, all the more, perhaps, in that the coal-black insects are very difficult to see. Produced by uncountable numbers of crickets, their sound takes on an effect of the uncanny; energetic and insistent, and lasting hours into the night, it is an innate biological acknowledgment of life force, but also one that people experience with the melancholic recognition of summer's end. The natural cycle of life immanent to the call will continue in the future as though the people and the events in the film never happened, and long after Malick's fictive narrative disappears from anyone's memory.

The "Days of Heaven" theme is first heard early in the film (table 4, cue 4), at the moment when the Farmer sees Abby as the migrants break off work for their noon meal near the fields they have been cutting.[51] The theme sounds at the moment he first catches sight of her, the wind blowing her hair. Written for solo piano, the only time this scoring is used in the film, the cue's twelve measures are played at a tempo (48 bpm) only half that employed at the film's end. The dynamic level is constant, approximately *piano*. The limited timbre of the single instrument, as well as the reduced dynamics and moderate performance tempo, matches the tentative nature of the one-sided visual encounter. The cues thereafter accompanying the Farmer and Abby, all orchestrated, gain musical complexity, while almost invariably underscoring the fragility of their relationship.

This music is heard again (table 4, cue 6, second part) at the precise moment when Abby and the Farmer accidentally first meet. Linda's voiceover has immediately preceded this scene, speaking of the Farmer's impending death as Malick shows us the Farmer, alone on his bed, contemplating the diagnosis he has just received. After sunset, Abby and Linda playfully chase after the Farmer's peafowl, and Abby ends up near the house. The Farmer, who has been reclining in the long grass, rises up, startling her. She apologizes for the intrusion. In a close-up, framed by the afterglow of the sunset, he reassures her ("Don't worry") and attempts a conversation while gazing intently at her. The "Days of Heaven" theme sounds briefly a second time, now orchestrated, the melody given to a bassoon; slow-moving, quiet, and still tentative, it trails off during a cut to Bill and Linda roasting a bird over a small bonfire.

The "Days of Heaven" theme emerges from the elegiac music that immediately precedes it, not otherwise heard in the film or included on the soundtrack album. The music is at odds with the shot of Abby and Linda playfully chasing peafowl, but well in keeping with the very brief vignette of the Farmer on his bed contemplating his untimely death, which will indeed soon arrive but by a means other than what his physician diagnosed. Thus there are two "worlds" at odds here, one seen (the young women at carefree sport) and the other heard (the music as a kind of transliteration of the Farmer's very different reality and, presumably, existential moment). These distinct phenomena are wholly separate, despite the physical proximity of Abby and the Farmer; they conjoin, as it were, when sight and sound come together moments later, with the sounding of the "Days of Heaven" motif, if only in the Farmer's imagination.

FIRE

The longest musical set-piece (lasting 5:41) in *Days of Heaven* is "Fire" (table 4, cue 21), which coincides with a crop-destroying plague of locusts, initially noticed by Linda, who finds insects in the kitchen while preparing vegetables and soon is furiously, if helplessly, swatting at them. Thereafter Abby, washing her face, finds a locust floating in her basin; Bill, outside and near his motorcycle, stares at the ground, now teeming with insects; the Farmer's ducks gorge themselves in the farmyard; and so on. The sounds of the limitless swarm are amplified at the moment a worker cranks a warning siren and a red disaster flag is hoisted. The migrant workers futilely attempt to drive the insects from the fields, an hours-long process that continues well into the night. Their frustrated efforts are intercut with extreme close-ups of grasshoppers eating the barley (not wheat), the ground virtually alive with them. Photographed near the farmhouse, a black swarm lifts from the ground, a kind of smoke-cloud of insects (the scene was photographed with a camera that ran backwards as peanut shells were dropped en masse from a hovering helicopter;

the six men in the scene rehearsed their movements in reverse and in slow motion, though the end result is visually imperfect). All of this is pretext to the fire that consumes the crop. The night scene opens with a fire-illuminated close-up of the Farmer's fixed stare. In the dark, men with lanterns and portable smudges attempt to smoke out the locusts, collecting them in baskets to pitch onto a huge bonfire.

Bill approaches the Farmer, placing his hand on his shoulder in a gesture of empathy. The Farmer pushes him back and moves to attack, angrily swinging at Bill with his kerosene lantern, which is attached to a pole. The gesture accidentally lights the field on fire, and the Farmer orders that it be allowed to burn. The conflagration, apocalyptic within the scale of the film, is soon out of control. The days of heaven have concluded, amidst a situation that will quickly worsen, only to end with the deaths of the two male protagonists. This long scene was foretold near the film's beginning in Linda's voiceover about the man Ding Dong and his vernacular account of the end of time by fire: "[Ding Dong] told me the whole earth is goin' up in flames. Flames will come out of here and there and they'll just rise up. . . . There's gonna be creatures runnin' every which way, some of them burnt, half their wings burnin'; people are gonna be screamin' and hollerin' for help." Smoke and flame fill the screen; terrified horses rear up and attempt to flee, as do hapless wild fauna. Any sense of order among the crowd of humans is lost; they run about helplessly, overwhelmed by something of their own making, a force they cannot hope to contain. The sounds of the conflagration are ever present.

Throughout most of this long scene, Morricone's underscore, alternately low-pitched and high-pitched, percussively rumbles. Thematic elements, when discernible, are jagged with successive intervallic leaps. Instruments sound at the extremes of their range. Beats are aggressively accented. Dissonance is prominent: tonal centers are variously blurred, shifting, or uncertain, sectional structural shifts abrupt. When the music finally concludes, more or less at the height of the firestorm, all that is heard are the pathetic shouts of the men, little competition for the sounds of the fire that, in long shot, extends the full width of the horizon. Only the cries of a lone, unseen hawk penetrate the noise-filled din. The music in this scene is unlike any other in the film, though it is never heard by itself; indeed, the music is thoroughly mixed with the sounds of the events just described: locusts chewing, a siren, people screaming, horses neighing, and above all the sounds of the fire. This is to say that the music works here not so much as a characteristic underscore, but as part and parcel of the unfolding events, almost as if it were part of the diegesis. At times, its sonic presence is pronounced; at others, it is pushed into the acoustic background by other sonic events, as though at once a sound event directly tied to the fire and a form of indirect commentary thereupon.[52]

The cue is initially heard as a low rumble when Bill, near his motorcycle, looks down at the ground teeming with the insects (1:08:16). The shot cuts to the peafowl near some outbuildings, and then to a close-up of a single locust crawling across the page of a handwritten letter (1:08:24), at which point the ominous rapid bass tremolo is readily apparent and disruptively threatening, all the more given the directionless nature of the drone:

intrusive, monstrous, and continuing in subsequent scenes of Linda in the kitchen noisily swatting grasshoppers (1:08:35), and in the farmyard with the noisy quacking of the ducks (1:08:42). All the sounds merge into a single acoustic mass of confusion and imminent danger. Indeed, though the dronelike bass remains part of the mix, at times it is overwhelmed to the point of near inaudibility by competing sounds such as the warning siren (first seen at 1:08:57, but heard slightly earlier). As the siren wails, Morricone's score changes. The string tremolo migrates into the top register, taking on the effect of a swarm—these sounds emerge during a close-up of locusts devouring heads of barley (1:09:22 and thereafter). Morricone then adds tympani to the mix, providing an intermittent rhythmic pulse.

The remainder of the cue heightens the sense of helplessness; the music and other sounds associated with the fire or the fighting of the fire drown out virtually all attempts at dialogue. We see mouths move, though we rarely can discern more than a word of two of what is said. It's fair to say that the sound mass in this sense is as overwhelming as the image track, and perhaps more so for the audience, who, unlike those fighting the fire, hear the music. In this cue, Morricone employs the strings percussively for the most part *(col legno)*, whereas in most of the rest of the film's score the strings supply lush, consonantly enveloping sonorities. Here, however, the lower strings in particular consistently punctuate beats, often in rhythmic unison with tympani and piano. Over this background, later in the cue and for the only time in the film, Morricone prominently employs the full range of brass instruments. The thematic material, in four distinct sections, is never developed, but only obsessively repeated with slight variation—the main motive repeats at least ten times, variously passed among the instruments. Further, no transitional material smooths out segues from motive to motive; each is simply introduced paratactically, the compositional technique complementing Malick's filmmaking. The acoustic disorder of Morricone's music perfectly matches the frantically hopeless disorder among the migrants fighting the flames. The motives are jagged; the emphasis is on intervallic leaps, supported by sharp harmonic dissonances. Throughout, the thematic material is as aggressively accented as the accompaniment. The music is forceful, though not teleological, and seemingly unstoppable until the cue ends, more than a minute before the fire scene itself concludes, as if the music has simply exhausted the sonic fuel that sustained it—as will be made apparent in the succeeding shot of the still-smoldering ash that was once cropland.

The high-decibel Dolby-articulated sound design, simultaneously incorporating both Morricone's underscore and the noises associated with a fire so severe that it creates its own audible wind, contributes to the dialectical opposite embedded in the metaphor of days of heaven: nights of hell. The heaven is principally imagined, start to finish; the hell is not. Hell *is* the film's beginning, the foundry furnace fueled by the coal Bill shovels into its maw; hell reappears during the harvest, in the "feeding" of fuel into the gigantic steam tractors by men worked to the end of their abilities, well described by Linda in a voiceover, and finally culminating at the film's climax that records horizon-to-horizon ruin.

Indeed, the aftermath—the deaths of the Farmer and Bill—are not more than a final working out, the last flicker of the flames expending the last bit of their fuel. The Farmer, after all, seeks to fire on Bill; Bill in turn is fired upon by the Law in a reemergence of an order defined on the principle of death. To fire upon, to put fire to: either way, conflagration.

Walter Benjamin once suggested that "only for the sake of the hopeless ones have we been given hope."[53] Each of Malick's feature films, however differently, engage grim realities of history, all of it twentieth century, except for *The New World* (2005), whose tale of colonization might as well be current. Yet these films are distinctly beautiful, and only in part on account of the nature photography for which Malick is so well known. What makes beautiful the *art* of his work is properly located in the formal structures, marked less by any form of argument that fictively, satisfyingly resolves the contradiction of the nature/culture dialectic, and far more akin to Adornian *Wahrheitsgehalt,* whose purpose is to emphasize the consequences of social contradictions that cannot be wished away either philosophically or aesthetically. In the end, Malick provides an account of an experiential dystopia, necessary if his films are to lay claim to the truth content of history; at the same time, he allegorically retrieves the shards of an alternative. As Adorno once put it, dialectics' "agony is the world's agony raised to a concept."[54] Its larger purpose resides in service toward reconcilement, with regard to which Adorno ended his last major work, *Aesthetic Theory:* "But then what would art be, as the writing of history, if it shook off the memory of accumulated suffering."[55] It is here that Malick's art makes its mark.

Der Begriff des Naturschönen rührt an eine Wunde: the concept of natural beauty rubs on a wound.[56] The aesthetic beauty of Malick's film, confronting the conflicted relationship of human subjects to nature, honors nature and natural beauty alike. The beauty of artworks reconciles with natural beauty by speaking for what in nature is mute. Artworks, Adorno suggests, "are a sign from heaven yet artifactual, an ominous warning, a script that flashes up, vanishes, and indeed cannot be read for its meaning. . . . In each genuine artwork something appears that does not exist." In brief, the artwork—this film—for all the dystopian actualities it encompasses, is finally a *promesse du bonheur,* an "instillable longing in the face of beauty."[57]

That longing is underwritten by Morricone's score at key moments throughout the narrative, but it is also visually referenced in Malick's inclusion of the lotus-horn gramophone, a modern-mechanical Horn of Plenty, from which emerge the orderly and contented sounds of Beethoven's Minuet in G to which Abby dances in one of the final moments of her happiness with the Farmer, immediately prior to Bill's fateful return (fig. 136). Again near the film's conclusion, shortly before Bill's death, Malick provides a final look at the gramophone, and in a situation for which its presence is strikingly improbable (the trio having fled with little more than the clothes on their backs), thus imbuing it with a function beyond the parameters of the plot (fig. 137). It is early morning, and Bill and Linda, on the lam, are still sleeping; Abby, resting under a blanket and leaning against the base of a long-dead and uprooted tree, stares into the distance. Next to her on the

FIGURE 136
Malick, *Days of Heaven:* Abby dancing; Bill's return (1:03:36).

FIGURE 137
Malick, *Days of Heaven:* on the lam (1:19:41).

ground sits the gramophone, its horn pointing toward the camera. The turntable does not appear to be moving, though there is a disk on the platter. Nonetheless, there is music to be heard: Leo Kottke's "Enderlin," the music that earlier underscored the journey to a new life on the western plains, and now hints of another such journey, despite the sadness in Abby's eyes and the silence of the apparatus. Shortly thereafter, in the film's penultimate scene, Abby again boards a train on her way in search of a future; now the musical accompaniment, diegetic and markedly upbeat, is the happily innocuous and insouciant "There'll Be a Hot Time in the Old Town" (table 3, cue 7). There is no way to know her future, but she leaves with a smile and an air of confidence matched perfectly to the spirit of the tune, never mind the ironies that emerge in the space between this singular moment and nearly everything in the narrative that precedes it.

The affirmative element of music, Adorno wrote in the notes to his never-completed Beethoven monograph, lies "merely in the fact that it is *a voice lifted up,* that it is music at all."[58] Malick and Morricone give us that, the semblance of the utopian imaginary, despite all odds. As Linda and her friend walk along the tracks leading out of the prairie town, Morricone's "Days on Heaven" plays through for the first and only time.

Linda's voiceover recollections are consistently spoken without sentimentality, or even emotion, their phatic impact severely muted. That said, her recollections are often musicalized by Morricone's score, just as the significance of the musical sonorities is visually underscored at key moments by reference to the gramophone, the device that accords *a voice lifted up* and at the same time the apparatus whose initial worth was in part explained by Edison, its inventor, as preserving the voices of the dead. Malick's film delineates the denaturalization of nature and the price paid for it; the art of his film, like the art of Morricone's music, at least hints that things could be otherwise. Artworks, as Adorno once put it, want "to keep nature's promise."[59] That promise, as he understood it, was the foundation for hope, and ultimately for some semblance of utopia, an issue to which I'll return in the Conclusion.

CONCLUSION

Acoustic Invocations of Crisis and Hope

> Brünnhilde then appeared in the background in the shape of the Statue of Liberty in New York. Sounding like a nagging wife, she screamed, "I want a ring, I want a beautiful ring, don't forget to take her ring from her." This was how Siegfried obtained the ring of the Nibelung.
>
> ADORNO, DESCRIBING A DREAM IN 1937 WHEN HE WAS WORKING ON *IN SEARCH OF WAGNER*

ADORNO'S DREAM

For many years Theodor Adorno kept notes of his dreams, writing down his recollections in each case shortly after waking. There was method to this labor to the extent that, as he put it, "our dreams are linked with each other not just because they are 'ours,' but because they form a continuum, they belong to a unified world."[1] A dream from August 10, 1944, while he was living in Los Angeles, involved his attending with actress Luise Rainer (they were friends) a press ball in a damaged, roofless opera house, either Frankfurt or Vienna. Taking notice only of each other, the couple entered a room where music was playing, thereafter slipping out and involving themselves in a "completely shameless" love scene. It was, he writes, "like a victory over those present, a frank act of disappearance, an unconscious challenge to the world. Woke up with a feeling of happiness that was still there when I phoned her up."[2]

I mention Adorno's dream for several connections it traces, wherein the opera house serves as a stand-in for opera *tout court*. First off, Adorno surmises its ruination is "probably as the consequence of an air raid" (fig. 138). Fair enough. But it's more likely, given the degree to which he regarded opera, as both a medium and an institution, to be "obsolete," that the destruction points to it existing in a state of "petrifaction."[3] In his aphoristic essay "Bourgeois Opera," principally a bitter critique of the well-commodified, socially regressive utility of opera in late modernity, Adorno incorporates a sharp dialectical turn by attempting to salvage what he regards as opera's echo of utopian promise—its

FIGURE 138
Achille Beltrame (1871–1945), *La Scala Opera House in Ruins (bombed August 16, 1943)*, engraving in newspaper *La Domenica del Corriere* (August 1943). Photo credit: Gianni Dagli Orti/The Art Archive at Art Resource, New York.

romanticism, explicitly a-rational (or even anti-rational)—as an aesthetic stop-gap against a modernity defined by instrumental rationality. What opera clings to, and in the best sense why its obsolescence falls short of delivering its own coup de grâce, is what Adorno names its "magic," for him a key element of aesthetic comportment and a defining principle of art's critique of reality. He sees in magic the inexplicable, the thrill of what exceeds our ability to control and explain; magic in this sense is coterminous with what he elsewhere terms the "non-identical" in a world dominated by the identicalness of identity: "It would be appropriate to think of opera as the specifically bourgeois genre that, in the midst of, and with the methods appropriate to, a world bereft of magic, paradoxically endeavors to preserve the magical element of art" (he has in mind *Die Zauberflöte, Der Freischütz,* and *Fidelio*).[4]

In magic he sees, and in music hears, the semblance of innocence, which is why this section of his essay engages issues surrounding certain operas' appeal to children even while they embarrass adults, given the silliness of opera's world of incantations.[5] Whereas for Adorno disillusionment is a byproduct of central planning, regulation, and the goal of predictability, magic preserves at least a hint of the price paid in the form of the general loss of spontaneity and all that figures for emancipation. Adorno acknowledges magic and myth as socially progressive elements ascribable to opera—a kind of wished-for remembrance of things past, and a protest against the hyperrationalized and wholly instrumentalized antireason of the here and now.

Adorno's insight derives from a particular—and strictly musical—event near the end of Beethoven's *Fidelio:* the fateful horn call, the small sonic detail of offstage brass, distant but approaching, an acoustic advance notice of historical change. He hears the fanfare as a micrological, historically sedimented moment that *magically* imposes itself to announce the promise of a last-minute (and logically inexplicable) rescue and the freeing of the prisoners: again, a general emancipation. The *Fidelio* horn call embeds the hope for an end to despair. "This interlocking of myth and Enlightenment defines the bourgeois essence of opera: namely, the combination of imprisonment in a blind and unselfconscious system with the idea of freedom, which arises in its midst. The metaphysics of opera cannot be simply separated from this social dimension." Adorno concludes with two sentences reiterating at once the dialectical turns fundamental to critical theory together with the potential social stakes that emerge from its exercise: "Metaphysics is absolutely not an unchanging realm to be grasped by looking out through the barred windows of the historical; it is the glimmer—albeit a powerless glimmer—of light which falls into the prison itself. The more powerful it becomes, the deeper its ideas embed themselves in history; the more ideological it becomes, the more abstractly it stands opposed to history."[6]

Adorno's assessment of opera, typified by this essay, complements what he heard in Mahler, whose music he deeply admired: a digging in the sonic garbage heap of history to discover a broken piece of acoustic glass; turning the shard variously to the light, bringing it from the shadows; recognizing what it once was or what it might have been, while treasuring the truths it might contain in its current state; and taking to heart the fragmented and fragmentary aesthetics of its actuality, manifested in the truth content of the whole within the particular: "It is precisely because opera, as a bourgeois vacation spot, allowed itself so little involvement in the social conflicts of the nineteenth century that it was able to mirror so crassly the developing tendencies of bourgeois society itself."[7] The "aesthetic semblance" of opera, he noted, is at once "the gilding of what already exists and the reflection of that which could be otherwise"; opera, in short, is "the surrogate for the happiness that is refused to people, and the promise of true happiness."[8] One understands opera, whether as an aesthetic event, an object, or a practice fit for sociology, only when the centrality of this contradiction lies at the heart of hermeneutic thought.

Besides reference to the opera house, Adorno's dream morphs to love-making, "completely shameless" but "without being exhibitionistic," as he puts it. The next sentence expands the thought, simultaneously referencing not only the physicality of the scene his psyche constructs but also the illicit (adulterous: he was married) nature of the coupling. He reads it as a "victory over those present," people he has described as including celebrities who, like the ruined building itself, "also seemed to look rather the worse for wear." So here's what we have: the memory of opera, for him an object of both love and antipathy; the sudden modulation of finding himself with Luise in a room "where music was being played," leading to love-making and finally to awakening in a state of happiness that "was still there when I phoned her up."[9] In other words, in the midst of ruins, hope and even happiness emerges and against considerable odds.

Adorno recognized the socio-cultural agency of opera as a still-prestigious cultural leftover of nineteenth-century bourgeois triumphalism, which he vigorously opposed. In its place, he labored to promote what he regarded as a more socially responsible musico-operatic practice to supplant the complacency, both aesthetic and social, of the established order—ideas that after his death have found considerable currency, nowhere more apparent than in late-modern opera productions in Europe, North America, and elsewhere, as well as in a significant body of recent musicological scholarship. In this regard, the cogent sociological issue for Adorno was that opera now, "in style, in substance, and in attitude," was no longer connected to the lives of the people to whom it had to appeal in order to justify its staggering costs, all the more given opera's "outwardly pretentious form."[10]

The "challenge" today revolves around the need to negotiate opera's contradictions, which constitute nevertheless its real truth. Salvage efforts, if I may call them that, on behalf of opera in the postmodernity of the young twenty-first century connect forthrightly to the ghosts of the nineteenth century that the twentieth never quite came to terms with. We might say that opera (specifically its quotient of magic to which Adorno refers) lives on because the moment to realize it beyond the confines of the theater was lost.[11]

VICTORY TO THE LOSERS

Adorno heard Mahler's music, caught between late Romanticism and modernity, as the sonoric engagement of history as well as the utopian echo of something better, read through the lens of nature and—not least—by self-reflexive appropriation of common (or popular) culture, including what he considered kitsch, reimagined and repurposed. Fundamentally, Adorno's Mahler is a progressive who wrung from the increasingly worn-out musical language of the nineteenth century the contradiction of its confrontation with history—Adorno once noted that Mahler "has absolutely nothing in common with the idea of originality."[12] The truth of Mahler, the character of his greatness, is located in his ability to imagine something different, paradoxically by using the detritus of an exhausted musical vocabulary, as it were, against itself. In Mahler, Adorno heard the acoustic trace of hope's realization.[13]

The society immanent to the music assures that the music will ultimately remain tied to that against which it protests—an entanglement that art would breach, if it could. For Adorno, Mahler's works "are rooted in what music seeks to transcend."[14] Formally, as Rose Rosengard Subotnik has pointed out, Mahler invokes Beethovenian totality, but negatively—as an "as-if," a totality irretrievably lost—by "constructing enormous symphonic patterns out of elements too discontinuous to effect any large-scale unity."[15] Adorno hears Mahler's protest in his works' perpetual motion, what he terms their "aimlessly circling, irresistible movements [which] . . . are always images of the world's course."[16] Simply put, Mahler renders problematic the supposed forward motion of frenetic modernity, trapped in activity, the "vain commotion" of a general unfreedom. Adorno suggested that "hope in Mahler always resides in change," a struggle against "blind functioning. . . . Mahler's symphonies plead anew against the world's course. They imitate it in order to accuse" and in the end decline to offer a counterfeit reconciliation.[17]

Mahler's utopia is "the forward motion of the past and the not-yet-past in becoming."[18] It looks back in order to discern a better future, which can only come about if the past is faced squarely. Mahler seeks out Otherness, whose conventionally hidden presence he brings forward into view. Nowhere does Mahler's pursuit of otherness come more significantly into play than in his incorporation of the musically common (Mahler's "symphonies shamelessly flaunt what rang in all ears, scraps of melody from great music, shallow popular songs, street ballads, hits").[19]

Adorno long lamented the social causes and effects of musical division, the increasingly absolute separation of light or popular music from its "serious" twin. Both high and low, stigmatized by capitalism, were but the sundered fragments of a whole, now extant only as an "unresolved contradiction."[20]

Mahler sets these musics against each other, and in extreme tension. Indeed, it's the tension between the musics that matters, not simply the incorporation of the "banal and vulgar" (Adorno's words) with the supposedly elevated. As a result, both musics are changed: "nothing sounds as it was wont to; all things are diverted as if by a magnet. What is worn out yields pliantly to the improvising hand; the used parts win a second life as variants."[21] Or, as he elsewhere remarked: "In his musical vagrancy [Mahler] picks up the broken glass by the roadside and holds it up to the sun so that all the colors are refracted. . . . In the debased and vilified materials of music he scratches for illicit joys."[22]

The scandal of Mahler's use of the banal and vulgar develops from his acknowledgment of the putative legitimacy of both. What conventionally goes unrecognized is not the otherness of banality and vulgarity but the fact of their worn-out character—precisely what Mahler preserves in order to reach his destination, defined by a utopia of truth that emerges from lies exposed.[23] And otherness arises from victims and victimization, the losers in "progress" with whom Mahler identifies.[24] Desperately, his music holds onto what culture has cast off as unworthy, mutilated.[25]

Mahler knew the social semiotics of sound, and he knew the effects of sound intrusions: the mandolin in the Seventh Symphony, as well as the guitar; the multiple mandolins in the Eighth; and the cowbells in the Sixth and Seventh. Yet it would be misleading simply to suggest that Mahler's music is principally a sonoric effort to scandalize smug urbanites by attacking haut-bourgeois solipsism and complacency. Mahler's setting in tension of high art and low functions as more than a sonoric comeuppance of privilege because the everyday itself is transformed, raised up, just as the high and mighty are taken to task—and maybe taken down a peg—by the presence of the otherwise suppressed Other. But the real point is that Mahler acknowledged and valorized difference without valorizing the current state of either the high or the low. Instead, his sprawling symphonies, for Adorno, hint of a utopia that develops both by articulating the inadequacy of the here and now and by positing an alternative—without however pretending that current reality has been rendered moot.[26] The lack of an organic totality that defines Mahler's musical structures acts to prevent such wishful thinking. Mahler, Adorno insists, works to reverse the direction of history's forward march: "He promises victory to the losers. His entire symphonic work is a reveille. Its hero is the deserter."[27]

MAHLER'S DREAM

The whole of nature finds a voice in it and reveals profound mysteries
such as one might perhaps intuit in dreams!

MAHLER ON THE THIRD SYMPHONY

I'd like to concretize the foregoing discussion by means of a single example drawn from the Third Symphony, completed in 1896 (revised in 1906) and receiving its first complete performance in 1902. In six movements, incorporating a female solo, a boys' choir, and a women's choir, the Third was the composer's longest symphony (running one hour and forty minutes) and, indeed, one of the longest in the history of the symphony (its first movement is longer than the entire Fifth Symphony of Beethoven). I'll principally confine my remarks to the third movement, Comodo, Scherzando.

The symphony has two parts. Part 1 comprises the gigantic first movement; part 2 the succeeding five. The whole is shaped by a program, which Mahler, postcomposition, officially renounced. Briefly stated, the symphony is a sonoric enactment of a progression toward enlightenment built on a foundation of love, and deeply informed in particular by reconciliation with nature. The third movement is titled "What the creatures in the forest tell me." Its extended opening defines a kind of animal paradise in raucous equilibrium. But at the height of the musical frenetics, a sudden silence is momentarily imposed, as if the creatures of the forest sense a new, unnerving, and unseen presence. Immediately thereafter, and from offstage, a posthorn sounds. It announces history: the arrival of man—and by means of an instrument not commonly associated with high-caste symphonic literature. Softly, it plays a distinctly simple, folklike, sentimental, and—as has often been suggested—(nearly) banal melody. The structure of this movement is complex and nuanced, and I cannot do justice to it here.[28] But I do at least want to make a couple of basic points relative to the larger themes explored in this volume.

Here is Mahler's program description: "[The movement] illustrates the quiet, undisturbed life of the forest before the appearance of man. Then the animals catch sight of the first human being and, although he walks calmly past them, the terrified [animals] sense that future trouble will come from him."[29]

FIGURE 139
John Cordrey (1765–1825), *The Portsmouth and Chichester Coach* (1812), oil. Whereabouts unknown.

FIGURE 140
Cordrey, *The London-Coventry-Birmingham Royal Mail Fifteen Miles from London* (1811), oil. Whereabouts unknown.

What Mahler actually scores does not precisely follow this program. First Man, or in reality Modern Man, doesn't "walk calmly past" the animals; rather, he approaches no closer than sufficient to make his aural, acousmatic presence known. He intrudes on nature from afar, sounding his posthorn, which the creatures of the forest read as a warning (in the orchestral score, at rehearsal nos. 14–16). This seems clear from the semiotics associated with the sonorities of the posthorn in the nineteenth century.

The posthorn was a signaling instrument, a harbinger.[30] As its name implies, it communicated the arrival of communication itself, the post, when, prior to the railroad, the post as well as passengers were delivered by horse-drawn coach. The speed of such travel, and the considerable distances covered—both critical to modernity's sense of itself—became popular subjects in visual culture during the early decades of the nineteenth century prior to being made redundant by the railroad. Such images, often oil paintings, provide a solid indication of the cultural sensitivity to the phenomenon. Images by English painters like John Cordrey (figs. 139 and 140), T. C. Cooper, and James Pollard tend to emphasize rapid movement, discernible from the pose of the horses' legs, and sometimes by direct reference to distances (the mile marker in figure 140). Many of these paintings incorporate a rider at the back atop the coach blowing the posthorn, whether coiled or straight, its sound confirming command of both space and time dependent on speed, the ultimate sign of—and cliché for—modernity and progress alike.

Mahler's posthorn communicates a notably particular message: it certifies change. The simple instrument and its equally simple, almost childlike tune (ex. 16) are thus appropriated by Mahler not as a nostalgic remembrance of things past, but as the critical warning of what is to come, and indeed of what has already arrived. The posthorn fulfills, for Nature, the role of the canary in the coal mine, and the fauna know it. In other words, however distant the sound and prettiness of the tune, for Mahler's musical Nature the posthorn is at best ambiguous. (The posthorn part is usually given to the flugelhorn, common to military bands at the time, since the music is essentially beyond the technical capability of the valveless posthorn.)

After the horn dies away the animals gradually return to their chatter, but now uneasily. And soon every instrument is expressing its concern in a cacophony of simultaneously sounding voices. Panic is audible not least in Mahler's scoring the music at the extreme limits of individual instruments' ranges, which as a result sound strained (an effect Mahler often exploited). Then, quite suddenly, as though without warning, the posthorn makes a second (and last) appearance, though here more briefly (rehearsal nos. 27–29). Thereafter, and within a few seconds of the horn's last sounds, now at the movement's close, there follows a fortissimo *tutti,* the orchestra playing in identical rhythm, registering the unanimity of hysterical response, as if Nature had all at once figured out the stakes, for better or worse, of the arrival in Paradise of the human subject.

Mahler's "creatures of the forest" tell of fear and impending conflict. The seeming innocence of the posthorn solos, clichés of pseudo-folk simplicity, are the not-so-innocent foretaste of the dialectic of enlightenment aestheticized, and the fauna, so to speak, like Mahler, recognize it. Mahler juxtaposes two distinctly different kinds of music, the high and the low, both of which he treats with equal honor. Neither music is the same as a result of the juxtaposition. That is, once the posthorn is first heard, the movement cannot continue as if the intrusion never happened. To be sure, the music of the opening attempts to reassert itself, but it just won't work; it's forced to deal with the ghost of the posthorn, even though the posthorn's music is wholly absented. And just at the moment when "nature" seems to have overcome the intrusion, by a return to the formal disorder of a happy sonoric fecundity, the posthorn sounds again, after which, simply put, no recovery is possible. Any resolution of the aporia produced by these two oppositional sound masses can only be addressed in the movements that follow—which is precisely what happens: the ultimate move, toward which Mahler aims, is reconciliation between nature and the subject, what Adorno hears in Mahler's music generally.

EXAMPLE 16. Gustav Mahler, *Symphony No. 3* (Vienna: Universal Edition, 1906), third movement, rehearsal no. 14, mm. 1–29.

In sum, for Adorno, the humane quality of music emerges not simply from the fact that music is made by and for human beings; rather, music's humaneness develops from the specific fact that music mediates human longing into an acoustics at once part of the social and cultural boundaries marked by history and language and at the same time reaching well beyond what language can pin down, gain control over, classify, regulate, and, not least, help market, all of this the result of a history that recognizes language first and foremost for its instrumental potential. The true "magic" of music lies in the degree to which it mirrors in its material objectivity the spirit and spirituality that enlivens it. Music makes audible both the materiality of human spirituality and the spirituality of our materiality, not as forever separate and oppositional entities but as momentarily reconciled: a microcosm of society in a state of bliss.[31]

QUESTIONING

Charles Ives's programmatic *The Unanswered Question* has a lengthy bibliography and is too well known to justify a lengthy précis of its musical unfolding.[32] In what follows, I'll make do with a brief sketch of the piece so as to elicit one particular point that connects to the preceding discussion.

The Unanswered Question, first performed only in 1946, was composed in 1908, though Ives revised it between 1930 and 1935, when he first added a brief statement describing the program and performance instructions. The composition is scored for string quartet or string ensemble, solo trumpet, and four flutes (Ives otherwise suggests two flutes, oboe, and clarinet); it's about seven minutes long.

The composition's basic design is easily summarized. A single question, posed by the trumpet, is heard seven times, to which the flutes attempt six different responses. At the end, the trumpet asks the question a seventh time, but the flutes offer nothing in return. Before, during, and after these exchanges, the strings play very quietly in the background. What, then, is the question, and what answers are attempted? Early on, Ives considered subtitling the piece "The Cosmic Landscape."[33] His later-added program statement makes clear what for him was embedded by the reference to the macrocosm.

It's often been pointed out that Ives's idea for *The Unanswered Question* was shaped by a poem, *The Sphinx* (1847), in seventeen stanzas, by transcendentalist Ralph Waldo Emerson. The poem's fifteenth stanza reads as follows:

> Thou art the unanswered question;
>   Couldst see thy proper eye,
> Always it asketh, asketh;
>   And each answer is a lie.
> So take thy quest through nature,
>   It through thousand natures ply;
> As on, thou clothed eternity;
>   Time is the false reply.[34]

EXAMPLE 17. Charles Ives, *The Unanswered Question* (New York: Southern Music Publishing, 1953), mm. 16–17, solo trumpet.

EXAMPLE 18. Ives, *The Unanswered Question,* mm. 20–21, flutes (first response).

Near the beginning of the poem Emerson makes clear that the secret held by the Sphinx is "The meaning of man," that is, the question of existence, in regard to which Ives's performance instruction reads: "The trumpet intones 'The Perennial Question of Existence', and states it in the same tone of voice each time."[35] The question doesn't change, because the answer isn't given, by either the Sphinx or Ives.[36] The question as posed seems simple enough, straightforward even, but the existential complexity of what it encodes is pronounced by its chromatic outline, intervallic angularity, and rhythm (ex. 17); musically, it gives the flutes more than what they may initially think they've bargained for. Their first response to the question is brief (two bars) but calm and seemingly tentative, thoughtful, and inconclusive (the dynamic marking is *piano* and without accentuation), ending on a weak beat (ex. 18).

The flutes, termed by Ives "The fighting Answerers," time after time give the question their best shot. The result is consistently unsatisfactory and frustrating, as is apparent in the increasing musical complexity, harmonic discord, and ensuing general agitation. Their initial response to the trumpet-sounded question plays at adagio; thereafter each response is at a faster tempo: andante to allegretto to allegro to allegro molto; the final response begins allegretto and accelerates to presto, then molto agitando con fuoco. In the end they sound angry. As Ives puts it, "after a 'secret conference', [they] seem to realize a futility, and begin to mock 'The Question'." Each time, the flutes

EXAMPLE 19. Ives, *The Unanswered Question,* mm. 52–56, flutes (final response).

respond only briefly, managing not more than four bars of response, and in their last response closing on something of a collective shriek (ex. 19). Ives suggests that what he terms "the hunt for 'The Invisible Answer' undertaken by the flutes and other human beings . . . need not be played in the exact time position indicated. It is played in somewhat of an impromptu way." In other words, the urgency of the question drives the response, sufficiently so as to suspend the temporal precision of the performance as notated.

I intend these brief remarks as the prelude to what principally interests me within the larger context of the music assigned to the trumpet and flutes, namely, the string ensemble.

The strings play softly *(ppp, con sordini)* throughout and in a very slow-moving tempo *(largo molto sempre)*. What barely passes for melodic material is confined to the violas, seven quarter-notes, completed by the cellos with four more, ending on a whole note held for three measures (bars 11–14). Everything assigned to the strings is diatonic, and the sustained harmonies are consonant and all but nonteleological. The sole change in performance marking is a diminuendo indicated for the last two bars: *ppp* to *pppp*. Ives calls for distinct spatial separation of the strings from the rest of the ensemble; ideally, they are to be offstage, hence invisible to auditors. Because we can't see the strings, absent a conductor, there is no certainty to our knowing when the performance actually begins (Ives's performance instruction simply states that in the absence of a conductor one of the flutes may serve to direct the other three). For that matter, even with a conductor, the strings play so softly that the audience may only gradually become aware of their playing: *as if their sound were always already extant.* Ives indicates that after the flutes, as he puts it, "disappear, 'The Question' is asked for the last time, and 'The Silences' are heard beyond in 'Undisturbed Solitude'." The strings, Ives indicates, represent "The Silences of the Druids—Who Know, See and Hear Nothing." So what exactly does he mean by Druids and by Silences—silences that are *heard?* The strings remain oblivious to the sounds of the trumpet and flutes that intrude on their all but unchanging ever-presence. Ives's invocation of the Cosmic Landscape to my way of thinking references something at once terrestrial and extraterrestrial that I would name Nature, perceived as both a material actuality and a spiritual (immaterial) essence. The question of existence is founded on the dilemma of what we are in relation to the otherness that we are not (or perhaps are as well). The cosmic landscape, put differently, *encompasses* us.

The seventh stanza of Emerson's poem incorporates text that echoes Rousseau in its condemnation of the human self-degradation voiced by the frustrated Sphinx:

But man crouches and blushes,
  Absconds and conceals;
He creepeth and peepeth,
  He palters and steals;
Infirm, melancholy,
  Jealous glancing around,
An oaf, an accomplice,
  He poisons the ground.

The following stanza suggests that it is Nature that humankind has offended: "Out spoke the great mother"; "'who," she asks, "with sadness and madness, / Has turned my child's head?'" At the poem's conclusion, in the last two stanzas, the Sphinx herself disappears into/as Nature:

She melted into purple cloud,
  She silvered in the moon;
She spired into a yellow flame;
  She flowered in blossoms red;
She flowed into a foaming wave:
  She stood Monadnoc's head.[37]

Thorough a thousand voices
  Spoke the universal dame;
"Who telleth one of my meanings
  Is master of all I am."

The strings, as a nature allegory, are nearly atemporal, as is apparent not least by comparison with the always-evident temporality of both the trumpet and flutes for which the parameter of rhythm is distinct. The strings, instead, evince spatiality, a kind of cosmic dimension that in its vastness remains indifferent and nonreactive to the dilemma of humankind attempting to make sense of itself within the macrocosm. In precisely this regard, *The Unanswered Question* engages the dialectical concerns of the principal artifacts considered in this volume: the relation of person to person within the existential domain of subjectivity; we and our relation to the other; nature as a redemptive force; and sound and music as expressive media and forms of knowledge. The Western world around 1910 had well prepared itself to respond to these issues structured on thinking that reached back to the Enlightenment (and even antecedents thereto), just as by 1910 it had—perhaps as never before and in no small part on account of its technological advancement, commonly instrumentalized for anti-enlightened function—remade the world into a shape that begged for redemption and to which art in various guises attempted to respond.[38]

TO END, IN CINEMA

Terrence Malick's *The Thin Red Line* (1998), a deeply moving elegy on the fractured relation of humans to themselves and to the nature that constitutes them, stages its narrative during World War II and the American effort between August 1942 and February 1943 to take the Pacific island of Guadalcanal from the Japanese, one of the bloodiest engagements of the war, with 7,100 American and 31,000 Japanese dead. Malick's story is loosely based on the novel of the same name by James Jones.[39] The film's impressive score was composed by Hans Zimmer.

As with other Malick films, there is relatively little dialogue and a considerable amount of voiceover. The film opens to the sound of a chordal drone, slowly and dramatically increasing in volume, principally incorporating an organ, presumably for its spiritual associations, and in conjunction with a series of related images beginning with a tight shot of a large crocodile. As the animal very slowly moves into the water, it pushes aside yellow-green slime covering the surface; this in turn permits the reflection onto the surface of the sky above, capturing a kind of cosmic wholeness. Malick cuts to a view of a dense forest, again a tight shot, now with acousmatic bird sounds; moments later he points the camera toward the sky, the rays of the sun radiating out behind the canopy, as the film's principal character, Private Witt, unseen, speaks in voiceover: "What's this war in the heart of nature? Why does nature vie with itself? The land contend with the sea? Is there an avenging power in nature? Not one power but two?" A new musical underscore begins near the end of this shot and continues into the next, a scene of Melanesian natives, children mainly, playing a game, swimming, and fishing, intercut with the AWOL Private Witt paddling in a borrowed canoe, now but briefly one of them and happy. Malick films it as a paradise, and the music confirms as much by incorporating the "In Paradisum" movement from Gabriel Fauré's *Requiem*. In image, Malick gives us an earthly paradise; in sound he gives us another one, equally beautiful, but achieved only in death.

The final voiceover, at the film's end and again voiced by Private Witt, now from beyond the grave, concludes with an invocation of reconciliation: "Darkness and light. Strive for love. Are they the working of one mind, the features of the same face? Oh, my soul let me be in you now. Look out through my eyes. Look out at the things you made. All things shinin'." Witt speaks softly, slowly, to the accompaniment of an orchestral elegy underscore heard earlier in the film. The image track to the voiceover opens with soldiers aboard ships departing the island, followed thereafter by a shot looking down at the waves and the ship's wake: water only. The moment that Witt's voiceover ends, Malick abruptly cuts back to the island, a fairly tight shot of three children in two canoes paddling quietly in a shallow river near the shore and nearly swallowed by the jungle encroaching around them. There is no music, only the sounds of their paddles in the water. Malick then cuts to a close-up of two multicolored parrots roosting on a branch, one grooming the other; a moment later he cuts again, now a low shot of a sprouting coconut in calm, shallow water and with a view of islands in the distance, accompanied by the gentle sound of waves; and then the screen goes black. As the credits roll, the underscore is an a cappella hymn ("God Yu Tekem Laef Blong Mi") joyfully and forcefully sung in unison by a Melanesian choir, to which a full-throated organ accompaniment is added in subsequent verses, producing the effect of a Melanesian/Bach-flavored chorale hybrid, completing in sound the acoustic frame that opened the film and sonically bringing together two different but related sound worlds.

The film's most dramatic moment involves a protracted scene leading up to and concluding with the American army's taking of so-named Hill 210, held by a well-fortified and dug-in Japanese contingent. The scene is brutally violent in both sight and sound. Midpoint, the sounds of the fighting are mixed with the elegiac, slow-moving underscore, incorporating the tolling of a bell (the same music heard again at the film's end). The Americans defeat the Japanese and gather prisoners, terrified and uncomprehending, surrounded by the dead from both sides. Gradually, the music swells and the diegetic sound effects diminish and fade to silence. To the accompaniment of the orchestral elegiac underscore, Private Witt speaks once again in voiceover (1:50:25 in the DVD release):[40] "This great evil, where's it come from? How'd it steal into the world? What seed, what root did it grow from? Who's doing this? Who's killing us, robbing us of life and light, mocking us with the sight of what we might have known? Does our ruin benefit the earth? Does it help the grass to grow, the sun to shine?"

As Witt speaks the last lines of the voiceover, "Is this darkness in you, too? Have you passed through this night?," the music seamlessly morphs into Ives's *The Unanswered Question,* at a point in the image track where Private Bell, pliers in hand, approaches a wounded, supine Japanese soldier, waiting for him to die so he can extract any gold-filled teeth (fig. 141). Bell speaks to the Japanese soldier, who cannot understand him: "I'm gonna sink my teeth into your liver. You're dying. See them birds up there? You know,

FIGURE 141
Terrence Malick (director), *The Thin Red Line* (1998): Private Bell with a dying Japanese solider (1:52:53).

FIGURE 142
Malick, *The Thin Red Line:* Private Bell weeping in shame, having cast off the teeth he has taken from dead enemy soldiers (2:06:58).

they eat you raw. Where you're going you're not coming back from." As the Japanese soldier begins to respond, telling the uncomprehending American that he too will one day die,[41] the initial iteration of the solo trumpet sounds, during which Malick provides other shots of the general scene of captors, prisoners, and the dead; as the trumpet sounds again, Malick's camera focuses on circling vultures. Just two of the seven iterations of the trumpet are included in the excerpt, but more to the point, Zimmer's inclusion of the Ives excerpt removes the flute responses, as if to suggest that the question posed by Private Witt in voiceover is unanswerable. Bell ends the pointless exchange with his prisoner by emphasizing his disregard for the dying man's otherness: "What are you to me? Nothin'." Near the film's end (2:06:12), Bell, filled with shame, in tears and trembling uncontrollably, haunted by flashbacks to his earlier mutilation of Japanese bodies, casts off the teeth he's collected (fig. 142). Only then is he reconciled with something approaching a sense of oneness with the other; only then does he become part of something greater than himself. The answer to the unanswered question is in behavior toward the self and toward the otherness within us and without.

APPENDIX

Chapter 5 Tables

NOTE: Timings in all four tables are from the 2010 Criterion Collection DVD *Days of Heaven* (1978).

TABLES 1 AND 2

Sonic and visual references to the prairie winds, common throughout *Days of Heaven*, are employed by Malick to signal change or even danger related to the unfolding narrative. Table 1 accounts for the wind that drives the propeller-generator that sits atop the Farmer's house. The device is photographed variously, both at a distance and in tight close-up, the latter at fraught moments as if underscoring the trope of impermanence ubiquitous to the film. At other times, the spinning propeller is heard but not seen, a more subtle acousmatic reminder of the nature/culture dialectic that organizes the lives of the principal characters.

Table 2 catalogues all references (visual and/or audible) to wind except those listed in Table 1, some of which simply reflect the fact that perfect stillness on the prairie is rare. More to the point, however, Malick repeatedly makes self-reflexive use of the visual and/or audible effects of wind in both close, medium, and long shots of his characters and the outdoor setting (waving grasses and grains, ripples on water, a fluttering scarecrow, etc.). The chapter discussion highlights the most significant references of this sort that are listed below.

TABLE 1. WIND CHARGER

Time	Scene	Visual reference	Audible reference
7:19–7:25	First close-up shot of house	x	x
7:38–7:41	Farmer eats apple by house		x
27:20–27:37	Bill and Abby near house	x	x
33:09–33:28	Farmer services wind charger; Abby walks toward outbuildings; shot of house	x	x
44:33–44:42	Wind charger close-up at night, followed by cut to black	x	x
44:43–45:08	Bill wakes Abby; they leave house; shots of gazebo, parasol, scarecrow, etc.		x
54:17–54:35	Farmer and Bill plucking pheasants; arrival of flying circus	x	x
1:06:12–1:07:15	Farmer by wind charger watches Bill and Abby embrace	x	x
1:16:08–1:16:12	Farmer ties Abby to porch post		x

TABLE 2. WIND *(principal references only; approximate timings)*

NOTE: Scenes tabulated in table 1 often connect directly to visual and/or audible reference to the wind charger atop the farmhouse as well.

Time	Scene	Visual reference	Audible reference
4:57–7:19	on train; arrival at farm	x	x
7:59–8:31	Bill in wheat field	x	x
9:20–9:38	first locust; immigrant reading	x	x
9:58–10:09	scarecrow; waving flags	x	
11:51–12:08	cutting oats; animals flee	x	
12:15–12:36	Farmer sees Abby; lunch break	x	
13:31–13:49	Bill fights	x	
14:14–14:41	cutting oats, collecting bundles	x	
14:58–15:28	stacking bundles into shocks	x	
16:37–16:57	frolicking after work	x	
17:22–17:30	Bill by doctor's wagon	x	
18:35–18:58	Abby meets Farmer	x	
19:17–19:54	early snow	x	x
19:55–20:07	ripe wheat close-up	x	
21:07–21:39	threshing tractors on move	x	
21:40–21:52	collecting bundles	x	
21:50–22:23	Farmer and accountant; spies on Abby	x	x

Time	Scene	Visual reference	Audible reference
23:07–23:14	steam tractors on the move	x	
23:39–25:11	Farmer on horse; later talks with Abby	x	
27:42–28:04	Bill and Linda talk	x	
28:15–28:57	Linda and young woman talk	x	x
28:58–29:26	Bill in close-up; men wrestle	x	
30:12–30:42	Bill and Abby on the prairie	x	
31:39–32:06	dance by bonfire	x	
33:29–33:42	Linda contemplates her future	x	x
34:46–35:00	foreman interrogates Linda	x	x
35:01–35:42	Bill and Abby as lovers; baseball	x	
38:51–40:00	wedding; trees rustling	x	x
40:28–40:32	locust on leaf, close-up, night	x	
40:32–41:04	honeymoon departure	x	
43:40–44:24	gazebo lunch; golfing	x	x
44:30–44:33	Farmer suspicious	x	
45:09–45:41	shots of gazebo, parasol, scarecrow, etc.	x	x
47:08–47:25	Farmer calls for Abby	x	
47:46–47:52	Linda flies kite	x	
48:35–49:55	foreman distrusts Bill and Abby	x	
51:29–51:42	wind on pond	x	x
52:14–52:31	evening	x	
52:42–52:48	near dark; scarecrow	x	x
53:04–54:20	Farmer and Bill hunting	x	x
54:36–55:08	flying circus arrives	x	
55:33–56:03	circus men and Linda on the prairie	x	x
57:02–57:48	night in gazebo; Bill and Abby kiss	x	
58:32–59:08	Abby and Bill next day	x	x
1:00:02–1:00:05	house; sleigh ride	x	
1:00:20–1:00:28	snow angels; gazebo	x	
1:00:43–1:00:49	spring, tree leaves	x	x
1:01:00–1:01:05	seeding	x	
1:01:55–1:02:10	wheat	x	x
1:02:11–1:02:30	harvest season; migrants return	x	
1:02:33–1:02:37	Farmer, Abby, Linda at beehives	x	
1:02:40–1:02:54	ripe wheat waving in wind	x	x
1:02:54–1:04:19	Bill returns	x	x
1:07:16–1:07:39	windy day; ducks scatter, gazebo shot; horses skitter; bison	x	x
1:08:04–1:09:21	Bill by his motorcycle; locusts in farmyard; locusts in house with curtains moving; siren alarm; battling insects	x	x
1:09:40–1:10:05	battling locusts, continued	x	

(continued)

TABLE 2 *(continued)*

Time	Scene	Visual reference	Audible reference
1:12:55–1:13:25	fire; Abby and Bill	x	
1:16:44–1:18:31	Farmer rides to find Bill; smoke blowing; Bill kills Farmer and runs; horses amid smoke; foreman finds Farmer's body	x	x
1:21:04–1:21:34	on river, on the run; campfire	x	
1:26:49–1:28:46	Abby says goodbye to Linda; boards a train; window curtains at Linda's school	x	
1:29:44–1:30:46	final scene, Linda and friend walk along railroad tracks; fade to black	x	

TABLES 3 AND 4

Tables 3 and 4 present the diegetic and the nondiegetic cues, respectively, for *Days of Heaven* (thirty-two in all), based on the published Paramount Cue Sheet (PCS) number and title. The PCS-supplied titles usually reflect the film action or event relating to the music; they are distinct from the track titles on the CD album release, *Ennio Morricone: Gli avvoltoi hanno fame (Two Mules for Sister Sara) & I giorni del cielo (Days of Heaven)*, Legend CD16 (1994), which contains only the music composed by Ennio Morricone. Table 4 references the titles on the CD in the text descriptions.

TABLE 3. DIEGETIC MUSIC

1. 29:20–30:13 / PCS NO. 8, LOST BOY BLUES

African-American man and Linda tap dance to the accompaniment of a harmonica played by Rick Smith. The tune, "Lost Boy Blues" by Palmer A. McAbee (1894–1970), is initially heard offscreen; at the end, the audio bleeds into the following scene.

2. 30:38–32:14 / PCS NO. 9, SWAMP DANCE

Night, the scene illuminated by a bonfire, with dancing. Cajun tune for fiddle and voice, "Swamp Dance," words and music by Doug Kershaw; performed by Doug Kershaw. Tune is initially heard offscreen; at the end, the audio bleeds into the following scene, next day, and the migrant workers departing.

3. 39:46–39:59 / PCS NO. 14, UNIDENTIFIED MELODY

Following the outdoor wedding of the Farmer and Abby, the couple and their friends walk along a trail in the woods to the accompaniment of a solo fiddler (uncredited).

4. 56:30–57:53 / PCS NO. 20, AZIZA

The flying-circus performers entertain in the Farmer's house. The woman belly dances, accompanying herself with finger cymbals and to Aziza music on a gramophone. The music continues through a clip from Chaplin's *The Immigrant* and during subsequent entertainments in the gazebo near the house (with clapping to the music), during which the Farmer observes

Bill and Abby flirting and kissing; the music continues offscreen as the Farmer, furious, in the couple's bedroom, scatters his medications onto the floor; the music continues throughout a brief vignette of the Farmer's peafowl roosting on the roof of the house, after which the screen goes black and the music fades.

5. 1:03:09–1:03:31 / PCS NO. 23, MINUET IN G AND BILL RETURNS

Bill returns to the farm, riding a motorcycle; dismounting near the house porch, he hears solo piano music on the gramophone (Beethoven, Minuet in G, WoO 10, no. 2); looking in through a window, he sees Abby dancing by herself to the music. Morricone's music overrides the fading sounds of the recording. (Slightly later, the gramophone is shown atop a side chair on the porch; Abby turns it off, though by now the piece has already concluded.)

6. 1:26:05–1:27:32 / PCS NO. 29, MINUET IN G

Linda arrives with Abby at the Academy for young girls; they come in on a group dance lesson. The scene opens with a close-up shot of a Story & Clark (Chicago and New York) upright player piano in action, playing the same music (Beethoven, Minuet in G, WoO 10, no. 2) heard in cue no. 23. The music continues in the background as the scene shifts to the grounds of the Academy as Abby and Linda part ways.

7. 1:28:01–1:28:45 / PCS NO. 30, HOT TIME IN THE OLD TOWN TONIGHT

The town band (clarinet, saxophone, trumpet, trombone, tuba, side drum), part of the send-off for soldiers leaving for World War I, performs near the railroad station. The tune, popular with military bands at the time, is "There'll Be a Hot Time in the Old Town" (1896, music by Theodore Metz). The band itself is shown only momentarily at the start of the scene and again briefly at the end, as the train pulls out.

TABLE 4. NONDIEGETIC MUSIC *by Ennio Morricone (except as noted)*

The nondiegetic orchestral cues for *Days of Heaven* are invariably scored for strings; in nearly all cues the melody line is carried by flute(s), often doubled on oboe; occasionally thematic material is given to a bassoon. Various cues also include clarinet, piano, celeste, vibraphone, guitar, horns, and organ. The score's longest set piece ("The Fire") is the most densely orchestrated; the score calls for 3 flutes, 2 oboes, clarinet, brass (4 trumpets, 4 horns [other cues use 2], 4 trombones, and tuba), piano, organ, guitar, percussion (including timpani, bass drum, cymbals, tam tam), and strings (18 violins, 8 violas, 8 violoncellos, 4 bass).

Characteristic of Morricone's work process, his nondiegetic orchestral music was recorded in Rome, with the composer conducting. Morricone insistently orchestrates his own scores (the more common practice is for film music composers to produce a short score, which is in turn handed over to one or more orchestrators).

The instrumentation heard both in the film and on the soundtrack album is somewhat scaled back from the orchestration in the manuscript score, which was made available to me in a PDF scan of a Paramount Pictures Music Archive photocopy (Morricone presumably retains the autograph). In some instances, it is obvious that parts were simply omitted during the recording; in other instances, it is possible that parts are present but otherwise lost in the sound mix.

There are, of course, significant differences between the soundtrack album's complete set pieces and the individual cues in the film. The film cues are typically shorter, which results in differences in orchestration to the extent that some instruments initially enter the mix in the complete pieces subsequent to what is included in the shorter cues.

Morricone composed a set piece entitled "The Chase" (1′57″) presumably to serve as underscore near the end of the film when Bill, Abby, and Linda flee following Bill's murder of the Farmer. Although this music is available on the soundtrack recording, it does not appear in the finished film.

1. 00–02:29 / PCS NO. 1, THE AQUARIUM FROM CARNIVAL OF THE ANIMALS

Camille Saint-Saëns, "Aquarium," part 7, *Le carnaval des animaux (Grande fantaisie zoologique)* (1886): title credits. Members of the Vienna Philharmonic, conducted by Karl Böhm, released in 1975 on the Polydor International label. *Carnival* was originally scored for a chamber ensemble of eleven instruments; the "Aquarium" section was written for flute, glass harmonica (a celeste or glockenspiel is commonly substituted), two pianos, two violins, viola, and violoncello. (Many modern recordings employ full orchestral string sections.)

2. 4:46–6:27 / PCS NO. 2, ENDERLIN

Bill, Abby, and Linda ride the rails to the Texas Panhandle, together with other migrant workers. Music: solo guitar, "Enderlin," composed and performed by Leo Kottke.

3. 10:35–11:28 / PCS NO. 3, MAIN TITLE

The harvest; blessing of the crops. A steam whistle on one of the five tractors signals the start; horse-drawn binders begin cutting oats. Music: "Harvest," composed by Ennio Morricone and based on material borrowed from the opening, two-bar motive of "Aquarium," which is immediately repeated and in turn expanded into an eight-bar theme, in turn repeated; music concludes with fast fade.

4. 12:18–12:55 / PCS NO. 4, THE FARMER AND THE GIRL

Outdoors: Farmer, during migrants' noon meal break, takes notice of Abby, as explained by Linda's voiceover. Music: initial use of the "Days of Heaven" theme; scored for piano solo.

5. 13:39–15:35 / PCS NO. 5, IN THE FIELD

Lunch break: Bill and Abby rest in the shade under a wagon; Linda plucks a chicken; following the break, workers gather and stack grain bundles into shocks; Farmer inquires about Abby's identity; field work continues. Music: repeats and expands cue no. 3, "Harvest," and concludes with formal closure on a full cadence.

6. 16:55–19:09 / PCS NO. 6, BAD NEWS

Sunset: Near the farmhouse, Bill steals salve from the doctor's medicine wagon; he hears the doctor inform the Farmer that he has perhaps a year to live; Farmer lies on his bed contemplating his situation. Music in approximate character of night music; scored for strings and celeste.

Fades directly into: Abby and Linda chase peafowl; Linda's voiceover concerning Farmer's illness; Abby and Farmer, near the farmhouse, speak for the first time; Linda and Bill sit at night near a fire while roasting a bird. Music: initially athematic, slow moving, and not heard elsewhere in the film, prior to entry of "Days of Heaven" theme (played on bassoon) first heard at the point when the Farmer and Abby first speak (18:30). Otherwise scored for strings only.

7. 20:36–21:06 / PCS NO. 7, NON-STOP WORK

Harvest work in the fields; Linda's voiceover describes the indifference of the boss to the workers. Music: "Threshing"; flute, oboe, piano, and strings.

8. 32:27–33:20 / PCS NO. 10, MAIN TITLE

A series of very short scenes: Linda and her young friend part ways as the migrants run to catch the slow-moving train. Silhouetted against the sky, Linda looks at those leaving. Screen goes black. The porch of the house with Abby doing the wash; Bill shuts down a steam tractor; Farmer services the wind charger; Linda walks towards the outbuildings; the music ends, after which only the whirling wind generator is heard offscreen. Music: repeats cue no. 3, "Harvest." (The piano is more prominent in this cue than in cue nos. 3 and 5.) Fade-out at end.

9. 35:01–35:50 / PCS NO. 11, OLD STORY

Bill and Abby lie in the grass; Bill and Farmer on porch; Bill describes his past. Music: "The Return"; sound mix emphasizes guitar, flute, bassoon, and strings.

10. 38.15–38:49 / PCS NO. 12, BAD NEWS

Bill, with Abby, expresses his anger at seeing the Farmer gazing at her. Music: brief, slow-moving, and quasi-elegiac; scored for strings only. The chirping of crickets is audible throughout the cue.

11. 38:54–39:46 / PCS NO. 13, AFTER THE WEDDING

Outdoor wedding of Farmer and Abby. Music: repeat of cue no. 3; tempo slows at end. Note: The ceremony is accompanied by three musicians playing a reed pump organ, violin, and trumpet; the soundtrack music, however, is nondiegetic; we hear the couple speak their vows but we do not hear the music played by the trio.

12. 41:23–41:56 / PCS NO. 15, EMPTY HOUSE

Bill moves about in the newlywed's house while the Farmer and Abby are on honeymoon. Music: "The Honeymoon"; scored for strings; slow-moving, contrapuntal miniature emphasizing minor mode and harmonic dissonances.

13. 42:07–43:40 / PCS NO. 16, ON THE ROAD

Honeymoon, followed by brief vignettes of the major characters frolicking in the shallows of the river, picnicking, playing with a dog, and Abby trying on new clothes. Music: "Happiness"; sound mix emphasizes strings, guitar, flute, oboe, and piano.

14. 46:27–48:39 / PCS NO. 17, THEY SHOULD LEAVE

Bill and Abby lying on the grass, having sneaked off in the night. Wind disturbs surface of a pond; haze covers the moon; close-up shot of a dropped wine glass in the river with a small fish swimming nearby. Music: opens with extended chordal drone in the bass, followed by a very slow, elegiac variant of cue no. 3. Cut to Bill and Abby at dawn running back to the house, with repeat of the bass drone suspending the repeat of the main motive. Bill discreetly disappears before the Farmer sees him. Abby makes excuses. The main six-note motive of "Aquarium" opens very slow, the tempo producing an aural sense of instability, uncertainty, and perhaps ominousness. The cue segues into a slowed-down version of Morricone's "Days of Heaven" track (cue nos. 4, 6, 27) as Linda looks at the illustrations in Kipling's *The Jungle Book,* continuing into the immediately subsequent shots of the Farmer, in pain, writhing on his bed; kite flying; Bill and Abby alone on the prairie and later riding horseback; Abby trying on a new dress in front of Bill; increasing signs of jealousy and tension; foreman confronting Farmer with his suspicions. Music: "Days of Heaven" theme in slow tempo, tentative, elegiac. Scored for strings, flute, and oboe.

15. 49:52–51:06 / PCS NO. 18, EMPTY HOUSE

Abby undresses; Farmer and Abby sit together on bed, the Farmer declaring his love. Abby closes bedroom door and walks back to the Farmer; they embrace. Music repeats cue no. 12.

16. 51:42–52:45 / PCS NO. 19, THE AQUARIUM FROM CARNIVAL OF THE ANIMALS

Newspaper headline announcing President Wilson's trip to the Texas Panhandle; Farmer, Abby, Bill, and Linda wave to the train as it slowly passes them on the prairie at night; they return to farm via buckboard; Bill jealously watches the couple; closed bedroom door; scarecrow looks over the field. Music: excerpt from "Aquarium."

17. 58:11–58:31 *[THIS CUE IS NOT ON THE PCS]*

In the couple's bedroom: Farmer confronts Abby after seeing her kiss Bill the previous night. Music: pianissimo strings at high pitch, a tone-cluster drone.

18. 59:49–1:01:56 / PCS NO. 21, ON THE ROAD

Bill has left the farm. Scenes of the Farmer and Abby on sleigh ride, making snow angels, Abby trying on new jewelry, the couple in bed; transition to spring, planting, seed germination; fireworks; Bill shows Abby the painted-stone outline of a large boat set out in the prairie grass; foreman holds seedlings in his hand. Music repeats "Happiness," cue no. 13.

19. 1:02:09–1:02:29 / PCS NO. 22, ENDERLIN

Harvest season and return of the migrants. Music: solo guitar, excerpt from Leo Kottke's "Enderlin," cue no. 2.

20. 1:03:27–1:05:54 / PCS NO. 23, MINUET IN G

Bill returns to the farm; realizes that Abby loves the Farmer. Music: "The Return," cue no. 9.

21. 1:08:13–1:13:54 / PCS NO. 24, THE LOCUSTS AND FIRE

Plague of locusts; angry Farmer confronts Bill in field at night as migrants attack the insects; Farmer accidentally ignites the ripe straw; field burns. Music: "The Fire"; expanded scoring (see discussion of orchestration in table headnote).

22. 1:16:11–1:16:42 / PCS NO. 25, THE FARMER AND THE GIRL

Next morning: Farmer rides his horse across the burned stubble; blackened prairie; Linda examines scorched farm machinery; a single sandhill crane stands in the midst of the ruin. Music: repeat of cue no. 10.

23. 1:17:53–1:18:50 / PCS NO. 26, THE KILLING

Bill prepares his motorcycle in advance of his intended departure; Farmer, with gun, comes to confront Bill, who fatally stabs him with a screwdriver. As the music begins, Bill runs, chasing after the Farmer's horse, which escapes; shot of six horses amidst the smoke from the burned-out fires; foreman finds Farmer's body; Bill, Abby, and Linda flee in Farmer's car. Music: "Ashes and Dust"; the cue consists of three identical iterations of the six-note motive described in cue no. 14; strings, flute, and oboe are audible in the sound mix.

24. 1:18:57–1:21:38 / PCS NO. 27, ENDERLIN

Bill, Abby, and Linda on the lam; at the river's edge, they pawn jewelry and the car in exchange for a boat; on the river; resting in woods; Bill spears a carp; river travel; foreman, with posse, shows photograph of Abby; sunrise, wild turkeys gobbling. Linda's voiceover is heard throughout the sequence. Music: solo guitar, repeat of Leo Kottke's "Enderlin," cue no. 2.

25. 1:25:21–1:25:58 / PCS NO. 28, HIS DEATH

Bill has been shot and killed; his body floats downstream; an officer pulls his body from river; Abby, crying, cradles the body as Linda looks on. Music: variant of cue no. 23.

26. 1:28:47–1:29:48 / PCS NO. 31, THE AQUARIUM FROM CARNIVAL OF THE ANIMALS

Linda makes her escape from the Academy, dropping tied sheets from a second-floor window. She runs with her young friend into town. Music: mm. 1–20 of the original Saint-Saëns score.

27. 1:30:22–1:33:36 / PCS NO. 32, THE FARMER AND THE GIRL

Linda and her friend light out, heading down the railroad tracks. Linda's voiceover describes her friend. Cut to credits, the music continuing. Music: "Days of Heaven" theme, scored for strings, flutes, oboe, bassoon, acoustic guitar, piano, synthesizer, celeste, organ, vibraphone, and strings (not all of these instruments can be discerned on the soundtrack).

NOTES

INTRODUCTION

1. Virginia Woolf, "Mr. Bennett and Mrs. Brown," in *Collected Essays,* ed. Leonard Woolf, 4 vols. (London: Hogarth, 1966), 1:319, available online at www.ric.edu/faculty/rpotter/temp/Woolf_bb.pdf (accessed 6 December 2011). The relevant passage reads in whole: ". . . On or about December, 1910, human character changed. I am not saying that one went out, as one might into a garden, and there saw that a rose had flowered, or that a hen had laid an egg. The change was not sudden and definite like that. But a change there was, nevertheless; and, since one must be arbitrary, let us date it about the year 1910."
2. Ibid., 332–33.
3. Luigi Russolo, *The Art of Noises,* Monographs in Musicology no. 6, trans. Barclay Brown (New York: Pendragon, 1986), 26–27, quoting Marinetti. Russolo charted among his "6 families of noises" to be realized mechanically in his would-be futurist orchestra the "Voices of animals and people," incorporating solely the sounds of distress and suffering: "Shouts, Screams, Shrieks, Wails, Hoots, Howls, Death rattles, Sobs" (28). Yet even in Russolo's neo-fascist rant there lies a not-quite-silent oppositional and utopian prospect, to the extent that the sounds he evokes are not only properly associated with suffering and abjection but also at heart pleas for life, against all odds.

   Marinetti published his poetic account of the experience in *Zang Tumb Tumb* (1914), employing onomatopeias and a variety of different typefaces, from small to very large, in an effort to represent as graphically as possible the sounds of war. The letter passage quoted reflects his so-named "words-in-freedom" style. He celebrated the outbreak of the First World War and in 1915 produced a volume of poems called *Guerra sola igiene del mundo* (War the Only Hygiene of the World). Later, Marinetti became an active supporter of Mussolini. See further Cinzia Sartini Blum, *The Other Modernism: F. T. Marinetti's Futurist Fiction of Power* (Berkeley: University of California Press, 1996).

4. Woolf, "Mr. Bennett and Mrs. Brown," 334 and 336, respectively.
5. Jean-Jacques Rousseau, *The First and Second Discourses,* ed. Roger D. Masters, trans. Roger D. Masters and Judith R. Masters (New York: St. Martin's Press, 1964), 47, emphasis added.
6. Ibid., 95.
7. Ibid., 95–96.
8. Ibid., 168.
9. See the insightful essay by Berthold Hoeckner, "Wagner and the Origin of Evil," *Opera Quarterly* 23, nos. 2–3 (2008): 151–83, considering Wagner's conception of the *Ring* cycle as well as post-Holocaust assessments of Wagner as the origin of evil for the Third Reich.
10. See Warren Darcy, "*Creatio ex nihilo:* The Genesis, Structure, and Meaning of the *Rheingold* Prelude," *Nineteenth Century Music* 13, no. 2 (1989): 80–91, incorporating and engaging research by John Deathridge.
11. Richard Wagner, *My Life,* 2 vols. (New York: Dodd, Mead, 1911), 2:603.
12. Ibid., 611.
13. Charles Ives employed the same technique, and for the same apparent purpose, in the string-ensemble opening of *The Unanswered Question* (1908/revised 1930–35).
14. Darcy, "*Creatio ex nihilo,*" 93. See especially 92–98 for Darcy's detailed discussion of the structure and meaning of the Prelude, from which some of my account is derived.
15. Adorno recognized precisely this feature in Wagner's music generally—though arguably the "tendency" is particularly pronounced in the telling opening to the *Ring* cycle; for example, *Philosophy of New Music,* ed. and trans. Robert Hullot-Kentor (Minneapolis: University of Minnesota Press, 2006), 190: "In no passage [in Wagner's music] does sound go beyond itself temporally; instead it is dissipated in space." Michel Foucault's discussion appears in *The Order of Things: An Archaeology of the Human Senses* (New York: Vintage, 1966), 307–11.
16. Arthur Schopenhauer, *The World as Will and Representation* (1818; 3rd and final ed., 1859), trans. Richard E. Aquila in collaboration with David Carus, 2 vols. (New York: Pearson Longman, 2008–10), 1:308–10, original emphasis.
17. Ibid., 313.
18. Ibid., 308, original emphasis. Schopenhauer continues: "Just for this reason, the effect of music is so very much more powerful and penetrating than that of the other arts. For the latter speak only of shadows; it, rather, speaks of the essence of things."
19. Ibid., 315.
20. The *Rheingold* Prelude appears at two other key moments in the film; see the discussion by Robert Sinnerbrink, "Song of the Earth: Cinematic Romanticism in Malick's *The New World,*" in *Terrence Malick: Film and Philosophy,* ed. Thomas Deane Tucker and Stuart Kendall (New York: Continuum, 2011), 186–93.

21. Ibid., 181. There is a fairly substantial literature concerning this film. To my way of thinking, the best of this work is Sinnerbrink's deeply insightful essay "Song of the Earth." See also, in the same volume, Elizabeth Walden, "Whereof One Cannot Speak: Terrence Malick's *The New World,*" 197–210. Other accounts include Lloyd Michaels, *Terrence Malick* (Urbana: University of Illinois Press, 2009), 78–99; Mark Cousins, "Praising *The New World,*" in *The Cinema of Terrence Malick: Poetic Visions of America,"* ed. Hannah Patterson, 2nd ed. (London: Wallflower Press, 2007), 192–98; James Morrison, "Making Worlds, Making Pictures: Terrence Malick's *The New World,*" ibid., 199–211; and Adrian Martin, "Approaching *The New World,*" ibid., 212–21.
22. Alexis de Tocqueville, "Two Weeks in the Wilderness," in *Democracy in America and Two Essays on America,* trans. Gerald E. Bevan (London: Penguin, 2003), 876.
23. Ibid., 897.
24. Ibid., 924.

1. THE CIVILIZING PROCESS

1. A good deal has been written about this opera in recent years, the work of Allan W. Atlas, Helen M. Greenwald, Annie J. Randall, and Rosalind Gray Davis (all cited in the notes that follow) being especially significant. My remarks are indebted to their research, though my thinking moves in a somewhat different direction.
2. Norbert Elias, *The Civilizing Process,* vol. 1: *The History of Manners,* trans. Edmund Jephcott (New York: Pantheon, 1978).
3. Michel de Certeau, *The Practice of Everyday Life,* trans. Steven Rendall (Berkeley: University of California Press, 1984), 115. He continues: "Every story is a travel story—a spatial practice"; and "Narrated adventures, simultaneously producing geographies of actions and drifting into the commonplaces of an order, do not merely constitute a 'supplement' to pedestrian enunciations and rhetorics. They are not satisfied with displacing the latter and transposing them into the field of language. In reality, they organize walks. They make the journey, before or during the time the feet perform it" (115–16).
4. Ibid., 117: "Space occurs as the effect produced by the operations that orient it, situate it, temporalize it, and make it function in a polyvalent unity of conflictual programs or contractual proximities. . . . In contradistinction to the place, [space] has thus none of the univocality or stability of a 'proper.' In short, *space is a practiced place*" (original emphasis); and 118: "Stories thus carry out a labor that constantly transforms places into spaces or spaces into places. They also organize the play of changing relationships between places and spaces." Henri Lefebvre, *The Production of Space,* trans. Donald Nicholson-Smith (Oxford: Blackwell, 1991), points out that space is not natural but cultural: it is socially produced—though not as a thing; as such, space responds to both the forces and relations of production. Accordingly, space "serves as a tool of thought and of action; that in addition to being a means of production it is also a means of control, and hence of domination, of power; yet that, as such, it escapes in part from those who would make use of it" (26); see also 71.
5. See further Gary F. Kurutz, "Yosemite on Glass," in *Yosemite: Art of an American Icon,* ed. Amy Scott (Berkeley: University of California Press, 2007), 54–89.

6. William Deverell, "'Niagara Magnified': Finding Emerson, Muir, and Adams in Yosemite," in Scott (ed.), *Yosemite,* 11–12. Kate Nearpass Ogden, "California as Kingdom Come," ibid., 23: "To a nation that was both insecure about the brevity of its history and struggling to rebuild following a brutal civil war, Yosemite was worth its weight in artistic metaphors."
7. John Muir, *Nature Writings: The Story of My Boyhood and Youth; My First Summer in the Sierra; The Mountains of California; Stickeen; Selected Essays* (New York: Library of America, 1997).
8. Frederick Jackson Turner, "The Significance of the Frontier in American History" (1893), online at http://xroads.virginia.edu/~Hyper/TURNER/chapter1.html (accessed April 20, 2014). Turner ends his paper thus: "The stubborn American environment is there with its imperious summons to accept its conditions; the inherited ways of doing things are also there; and yet, in spite of environment, and in spite of custom, each frontier did indeed furnish a new field of opportunity, a gate of escape from the bondage of the past; and freshness, and confidence, and scorn of older society, impatience of its restraints and its ideas, and indifference to its lessons, have accompanied the frontier. What the Mediterranean Sea was to the Greeks, breaking the bond of custom, offering new experiences, calling out new institutions and activities, that, and more, the ever retreating frontier has been to the United States directly, and to the nations of Europe more remotely. And now, four centuries from the discovery of America, at the end of a hundred years of life under the Constitution, the frontier has gone, and with its going has closed the first period of American history."
9. See Lee Clark Mitchell, *Westerns: Making the Man in Fiction and Film* (Chicago: University of Chicago Press, 1996), 59–70.
10. Ogden, "California as Kingdom Come," 24.
11. Mitchell, *Westerns,* 89.
12. The West was also in part the product of popular literature, the dime novel especially, a genre noted for its sensationalist narrative and published in staggering quantities during the last four decades of the nineteenth century. The Beadle Dime Novel series, produced by the firm Beadle and Co., later Beadle and Adams, between 1860 and 1885, for example, reached number 631, with western subjects among the most popular in the aftermath the Civil War. Few of the Beadle narratives achieved the popularity of the stories about Buffalo Bill, a man large in fiction and perhaps even larger in life. Buffalo Bill (William Cody, 1846–1917), Pony Express rider, army scout in the Civil War, and both a scout and fighter in the Indian wars in the West, gained mythic status from Ned Buntline's dime novel *Buffalo Bill, King of the Border Men,* serialized in the *New York Weekly* in 1869 when Buffalo Bill was only twenty-three years old. All told, he was the subject of more than 550 conventionally exaggerated written accounts. See William H. Goetzmann and William N. Goetzmann, *The West of the Imagination* (New York: Norton, 1986), 288. See also Henry Nash Smith, *Virgin Land: The American West as Symbol and Myth* (Cambridge, MA: Harvard University Press, 1970), 90–111, on the dime novel in general and the Buffalo Bill stories in particular.

    In 1872, with art (however loosely described) imitating life, Buffalo Bill acted on a Chicago stage with Buntline (Edward Zane Carroll Judson) in a Buntline melodrama,

The Scouts of the Prairie, supposedly written in four hours. Firing his six-guns at the critical moment, he saved a young couple from certain death at the hands of hostile Indians. The play was a sensation, in large part because the hero was playing himself, as the saying goes, live and in person. The play had a long run, much of it on tour. See further, Goetzmann and Goetzmann, *West of the Imagination,* 288–91. In the early 1880s, Cody cashed in on his ever-increasing fame by mounting what became his fabled "Buffalo Bill's Wild West," a multipart melodrama of "historical" scenes, ranging from episodes from pioneer life to a kind of cowboy-and-Indians extravaganza, involving as many as 1,200 participants in reenactments of pitched battles of whites against invariably-to-be-vanquished Native Americans. (The exception was Custer's Last Stand with Cody playing Custer, though Buffalo Bill symbolically triumphed by reenacting his long-held claim to having taken the first scalp in revenge following the Custer massacre.) Cody took the show to Europe beginning in 1887. Puccini saw it in Milan in 1890 and reported enjoying himself. See Emanuele Senici, *Landscape and Gender in Italian Opera: The Alpine Virgin from Bellini to Puccini* (Cambridge: Cambridge University Press, 2005), 248.

Puccini's acquaintance with the American West was otherwise formed from his reading of Bret Harte's melodramatic short stories in Italian translation, many of which were set in California gold-mining camps (for example, "The Luck of Roaring Camp" and "The Outcasts of Poker Flat"). See Senici, *Landscape and Gender in Italian Opera,* 248–49. On Harte's creation of recurring characters and tropes in Western-themed fiction, see Mitchell, *Westerns,* 77–78. See also Ray Allen Billington, *Land of Savagery, Land of Promise: The European Image of the American Frontier in the Nineteenth Century* (New York: Norton, 1981). Billington points out that Europeans were more interested in the western plains and deserts than in the mountains.

13. Mary Douglas, *Purity and Danger: An Analysis of Concepts of Pollution and Taboo* (Harmondsworth, UK: Penguin, 1970), 137, 145, respectively.
14. Elias, *Civilizing Process,* 1:3–4, suggests that the noun *civilization* acknowledges Western self-consciousness: "by this term Western society seeks to describe what constitutes its special character and what it is proud of: the level of *its* technology, the nature of *its* manners, the development of *its* scientific knowledge or view of the world, and much more" (original emphasis). However, as Elias points out, German usage is different. *Zivilisation* referenced a value of second rank, one "comprising only the outer appearance of human beings, the surface of human existence." By contrast, *Kultur* expresses a uniquely German sense of national achievement and essence. *Kultur* in German "refers essentially to intellectual, artistic, and religious facts, and has a tendency to draw a sharp dividing line between facts of this sort, on the one side, and political, economic, and social facts, on the other." In French and English, Elias, suggests, the concept of civilization, while acknowledging accomplishment, refers as much to attitudes of behavior of people, whereas *Kultur* in German places little value on behavior in the absence of accomplishment. Herbert Marcuse, "Remarks on a Redefinition of Culture," in *Science and Culture: A Study of Cohesive and Disjunctive Forces,* ed. Gerald Holton (Boston: Houghton Mifflin, 1965), 218–35, elaborates the distinction between *Zivilisation* and *Kultur* by describing the former as a realm of necessity and the latter as a realm

of higher fulfillment, though one located in class privilege; the former as fact and means, the latter as value and ends. If *Zivilisation* marks what is, for Marcuse *Kultur* marks what ought to be: utopia. I am not keen to parse the problematic and indeed politically suspect binary that Marcuse advances; rather, I reference it as a means of delineating the progressive aspects of both Belasco's play and Puccini's opera, and this despite a panoply of profoundly regressive problematics immanent to both.

15. Norbert Elias, *Time: An Essay,* trans. Edmund Jephcott (Oxford: Blackwell, 1992), 13.
16. Ibid., 21.
17. Michael L. Johnson, *Hunger for the Wild: America's Obsession with the Untamed West* (Lawrence: University Press of Kansas, 2007), 204; see further to 213.
18. Stuart Hall, "Ethnicity: Identity and Difference," *Radical America* 23, no. 4 (1989): 12.
19. Re Puccini's deep-seated love of nature—and his dislike of urban life and the trappings of "civilization" (the material benefits of which he unambiguously enjoyed), see Mary Jane Phillips-Matz, "Puccini's America," in *The Puccini Companion,* ed. William Weaver and Simonetta Puccini (New York: Norton, 2000), e.g. 215: "I long for the woods with its many perfumes . . . I long for the wind that blows my way from the sea, free and smelling of salt water . . . I hate pavements! I hate palaces! I hate ornate pillars! I hate styles! I love the beautiful shape of the poplar and the pine tree." See also Mosco Carner, *Puccini: A Critical Biography,* 3rd ed. (London: Duckworth, 1992).
20. David Belasco, *The Girl of the Golden West: Novelized from the Play* (New York: Grosset & Dunlap, 1911).
21. The film exists in a couple of prints; seven excerpts totaling fourteen minutes are available online at www.fanciulla100.org/fan_video_silent_dvd (accessed May 1, 2014), part of a valuable assemblage by Deborah Burton in recognition of the centennial of the opera's premiere (notes that follow reference several other parts of the website). According to Lisa-Lone Marker, *David Belasco: Naturalism in the American Theatre* (Princeton: Princeton University Press, 1975), 43, 48, Belasco had collaborated on both playwriting and directing with Cecil's father, Henry, in the late 1880s, though Cecil B. DeMille, *The Autobiography of Cecil B. DeMille,* ed. Donald Hayne (Englewood Cliffs, NJ: Prentice-Hall, 1959), 113–14, says almost nothing about the film. What DeMille principally reports is a close call involving a near car accident in the "extremely crude mountain roads of San Diego County," where the location shooting of mountain scenes took place (near the present site of Mount Palomar). See also Robert S. Birchard, *Cecil B. DeMille's Hollywood* (Lexington: University of Kentucky Press, 2004), 34–36.

    According to Larry Langman, *A Guide to Silent Westerns* (New York: Greenwood Press, 1992), ix, the first western, Edison's brief *Cripple Creek Barroom* from 1898, within five years was superseded by narrative films, such as Edison's *Brush between Cowboys and Indians* (1904), which quickly grew to feature length. Between 1898 and 1930, 5,400 silent western films were produced, including documentaries, shorts, and serials as well as features. The earliest were made on the East Coast and with painted scenery, but by the second decade of the century, westerns were made in the West, often partly on location.
22. "She's a gal who would fight for a Buddy / Just a pal who could weather a test / She's a devilish sort / But an angel at heart / She's the girl of the olden west." The song was recorded in 1923 for the Victor label (10″, 78 rpm, Victor #19104-A) by the popular

Canadian ballad singer Henry Burr (born McClaskey, 1885–1941), who began recording in 1902. In all, he recorded a staggering 12,000 titles, according to the online *Canadian Encyclopedia Historica.*

23. The musical numbers include a jarringly incorporated "Ave Maria" (Gounod version) and Liszt's "Liebestraum," both sung by the Girl, the latter song accompanied on the saloon piano by the town drunk. Of these four films, only the first, by DeMille, and the 1938 musical are known to have survived.
24. For details of Belasco's life and work, see Marker, *David Belasco;* William Winter, *The Life of David Belasco,* 2 vols. (New York: Moffat, Yard, 1918); Richard Wattenberg, *Early-Twentieth-Century Frontier Dramas on Broadway: Situating the Western Experience in Performing Arts* (New York: Palgrave Macmillan, 2011), 156–68; and Roger A. Hall, *Performing the American Frontier, 1870–1906* (Cambridge: Cambridge University Press, 2001), 206–11.
25. Marker, *David Belasco,* 30.
26. Ibid., 63.
27. David Belasco, *The Girl of the Golden West: A Play in Four Acts* (New York: Samuel French, 1915, 1933), 134–58. The production script also includes scene and light plot design sketches for each act, as well as placement instructions for the special-effects machinery. Only this edition of the play provides this information. See also the accounts in Marker, *David Belasco,* 139–60; and Winter, *Life of David Belasco,* 2:205–7.
28. David Belasco, *The Theatre through Its Stage Door,* ed. Louis V. Defoe (New York: Harper & Brothers, 1919), 61.
29. The other songs used in the show were "I'll Build Me a Little Home," "Bonnie Eloise," "Sweet Annie of the Vale," "Jim along Josie," "Wait for the Wagon," and "The Old Armchair." The complete set of costume instructions and song cues for the quartet of singers is in Belasco, *Girl of the Golden West,* 159–62; the song list appears on 163. The play text, however, lists additional songs. In *Theatre through Its Stage Door,* 61, Belasco stated: "I always aim to avoid fitting old or familiar music to a new play." *The Girl of the Golden West* obviously does not adhere to this claim. At the end of *Theatre through Its Stage Door,* 245, Belasco indicates a change in his thinking that occurred within the last few years preceding the book's publication in 1919: "I became convinced that the use of orchestras and entr'acte music in the theatre was often destructive to the illusion of what was taking place on stage and calculated to interfere with the imaginative quality of what I was attempting to put into my productions. In other words, I came to believe that an orchestra, however delightful its music, produced a discordant note in the theatre. Therefore I resolved to do away with my orchestra altogether. I dismissed my musicians and concealed my orchestra pit beneath a canopy of flowers."
30. The New York Public Library's Billy Rose Theatre Division at Lincoln Center holds several more or less complete copies of the music for the play. Furst's work is hand copied; the play's popular tunes (solo and ensemble) are in the form of published sheet music with piano accompaniment, again several copies of each. The conductor's score (marked "Leader") is simply the first violin part; there is no full orchestral score. One set has a great deal of the music crossed out (most of the prelude and about half the entr'acte music, for example, indicating changes made somewhere along the way, perhaps for a scaled-back touring production). There are also copies of published piano-vocal sheet

music that Furst used as source material for orchestral entr'acte medleys, including a few tunes not listed in the printed script for the play. The sixteen music cues for orchestra in *The Girl of the Golden West* are most heavily concentrated in act one (nine individual cues plus repeats, for a total of fourteen); throughout the play, the cues are mostly short, usually sixteen bars or fewer. (In the New York Public Library's extensive Belasco holdings, seventy-five reels of microfilm are given to incidental music for his plays.) For additional information on Furst and the New York Public Library holdings of music for the play, see Allan W. Atlas, "Belasco and Puccini: 'Old Dog Tray' and the Zuni Indians," *Musical Quarterly* 75, no. 3 (1991): 394–95nn19–20. In 1905, Furst also published a sheet-music arrangement of the play's first-act waltz music, "The Girl of the Golden West Waltz," in seven pages; the cover reproduces a photograph of Blanche Bates.

31. Belasco's representation of the play's Native Americans, Wowkle and Billy Jackrabbit, by contrast, is both clichéd and fundamentally racist. The character description for Billy registers him as "shifty, beady-eyed, lazy and lying; toes in" (Belasco, *Girl of the Golden West*, 7). Wowkle and Billy speak largely in monosyllables, in a combination of broken English and gutturals, "Ugh" and "Huh" being the favorites. Regarding antiracist aspects of the play, see Roxana Stuart, "Uncle Giacomo's Cabin: David Belasco's Direction of *La fanciulla del West*," in *Opera and the Golden West: The Past, Present, and Future of Opera in the U.S.A.*, ed. John L. DiGaetani and Josef P. Sirefman (Rutherford, NJ: Fairleigh Dickinson University Press, 1994), 145.

32. Belasco's voluminous papers were left to the New York Public Library following his death, forming the initial core of the extensive theater history collections. Belasco meticulously clipped reviews and saved programs, which he mounted in large scrapbooks. The scrapbooks were eventually microfilmed by the library; unfortunately, the originals were then destroyed. Belasco's plays were well documented in production photographs as well; the NYPL retains these scrapbooks. The clippings records for *The Girl of the Golden West* are extensive. Reviews for the play were mixed. While acknowledging Belasco's lavish production qualities and the solid cast, Bates especially, some critics were notably weary of the predictable nature of the playwright's melodramas, which to some seemed very old hat.

33. Belasco, *Girl of the Golden West*, 11–12. A critic for the *New York Evening World* (November 15, 1905) noted, "The pictures were better than the play." The *Fanciulla 100* website (www.fanciulla100.org/virtualmuseum_BelascoToscanini01.html; accessed March 1, 2014) reproduces the full text of the play, in typescript, a copy given by Belasco to Toscanini (the descriptions of the pictures are slightly different from the published text). The "Virtual Museum" section of the website reproduces a number of valuable textual and visual primary sources, as well as several scholarly papers.

34. Louis Hartmann served as Belasco's lighting designer beginning in 1901 and continued in that capacity until Belasco's death nearly thirty years later. For an account of his work, see Louis Hartmann, *Theatre Lighting: A Manual of the Stage Switchboard* (New York: D. Appleton, 1930); regarding Belasco's lighting rehearsals, see 14, 19, 21. See also Belasco, *Theatre through Its Stage Door*, especially 50–57 and 162–83, for extensive discussion of Belasco's interest in, and the effort spent on, the lighting of his plays.

35. Donald R. Anderson, "The West of Frederick Jackson Turner in Three American Plays," *Journal of American Culture* 23, no. 3 (2000): 89–97, briefly discusses Belasco's play.
36. Belasco's novel *The Girl of the Golden West,* 78–80, provides the initial view of the Sierra Nevada; the description is based on the First Picture panorama.
37. Ibid., epigraph.
38. The effect of Belasco's lighted sunburst curtain seems to have been magical. Here is the report of an enthused critic in the *Red Book,* January 1906, 404: "As you seat yourself in your orchestra chair you are confronted with a drop-curtain of dazzling beauty. It is made of embossed leather, and shows in shadowy outline a dark green and red valley, a chain of inky black mountains surmounted by a blazing sunset scene. A skillfully concealed spot-light kept always focused upon this sun makes it seem a living ball of fire." And here is the main point: "Under the spell of this curtain you gradually drift far, far away from Forty-second Street on your long journey across the continent. In less than two minutes you have arrived."

    Another critic, writing in the *New York Sun* in a piece titled "Belasco and His Three Aces" (December 1905 [precise date illegible]), reacted in kind, repeating the metaphor of time and space travel. Referring to "the decorative beauty, the apt symbolism" of the act curtain, he noted: "Words cannot describe such beauty. . . . The disc of the sun and its flaring streamers were laid on in opaque gold. Their light was reflected from a spotlight in the gallery. How were the beams kept from striking also beneath the summits? The sides of the mountains were of rich, nappy cloth, which drank in every straying beam. . . . Only Belasco could be the father of such striking and perfect scenic art. . . . The curtain had transported us to the golden West, and the panorama view . . . showed us the spot in which *The Girl* lived . . . in which the story of her fate was to be enacted." Belasco's play and novel both incorporate a variety of nature tropes, including that of a pastoral paradise (the novel: 94–95), stormy violence (218), and a gift from the Almighty (200), the last of these in an account Minnie gives to Dick Johnson in response to his comment that she must be lonely living in the wilderness: "Oh, my mountains! My beautiful peaks, my Sierras! God's in the air here, sure! You can see Him layin' peaceful hands on the mountain tops. He seems so near you want to let your soul go right on up." (Approximately the same text occurs in act two of the play; see David Belasco, *Six Plays* [Boston: Little, Brown, 1929], 357.)
39. Belasco, *Six Plays,* 402, in typical fashion, precisely describes the stage set, the gist of which is as follows: "The scene is a great stretch of prairie. In the far background are foothills in *[sic]* with here and there a suggestion of a winding trail leading to the West. The foliage is the pale green of sage brush,—the hills the deeper green of pine and hemlock."
40. The act four lighting design is reproduced in Belasco, *The Girl of the Golden West: A Play in Four Acts,* last page (unpaginated).
41. Belasco, *Six Plays,* 403.
42. Here the music reprises the G-major waltz tune first heard at the end of act one when the new lovers have first declared themselves to each other. Belasco worked three months on the sunrise for act four, spending, he says, the considerable sum of five thousand

dollars to replicate correctly the magic of the California sunrise, though in the end he was displeased with the result, thereafter selling it to another manager for a different production. "It was a very beautiful sunset *[sic]* that we contrived, but it was not even remotely Californian" (Belasco, *Theatre through Its Stage Door,* 173). Belasco further discusses the "sunset," obviously having forgotten that the effect was for a sunrise, on 56–57. For more on Belasco's lighting, see Helen M. Greenwald, "Realism on the Opera Stage: Belasco, Puccini, and the California Sunset," in *Opera in Context: Essays on Historical Staging from the Late Renaissance to the Time of Puccini,* ed. Mark A. Radice (Portland, OR: Amadeus Press, 1998), 292–93; and Marker, *David Belasco,* 78–98.

43. Belasco, *Girl of the Golden West: Novelized from the Play,* 340–41.
44. Ibid., 343.
45. Ibid., 345.
46. For a detailed accounting of the opera's advance publicity, see Annie J. Randall and Rosalind Gray Davis, *Puccini and the Girl: History and Reception of "The Girl of the Golden West"* (Chicago: University of Chicago Press, 2005), 96–98, 107–13. See also John Dizikes, *Opera in America: A Cultural History* (New Haven: Yale University Press, 1993), 337–44; and Alan Mallach, *The Autumn of Italian Opera: From Verismo to Modernism, 1890–1915* (Boston: Northeastern University Press, 2007), 267–73.
47. John C. Freund, "First Production of Puccini's Opera," *Musical America* 13, no. 6 (December 17, 1910): 1. Freund (1848–1924) founded the journal, first published in 1898.
48. Ibid., 2. Among the likely lesser-known names in this list, Clarence Mackay (1874–1938) was a fabulously wealthy financier whose daughter married Irving Berlin (for which she was disinherited). Mackay's father, John William Mackay, made his fortune in silver mines and the telegraph. Clarence's second wife was Anna Case (1888–1984), a soprano who sang at the Metropolitan Opera and recorded for Edison, for whom she participated in his gramophone "Tone Tests" (see chapter 3 below). German-born Andreas Dippel (1866–1932) was a tenor who performed at the Metropolitan Opera from 1890 until 1908, when he began service, ending in 1910, as the company's joint manager, with Giulio Gatti-Casazza. Louise Homer's composer husband was Sidney Homer (1864?–1953). Prussian soprano Johanna Gadski (1872–1932) sang at the Met, on and off, between 1898 and 1917. The Humperdinck opera mentioned was *Königskinder,* premiered at the Met on December 28, 1910, in which Louise Homer had a role. The foregoing information is from Wikipedia online.

    More description of the opening-night audience: "Such was the beauty of the women [in the audience], and the magnificence of the toilettes, that the filmy attire, the revealed physical charms, and the jewels, which seemed a sort of mediaeval armor, conspired to make a background that was simply overwhelming" (from Metropolitan Opera Archives, microfilm [1910], review: "'The Girl' Proves Puccini Triumph," December 11, 1910, source unidentified). And: "Many of the socially elect sat in the orchestra, where jeweled coronets and necklaces worth several kings' ransoms vied with the electrics overhead. Silks, satins, and rare old laces were still trailing in from the corridor when Toscanini, looking thinner than ever after long rehearsals, hurried out to the conductor's desk amid a general salvo of applause" (from Metropolitan Opera Archives, microfilm [1910]; the newspaper source cannot be identified, but the date is almost certainly December 11,

1910). Such lead-ins are typically followed by long lists describing the costumes of individual society women, of the sort: "Mrs James W. Gerard wore white satin, with a tunic of tangerine chiffon and embroidery with pearl ornaments" (from Metropolitan Opera Archives, microfilm [1910]: Cholly Knickerbocker, "First Night Any City in the World Might Envy: Society Flock to Greatest Opera Opening City Ever Saw," *New York American,* December 11, 1910). The Metropolitan Opera Archive has microfilmed its numerous scrapbooks of clippings. Those from the early twentieth century were already in poor condition when photographed, and the quality of the photography is very uneven. Many clippings are incomplete due to deterioration, and the source data, as a result, is often impossible to discern.

49. See Belasco, *Theatre through Its Stage Door,* 101–8. The critics were divided, not only about the production but also about the music and, for some, on the very question of a wild-west western as the subject for an opera, especially one written by an Italian who—so obviously, some surmised—knew so little about the country. The reviews were lengthy, many requiring a half page and more, often with pictures of the principals as well as Puccini and Belasco and the stage sets. For a sampling of the reviews, see Randall and Davis, *Puccini and the Girl,* 113–15; for reviews of early productions in Europe, 118–24; and for the history of Metropolitan Opera productions to the present, 208–25. Anton Webern saw *La fanciulla del West* in 1918 and confided his impressions to Schoenberg in a letter of March 27, 1918: "I am a little surprised that it is a score that sounds original in every way. Splendid. Every measure astonishing. Very special sounds. Not a shade of kitsch! And mine is a first-hand impression. I have to say I really liked it" (quoted in Michele Girard, *Puccini: His International Art,* trans. Laura Basini [Chicago: University of Chicago Press, 2000], 283–84).

50. Theodor W. Adorno, "On Some Relationships between Music and Painting," trans. Susan H. Gillespie, *Musical Quarterly* 79, no. 1 (1995): 66; and "On the Contemporary Relationship of Philosophy and Music," in *Theodor W. Adorno: Essays on Music,* ed. Richard Leppert, trans. Susan H. Gillespie (Berkeley: University of California Press, 2002), 144: "The time that is immanent in every music, its inner historicity, *is* real historical time, reflected as appearance" (original emphasis).

51. Giacomo Puccini, *The Girl of the Golden West* (New York: F. Rullman, 1910), edition for the Chicago Grand Opera Company, 5. Concerning the redemption trope—far more important to Puccini's opera than to Belasco's play—see the detailed and insightful discussion, including its history in the creative process and advancement in the publicity efforts of both Puccini himself and the Metropolitan Opera, in Randall and Davis, *Puccini and the Girl,* 148–56.

52. Randall and Davis, *Puccini and the Girl,* 45n17, 57. On August 27, 1907, Puccini wrote to his librettist Zangarini: "Increasingly the California-disease takes hold of me. I have copied several photographs of the most beautiful part of the forest where the highest and largest trees are, all for the scene in the third act. I am *determined* that it must be in the open air in a large clearing of a forest with colossal trees and with ten or more horses and sixty men" (ibid., 59, original emphasis).

53. Giacomo Puccini, *La fanciulla del West* (full score) (Mineola, NY: Dover, 1997).

54. William Ashbrook, *The Operas of Puccini* (New York: Oxford University Press, 1968), 146, is reminded by the second motif of "the swaying branches of huge trees."

55. There are good discussions of the prelude in Randall and Davis, *Puccini and the Girl,* 12–15; and Girard, *Puccini,* 286–89, though the points made in each are somewhat different from mine.

56. Concerning Puccini's unusual orchestrations, see Ashbrook, *Operas of Puccini,* 146–47.

57. Carner, *Puccini,* 460. As Richard Specht remarks in *Giacomo Puccini: The Man, His Life, His Work,* trans. Catherine Alison Phillips (London: J. M. Dent and Sons, 1933), 198, "It is significant to note how often the expression-mark *ruvido* (harsh) occurs in the score," adding that "the rough, jagged, untamed quality of the [opera's] natural surroundings imparts itself to the melodies too" (201).

58. For a list of recordings of individual arias and duets, see *La fille du Far West* (Paris: Editions Premières Loges, 1995), 128–29. The opera's lack of conventional arias had negative financial consequences for Puccini, who realized considerable income from sheet music royalties; see Ashbrook, *Operas of Puccini,* 146.

59. Lawrence Kramer, *Opera and Modern Culture: Wagner and Strauss* (Berkeley: University of California Press, 2004), 128–66.

60. Walter Benjamin, "On the Concept of History," in *Walter Benjamin: Selected Writings,* vol. 4: *1938–1940,* ed. Howard Eiland and Michael W. Jennings, trans. Harry Zohn (Cambridge, MA: Belknap Press of Harvard University Press, 2006), 395.

61. See the excellent essay by Arman Schwartz, "Puccini, in the Distance," *Cambridge Opera Journal* 23, no. 3 (2012): especially 169, 179, for comments concerning *La fanciulla del West.* The essay as a whole focuses on Puccini's later operas *Il tabarro* and *Suor Angelica.*

62. Atlas, "Belasco and Puccini: 'Old Dog Tray' and the Zuni Indians," has carefully traced the sources for the tune that Jake Wallace sings in both Belasco's play and Puccini's opera. In the play, the tune is "Old Dog Tray," also known as "Echoes of Home," for which more than one version exists, though today the best known is by Stephen Foster. Foster's setting was performed by minstrels in the California mining camps. Contrary to oft-repeated claims by scholars prior to Atlas, Puccini's source, identified by Atlas, is entirely unrelated to what Belasco employed, though the imagery and sentimentality of the lyrics are similar.

63. Belasco describes Wallace in Winter, *Life of David Belasco,* 1:74–75. See also Margaret A. Estabrook, "Minstrel Jake Wallace and 'The Girl of the Golden West,'" *California History* 64, no. 2 (1985): 118–21.

64. Belasco, *Six Plays,* 321–22; and Belasco, *Girl of the Golden West: Novelized from the Play,* 43–48.

65. Allan W. Atlas has also written about this song in a second essay that lays out what he perceives to be the opera's three interrelated tropes: distance, return, and redemption. In "*Lontano-Tornare-Redenzione:* Verbal Leitmotifs and Their Musical Resonance in Puccini's *La fanciulla del West,*" *Studi Musicali* 21, no. 2 (1992), he points out that by the time Jake Wallace first sings the word *lontano,* it has already appeared ten times in the stage directions as well as one other time in the opera's "Preliminary Note" (364–65); that the word *lontano* appears a total of twenty-four times in the opera's dialogue and seventeen times in the stage directions and the score's prefatory note (361n7); further, that *tornare* appears twenty-one times in dialogue and four times in the stage directions; and finally, that Puccini uses *redenzione* four times, whereas its English equivalent never

appears in Belasco's play (ibid.). See also Senici, *Landscape and Gender in Italian Opera,* 252.

66. Belasco, *Six Plays,* 356–57; cf. Belasco, *Girl of the Golden West: Novelized from the Play,* 199–200, repeating the play's dialogue. Puccini, *La fanciulla del West,* act two, rehearsal no. 19 m. 1 to 21 m. 2.

67. Belasco, *Six Plays,* 337–38; and Belasco, *Girl of the Golden West: Novelized from the Play,* 129–30.

68. Belasco, *Six Plays,* 334. This unlikely utterance does not appear in the novel.

69. Catherine Clément, *Opera, or the Undoing of Women,* trans. Betsy Wing (Minneapolis: University of Minnesota Press, 1988), 95, judging *La fanciulla del West* a "masterpiece," refers to Minnie as "the rising sun; contrasted to her nocturnal sisters, she is the day that does not close on an act of mourning. Opera lovers do not love this antiheroine. She is made for tomorrow. Tomorrow she will set out, lit by the brilliance of her victory."

70. Schwartz, "Puccini, in the Distance," 180: The Met unsuccessfully attempted its first broadcast of live opera already in 1910, with Caruso and Destinn performing in *Cavalleria rusticana* and *Pagliacci.*

71. The primeval western setting of the final act attracted some critics' attention: "And so, the opera ends, amid one of the loveliest of stage settings [the review includes a reproduction of the set], a forest of huge redwoods, through which one sees the snow clad Sierras lit with the pink light of dawn, a regular Maxfield Parrish study with the two [lovers] turning their faces toward the East[,] the sunlight, and with an adieu, the familiar Italian 'addio' to their beloved California, the snowy Sierras and the Golden West" (Metropolitan Opera Archives, microfilm [1910]: "'The Girl' Proves Puccini Triumph," December 11, 1910, source unidentified).

72. Indeed, at the opera's end, as Atlas, "*Lontano-Tornare-Redenzione,*" 377, has shown, Puccini quotes the tune one final time (act three, rehearsal no. 42 mm. 12–14), giving it to Minnie as she successfully pleads for Johnson's life. Senici, *Landscape and Gender in Italian Opera,* 255, suggests that in *La fanciulla del West* Puccini has created "a particularly powerful ear, a giant one, capable of hearing the action beyond the fixed field of visibility—an ear capable of 'seeing' the action that the eye cannot see." Senici further suggests that "the capabilities of the giant ear that the opera offers its audience go beyond anything of which any human ear is capable: they allow us to hear beyond reality" (259).

73. Quoted in Girard, *Puccini,* 260–61. In a letter to Sybil Seligman of July 14, 1907, Puccini wrote: "But the scene must take place outside the *Polka* in a big wood, and in the background . . . there are paths leading to the mountains—the lovers go off and are lost from sight, then they are seen again in the distance embracing each other, and finally disappear—how does that strike you?" (quoted in Vincent Seligman, *Puccini among Friends* [New York: Macmillan, 1938]), 139). See also Randall and Davis, *Puccini and the Girl,* 171n3, regarding the stage directions that describe the act three setting. On the elaborate act three scenery used for the Boston production, used again in 1911 in Rome—the trees modeled in plaster and the foliage cut from leather—see Specht, *Giacomo Puccini,* 195.

74. Greenwald, "Realism on the Opera Stage," 284–85, points out that Puccini began seven of his twelve operas at sunset.

75. Byron Nelson, "The Isolated Heroine and the Loss of Community in Puccini's Belasco Operas," *Yearbook of Interdisciplinary Studies in the Fine Arts* 2 (1990): 404–5, makes a similar point, and also compares the opera's conclusion to the final act of *Aida*. Concerning Puccini's unusual orchestral scoring of the closing measures, see Girard, *Puccini*, 324.
76. The stage manual likely used for the 1910 production calls for the mountains to be visible even in the first and second acts, both of which are interior settings, through a door and windows. See the insightful commentary in Senici, *Landscape and Gender in Italian Opera*, 229, 250–51, and 318nn4–5. A copy of the rare stage manual by Jules Speck, *La fille du West: Opéra en trois actes* (Paris: G. Ricordi, c. 1911–12), is in the Cornell University Music Library. The full text is reproduced online as part of the *Fanciulla 100* website; see www.fanciulla100.org/FanciullaMiseEnSceneswf.html (accessed March 1, 2014). Speck at the time of the Puccini première was the stage manager at the Metropolitan Opera. For a detailed discussion of this text, see Ellen Lockhart, "Photo-Opera: *La fanciulla del West* and the Staging Souvenir," *Cambridge Opera Journal* 23, no. 3 (2011): 145–66; and the paper by David Rosen on stage manuals, *Fanciulla*'s in particular, delivered as part of the *Fanciulla 100* symposium and available online in video form at www.bu.edu/buniverse/view/?v=2BU6vnTx (accessed March 1, 2014). Rosen notes that the *Fanciulla* stage manual is based on a version of the piano-vocal score that was already obsolete by March 1911 (Puccini was an inveterate reviser of his scores).
77. Max Horkheimer and Theodor W. Adorno, *Dialectic of Enlightenment: Philosophical Fragments*, ed. Gunzelin Schmid Noerr, trans. Edmund Jephcott (Stanford: Stanford University Press, 2002), 42–43.

2. OPERA, AESTHETIC VIOLENCE, AND THE IMPOSITION OF MODERNITY

1. Manaus is in western Brazil. The first performance in the lavishly decorated Teatro Amazonas took place on New Year's Eve, 1896. The rubber boom lasted from 1880 to 1914. See Lester Caltvedt, "Herzog's *Fitzcarraldo* and the Rubber Era," *Film & History* 18, no. 4 (1988): 74–84. According to Richard Collier, *The River That God Forgot: The Story of the Amazon River Rubber Boom* (New York: Dutton, 1968), 56, Caruso was in fact invited to sing at the Manaus opera house but never did so; the closest he got was Rio de Janeiro for performances in 1903 and again in 1914. The historical character on whom Herzog loosely based his film was Carlos Fermin Fitzcarrald (1862–97), a rubber baron and merchant. Like Herzog's character, Fitzcarrald brought a boat over a hill—a much higher one than Herzog's—but only by first disassembling it. For the basic biographical details, see Ronald H. Dolkart, "Civilization's Aria: Film as Lore and Opera as Metaphor in Werner Herzog's *Fitzcarraldo*," *Journal of Latin American Lore* 11, no. 2 (1985): 129.
2. *Fitzcarraldo* is not the first film to document such an engineering feat. A French documentary, *La croisière jaune* (1934), directed by André Sauvage, a promotional record of an expedition sponsored by Citroën intended to advertise the advanced technology of their automobiles, includes scenes involving the feat of taking the cars across the Himalayas. The vehicles were disassembled and their parts toted by Sherpas through the mountain passes. The use of native labor to facilitate the penetration of Western tech-

nology into other worlds, a hoary trope to be sure, is used in both films. See Charles Musser, "Engaging with Reality: Documentary," in *The Oxford History of World Cinema*, ed. Geoffrey Nowell-Smith (Oxford: Oxford University Press, 1996), 322. Thanks to Hisham Bizri for telling me about this film.

3. A very brief quotation from another piece of classical instrumental music occurs, this time diegetically, near the film's end, a quotation from Beethoven's *Emperor* Concerto, discussed below.
4. Lutz P. Koepnick, "Colonial Forestry: Sylvan Politics in Werner Herzog's *Aguirre* and *Fitzcarraldo*," *New German Critique* 60 (1993): 135–36: "Herzog promotes nature to the role of an actor in and of itself. . . . Herzog's films tend to represent nature as a text abounding with inscriptions of human desire. Within Herzog's expressionist vocabulary of nature, however, the jungle seems to denote a text that frustrates all hermeneutic efforts from the outset; with course *[sic]* brutality, the chaotic diversity of the rain forest exposes the systematic inappropriateness of Western routines of cognition and ordering. . . . Herzog's rain forest delineates a unique training ground for sentiments of sublime terror."
5. Werner Herzog, *Fitzcarraldo: The Original Story*, trans. Martje Herzog and Alan Greenberg (San Francisco: Fjord Press, 1982), 23, in his original story for the film, described the opening shot as follows: "As immense as an ocean extending to the edge of the universe, the jungle stretches out, steaming, as on the morning of Creation, still indistinct, full of animal noise. A music swells up, magnificent, breathtaking, and measured, as a hundred million birds awaken far below our feet. The earth lies in wait, calmly and patiently, but the sky begins to quiver as if this were some painful quaking of the heavens, something like the birth throes of heaven."
6. Oscar Hammerstein I held similar views. The following is quoted from an interview in Vincent Sheean, *Oscar Hammerstein I: The Life and Exploits of an Impresario* (New York: Simon & Schuster, 1956), 252–53, as cited by Dolkart, "Civilization's Aria," 131: "Grand opera is, I truly believe, the most elevating influence upon modern society, after religion. . . . I sincerely believe that nothing will make better citizenship than familiarity with grand opera. *It lifts one so out of the sordid affairs of life and makes material things seem so petty, so inconsequential, it places one for the time being, at least, in a higher and better world. . . .* [Opera] will establish a brotherhood of art which knows not race or creed and makes all the civilized world akin; that will erect a shrine of beauty in form, color, and tone, before which all may bend the knee" (emphasis added). To be sure, Hammerstein seems oblivious of the material reality that makes grand opera possible, and that in turn preserves it as elite entertainment.
7. Opera has long been linked to film, beginning in the silent era. See Joengwon Joe and Rose Theresa, eds., *Between Opera and Cinema* (New York: Routledge, 2002); Jeremy Tambling, *Opera, Ideology, and Film* (New York: St. Martin's Press, 1987); and Marcia J. Citron, *Opera on Screen* (New Haven: Yale University Press, 2000).
8. Sarah Bernhardt (1844–1923) was the most famous actress of her age, with a career that spanned six decades. She toured widely in Europe and the United States; in 1886 she made one trip to South America, including a visit to Lima, her closest approach to the film's setting. In 1877, Bernhardt had performed in Victor Hugo's *Hernani*, the source

for Verdi's opera. Cross-dressed, she played the title role in *Hamlet* in 1899 and toured it across Europe for two years. Interested in modern technology, she recorded her voice and, late in her career, made eight films, of which five were hits; she also made a number of home movies between 1913 and 1915. Bernhardt starred in several films whose subjects had been used for opera, including *La Tosca* (1908; reprising a stage role she first performed in 1887); *La dame aux camélias* (1911), the source for *La traviata;* and *Adrienne Lecouvreur* (1913). At the time of her death at age seventy-eight she was at work on a film, *La voyante* (The Fortune), which was never completed. Bernhardt, after seeing the final cut of her greatest film hit, the seven-reel *La Reine Elizabeth* (1912), is reputed to have exclaimed: "I am immortal! I am film!" On Bernhardt's film career, see Ruth Brandon, *Being Divine: A Biography of Sarah Bernhardt* (London: Secker & Warburg, 1991), 433–35. In real life, Caruso and Bernhardt only once performed at the same event, though not together: a war benefit at the Metropolitan Opera House on April 17, 1917, together with Frances Alda. See Francis Robinson, *Caruso: His Life in Pictures* (New York: Studio Publications in association with Thomas Y. Crowell, 1957), 90–91, which reproduces the program.

9. The film's consistent dependence on the displaced singing voice is mirrored in the fact that *Fitzcarraldo* was actually filmed with dialogue spoken in English; the German "original" is dubbed.
10. Herzog, *Fitzcarraldo: The Original Story,* 11–14, 17–18. Numerous differences exist between Herzog's original story and the finished film.
11. Werner Herzog, *Herzog on Herzog,* ed. Paul Cronin (London: Faber & Faber, 2002), 188. Indeed, for Herzog, it is precisely the plausible within the implausibility of opera that attracts him. "It matters little that most of the libretti are bad or . . . [even] a true catastrophe. In fact, so many of the opera plots are not even within the calculus of probability; it would be like winning the lottery jackpot five consecutive times over. And yet, when the music is playing, the stories do make sense. Their strong inner truths shine through and they seem utterly plausible" (ibid., 259). Since making *Fitzcarraldo,* Herzog has directed a number of opera productions throughout Europe, as well as in Japan and the United States. For a list, current to 2002, see Beat Presser, ed. and photog., *Werner Herzog* (Berlin: Jovis Verlag and Arte Edition, 2002), 119.
12. The situation is similar to an operatic drag-act performed by Larry, Moe, and Curly in the Three Stooges' short *Micro-Phonies* (1945). The music they attempt to lip-sync is the sextet from *Lucia,* or as they would have it, the sextet from *Lucy.*
13. Oscar Wilde wrote *Salomé* for Bernhardt. In 1892 the play, in French, was in rehearsal for a London premiere, but the Lord Chancellor banned it; the play opened in Paris in 1896, by which time Wilde was in prison. See Brandon, *Being Devine,* 344. An acquaintance seeing Bernhardt in old age, not long before her death, wrote that she looked "both tragic and sinister" (ibid., 429).
14. Pulling a riverboat over a steep hill is—obviously enough—absurdly comic, all the more given the extraordinary seriousness, utterly nonironic, with which Fitzcarraldo engages in his harebrained scheme. The feat is also operatic, a fact not lost on Herzog: "I pulled the ship over the mountain not for the sake of realism. . . . What you actually see is a very stylized thing. It looks like an operatic event, like a dream-event, and that's what's

so strange about it. It's not really a paradox" (quoted in Guido Henkel, "Werner Herzog: The Real Fitzcarraldo," *DVD Review* [November 1, 1999], online review, www.dvdreview.com/1999/11/werner-herzog-the-real-fitzcarraldo/ [accessed in 2004]).

15. The French actor Jean-Claude Dreyfuss plays the part of Bernhardt, whom he had previously impersonated. (Herzog's commentary accompanying the DVD release of *Fitzcarraldo* refers to the actor as a transvestite.) See further Dolkart, "Civilization's Aria," 132; and Presser, *Werner Herzog,* 38. For more on Herzog's opera directing, see *Herzog on Herzog,* 253–54, 258–60.
16. There are historical antecedents to the cross-dressing, as in an 1865 production of an English burlesque of *Ernani* by William Brough, *Ernani, or, The Horn of a Dilemma,* in which the two male characters, including Ernani himself, were played by women. See Roberta Montemorra Marvin, "Verdian Opera Burlesqued: A Glimpse into Mid-Victorian Theatrical Culture," *Cambridge Opera Journal* 15, no. 1 (2003): 47. Marvin points out that *Ernani* was the Verdi opera most subjected to burlesquing, though *Il trovatore* and *La traviata* were also popularly mocked. On the extraordinary popularity of *Ernani* in the United States for several decades beginning in 1847, only three years after the opera's premiere, see George Martin, "Verdi Onstage in the Unites States: *Ernani,*" *Opera Quarterly* 20, no. 2 (Spring 2003): 171–96. In short, there is good historical reason for Herzog's choice of this opera. Not the least sign of *Ernani*'s popularity at the time of *Fitzcarraldo*'s setting is evident in the fact that the Victor Talking Machine Company by 1912 had released no fewer than forty-five recordings of its arias and choruses (ibid., 183).
17. See also the discussion of this scene in Roger Hillman, *Unsettling Scores: German Film, Music, and Ideology* (Bloomington: Indiana University Press, 2005), 141–44.
18. Dolkart, "Civilization's Aria," 125: "The most significant and enduring lore embraced by elites in Latin America is the division between civilization and barbarism. The separation into two Latin Americas, one civilized, that is positive and progressive, another barbaric, that is negative and regressive, has shaped the foreigner's views, as well as the self-image of the region, as has no other concept." Dolkart explains that opera in particular constituted a sign of civilization among nineteenth-century Latin American elites, concerning which see Ronald H. Dolkart, "Elitelore at the Opera: The Teatro Colón of Buenos Aires," *Journal of Latin American Lore* 9, no. 2 (1983): 231–50.
19. Werner Herzog, "The Minnesota Declaration: Truth and Fact in Documentary Cinema," in Herzog, *Herzog on Herzog,* 301: "There are deeper strata of truth in cinema, and there is such a thing as poetic, ecstatic truth. It is mysterious and elusive, and can be reached only through fabrication and imagination and stylization."
20. Ulrike Sieglohr, "Excess and Yearning: The Operatic in Werner Schroeter's Cinema," in *A Night in at the Opera: Media Representations of Opera,* ed. Jeremy Tambling (London: John Libbey, 1994), 197: "Schroeter's conception of cinema relies on intense stylization, deploying manneristic prolonged gestures. The characters are framed in sumptuous tableaux compositions and a highly manipulated post-synchronized soundtrack underscores the visuals."
21. Werner Herzog, *Conquest of the Useless: Reflections from the Making of "Fitzcarraldo,"* trans. Krishna Winston (New York: Ecco, 2010), 175.
22. Herzog, in his commentary accompanying the DVD release of *Fitzcarraldo.*

23. Herzog, in his commentary to the *Fitzcarraldo* DVD, indicates that the music is "authentic," but it was recorded in Burundi; acknowledging that the African drumming is "totally different" from the kind of drumming employed by the Indians native to the rain forest, he chose it because of what he terms the "certain danger" and "certain menace" he associates with its sound.

24. Caruso recorded the aria in 1904. See J. Freestone and H. J. Drummond, *Enrico Caruso: His Recorded Legacy* (London: Sidgwick & Jackson, 1960), 27.

25. Martin Scherzinger, in a private communication: "One reason the Burundi segment synchronizes so easily—too easily—with the phonograph's song fragment is because both are hyperbolic indexes of contrasting culture: 'Western' music as individualized expressive song, primarily harmonic-melodic in construction (mechanically produced even); non-Western music as functional, primarily rhythmic, collectivist (apparently not mechanically produced, but of course, the latter music stops like a recording stops, not like a group of performers stop—an indication that mischief of another sort is afoot). This extreme, almost mannerist, presentation of dualized musical worlds must work well musically because the one fills the obvious inadequacy of the other. This is why the phonograph sounds so isolated when the drumming is switched off."

26. Herzog, *Conquest of the Useless*, 175. Compare this scene in the film with Michael Taussig, *Mimesis and Alterity: A Particular History of the Senses* (New York: Routledge, 1993), 194, an account by Richard Oglesby Marsh of the impact of a phonograph when first experienced by the Kuna Indians in Panama's Darién province during the Marsh Darién expedition in 1924–25, which includes the following: "After my experiences in the Darién, I would never think of going into a 'wild' Indian territory without a phonograph. . . . That victrola, our fireworks, outboard motors and dynamite were four essentials without which we could never have traversed interior Darién." By Marsh's telling, the Indians were as much interested in the apparatus itself as in the sound emanating from its horn.

27. Caruso recorded the aria three times between 1903 and 1907, of which the last recording seems to be the one used in the film. For details on the recordings, see Freestone and Drummond, *Enrico Caruso: His Recorded Legacy*, 17–18, 27–28, 36–37.

28. Herzog, *Fitzcarraldo: The Original Story*, 26, describes the scene as follows: "Among [the Indian children] an unusually long-legged, wooly pig, a real sprinter, has pushed its way to the front in breathless curiosity. Drunk with sleep, Fitzcarraldo gropes with one hand toward a little table, as if it were wandering away in a dream, upon which sits one of the very earliest phonographs. It is one of Edison's machines with needle and horn which, in those days, worked by sensing the grooved cylinder. The machine starts to move, the morning concert begins: these are the first recordings of Enrico Caruso, terribly scratched, but of an unspeakably dignified beauty, sad and strong and moving. Fitzcarraldo now opens his eyes completely. 'When one day my opera house is built, you will have your own box and an armchair covered in velvet,' he tells the pig. It stands there as if rooted to the ground, listening." In the film, Herzog employs a disk phonograph, aptly so, since Caruso recorded exclusively for Victor, which produced only disk recordings (Edison produced both cylinder and disk records and phonographs), details regarding which are discussed in chapter 3, below.

29. The penetration of the jungle by the riverboat, traveling where no white man has ventured previously, anticipates the resolutely male enterprise of creating the deep gash in the jungle, a literal deflowering, clearing the way for the boat to, as it were, mount the mountain. The scene resonates with the iconography of Watteau's *Embarkation from the Isle of Cythera,* in which a boatload of would-be lovers has penetrated a landmass whose form is analogous to the shape of two legs. At the shoreline stands a small hill, replete with a Venus figure atop the mound. Koepnick, "Colonial Forestry," 157, referring to Herzog's "green essentialism," argues that he clear-cuts forest and levels hills for the land journey of the riverboat in the name of filmic authenticity. Lutz regards Herzog as "a master in the jargon of authenticity," summing up (158): "Herzog, in other words, uses the diegetic text of *Fitzcarraldo* to exercise his own colonial practice, an exercise that cannot but forfeit its alleged aspiration to obliterate the grounds and politics of what I call here colonial forestry." See also John E. Davidson, "Contacting the Other: Traces of Migrational Colonialism and the Imperial Agent in Werner Herzog's *Fitzcarraldo,*" *Film & History* 24, nos. 3–4 (1994): 66–83; and by the same author, "As Others Put Plays upon the Stage: *Aguirre,* Neocolonialism, and the New German Cinema," *New German Critique* 60 (Fall 1993): 101–30; see also Les Blank and James Bogan, eds., *Burden of Dreams: Screenplay, Journals, Reviews, Photographs* (Berkeley: North Atlantic Books, 1984). For Herzog's response, see *Herzog on Herzog,* 169–70, 177–84, 188–89.
30. The trademark was established in 1902. See Friedrich A. Kittler, *Gramophone, Film, Typewriter,* trans. Geoffrey Winthrop-Young and Michael Wutz (Stanford: Stanford University Press, 1999), 69. For an illustrated account of the logo, see Leonard Petts, *The Story of "Nipper" and the "His Master's Voice" Picture Painted by Francis Barraud* (Bournemouth, UK: Talking Machine Review International, 1973/1983).
31. Herzog, *Herzog on Herzog,* 177: "I wish we had shot in Dolby stereo because the sound of this boat [being pulled up the hill] was so stunning and so amazing no sound engineer could ever have invented what we heard on location. There is a mysterious truth in what we did, and I wanted the audience in a position where they could trust their own eyes." For more on the discursive potential of Dolby, see Michel Chion, *Audio-Vision: Sound on Screen,* ed. and trans. Claudia Gorbman (New York: Columbia University Press, 1994), 152–56. Herzog, in his commentary accompanying the DVD release of *Fitzcarraldo,* refers to the scene as a "fever dream"—despite its documentary look—"having the quality of farce." He also refers to it as looking "like an operatic event" and later as "an event out of Italian opera." Cf. Peter Conrad, *A Song of Love and Death: The Meaning of Opera* (New York: Poseidon Press, 1987), 236: "Opera is the most grandiose technological dream money can buy."
32. Caruso recorded the sextet three times, the ensembles varying each time, in 1908, 1912, and 1917 (here with Amelia Galli-Curci, Minnie Egener, Marcel Journet, Giuseppe De Luca, and Angelo Badà). The film seems to use the 1917 recording. See Freestone and Drummond, *Enrico Caruso: His Recorded Legacy,* 40–41, 75, and 104. For a photograph of the ensemble taken the day of the recording session in January 1917, see Robinson, *Caruso: His Life in Pictures,* 99. The *Lucia* sextet, performed as an instrumental, was often used to accompany scenes in silent films—in other words, films made at the same time of *Fitzcarraldo*'s setting.

33. Chion, *Audio-Vision,* 54: "The cinema is a realist art: but it remains that this realist art has progressed only by means of straining against its own principle, through forceful doses of unrealism." On Herzog's obsession with dreams, dreamers, and dreaming, see also Michael Goodwin, "Up the River with Werner Herzog," in Blank and Bogan, *Burden of Dreams,* 212–34.

34. Theodor W. Adorno and Hanns Eisler, *Composing for the Films* (London: Athlone Press, 1994), 75. The text for this monograph was revised for its appearance in a German edition. The somewhat clumsy sentence as rendered in the original English is rearranged and simplified in Adorno, *Gesammelte Schriften,* ed. Rolf Tiedemann et al. (Frankfurt am Main: Suhrkamp Verlag, 1976), 15:75: "Kinomusik hat den Gestus des Kindes, das im Dunkeln vor sich hinsingt."

35. Re the riverboat "configured to be suggestive of an opera house," as well as a brief comment concerning the Beethoven citation, see Hillman, *Unsettling Scores,* 144–45.

36. Herzog, *Fitzcarraldo: The Original Story,* 155–59, calls for an unspecified scene from *Die Walküre.*

37. See on this point Dolkart, "Civilization's Aria," 141. Susan Sontag, "Notes on 'Camp,'" in *Against Interpretation and Other Essays* (New York: Noonday Press/Farrar, Straus & Giroux, 1966), 275, specifies: "The essence of Camp is its love of the unnatural: of artifice and exaggeration," then provides a shopping list of canonic camp at the time that includes among its musical artifacts *Swan Lake,* Strauss operas (she cites *Der Rosenkavalier*), and, among the Italian works, *Il trovatore* and, as she gives it, "Bellini's operas" (277, 280, 286).

38. Alexander Kluge, in his 1983 film *The Power of Emotion (Die Macht der Gefühle),* took on the institutionality of opera in a scathing critique. See also the book volume, with numerous stills, by Kluge, *Die Macht der Gefühle* (Frankfurt am Main: Zweitausendeins, 1984). Caryl Flynn has devoted an excellent essay to this film, "Undoing Act 5: History, Bodies, and Operatic Remains: Kluge's *The Power of Emotion,*" in *The New German Cinema: Music, History, and the Matter of Style* (Berkeley: University of California Press, 2004), 138–69. As she explains, "Kluge turns to [opera] productions, focusing on the material *behind* the fantasies and *underneath* the spectacle, blasting them out in so many directions" (139, original emphasis). For Kluge, she continues, opera "is an industry that capitalizes on human misery, glorifies defeat, and disguises the material aspects of its production. Especially cruel is how tragic opera encourages audiences to buy into its fatalistic worldview, and Kluge aggressively directs his line of fire in that direction" (141).

39. Jacques Attali, *Noise: The Political Economy of Music,* trans. Brian Massumi (Minneapolis: University of Minnesota Press, 1985), 6. Attali's insight is indebted to Adorno, whose work he knows well. See Theodor W. Adorno, *Aesthetic Theory,* ed. Gretel Adorno and Rolf Tiedemann, trans. Robert Hullot-Kentor (Minneapolis: University of Minnesota Press, 1997), 53–54 and 228.

40. Rainer Maria Rilke, *An Unofficial Rilke: Poems 1912–1926,* ed. and trans. Michael Hamburger (London: Anvil, 1981), 12. My thanks to Richard Kurth for bringing this text to my attention.

41. Holly Rogers, "Fitzcarraldo's Search for Aguirre: Music and Text in the Amazonian Films of Werner Herzog," *Journal of the Royal Musical Association* 129 (2004): 102, points

out that Fitzcarraldo's operatic music is "supported by the pillars of Western tonality, a music that constantly drives towards closure," which she appropriately contrasts with the acoustic circularity of the music provided by Popol Vuh against which Caruso is heard. And yet such sonic closure is repeatedly set in opposition to the failure textually narrated by the arias and ensembles. In other words, the dream-claims of the operatic excerpts employed in the film are consistently mediated by their own internal dialectics: outright failure (the narrative) and apparent success (musical climax/closure). This fact notwithstanding, opera serves in the film as a protest against the overdetermined inadequacy of modern life.

João Pedro Cachopo, "Tales of a Technologically Mediated Passion: Re-reading Beineix's *Diva* (1981), Herzog's *Fitzcarraldo* (1982), and Fellini's *E la nave va* (1983)," in *Kinetophone* [online journal] 1 (2014): 69, suggests of my account of the film in an earlier published version of this chapter (see Acknowledgments) that "in order to rescue opera—at least part of it—from instrumental rationality one could do nothing else but resort to the dichotomy between opera *qua* spectacle and opera *qua* music, and side with the latter. Only as music (as a sonic manifestation rather than as an institutional practice) could opera stand for the grandiose uselessness of art. If anywhere, the core of cinema's affinity with opera would lie in the *promesse du bonheur* kept safe within this uselessness, a major trait of beauty at least since the first paragraphs of Kant's third *Critique*." Cachopo's thoughtful, intellectually nuanced essay critically engages previous readings of the three films mentioned in his title, mine included; his take is well worth incorporating into any consideration of these films and, for that matter, of opera more generally. There's not space here either to account adequately for his reading, let alone to respond, but I very much appreciate the argument he advances. In the end, he and I are pursuing in part some similar questions. Perhaps the greatest difference between us is encapsulated in the following remark (ibid., 73): "I would maintain that the link between opera and the darker side of modernity is hardly less apparent when it comes to music than when any other aspect of opera is at stake. . . . Neither music nor image could arguably rescue opera from the clutches of modernity. But, before making such a claim, I would probably be willing to question, too, the extent to which it is fair to assume that opera should be 'rescued,' or, in other words, the extent to which the dialectic between guilt and expiation is the best framework with which to put the relationship between opera and modernity in perspective."

EXCURSUS: OPERA, MONUMENTALITY, AND LOOKING AT LOOKING

1. Henri Lefebvre, *The Production of Space*, trans. Donald Nicholson-Smith (Malden, MA: Blackwell, 1991), 42.
2. See Emily Thompson, *The Soundscape of Modernity: Architectural Acoustics and the Culture of Listening in America, 1900–1933* (Cambridge, MA: MIT Press, 2002), 1–57; and Evan Baker, *From the Score to the Stage: An Illustrated History of Continental Opera Production and Staging* (Chicago: University of Chicago Press, 2013). The mid-eighteenth-century, 450-seat, outlandishly baroque Margrave Opera House in Bayreuth, not for nothing a UNESCO World Heritage site, anticipates the far larger if similarly ornate

opera theaters built in the principal urban centers of the nineteenth century (although the Margrave was a court theater, it was nonetheless located in an urban setting). For a detailed description of the building, see http://whc.unesco.org/en/list/1379 (accessed November 22, 2012).

3. Lefebvre, *Production of Space,* 220. On the design and history of the Paris Opéra, see Christopher Curtis Mean, *Charles Garnier's Paris Opéra: Architectural Empathy and the Renaissance of French Classicism* (New York: Architectural History Foundation; Cambridge, MA: MIT Press, 1991). Regarding the Grand Escalier and Grand Foyer designs, see 76, 80–81, 93–97.
4. A sense of the importance of the Opéra to the layout of the district surrounding the structure is evident in aerial photographs; see Mean, *Charles Garnier's Paris Opéra,* 108.
5. Lefebvre, *Production of Space,* 220.
6. See Ruth Solie, "Fictions of the Opera Box," in *Music in Other Words: Victorian Conversations* (Berkeley: University of California Press, 2004), 187–218, a study of the opera-box trope in novels by American authors between about 1870 and 1920, that is, during the so-named Gilded Age.
7. See www.google.com/search?q=wedding+photographs,+running+through+mud&client=safari&rls=en&tbm=isch&tbo=u&source=univ&sa=X&ei=QwMiU9ibEcKbygGJj4CICA&ved=0CCYQsAQ&biw=1420&bih=1206 (accessed March 13, 2014).
8. Lefebvre, *Production of Space,* 50 (original emphasis).
9. James H. Johnson, *Listening in Paris: A Cultural History* (Berkeley: University of California Press, 1996); and Richard Sennett, *The Fall of Public Man* (New York: Vintage, 1978), 18–19, 206.
10. See Mary Cowling, *The Artist as Anthropologist: The Representation of Type and Character in Victorian Art* (Cambridge: Cambridge University Press, 1989).
11. Theodor W. Adorno, "The Natural History of the Theatre," in *Quasi una fantasia: Essays in Modern Music,* trans. Rodney Livingstone (London: Verso, 1992), 74.
12. Lefebvre, *Production of Space,* 220.
13. Adorno, "Natural History of the Theatre," 74.
14. Carolyn Abbate has written extensively and well on this matter; see *In Search of Opera* (Princeton: Princeton University Press, 2001), especially 147–60. Brian Kane's *Sound Unseen: Acousmatic Sound in Theory and Practice* (New York: Oxford University Press, 2014) is a lengthy and brilliant investigation of the subject, including extensive engagement of the work by Pierre Schaeffer and Michel Chion. His intention is "to develop a theory of acousmatic listening as a historical and cultural practice with clearly defined characteristics" (7). On the relation between early phonography and "silent" (i.e., nontalking) cinema, and in particular the impact of the former on the latter, see Tom Gunning, "Doing for the Eye What the Phonograph Does for the Ear," in *The Sounds of Early Cinema,* ed. Richard Abel and Rick Altman (Bloomington: Indiana University Press, 2001), 13–31.

3. CARUSO, PHONOGRAPHY, AND OPERATIC FIDELITIES

1. Shellac is a nontoxic bio-plastic, a secretion of the lac insect native to India, Thailand, and Burma. Shellac was a critical component of phonograph disks from the early twen-

tieth century into the 1940s, after which vinyl disks took control of the market. On the ecology of shellac manufacture and the use of shellac in the making of sound recordings, see the fascinating study by Jacob Smith, *Eco-Sonic Media* (Berkeley: University of California Press, 2015).

2. Regarding the early history of the Victor Talking Machine Company and its Red Seal label, see Roland Gelatt, *The Fabulous Phonograph, 1877–1977*, 2nd rev. ed. (New York: Macmillan, 1977), 130–57.
3. The numbers specified in the subtitle of this and subsequent editions are in fact only approximate, having been rounded up or down to create a tractable evenness.
4. The first three editions were published in 1912; thereafter, 1917 (4th), 1919 (5th), 1921 (6th), 1924 (7th), 1929 (8th), 1936 (10th), and 1976 (13th, the final edition). (I have been unable to locate the 9th, 11th, and 12th editions.) The book originally sold for seventy-five cents. The Library of Congress "National Jukebox" reproduces the 5th edition online, to which are linked audio files of hundreds of the recordings listed in the catalogue: www.loc.gov/jukebox/ and www.loc.gov/jukebox/victor-book-of-the-opera/interactive.
5. In 1922, Victor released its first jigsaw-puzzle advertising, disk-shaped and in color, replete with a Victrola Red Seal label that reads, "The Names That Everybody Knows, *[sic]* Are In The *Victor* Catalogue." Headshots of Victor recording artists, mostly opera singers, form the puzzle pieces, Caruso receiving best billing. The puzzle is reproduced in color in Arnold Schwartzman, *Phono-Graphics: The Visual Paraphernalia of the Talking Machine* (San Francisco: Chronicle Books, 1993), 67. In 1921, the L. H. Soper Company of Waterville, Maine, produced a cardboard fan advertising Victor/Victrola; the ad imagery featured opera singers in costume. (One of these fans was available for auction on eBay as recently as May 2014.)
6. According to Eleanor Selfridge-Field, "Experiments with Melody and Meter, or the Effects of Music: The Edison-Bingham Music Research," *Musical Quarterly* 81, no. 2 (1997): 309, Edison's National Phonograph record labels did not include performers' names until 1915. Regarding primary source material on Edison's phonograph (invention, improvements, marketing potential) as perceived in 1877–78, see *The Papers of Thomas A. Edison*, vol. 3: *Menlo Park: The Early Years, April 1876–December 1877*, ed. Robert A. Rosenberg et al.; and vol. 4: *The Wizard of Menlo Park 1878*, ed. Paul B. Israel et al. (Baltimore: Johns Hopkins University Press, 1994 and 1998, respectively). The papers for the years at the century's end, when Edison returned once again to the phonograph, have not as yet been published. A great deal of information concerning the development, technical details, marketing, sales figures, and cost of Edison disk phonographs and record manufacture is available in George L. Frow, *The Edison Disc Phonographs and the Diamond Discs: A History with Illustrations*, rev. ed. (Los Angeles: Mulholland Press, 2001). Frow provides extensive information concerning the many different phonograph models Edison produced from the early teens through the end of all production in 1929.
7. Theodor W. Adorno, "Analytical Study of the *NBC Music Appreciation* Hour," in *Current of Music: Elements of a Radio Theory*, ed. Robert Hullot-Kentor (Cambridge: Polity, 2009), 163–215, provides a withering critique of such efforts. The NBC program was broadcast between 1928 and 1942 and was linked to public school classroom music education.

8. *The Victor Book of the Opera,* 3rd ed. (Camden, NJ: Victor Talking Machine Company, 1912), 7.
9. Ibid.
10. On the cost of recordings, see further Timothy Day, *A Century of Recorded Music: Listening to Musical History* (New Haven: Yale University Press, 2000), 103; and Walter L. Welch and Leah Brodbeck Stenzel Burt, *From Tinfoil to Stereo: The Acoustic Years of the Recording Industry, 1877–1929* (Gainesville: University of Florida Press, 1994), 113–14.

Regarding the Caruso discography, see John Richard Bolig, *The Recordings of Enrico Caruso: A Discography* (Dover: Eldridge Reeves Johnson Memorial, Delaware State Museum, 1973), listing 496 recordings between c. 1901 and Caruso's last recording session, September 16, 1920. The first Victor recordings date from a recording session on February 1, 1904; although the earliest Victor Caruso recordings were issued in 1903, they were made in Italy by the Gramophone and Typewriter Company. The number of recordings released by Victor during Caruso's lifetime, upward of three hundred, was considerably smaller than the total he recorded for Victor over the course of many sessions. Caruso's Victor records accounted for all but thirty-two of his total output. James P. Kraft, *Stage to Studio: Musicians and the Sound Revolution, 1890–1950* (Baltimore: Johns Hopkins University Press, 1996), 62, states that for the initial 1904 session, Caruso was paid the handsome sum of $4,000 for ten "sides," though later royalties far exceeded such initial payouts. (Throughout his career, Caruso reaped ample financial benefits; his record royalties by themselves made him a multimillionaire.) J. Freestone and H. J. Drummond's *Enrico Caruso: His Recorded Legacy* (London: Sidgwick & Jackson, 1960) is particularly valuable for the extended commentary provided for each recording. See also Francis Robinson, *Caruso: His Life in Pictures,* discography by John Secrist (New York: Studio Publications, 1957), 149–60; and Aida Favia-Artsay, *Caruso on Records* (Valhalla, NY: Historic Record, 1965).

The University of California/Santa Barbara, partnering with the Library of Congress "National Jukebox," produces an online *Encyclopedic Discography of Victor Recordings,* including thousands of audio files linked to the catalogue, principally acoustic recordings from 1900 to 1925, though the project will eventually extend to the end of the 78-rpm era in the 1950s. See http://victor.library.ucsb.edu/. The resources section of the website includes a link to the 1912 first edition of *The Victor Book of the Opera.* For a brief account of the process for making acoustic recordings, see David Suisman, *Selling Sounds: The Commercial Revolution in American Music* (Cambridge, MA: Harvard University Press, 2009), 107–8.

For details of the history of Victor's Red Seal label, introduced in the United States in 1903, including Red Seal advertising campaigns, see William Howard Kenney, *Recorded Music in American Life: The Photograph and Popular Memory, 1890–1945* (New York: Oxford University Press, 1999), 44–64.
11. Lisa Gitelman, *Always Already New: Media, History, and the Data of Culture* (Cambridge, MA: MIT Press, 2006), 62–63. She continues: "Perhaps because they are media in addition to being technologies and commodities, phonographs and records seem to have possessed an extraordinary 'interpretative flexibility,' a range of available meanings wherein neither their inventor nor the reigning authorities on music possessed any special authorial status."

12. Suisman, *Selling Sounds*, 112.

13. Regarding the collapse of record sales during the Great Depression, see David Morton, *Off the Record: The Technology and Culture of Sound Recording in America* (New Brunswick, NJ: Rutgers University Press, 2000), 28–29; and Frow, *Edison Disc Phonographs and Diamond Discs*, 87–94, on the decline and end of Edison's National Phonograph Company.

14. *Victor Book of the Opera*, 3rd ed. (1912), 7. Caruso's voice was well suited for the limitations of early acoustic recording. Stated broadly, tenors recorded best, sopranos worst. According to Andre Millard, *America on Record: A History of Recorded Sound*, 2nd ed. (Cambridge: Cambridge University Press, 2005), 59–60, Caruso's voice "emerged from the horn with such clarity and power that it seemed to fill the room with music. Unlike sopranos and bass voices, the full range of the tenor fell within the narrow band of sound frequencies picked up by the recording horn. The warmth of Caruso's tone and the emotion of his singing were also captured on disc and faithfully recreated through the horn of the gramophone." Regarding the difficulty of recording women's voices, sopranos especially, see Gitelman, *Always Already New*, 70–71.

15. *Victor Book of the Opera*, 3rd ed. (1912), 7.

16. Ibid.

17. On the wide availability of recordings through retail outlets (department stores, music shops, hardware stores, sporting goods emporiums, dry goods shops, drug stores, and the like), see Gitelman, *Always Already New*, 82–83.

18. *Victor Book of the Opera*, 3rd ed. (1912), 9.

19. *The Victrola Book of the Opera*, 7th ed. (Camden, NJ: Victor Talking Machine Company, 1924), 12–13.

20. Ibid., 13–14.

21. Gitelman, *Always Already New*, 76, however, points out that many small American towns sported so-named opera houses, without necessary reference to opera proper; in other words, the noun *opera* had considerable currency beyond reference to opera as such. Gitelman: "*Allusions* to opera operated as cultural currency, circulating as 'consensus builders' and 'distinction makers' in different contexts" (original emphasis). She adds that "opera was newly a style of material possession, rather than just a kind of music, and opera records apparently did much to elevate the medium of recorded sound in the public eye, even if popular music and other 'Coney Island' fare formed the real bread and butter of the incipient recording industry" (78).

22. Victor signed contracts with singers of the first rank; Edison by intention did not, regarding this to be a poor investment, a bet that in the end served his company poorly. See Welch and Burt, *From Tinfoil to Stereo*, 131–33.

23. Suisman, *Selling Sounds*, 111, points out that Victor held off issuing double-sided records until 1923, "for no other reason than to present each as a singular work of art. Taken to its logical extreme, this aim even implied a kind of counter-narrative to consumer society itself—an illusion of uniqueness based on mass-produced intimacy." See further 110–14. (Suisman is incorrect re the date; the 1917 fourth edition of *The Victrola Book of the Opera* already advertised two-sided disks.)

24. *New Victor Records*, March 1919 [Victor Talking Machine Company monthly catalogue], 3.

25. *Victor Book of the Opera,* 3rd ed. (1912), 16.

26. Ibid., 33. These sorts of comments are less evident in subsequent editions that I have examined, sometimes dropped altogether, sometimes abbreviated. By the 7th edition (1924), the format has changed considerably. The list of Victor recordings is now placed at the end of each opera's description, as is the English text of arias; further, comparatively few aria texts are provided, unlike the case with the first editions. The 8th edition (1929) restores the practice of listing recordings within the description of the narrative.

    Concerning Victor's promotion of Caruso to celebrity status, see Suisman, *Selling Sounds,* 125–45; and on 128: "Many singers and performers made records, but Victor advanced Caruso as a symbol of sound recording technology itself—both its artistic potential as a medium and its value as an industry."

27. Lewis Foreman, *Systematic Discography* (North Haven, CT: Linnet Books, 1974), 13.

28. The Columbia recordings were advertised in the October 2, 1929, issue of *Punch, or the London Charivari,* p. xxxi.

29. *Grand Opera with a Victrola,* arranged by Albert E. Wier, published with record annotations by courtesy of the Victor Talking Machine Company (New York: D. Appleton, 1915–16).

30. Wayne Koestenbaum, *The Queen's Throat: Opera, Homosexuality, and the Mystery of Desire* (New York: Poseidon Press, 2003).

31. *New Victor Records,* March 1919, 12–13.

32. Carolyn Abbate, *In Search of Opera* (Princeton: Princeton University Press, 2001), 18: "Opera in performance is an embodiment, which makes the force of music palpable."

33. *New Victor Records,* March 1919, 23.

34. The advertisement also ran in the *Cosmopolitan* 72, no. 3 (March 1922): 1, its text replicating the prediction made in a short essay, "The Talking Phonograph," published in *Scientific American* 37 (December 22, 1877): 384–85: "We have already pointed out the startling possibility of the voices of the dead being reheard through this device, and there is no doubt but that its capabilities are fully equal to other results just as astonishing. When it becomes possible as it doubtless will, to magnify the sound, the voices of such singers as Parepa and Titiens will not die with them, but will remain as long as the metal in which they may be embodied will last" (385). The singers referred to, both operatic sopranos, were recently deceased: Euphrosyne Parepa-Rosa (1836–74) and Thérèse Tietjens (1831–77).

35. *New Victor Records,* October 1922, 2.

36. Jason Stanyek and Benjamin Piekut, "Deadness: Technologies of the Intermundane," *TDR: The Drama Review* 54, no. 1, T205 (2010): 21–22, discuss the overdubbing of Caruso's 1907 recording of "Vesti la giubba" from Leoncavallo's *I Pagliacci,* a million-copy seller in its original release, and a remake they describe as what "may very well be the first case of a dead performer recording with live musicians" (22). A three-minute film short from British Pathé, filmed at HMV Studios, London, titled "Voice Grafting—The Latest Miracle of 'Sound' Science" (1932) shows the remake in progress. The film is available online at several sources, including www.britishpathe.com/video/voice-grafting (accessed October 23, 2013). The narrator refers to long-term sound engineering efforts to "revitalize" the voice of Caruso. The Stanyek and Piekut essay, theoretically

sophisticated and well historicized, principally focuses on the phenomenon of modern duet recordings with one of the performers singing anew from beyond the grave via a preexisting recording, the main example being Natalie Cole's "Unforgettable," recorded in 1991 in duet with Nat King Cole, her deceased father, from a recording of 1961.

37. Ibid., 15.

38. See, for example, the 2014 list, at www.forbes.com/dead-celebrities.

39. The Edison Company only began marketing disk-playing machines in 1912, and it stubbornly continued to produce cylinder recordings until 1929, the year Edison departed the recording industry altogether.

40. Emily Thompson, "Machines, Music, and the Quest for Fidelity: Marketing the Edison Phonograph in America, 1877–1925," *Musical Quarterly* 79, no. 1 (1995): 166n61.

41. *Edison and Music* (Orange, NJ: Thomas A. Edison, 1919), 15, 21. Selfridge-Field, "Experiments with Melody and Meter," 291: "In 1912, [Edison] took complete charge of all recording auditions and decisions. Management of recording operations must have consumed most of his waking hours over the next decade of his life, since he auditioned approximately 120,000 test recordings." Between 1903 and 1922 Edison published a sales catalogue under various names, *Edison Phonograph Monthly* being the title longest used, intended for the company's dealers: new record advertisements, promos for Edison artists, product pricing, recommended copy for print advertising, numerous stories about various ways dealers had found to market Edison phonographs and recordings, and, finally, photographs of window displays. The January 1913 issue (volume 11, no. 1), 6, for example, offers dealers the "Edison Window Display No. 27—Price $2.50," together with an accompanying text that opens: "Repeat the goodness of the Edison Phonograph often. You cannot tell it too often. You cannot tell it all at once. Window display advertising should be continuous to be successful." The same issue, 9–10, includes a story reprinted from the *Boston Journal* about a "Phonograph Used at Funeral," providing an indication of the "significant esteem in which the deceased man held the Phonograph." The totality of the service involved one hour of the deceased man's favorite music played on a phonograph placed at the head of the coffin, with a dedicated attendant responsible for the phonograph, all of this carried out according to the wishes of the decedent.

42. For additional information on phonograph prices, see Frow, *Edison Disc Phonographs and Diamond Discs,* 49–52 and 133–43; see also 286–88 concerning two recently discovered examples of these rare phonograph cabinets, a so-named French Gothic #1 and a French Gothic #2. Frow suggests that it's likely that only a single example of these models was ever made. The design is impractical: in order to change a record, a person of less than average height would need to stand on a stool. See also Thompson, "Machines, Music, and the Quest for Fidelity," 146. Regarding cheap machines, see Mark Katz, *Capturing Sound: How Technology Has Changed Music,* rev. ed. (Berkeley: University of California Press, 2010), 60; and Timothy C. Fabrizio and George F. Paul, *The Talking Machine: An Illustrated Compendium, 1877–1929,* 2nd ed., rev. and enlarged (Atglen, PA: Schiffer, 2005). For early sales figures of Victrolas (in 1911, 124,000 were sold) and more on phonograph prices, Victrolas and otherwise, see Millard, *America on Record,* 49 and 123–24, respectively.

43. Edison also marketed concrete furniture, refrigerators, fireplaces, stairways, bathtubs, and prefab houses; see Frow, *Edison Disc Phonographs and Diamond Discs,* 275–78; and Welch and Burt, *From Tinfoil to Stereo,* 143–44.
44. Mary Ann Doane, "The Indexical and the Concept of Medium Specificity," *differences: A Journal of Feminist Cultural Studies* 18, no. 1 (2007): 129.
45. Gilles Deleuze, *Cinema 2: The Time-Image,* trans. Hugh Tomlinson and Robert Galeta (Minneapolis: University of Minnesota Press, 1991), 81.
46. Jonathan Sterne, *The Audible Past: Cultural Origins of Sound Reproduction* (Durham, NC: Duke University Press, 2003), 310. See also Jacques Attali, *Noise: The Political Economy of Music,* trans. Brian Massumi (Minneapolis: University of Minnesota Press, 1985), 145, who argues that sound recording, record collecting especially, constitutes the stockpiling of other people's time; and Donald M. Lowe, *The History of Bourgeois Perception* (Chicago: University of Chicago Press, 1982), on temporality (including acute time consciousness) in modernity.
47. For accounts of the technological development of acoustic recording by Edison, as well as subsequent improvements, business issues, and assorted litigious competition, see Welch and Burt, *From Tinfoil to Stereo;* for a more general discussion of acoustic recording technology, see Morton, *Off the Record,* 13–29; and Day, *A Century of Recorded Music,* 6–12 and 16, for more on the advent of electrical recordings as regards increased frequency response over the acoustic predecessors. Concerning the relation of recorded sound fidelity to an imagined original in the early history of the phonograph record, see the lengthy discussion in Sterne, *Audible Past,* 215–86. The Victor Orthophonic models, first sold in 1924, were provided with an electrical drive mechanism and vacuum tubes already in use in both electrical recording and radio. Orthophonic phonographs were heavily advertised over the next several years, with emphasis placed on sound fidelity claiming to have closed the gap between live and recorded. For details, see Sterne's commentary, 275–76. The first Victrolas with an electric motor option were manufactured in 1913. Whereas the earliest models still used a horn—a more effective folded horn that improved both volume and frequency response—later models, called Electrolas, employed speakers.
48. According to Gelatt, *Fabulous Phonograph,* 142, "By 1912, Victor's annual advertising budget was to surpass $1,500,000." On the ability to discriminate between live performance and a recording, see John Mowitt, "The Sound of Music in the Era of Its Electronic Reproducibility," in *Music and Society: The Politics of Composition, Performance, and Reception,* ed. Richard Leppert and Susan McClary (Cambridge: Cambridge University Press, 1987), 173–97.
49. See the excellent discussion in Sterne, *Audible Past,* 259–66; and Welch and Burt, *From Tinfoil to Stereo,* 146–49.
50. Frow, *Edison Disc Phonographs and Diamond Discs,* 236.
51. Regarding uncertainties over the capacity of the early phonograph to record sound (here, spoken word) accurately, see Lisa Gitelman, *Scripts, Grooves, and Writing Machines: Representing Technology in the Edison Era* (Stanford: Stanford University Press, 1999), 148–50. Anxieties on this issue obviously continued once music began to be released on records.

52. Victor ran Tone Tests; Edison's were termed both "Tone Tests" and "Realism Tests." According to Thompson, "Machines, Music, and the Quest for Fidelity," 144, however, by 1915, the same year the Edison company initiated the company's public listening tests, its dealers were told to insist that Edison phonographs had no "tone" at all, again a plea for the medium's transparency.
53. The printed stage-set instruction sheet is reprinted in Thompson, "Machines, Music, and the Quest for Fidelity," 150; and in Frow, *Edison Disc Phonographs and Diamond Discs,* 246.
54. Thompson, "Machines, Music, and the Quest for Fidelity," 153.
55. *Ladies' Home Journal* 36 (December 1919): 100–101. See *McClure's Magazine* 50 (December 1918): 34, for a full-page advertisement, "The Final Test," featuring Anna Case singing the Mad Scene from *Lucia di Lammermoor.* Replicating the usual mis-en-scène for this ad campaign, she stands next to an Edison phonograph; nine men and two women listen.
56. Steven Connor, *Dumbstruck: A Cultural History of Ventriloquism* (New York: Oxford University Press, 2000), 35.
57. Katz, *Capturing Sound,* 24; see as well his longer discussion, 22–24.
58. Connor, *Dumbstruck,* 35. Thanks to Brian Kane for drawing my attention to this text.
59. Brian Kane, *Sound Unseen: Acousmatic Sound in Theory and Practice* (New York: Oxford University Press, 2014), 37 and 105, respectively (original emphasis). On acousmatic live-music performance in the late nineteenth century, see 97–118.
60. Pierre Schaeffer, *Traité des objets musicaux* (Paris: Éditions du Seuil, 1966), 93: "la pure écouter."
61. Katz, *Capturing Sound,* 23, a reproduction of the Realism Test; the text of the Realism Test is also reprinted in Timothy D. Taylor, Mark Katz, and Tony Grajeda, eds., *Music, Sound, and Technology in America: A Documentary History of Early Phonograph, Cinema, and Radio* (Durham, NC: Duke University Press, 2012), 44.
62. See, for example, Welch and Burt, *From Tinfoil to Stereo,* 153–54.
63. Adorno wrote about the problem of acoustic interference, which he named "hear-stripe," repeatedly even into the late 1930s, though with particular regard to AM radio. His fundamental insight is that radio is not a neutral or transparent technology for sound transmission. He gets at the issue in two complementary ways as regards music, in essence considering sound production as well as its consumption by listeners. Regarding the former, Adorno points to radio's ever-present background noise as a factor of technological interference between the live performance broadcast and the radio listeners' ears. See Theodor W. Adorno, "The Radio Symphony," in Adorno, *Essays on Music,* ed. Richard Leppert (Berkeley: University of California Press, 2002), 251. In an as-yet unpublished 161-page typescript mimeograph, "Memorandum: Music in Radio" from 1938, a copy of which is in the Paul Lazarsfeld Papers at Columbia University, Adorno discusses the "hear-stripe" in detail. He likens radio background noise to the groove noise heard on 78-rpm recordings at the start, before the music begins, noise that recedes—but does not disappear—once the music starts. "This slight, continuous and constant noise is like a sort of acoustic stripe," which Adorno then likens to film noise; a more recent technological analog is tape hiss. His interest in the "hear-stripe" involves

more than any overt listener distraction it might produce. He posits that the "hear-stripe" likely changes the listener's relation to the music to the extent that the music "appears to be projected upon the stripe and is only, so to speak, like a picture upon that stripe" (30–31). In other words, music, though performed live over radio, is compromised by a second-order presence, a technological filter whose effects, Adorno believes, may function only at the level of the unconscious. See also Theodor W. Adorno, *Current of Music,* ed. Robert Hullot-Kentor (Cambridge: Polity, 2008), in particular the editor's introduction, 19–22, and Adorno's "Radio Physiognomics," 114–16, for more on the "hear-stripe."

64. Thompson, "Machines, Music, and the Quest for Fidelity," 160. See further 142: Only Diamond Disk recordings could be played on Edison Diamond Disk phonographs, and they could not be played on Victrolas, this due to the different groove designs (vertical "hill and dale" for Edison, and lateral "to-and-fro" for Victrola); other companies, however, produced adaptors intended to get around this limitation. Edison went to considerable effort to curtail the use of such devices, concerning which see Frow, *Edison Disc Phonographs and Diamond Discs,* 40. (That said, the New Edison phonographs could play recordings by other manufacturers.)

    Edison's tone arm employed a long-life diamond stylus, superior to the standard steel needles that required frequent changing, ideally after a single playing of one disk, not only for proper sound quality but also to avoid damaging records.

65. Doane, "The Indexical and the Concept of Medium Specificity," 130 (original emphasis). The text to which she refers is E. H. Gombrich, "Conditions of Illusion," in *Art and Illusion: A Study in the Psychology of Pictorial Representations* (Princeton: Princeton University Press, 1960), 203–41.
66. Thompson, "Machines, Music, and the Quest for Fidelity," 146.
67. Gitelman, *Scripts, Grooves, and Writing* Machines, 137.
68. See further Welch and Burt, *From Tinfoil to Stereo,* 127–36.
69. *Ladies' Home Journal* 36 (November 1919): 159.
70. Theodor W. Adorno, "The Curves of the Needle," trans. Thomas Y. Levin, in Adorno, *Essays on Music,* ed. Richard Leppert (Berkeley: University of California Press, 2002), 273. Barbara Engh, "After 'His Master's Voice,'" *new formations* 38 (1999): 54, borrowing from Roland Barthes's comments on the impact of photography, suggests that the phonograph "represents an anthropological revolution in human history—not just another in a series of technological innovations, but one which profoundly interrupts and problematises what it means to be human. The phonograph dissociated the voice and embodied consciousness, which formerly had been thought to be so coterminous as to virtually define each other."
71. Sterne, *Audible Past,* 216, aptly points out that "fidelity" was "an amazingly fluid term"; and further that "sound fidelity is much more about faith in the social function and organization of machines than it is about the relation of a sound to its 'source'" (219).
72. John Philip Sousa, "The Menace of Mechanical Music," *Appleton's Magazine* 8 (1906): 278–84; quotation from 278, emphasis added (reprinted in Taylor, Katz, and Grajeda, *Music, Sound, and Technology in America,* 113–22). See also Patrick Warfield, "John Philip Sousa and 'The Menace of Mechanical Music,'" *Journal of the Society for American Music* 3, no. 4 (2009): 431–63, an important investigation of the larger concerns over composers'

rights and copyright driving Sousa's invective, and applied to player pianos and piano rolls as well as to recordings; and Timothy D. Taylor, "The Commodification of Music at the Dawn of the Era of 'Mechanical Music,'" *Ethnomusicology* 51, no. 2 (2007): 281–305, likewise focused on the cultural impact of player pianos as regards domestic music-making.

73. Virgil Thomson, *The Musical Scene* (New York: Alfred A. Knopf, 1945), 249–50. See also the excerpt by Joseph N. Weber, "Canned Music—Is It Taking the Romance from Our Lives?" *Musician,* November 1930, 7–8 (reprinted in Taylor, Katz, and Grajeda, *Music, Sound, and Technology in America,* 123–26).

74. Theodor W. Adorno, *Towards a Theory of Musical Reproduction: Notes, a Draft, and Two Schemata,* ed. Henri Lonitz, trans. Wieland Hoban (Cambridge: Polity, 2006), 134–45.

75. Adorno, "Curves of the Needle," 271–72. Adorno's dependence on Marx's account of commodity fetishism is readily apparent in this passage.

76. Ibid., 273.

77. Theodor W. Adorno, "The Form of the Phonograph Record," trans. Thomas Y. Levin, in Adorno, *Essays on Music,* ed. Richard Leppert (Berkeley: University of California Press, 2002), 277.

78. Ibid., 279. Concern with preservation (and restoration) is nowadays a matter of concern, as well as debate, in cinema studies. See, for example, André Habib, "Ruin, Archive and the Time of Cinema: Peter Delpeut's 'Lyrical Nitrate,'" *SubStance* 35, no. 2, issue 110 (2006): 120–39; and André Habib, "Thinking in Ruins: Around the Films of Bill Morrison," *Offscreen* 8, no. 11 (November 2004), online at www.horschamp.qc.ca/new_offscreen/cinematic_ruins.html (accessed October 16, 2013).

79. Robert Haven Schauffler, "Canned Music—The Player-Piano Fan," *Collier's: The National Weekly* 67 (March 26, 1921): 11–12.

80. Robert Haven Schauffler, "Canned Music—The Phonograph Fan," *Collier's: The National Weekly* 67 (April 23, 1921): 10.

81. Ibid., 23.

82. Ibid., 10.

83. Suisman, *Selling Sounds,* 118; a photo of the sign is reproduced on p. 120, as well as in Gitelman, *Always Already New,* 81.

84. Suisman, *Selling Sounds,* 115: "By the mid-1910s, Victor was one of the top five magazine advertisers in the United States. . . . In 1923 Victor was the single largest magazine advertiser in the country, the fourth-largest newspaper advertiser, and the first overall." See further 114–21 and 180–91.

85. See Suisman, *Selling Sounds,* 191–95; and Katz, *Capturing Sound,* 68–74.

86. On the relatively high degree of musical literacy at the turn of the twentieth century, see Gitelman, *Always Already New,* 74.

87. On women as phonograph purchasers, see Katz, *Capturing Sound,* 57–59, 62–68; and Kenney, *Recorded Music in American Life,* 88–108. Gitelman, *Always Already New,* 65–66, points out that the aggregate circulation of monthly magazines in the United States in 1905 was sixty-four million. Print advertising for consumer goods in these magazines was heavily geared to women. Gitelman notes that in 1906 Victor claimed that its ads reached forty-nine million people every month, more than half the country's population. The role of magazines in the advancement of music recording and the phonograph was

profound. By 1909, 27.2 million records were produced, though only a minority of these involved classical music. Although sales of around 5,000 of a given record over a two-year period constituted a best-seller early in the century, the first million-selling recording appeared between 1903 and 1905; anecdotally, Caruso recordings were among the earliest such success stories.

88. *Ladies' Home Journal* 42 (November 1925): 1: "The Victrola and the Radio combined!," priced between $300 and $1,000.
89. *Collier's: The National Weekly* 54, no. 3 (October 3, 1914): 36 (back cover); *Country Life in America* 25 (November 1913): back cover; *Life* 64, no. 1662 (September 3, 1914): 416; *McClure's Magazine* 47, no. 5 (September 1916): 1; *Saturday Evening Post* 185, no. 41 (April 12, 1913): 78 (back cover); and *The World's Work* 32 (August 1916): 474.
90. Concerning mass culture and repetition, see Gitelman, *Always Already New,* 66–68.
91. Adorno, "Curves of the Needle," 274.
92. *Collier's: The National Weekly* 55, no. 4 (April 10, 1915): 48 (back cover); *Country Life in America* 29, no. 1 (November 1915): back cover; and *Theatre Magazine* 22 (December 1915): inside front cover.
93. "Open your heart to the world's great music," advertisement for four Victrola recordings of "Caro nome" from Verdi's *Rigoletto,* appearing in *Collier's: The National Weekly* 63 (April 5, 1919): 52.
94. *The Victrola Book of the Opera,* 4th ed. (Camden, NJ: Victor Talking Machine Company, 1917), 427, lists these as Victor 12-inch disks, catalogue nos. 96200, 96201, and 95212. The Caruso et al. versions in 1917 sold for $6 ($5 for 95212); by the 5th ed. (1919), the same recordings were listed at $3 ($2 for 95212). Two other recordings by the vaguely identified "Victor Opera Sextette" were available for $1.25 and $1.50, and band arrangements for as little as $1.
95. Though the text emphasizes opera, only Nellie Melba and Caruso are illustrated among the classical musicians.
96. Roland Barthes, "Rhetoric of the Image," in *Image—Music—Text,* trans. Stephen Heath (New York: Hill & Wang, 1977), 45: "The denoted image naturalizes the symbolic message, it innocents the semantic artifice of connotation, which is extremely dense, especially in advertising." My commentary in the preceding is indebted to Barthes's semiotics, of which this essay is particularly significant regarding codes that operate through text and language, on the one hand, and images on the other. Barthes speaks of cultural (connoted) messages as well as what he calls perceptual (denoted) messages. Connotations implicit in advertising are ideological. Linguistic messages work to fix meanings (anchorage) that images alone may by themselves leave unstable. Language guides interpretation, in other words, and represses unwanted readings. The rhetoric of advertising images seeks in particular to naturalize its claims. In this and in other regards, in Barthes's terminology, linguistic messages serve as relays, or backup, to the semiotics of imagery alone. The appeal is impacted by the venue in which the ad is placed (presumed audience), where it appears in the magazine (inside pages or covers), size, black/white or colored, and so on. See further James N. Weber, *The Talking Machine: The Advertising History of the Berliner Gramophone and Victor Talking Machine* (Midland, ONT: Adio, 1997).

97. *Edison and Music,* 5: "The marvelous realism of the New Edison caused the New York *Globe* to refer to it as 'the phonograph with a soul,' and the New York *Tribune* to announce that 'Edison snares the soul of music.'" According to Frow, *Edison Disc Phonographs and Diamond Discs,* ix: Edison used the phrase as a trademark in 1918 with reference to the New Edison phonographs, which replaced the phonograph that had first appeared in 1912. In 1922, Edison released the New Diamond Disc Phonograph.
98. Edison advertisement, *Ladies' Home Journal* 37 (May 1920): 87.
99. Though the ad's text prints the headline "Noted Psychologists try the Realism Test," in fact only Bingham is identified as a psychologist (see n. 104 below). The others, C. H. Farnsworth and Wilson Follett, were, respectively, director of music, Columbia University Teachers College, and "distinguished author and music critic."
100. Edison required an ear trumpet in order to experience music at all; in that regard, Edison ads often posed the inventor with an ear all but touching the grill of one of his cabinet phonographs, but omitting the unsightly ear trumpet. On Edison's deafness, see Welch and Burt, *From Tinfoil to Stereo,* 156.
101. The Mood Change Chart was designed by Edison's assistant, William Maxwell.
102. http://en.wikipedia.org/wiki/Alice_blue, accessed September 16, 2013: "'Alice Blue' is a pale tint of azure that was favored by Alice Roosevelt Longworth, daughter of Theodore Roosevelt, and which sparked a fashion sensation in the United States." The song reflects this fashion; the musical was made into a 1940 film.
103. *Edison and Music,* 5: "The manufacture of ordinary talking machines and phonographs having adopted the words 'reproduction of music' as descriptive of the results which their various machines accomplish, a new phrase was needed to indicate the incomparably superior realism of the New Edison. A newspaper writer, in his enthusiastic description of Mr. Edison's wonderful new invention, hit upon the phrase 'Music's RE-CREATION.' The United States Government has granted Mr. Edison the exclusive right to use the word 'RE-CREATION' as applied to the phonographic reproduction of music."
104. Anonymous, *Mood Music* (Orange, NJ: Thomas A. Edison, Inc., 1921), 9 and 1, respectively. Walter Van Dyke Bingham (1880–1952) established the department of applied psychology at Carnegie Institute of Technology (forerunner of Carnegie Mellon University), where he was a faculty member from 1915 to 1924. He had a distinguished career and was influential in applied psychology, particularly in the areas of personnel and employment psychology. His papers are housed at Beloit College, where he earned his undergraduate degree. For biographical information, see www.encyclopedia.com/doc/1G2-3045000113.html (accessed September 9, 2013). For information on his early-career work on music, including his association with Edison, see Selfridge-Field, "Experiments with Melody and Meter."
105. Selfridge-Field, "Experiments with Melody and Meter," 296–300, provides additional background to this project, including Edison's own doubts as to, as Edison put it, "the real ability of professors to do anything of use in this line" (296). See also Frow, *Edison Disc Phonographs and Diamond Discs,* 247–50.
106. *Mood Music,* 5–6.
107. Ibid., 14.

108. Ibid., 19.
109. Ibid., 28–31. Bingham's narrative makes detailed allusion to the positive effects of music in the workplace in language coterminous with Muzak promotions, for example: "We have found music, as Re-Created by the New Edison, being used in business schools, to control and accelerate the speed of learners at the typewriter" (28).
110. Ibid., 31; and Selfridge-Field, "Experiments with Melody and Meter," 298, 300.
111. *Mood Music,* 32.
112. Frow, *Edison Disc Phonographs and Diamond Discs,* 250.
113. On the allegorical meanings of Five Senses paintings, see Norbert Schneider, *The Art of the Still Life: Still-Life Painting in the Early Modern Period,* trans. Hugh Beyer (Cologne: Benedikt Taschen, 1990), 65.
114. *1923 Catalogue of Victor Records* (Camden, NJ: Victor Talking Machine Company, 1923), 6–9 (unpaginated).
115. *1925 Catalogue of Victor Records* (Camden, NJ: Victor Talking Machine Company, 1925), 5–8 (unpaginated).
116. The fiddle player represents hearing; the lute-tuner, touch; the nose-holder, smell; the woman at the table reading, sight; and the drinkers, taste.
117. Theodor W. Adorno, "Opera and the Long-Playing Record," trans. Thomas Y. Levin, in Adorno, *Essays on Music,* ed. Richard Leppert (Berkeley: University of California Press, 2002), 283–87). The piece first appeared in the mass-circulation magazine *Der Spiegel.*
118. Ibid., 284.
119. Ibid., 285.
120. Ibid.

4. AESTHETIC MEANDERINGS OF THE SONIC PSYCHE

1. On bourgeois self-discipline in the concert hall and opera, see Richard Sennett, *The Fall of Public Man: On the Social Psychology of Capitalism* (New York: Vintage Books, 1978), 191 and 206–10; Peter Gay, *The Naked Heart,* vol. 4 of *The Bourgeois Experience (Victoria to Freud)* (New York: Norton, 1996), 18–19; and, more generally, James H. Johnson, *Listening in Paris: A Cultural History* (Berkeley: University of California Press, 1996).
2. Gay, *Naked Heart,* 18.
3. Jeremy Tambling, "Towards a Psychopathology of Opera," *Cambridge Opera Journal* 9, no. 3 (1997): 263 and 268–69; Kaja Silverman, *The Acoustic Mirror: The Female Voice in Psychoanalysis and Cinema* (Bloomington: Indiana University Press, 1988).
4. Paul Robinson, *Opera and Ideas: From Mozart to Strauss* (New York: Harper & Row, 1985), 264.
5. Stendhal [Marie-Henri Beyle], *Life of Rossini,* trans. Richard N. Coe (Seattle: University of Washington Press, 1972), 347: "Music as an art, suffuses the soul of man with sweet regret, by giving it *a glimpse of happiness;* and a glimpse of happiness, even if it is no more than a *dream* of happiness, is almost the dawning of hope" (original emphasis). [Stendhal, *Vie de Rossini* (Paris: Michel Lévy Frères, 1854), 269: "Voilà un peu le genre de plaisir et de consolation que j'ai trouvé dans la musique. Cet art donne des regrets

tendres en procurant la *vue du bonheur;* et faire voir le bonheur, quoique en songe, c'est presque donner de l'espérance." (*Songe* is not italicized in the French edition I consulted, vol. 19 of the *Oeuvres complètes*.)] Tambling, "Towards a Psychopathology of Opera," 279, reads the phenomenon, dialectically, through Lacan: "What we go to the opera for is something unattainable and unobtainable, but may involve in sound the object of desire that guarantees the subject's existence by being the *objet petit a*. Yet in the same way it may produce repulsion, or abjection, feelings of horror at the bodily image being shattered, fragmented, as though the subject were being taken into the unrepresentable, outside the field of acceptable vision."

6. Wayne Koestenbaum, *The Queen's Throat: Opera, Homosexuality, and the Mystery of Desire* (New York: Poseidon Press, 1993), 44.
7. Theodor W. Adorno, "Commodity Music Analysed," in *Quasi una fantasia: Essays on Modern Music,* trans. Rodney Livingstone (London: Verso, 1992), 50: "The positive element of kitsch lies in the fact that it sets free for a moment the glimmering realization that you have wasted your life."
8. Koestenbaum, *Queen's Throat,* 44.
9. Otherwise Musetta has only four other grace notes: three in act two and one in act three. The grace notes sung by Schaunard and Colline in act one, one each, relate to the comic horsing around of the boys prior to Mimì's appearance. Marcello's three grace notes in the second act don't add up to much, except for the fact that in both instances he is singing about love, as always with him a heady mix of desire and hope, usually tinged with irony if not sarcasm. In brief, the grace notes sung by Musetta and Marcello, markedly contrary to those assigned to Rodolfo and Mimì, function as counterpoints to the argument I'm pursuing.
10. My sources were Giacomo Puccini, *La bohème* [piano-vocal score] (Mineola, NY: Dover, 2000) and Puccini, *La bohème* [full score] (Milan: Ricordi, 1920/1999). On the instability of Puccini's scores given the composer's obsession to revise, see Arthur Groos and Roger Parker, *Giacomo Puccini: La bohème* (Cambridge: Cambridge University Press, 1986), 102–14, with Musetta's Waltz aria in act two as the principal example.

    In act one, Mimì's grace notes occur in her aria. Four of Rodolfo's six appear in his aria and the remaining two during the earlier comic playacting. At various points throughout the opera, especially for these two characters, Puccini scores what for want of a perfect term I'll call double graces (mordents or turns might do about as well), a kind of upping the ante of the "normal" grace notes, for precisely the same semiotic function. Written as small sixteenth-notes next to the pitch to which they connect, the totals are these:

	RODOLFO	MIMÌ
Act 1	3	2
Act 2	2	2
Act 3	**3**	**6**
Act 4	2	2

    For the two lovers both types of grace notes are used in close proximity, either in adjacent arias as in act one or in duet/dialogue in act three during the extended exchange that begins with their goodbyes and ends with their temporary reuniting. Concerning the unstable nomenclature for ornaments, see Clive Brown, "Ornaments: Late 18th Century and the 19th," in *Grove Music Online*, www.oxfordmusiconline.com/subscriber/article/grove/music/49928pg9#S49928.9 (accessed February 13, 2013).

11. Act three employs strongly punctuated unison dominant-tonic framing; it establishes itself in D minor, opening with a *fortissimo tutti* (implied) dominant to tonic A to D, immediately followed by a *subito pianissimo;* the act ends in opposite fashion, a *pianississimo* two-bar hold on the tonic (G-flat major), followed by a sixteenth rest and a *fortississimo tutti* D-flat to G-flat unison.

12. Puccini, *La bohème* [piano-vocal score], p. 191, rehearsal no. 9, m. 11. All other measure references are keyed to this edition of the score.

13. The "buddy music" duet appears only in the original version of the score (piano-vocal, 1863); thereafter the opera was considerably altered and not by the composer (scores were published in 1885 or 1886 and again in 1893). Bizet's original orchestration has not been found. See the original-version recording from 1978, conducted by Georges Prêtre, released on Angel SBLX-3856 and rereleased on CD in 1994 on the label Classics for Pleasure B000003X6Y. The "original"-version (1863) score, republished in 1975, includes this music (but only in an appendix, 226–35), of which the editor, Michel Poupet, writes: "In the first act, Zurga's and Nadir's duet originally ended in a somewhat trite hymn of friendship, instead of the substituted reprise of the *'Goddess theme.'* Although this reprise appears more effective in performance, the original ending [again, in the appendix] is psychologically truer, as the *'Goddess theme'* is associated with the quarrel rather than its reconciliation" (from unpaginated frontmatter). See Georges Bizet, *Les pêcheurs de perles* [piano-vocal score] (Paris: Editions Choudans, 1975).

14. Lawrence Kramer, *After the Lovedeath: Sexual Violence and the Making of Culture* (Berkeley: University of California Press, 1997), 39 and 88, respectively.

15. Lawrence Kramer, "Opera: Two or Three Things I Know about Her," in *Siren Songs: Representations of Gender and Sexuality in Opera,* ed. Mary Ann Smart (Princeton: Princeton University Press, 2000), 202: "Opera is always in danger of being exposed as a purveyor of what Freud called the 'forepleasure' that screens fantasy; opera as high art continually risks being reduced to an alibi for the practical art of psychosexual equivocation." An expanded version of this essay appears in Kramer's *Opera and Modern Culture: Wagner and Strauss* (Berkeley: University of California Press, 2004), 19–41.

16. Kramer, *Opera and Modern Culture,* 222. Cf. Peter Brooks, "Body and Voice in Melodrama and Opera," in Smart, ed., *Siren Songs,* 122, who refers to the "hystericization of voice in opera."

17. Lawrence Kramer, *Expression and Truth: On the Music of Knowledge* (Berkeley: University of California Press, 2012), 75.

18. Slavoj Žižek and Mladen Dolar, *Opera's Second Death* (New York: Routledge, 2002), 107. Dolar also suggests, "perhaps it is no coincidence that the fall of the opera coincides with the advent of psychoanalysis" (4).

19. Catherine Clément, *Opera, or the Undoing of Women,* trans. Betsy Wing (Minneapolis: University of Minnesota Press, 1988), 85.

20. Michel Chion, *The Voice in Cinema,* ed. and trans. Claudia Gorbman (New York: Columbia University Press, 1999), 5. Chion adopts his insight from a remark by Christine Sacco ("The presence of a body structures the space that contains it").
21. Puccini, *La bohème* [piano-vocal score], pp. 216–17, rehearsal no. 29, mm. 4–6.
22. Sigmund Freud, "Mourning and Melancholia," in *On Murder, Mourning, and Melancholia,* trans. Shaun Whiteside (London: Penguin Books, 2005), 204. Tambling, "Towards a Psychopathology of Opera," 274, cites this essay.
23. Puccini, *La bohème* [piano-vocal score], p. 217, rehearsal no. 29, mm. 11–13.
24. Brooks, "Body and Voice in Melodrama and Opera," 122.
25. The vocal "weakness" in Rodolfo's self-presentation contrasts sharply with the concurrent assertions of Marcello jealously confronting Musetta, his protestations no more credible on the "masculinity" scale than Rodolfo's despite the volumetric, overwrought anger with which they are delivered.
26. See Richard Leppert and George Lipsitz, "'Everybody's Lonesome for Somebody': Age, the Body, and Experience in the Music of Hank Williams," *Popular Music* 9, no. 3 (1990): 259–74; and Richard Leppert, "Gender Sonics: The Voice of Patsy Cline," in *Musicological Identities: Essays in Honor of Susan McClary,* ed. Raymond Knapp, Steven Baur, and Jacqueline Warwick (Aldershot, UK: Ashgate, 2008), 191–203.
27. Lawrence Kramer, "Philosophizing Musically: Reconsidering Music and Ideas," *Journal of the Royal Musical Association* 139, no. 2 (2014): 398 (original emphasis).
28. Stanley Cavell, *A Pitch of Philosophy: Autobiographical Exercises* (Cambridge, MA: Harvard University Press, 1994), 144.
29. Žižek and Dolar, *Opera's Second Death,* 4: "Obviously, if opera were measured by realistic standards (whatever one chooses to mean by that), then it would look totally absurd, but the more absurd it appears, the more this proves its authenticity."
30. Theodor W. Adorno, "On the Contemporary Relationship of Philosophy and Music," in *Essays on Music,* ed. Richard Leppert, trans. Susan H. Gillespie (Berkeley: University of California Press, 2002), 136, commenting on the Marx Brothers film *A Night at the Opera* (1935), involving a performance of *Il trovatore,* the scenery for which the boys manage to destroy.
31. Michal Grover-Friedlander, *Vocal Apparitions: The Attraction of Cinema to Opera* (Princeton: Princeton University Press, 2005), 23. The text continues: "With the entry into language, the object [the void that is the Other] is felt as irretrievably lost, and the trajectory of life is an endless search for the always already lost object. The object voice stands for what, in the object, is more than itself; the unarticulated cry comes close to representing it." Grover-Friedlander holds that "opera is the endless and painful quest for the original Object (Mother, Woman, *jouissance*)."
32. Clément, *Opera, or the Undoing of Women,* xv (original emphasis).
33. Sigmund Freud, *Civilization and Its Discontents,* trans. James Strachey (New York: Norton, 1961), 24.
34. Ibid., 25.
35. Ibid.
36. Ibid., 32. He adds that "psychoanalysis, unfortunately, has scarcely anything to say about beauty either," though he associates the impulse toward beauty with the sexual, ending

his paragraph with a somewhat jarring remark about the human genitals (and here I assume he means those of the male variety, since he's writing about visuality) to the effect that while "always exciting" as signs, they are "nevertheless hardly ever judged to be beautiful," a position maintained by the ancient Greeks, whose sculpture consistently underplays the dimensions of these biological appendages, almost as though their very actuality required apology.

37. A great deal has been written about Bartók's only opera, including two impressive monographs in English, both of which provide detailed analyses of the composition's inner workings: Elliott Antokoletz, in collaboration with Juana Canabal Antokoletz, *Musical Symbolism in the Operas of Debussy and Bartók: Trauma, Gender, and the Unfolding of the Unconscious* (New York: Oxford University Press, 2004); and Carl S. Leafstedt *Inside Bluebeard's Castle: Music and Drama in Béla Bartók's Opera* (New York: Oxford University Press, 1999).

38. Nicholas Vázsonyi, "*Bluebeard's Castle:* The Birth of Cinema from the Spirit of Opera," *Hungarian Quarterly* 46, no. 178 (2005): 132–44 (accessed online at www.hungarian-quarterly.com/no178/17.shtml on December 10, 2011), takes issue with the prevailing accounts of the opera as an exploration of Bluebeard's soul by "explorer" Judith. Regarding the libretto as distinctly open-ended, Vázsonyi suggests that its "vagueness resists definitive interpretation." In light of Balázs's subsequent film theory (n. 40, below), Vázsonyi sees the opera as "a remarkably early operatic response to film," an argument developed in detail throughout the essay, though almost entirely in the absence of any discussion of what happens musically.

39. Judit Frigyesi, "In Search of Meaning in Context: Bartók's *Duke Bluebeard's Castle,*" *Current Musicology* 70 (2000): 5–31, argues against the grain of most analyses of the opera, suggesting that Judith "is an inner desire, an attitude—she *is* Bluebeard. . . . The opera is not about man and woman in the biological or social sense, but about a duality of desires in constant conflict within all human beings (which perhaps some would identify as masculine and feminine desires)" (9).

40. On Béla Balázs's contribution to cinema theory, see his *Early Film Theory: Visible Man and the Spirit of Film*, ed. Erica Carter, trans. Rodney Livingstone (New York: Berghahn Books, 2011), and *Theory of the Film: Character and Growth of a New Art* (1949; reprint New York: Dover, 1970).

41. Susan McClary, *Feminine Endings: Music, Gender, Sexuality* (Minneapolis: University of Minnesota Press, 2002), 4.

42. Béla Bartók, *Herzog Blaubarts Burg* (Vienna: Universal-Edition, 1963), 100: "Judith hält, geblendet, die Hände über die Augen" (the orchestral score provides the text in German and English, but not Hungarian). In what follows, I have also consulted Béla Bartók, *Herzog Blaubarts Burg* [piano-vocal score] (Vienna: Universal-Edition, 1921).

43. Cf. Philip Friedheim, "Wagner and the Aesthetics of the Scream," *Nineteenth Century Music* 7, no. 1 (1983): 63–70. In Wagner operas most screams are not notated but confined to stage directions. Screams for Wagner reflect not physical pain but inner psychological anxiety and trauma. Friedheim also traces the scream, post-Wagner, in the operas of Richard Strauss and Alban Berg, and in Schoenberg (*Gurre-Lieder* and *Pierrot lunaire*), as well as in German expressionist literature and visual art, ending with com-

ments on Edvard Munch's *The Scream* (1896). The one operatic example he cites of vocalized physical pain is in *Tosca,* occurring offstage in the second act and involving the torture of Mario Cavaradossi, whose defiance of Scarpia is in fact sung (high A) and not a simple, unpitched cry of pain.

44. Libretto translation by Christopher Hassall, included with the Deutsche Grammophon CD 289 447 040–2 (1998) recording of the opera.
45. The opening of the Door Five scene is scored for 4 flutes, 2 oboes, English horn, 3 clarinets, 3 bassoons, contrabassoon, 4 horns, 4 trumpets, 3 trombones, bass trombone, timpani, organ and strings, as well as the offstage brass.
46. Bartók, *Herzog Blaubarts Burg,* 102: "Schaut starr hinaus, zerstreut."
47. The penultimate chord, passing quickly in eighth-notes, is D major with an added F-natural. The other harmonies are triadic only, except for a similar eighth-note F-natural also added to a long-held D-major chord earlier in the sequence (see rehearsal no. 76, mm. 1–14).
48. Detailed analyses of the scene are provided in (1) Antokoletz, *Musical Symbolism in the Operas of Debussy and Bartók,* 234–47; see 15–17 for a discussion of Bartók's use of nonfunctional diatonicism; and (2) Leafstedt, *Inside Bluebeard's Castle,* 107–11; concerning Bartók's use of tritone F#-C relationship as a harmonic organizational principle, see 55–61.
49. Linda B. Fairtile, "*Duetto a tre:* Franco Alfano's Completion of *Turandot,*" *Cambridge Opera Journal* 16, no. 2 (2004): 163–85 (see p. 172 regarding the specifics of the cuts and changes to Alfano's first version of the opera's conclusion); and Marco Uvietta, "'É l'ora della prova': Berio's Finale for Puccini's *Turandot,*" trans. Cormac Newark and Arman Schwartz, *Cambridge Opera Journal* 16, no. 2 (2004): 187–238. See also, on the Berio ending, Roger Parker, *Remaking the Song: Operatic Visions and Revisions from Handel to Berio* (Berkeley: University of California Press, 2006), 90–120, but especially 101–17. See also, on the Alfano ending, Jürgen Maehder, "Studi sul carattere di frammento della *Turandot* di Giacomo Puccini," *Quaderni pucciniani* 2 (1985): 79–163. For a detailed account of the opera as a whole, see William Ashbrook and Harold Powers, *Puccini's "Turandot": The End of the Great Tradition* (Princeton: Princeton University Press, 1991).
50. Alexandra Wilson, "Modernism and the Machine Woman in Puccini's *Turandot,*" *Music and Letters* 86, no. 3 (2005): 432–51, makes clear that Turandot, perceived as dehumanized, hence unfavorably compared to the all-too-human Liù, was deeply troubling to some critics already in the early reception of the opera. Wilson traces resemblances of the machine-woman trope to contemporaneous Italian theater and Futurist aesthetics. She also notes the resonance between this reading of Turandot and robotic characters in 1920s–30s cinema, Fritz Lang's *Metropolis* (1927) serving as the *locus classicus. The Bride of Frankenstein* (1935) is cut from the same broad cloth.
51. Žižek and Dolar, *Opera's Second Death,* 205–6; see also Fairtile, *Duetto a tre,* 178.
52. Žižek and Dolar, *Opera's Second Death,* 206.
53. James Inverne, "Beginning of the End," *Time Magazine World,* August 18, 2002, online at www.time.com/time/magazine/article/0,9171,338591,00.html (accessed December 7, 2011). Inverne reviews the Salzburg production with Berio's ending, available on DVD (TDK Recording Media Europe, DV-OPTURFS).
54. Uvietta, "'É l'ora della prova,'" 231.

EXCURSUS: NATURAL BEAUTY / ART BEAUTY

1. On the complex history of the words *civilization, culture,* and *nature,* see the separate entries in Raymond Williams, *Keywords: A Vocabulary of Culture and Society,* rev. ed. (New York: Oxford University Press, 1983). Nature, Williams suggests (219), "is perhaps the most complex word in the language"; and "culture is one of the two or three most complicated words in the English language" (87).
2. Max Horkheimer and Theodor W. Adorno, *Dialectic of Enlightenment: Philosophical Fragments,* ed. Gunzelin Schmid Noerr, trans. Edmund Jephcott (Stanford: Stanford University Press, 2002), 2.
3. Adorno is thus bluntly positioning himself against Hegel, whose disregard for nature is well known. On this point, see Theodor W. Adorno, *Aesthetic Theory,* ed. Gretel Adorno and Rolf Tiedemann, trans. Robert Hullot-Kentor (Minneapolis: University of Minnesota Press, 1997), 63, 75–77; and Richard Wolin, "Utopia, Mimesis, and Reconciliation: A Redemptive Critique of Adorno's *Aesthetic Theory,*" *Representations* 32 (Fall 1990): 42.
4. Adorno, *Aesthetic Theory,* 61–62; see also Heinz Paetzold, "Adorno's Notion of Natural Beauty: A Reconsideration," in *The Semblance of Subjectivity: Essays in Adorno's Aesthetic Theory,* ed. Tom Huhn and Lambert Zuidervaart (Cambridge, MA: MIT Press, 1997), 213–35.
5. Adorno, *Aesthetic Theory,* 347: "There is no artwork that does not participate in the untruth external to it, that of the historical moment"; and this untruth marks the perpetual failing of art to attain the Absolute, for which it nonetheless perpetually strives.
6. Ibid., 65–66. "Under its optic, art is not the imitation of nature, but the imitation of natural beauty" (ibid., 71). See also Roger Behrens, "On Music in Nature and Nature in Music," *Issues in Contemporary Culture and Aesthetics* 5 (1997): 17–26. Cf. composer-philosopher David Dunn, "Nature, Sound Art, and the Sacred," in *The Book of Music and Nature,* ed. David Rothenberg and Marta Ulvaeus (Middletown, CT: Wesleyan University Press, 2001), 95; alluding to a lengthy passage in James Agee's *Let Us Now Praise Famous Men* describing the meanings and intelligence audible in the late-night calls of two foxes, Dunn comments: "We hear in the world talking to itself a sense of otherness that simultaneously mirrors our deepest sense of belonging." And further: "Perhaps music is a conservation strategy for keeping something alive that we now need to make more conscious, a way of making sense of the world from which we might refashion our relationships to nonhuman living systems" (97).
7. Adorno, *Aesthetic Theory,* 65. He continues: "Times in which nature confronts man overpoweringly allow no room for natural beauty."
8. Nowhere is this phenomenon more apparent than in the United States, where, as Lee Clark Mitchell, *Witnesses to a Vanishing America: The Nineteenth-Century Response* (Princeton: Princeton University Press, 1981), has shown, nostalgia for the disappearance (better, disappearedness) of the Native (or, in this context, "Natural") American was at once acknowledged and, from a safe distance, lamented already by the 1830s, a half century in advance of the final slaughter at Wounded Knee in 1890.
9. The Greek poet Simonides of Ceos (556–468 B.C.) is the principal source for this story.

10. The foregoing summarizes research by Scott A. Sullivan, *The Dutch Gamepiece* (Totowa, NJ: Allanheld & Schram, 1984), especially the chapter "Hunting and Dutch Society," 33–45; see also by the same author, "Rembrandt's *Self-Portrait with a Dead Bittern*," *Art Bulletin* 62 (1980): 236–43; Norbert Schneider, *The Art of the Still Life: Still Life Painting in the Early Modern Period*, trans. Hugh Beyer (Cologne: Benedikt Taschen Verlag, 1990), 50–63; and Ingvar Bergström, *Dutch Still-Life Painting in the Seventeenth Century*, trans. Christina Hedström and Gerald Taylor (London: Faber & Faber, 1956), 247–59.
11. Sullivan, *Dutch Gamepiece*, 64.
12. See Richard Leppert, *Music and Image: Domesticity, Ideology, and Socio-Cultural Formation in Eighteenth-Century England* (Cambridge: Cambridge University Press, 1989), the chapter "Music and the Body: Dance, Power, Submission," 71–106.
13. Sullivan, *Dutch Gamepiece*, 62, indicates knowledge of approximately 130 gamepieces by Weenix.
14. Covering a slightly later period, the classic account is that by Michel Foucault, *Discipline and Punish: The Birth of the Prison*, trans. Alan Sheridan (New York: Vintage Books, 1979).
15. Adorno, *Aesthetic Theory*, 62.
16. Ibid., 63.
17. George Gordon Lord Byron, *Childe Harold's Pilgrimage: A Romaunt*, 3 vols. (London: J. Murray, 1812–18), Canto III, stanza 75, lines 1–2. The lines echo Goethe: "Is not the core of nature already inside the heart of human kind?" ("Ist nicht der Kern der Natur / Menschen im Herzen"), quoted in Georg Simmel, "Kant and Goethe: On the History of the Modern *Weltanschauung*," trans. Josef Bleicher, *Theory, Culture, and Society* 24, no. 6 (2007): 166.
18. Adorno, *Aesthetic Theory*, 65.
19. Ibid.
20. Ibid.: "Like the experience of art, the aesthetic experience of nature is that of images."
21. Adorno, *Minima Moralia: Reflections from Damaged Life*, trans. E. F. N. Jephcott (London: Verso, 1978), 48. Subsequent quotations are all from this page.
22. The aphorism concludes: "And it [the landscape] is perceived in a corresponding way. For what the hurrying eye has seen merely from the car it cannot retain, and the vanishing landscape leaves no more traces behind than it bears upon itself."
23. Arthur Schopenhauer, *The World as Will and Representation* (1819/1859), trans. Richard E. Aquila, in collaboration with David Carus, 2 vols. (New York: Pearson Longman, 2008–10), 1:249.
24. Sergei Eisenstein, *Nonindifferent Nature*, trans. Herbert Marshall (Cambridge: Cambridge University Press, 1987), 356, quoting D. H Lawrence. Cf. Horkheimer and Adorno, *Dialectic of Enlightenment*, 211: "Human beings are so radically estranged from themselves and from nature that they know only how to use and harm each other. Each is merely a factor, the subject or object of some praxis, something to be reckoned with or discounted." And Michel Chion, *The Thin Red Line*, trans. Trista Selous (London: British Film Institute, 2004), 49: "The image often associated with American cinema is that of the road or trail: a route crossing virgin landscape, with telegraph poles, wires, a metallic voice sent over thousands of kilometers; that is American cinema itself."

25. See further Martin Donougho, "West of Eden: Malick's *Days of Heaven*," *Post Script* 5, no. 1 (1985): 18–19; and Lloyd Michaels, *Terrence Malick* (Urbana: University of Illinois Press, 2009), 56.
26. Georg Simmel, "The Philosophy of Landscape," trans. Josef Bleicher, *Theory, Culture, and Society* 24, nos. 7–8 (2007): 21–22.
27. Simmel, "Philosophy of Landscape," 23.
28. Adorno, *Aesthetic Theory*, 66
29. Ibid.: "No feeling person in whom something of the European tradition survives fails to be moved by the sound of a robin after a rain shower. Yet something frightening lurks in the song of birds precisely because it is not a song but obeys the spell in which it is enmeshed."
30. Stanley Cavell, *The World Viewed: Reflections on the Ontology of Film*, enlarged ed. (Cambridge: Harvard University Press, 1979), xvi: "Objects projected on a screen are inherently reflexive, they occur as self-referential, reflecting upon their physical origins. Their presence refers to their absence, their location in another place. Then if in relation to objects capable of such self-manifestation human beings are reduced in significance, or crushed by the fact of beauty left vacant, perhaps this is because in trying to take dominion over the world, or in aestheticizing it (temptation inherent in the making of film, or of any art), they are refusing their participation with it." Malick studied philosophy with Cavell at Harvard University. On Cavell's impact on Malick, see Michaels, *Terrence Malick*, 15, 51; and James Morrison and Thomas Schur, *The Films of Terrence Malick* (Westport, CT: Praeger, 2003), 67–68.
31. Adorno, *Aesthetic Theory*, 68.
32. Ibid., 69.
33. Ibid., 70–71.
34. Ibid., 73–74.
35. Adorno, *Minima Moralia*, 247. Adorno's debt here to Walter Benjamin is obvious.
36. Theodor W. Adorno, "Is Art Lighthearted?," in Adorno, *Notes to Literature*, ed. Rolf Tiedemann, trans. Shierry Weber Nicholsen (New York: Columbia University Press, 1992), 2:248. Cf. Adorno, *Aesthetic Theory*, 51: "Works become beautiful by the force of their opposition to what merely exists."
37. Theodor W. Adorno, "The Schema of Mass Culture," in Adorno, *The Culture Industry: Selected Essays on Mass Culture*, ed. J.M. Bernstein (London: Routledge, 1991), 83. See further Ron Mottram, "All Things Shining: The Struggle for Wholeness, Redemption, and Transcendence in the Films of Terrence Malick," in *The Cinema of Terrence Malick: Poetic Visions of America*, ed. Hannah Patterson, 2nd ed. (London: Wallflower Press, 2007), 14–26.
38. William Faulkner, *The Mansion* (New York: Vintage Books, 1959), 435.
39. Ibid., 435–36.
40. Johann Wolfgang von Goethe, *The Sorrows of Young Werther and Selected Writings*, trans. Catherine Hutter (New York: New American Library, 1962), 24 and 63, respectively. Further regarding the issues raised here, see James D. Proctor, "Whose Nature? The Contested Moral Terrain of Ancient Forests," and Kenneth R. Olwig, "Reinventing Common Nature: Yosemite and Mount Rushmore—A Meandering Tale of a Double

Nature," both in *Uncommon Ground: Rethinking the Human Place in Nature*, ed. William Cronon (New York: Norton, 1996), 269–97 and 379–408, respectively.

5. SOUND, SUBJECTIVITY, AND DEATH

1. Jacob A. Riis, *How the Other Half Lives: Studies among the Tenements of New York* (1890), 2nd ed., ed. David Leviatin (New York: Bedford/St. Martin's, 2010). The title-sequence period photographs are by Lewis Hine (1874–1940), Henry Hamilton Bennett (1843–1908), Frances Benjamin Johnston (1864–1952), Chansonetta Stanley Emmons (1858–1937), and William Notman (1826–91), and were shot, roughly speaking, around the time of the film's setting, some before, others after. See Lloyd Michaels, *Terrence Malick* (Urbana: University of Illinois Press, 2009), 52. James Morrison and Thomas Schur, *The Films of Terrence Malick* (Westport, CT: Praeger, 2003), 46–47, suggest that the sequence captures an outline of the film's narrative.
2. Philippe Ariès, *Centuries of Childhood: A Social History of Family Life*, trans. Robert Baldick (New York: Vintage Books), 1962.
3. Henry Hamilton Bennett, "Canoeists in a Boat Cave, Wisconsin Dells" (c. 1890–95) and "Leaping the Chasm" (1886).
4. Malick touches on the miseries of immigrants and the poor later in the film, following the arrival of the circus performers who, one evening, stage theatricals and screen Chaplin's *The Immigrant* (1917) (56:56–57:01 in *Days of Heaven*, DVD [2010], The Criterion Collection). Three shots are briefly shown. The first, in close-up, is of nine immigrants looking intently at what is established by the succeeding shot to be the Statue of Liberty, seen now in the distance as the ship approaches the New York harbor. One of the viewers (probably the Farmer) points directly at the Statue, the shadow of his arm and extended finger cutting diagonally across the screen. The third shot puts into question the implied hopeful emancipation asserted by the statue; the immigrants, *en masse*, are herded behind a rope in preparation for their shipboard encounter with immigration officials. Early on in the narrative, Malick clarifies that many of the itinerant farm workers are immigrants, by including, for example, a very brief shot of two older men speaking Swedish—to say nothing of the Italian-speaking flying-circus performers.
5. Charles Kronengold, from his reading of an early draft of this chapter, pointed out that the instrumentation of "Aquarium" "is notably 'miniature' (neither traditionally orchestral nor an 'orchestral' treatment of solo piano)—very forward looking, one has to admit, in its use of an ad-hoc changing multiple-keyboard-dominated chamber ensemble . . . : its jewel-box qualities are hard-earned . . . and in their obsolete newness match the distancing 'enframed' qualities . . . of the b/w photos."
6. Stuart Kendall, "The Tragic Indiscernibility of *Days of Heaven*," in *Terrence Malick: Film and Philosophy*, ed. Thomas Deane Tucker and Stuart Kendall (New York: Continuum, 2011), 150, suggests that the music is destabilizing, conveying "a flowing, dreamlike effect over those portions of the film, as if we were entering and leaving a dream."
7. Royal S. Brown, *Overtones and Undertones: Reading Film Music* (Berkeley: University of California Press, 1994), 53, points out that a number of early-century French silent films

employed the *"Le Cygne"* section from *Le carnaval des animaux* as accompaniment. Concerning music, Sergei Eisenstein asks: "Why is music spoken of here as of something *generally* necessary, a priori, and taken for granted in film? I think the answer is quite clear. It is not so much a question of strengthening the effect (although to a great extent, it is) *as in emotionally expressing what is inexpressible by other means*" (original emphasis). He then quotes Saint-Saëns: "Music begins where the world ends; it expresses the unutterable; it forces us to find in ourselves unknown depths; it conveys moods and 'states of the soul' which no words can convey." Sergei Eisenstein, *Nonindifferent Nature,* trans. Herbert Marshall (Cambridge: Cambridge University Press, 1987), 217.

8. The "Aquarium" section of *Le carnaval des animaux* has been used in a number of other films and trailers and in television programs and video games. See "The Carnival of the Animals," Wikipedia online, accessed March 31, 2010.
9. For detailed consideration of Linda's voiceover narration, all of which was added in postproduction, see Anne Latto, "Innocents Abroad: The Young Woman's Voice in *Badlands* and *Days of Heaven,* with an Afterward on *The New World,*" in *The Cinema of Terrence Malick: Poetic Visions of America,* ed. Hannah Patterson, 2nd ed. (London: Wallflower Press, 2007), 94–98; and Charlotte Crofts, "From the 'Hegemony of the Eye' to the 'Hierarchy of Perception': The Reconfiguration of Sound and Image in Terrence Malick's *Days of Heaven," Journal of Media Practice* 2, no. 1 (2001): 20–24. For a general commentary on Malick's use of voiceover in his films, see Steven Rybin, "Voicing Meaning: On Terrence Malick's Characters," in Tucker and Kendall, eds., *Terrence Malick: Film and Philosophy,* 26–32.
10. Michel Chion, *Film: A Sound Art,* trans. Claudia Gorbman (New York: Columbia University Press, 2009), 80. In an adult voiceover, the putative and logical passage of time doesn't matter all that much, precisely to the extent that we take the character, as an adult (even one who narrates after his own murder like Joe Gillis/William Holden in *Sunset Boulevard* [1950]), to be more or less fixed, a trait we don't assume for a child.
11. The film's characters matter less on account of the dialogue they utter than, simply, how they look: their *visuality,* which Malick presents in two complementary, but very different, ways: close-ups and distance shots. Close-ups frame the characters' individualities, just as long shots diminish identity. If the close-up manifests modernity's notion of human uniqueness and selfhood, the long shots put all that into question. Put differently, very few characters in the film, which at times fairly teems with human beings, have any individuality whatsoever. Most are like "staffage" in eighteenth-century English landscape paintings. Indeed, Malick often seems to emphasize the ambiguous relation between individuality, selfhood, and subjectivity, on the one hand, and some sort of bare existence and mass consciousness, on the other. It's fair to say that the very characters who seem to inhabit realms of selfhood are in actuality rather less than fully rounded individuals, evident in particular in the degree to which, to a person, they seem to have distinctly circumscribed emotional lives. In other words, the modern notion of human subjectivity upon which the very ideas of selfhood, individuality, and uniqueness are based—part and parcel of modern thought—is perhaps not more than an operational mythology in the film.

12. On the destabilizing effects of voiceover narration in Malick's films, see Joan McGettigan, "Interpreting a Man's World: Female Voices in *Badlands* and *Days of Heaven*," *Journal of Film & Video* 52, no. 4 (2001): 33–43.
13. Chion, *Film: A Sound Art*, passim, has much to say on this subject.
14. Eric Repphun, "Look Out through My Eyes: The Enchantments of Terrence Malick," *Sydney Studies in Religion* 9 (2009): 1; also available online at http://escholarship.usyd.edu.au/journals/index.php/SSR/article/viewFile/711/703, accessed May 13, 2010.
15. A great deal has been written about Heidegger's influence on Malick's filmic worldview, a sense of which can be gained from Marc Furstenau and Leslie MacAvoy, "Terrence Malick's Heideggerian Cinema: War and the Question of Being in *The Thin Red Line*," in Patterson, ed., *Cinema of Terrence Malick*, 179–91; and Rybin, "Voicing Meaning: On Terrence Malick's Characters," 19–22.
16. A *locus classicus* argument on this score is Max Horkheimer and Theodor W. Adorno, *Dialectic of Enlightenment: Philosophical Fragments*, ed. Gunzelin Schmid Noerr, trans. Edmund Jephcott (Stanford: Stanford University Press, 2002).
17. On the biblical aspects of the film, see Hubert Cohen, "The Genesis of *Days of Heaven*," *Cinema Journal* 42, no. 4 (2003): 46–62, who suggests that key moments in the film's narrative are drawn from the Old Testament, including—as has many times been noted—the title, taken from Deuteronomy 11:21: "That your days may be multiplied, and the days of your children, in the land which the Lord sware unto your fathers to give them, as the days of heaven upon the earth." Cohen's conclusion, however, strikes me as considerably too precise and certain: "The more I considered this evidence, the more I thought that . . . Malick was presenting the Old Testament God as a force in the film" (59). See also Kendall, "Tragic Indiscernibility," 154–57, for a précis of the film's plot resemblances to the Genesis (12:10–20) story of Abram and Sarai, and, from the book of Ruth (2:1–23), the story of Ruth, Boaz, and Naomi.
18. The gate aestheticizes the principle of possession and ownership. Its absurdity, given the setting, is patently ironic; Malick takes care to burn the gate as part of the conflagration near the film's end. A wildly comic version of the will to order nature, more or less employing the same visual device, is the electric toll gate set into the otherwise unbounded (and nonelectrified) western landscape in Mel Brooks's *Blazing Saddles* (1974).
19. See Nestor Almendros, *A Man with a Camera*, trans. Rachel Phillips Belash (New York: Farrar, Straus & Giroux, 1984), 182. The esteemed Almendros was the original cinematographer for *Days of Heaven;* Haskell Wexler took over when Almendros had to leave for a project with François Truffaut. Almendros's memoir of his work on *Days of Heaven* is reprinted from *A Man with a Camera* in the booklet accompanying the DVD release; concerning the magic hour, see 31–32.
20. Béla Balázs, "Visible Man or the Culture of Film," in *Béla Balázs: Early Film Theory*, ed. Erica Carter, trans. Rodney Livingstone (New York: Berghahn Books, 2010), 53.
21. Ibid.
22. Kendall, "Tragic Indiscernibility," 163: "Malick's cinema is a cinema of discontinuities, designed with a distinct purpose."
23. Eisenstein, *Nonindifferent Nature*, 217: "The greatest share in 'making sound' fell to landscape. For landscape is the freest element of film, the least burdened with servile,

narrative tasks, and the most flexible in conveying moods, emotional states, and spiritual experiences. In a word, *all that,* in its exhaustive total, is accessible only to music, with its hazily perceptible, flowing imagery" (original emphasis). Eisenstein is speaking of silent film. Eisenstein's comment bears relation to one by Theodor W. Adorno, *Beethoven: The Philosophy of Music,* ed. Rolf Tiedemann, trans. Edmund Jephcott (Stanford: Stanford University Press, 1998), 223n172, concerning the philosophy of music: "In one of its dimensions, music is to be assigned to the realm of natural beauty rather than of art. The ineffable quality of a gentle dusk, the depth of night, dawn—these and the speechlessness of music are deeply related. Manifestations of a beauty which has not been absorbed into the sphere of meaning." My thanks to Stephen Decatur Smith for drawing my attention to the Adorno remark.

24. Cf. Vlada Petric, Review of *Days of Heaven, Film Quarterly* 32, no. 2 (1978–79): 40: "The fractional structure of the narrative is emphasized by long fade-out/fade-in transitions between the sequences: they are consequently perceived like loosely related 'pages' from a memoir. Malick obviously wants his audience to contemplate the previous sequence and to *think* of its meaning before the next event begins to unfold. . . . Malick belongs with those directors who resist the dominance of the narrative in film by developing events which are linked associatively instead of dramatically. In doing so, he intentionally detaches the audience from the story and the characters' destinies, urging us to experience the film's real meaning *via* means that cannot be and are not supposed to be conveyed through the plot line." A propos Petric's last remark is a comment by Theodor W. Adorno: "By emphatically separating themselves from the empirical world, their other, [artworks] bear witness that that world itself should be other than it is; [artworks] are the unconscious schemata of that world's transformation" (*Aesthetic Theory,* ed. Gretel Adorno and Rolf Tiedemann, trans. Robert Hullot-Kentor [Minneapolis: University of Minnesota Press, 1997], 177).

25. Chion, *Film: A Sound Art,* 166. It is highly unlikely that migrant workers would have been permitted to wander through fields of ripened grain, since so doing tramples crops for no good purpose.

26. Eisenstein, *Nonindifferent Nature,* 355. See also P. Adams Sitney, "Landscape in the Cinema: The Rhythms of the World and the Camera," in *Landscape, Natural Beauty, and the Arts,* ed. Salim Kemal and Ivan Gaskell (Cambridge: Cambridge University Press, 1993), 103–26, a capsule history of the trope in film; and Ben McCann, "'Enjoying the Scenery': Landscape and the Fetishisation of Nature in *Badlands* and *Days of Heaven,*" in Patterson, ed., *Cinema of Terrence Malick,* 77–87.

27. The presence of animals, mostly wild but some domestic, is striking, to say nothing of insects: locusts, often in close-up, or the sound of (unseen) crickets. The domestic animals include several dogs, ducks, peafowl, horses, and a chicken being plucked by Linda; the wild animals include bison, pronghorn, deer, fox, skunk, rabbit, beaver, wild turkey, sandhill crane, pheasant, white-tail hawk, perhaps an eagle (soaring at high altitude), ducks, geese, a speared carp, and a frog. Beyond actual fauna, Linda at one point (47:24) lies on her bed looking at the color illustrations, shown in close-up, of exotic animals in an edition of Rudyard Kipling's *Jungle Book* (1894): tiger, water buffalo, elephants, and finally, in a longer hold, coiled snakes, for which two conflicting scrip-

tural associations may apply—evil, of course, from the Genesis story, but perhaps more aptly, given their plurality in the illustration, Matthew's advisory from the New Testament (10:16): "Behold, I send you forth as sheep in the midst of wolves: be ye therefore wise as serpents and harmless as doves." Linda's long look is apt to the extent that she serves as a kind of moral compass for the film, gently making judgments (in a nonjudgmental way) and deeply concerned with both the past (she tells the story, after all) and the future, notably her own, including the brief and otherwise nearly weird vignette as she lies on the ground, holds a clod of earth in her hand, and muses about being a "mud doctor," like a healing angel, reconciling her kind to the earth, dressing the wound: a life option, however naive, of both social and moral consequence.

28. Francisco de Goya y Lucientes (1747–1828), *The Snowstorm* (also called *Winter*) (1786/87), oil on canvas, Madrid, Museo del Prado. Nestor Almendros, *A Man with a Camera,* 169: Malick "has an exceptional visual sense and an equally exceptional knowledge of painting." Concerning possible oblique mise-en-scène references in the film to other painters' works (Pieter Brueghel the Elder, Jean-François Millet, Gustave Courbet, Charles Sheeler, and Andrew Wyeth, as well as the aforementioned Edward Hopper), see Kendall, "Tragic Indiscernibility," 150–51; and Ian Rijsdijk, "The Belvedere and the Bunkhouse: Space and Place in *Days of Heaven,*" in Tucker and Kendall, eds., *Terrence Malick: Film and Philosophy,* 139, 142.
29. The beautiful film *Northern Lights,* released the same year as *Days of Heaven* (1978), directed by John Hanson and Rob Nilsson, incorporates a particularly dramatic harvest scene filmed during a snowstorm that develops into a blizzard (30:52–35:28); as in Malick's film, the scene's sound design, a mix of machine noise and howling wind, adds to the powerful impact of the black-and-white cinematography. *Northern Lights* won the Golden Camera award at Cannes in 1979. The film tells the story of the Nonpartisan League in North Dakota in 1915, thus directly contemporaneous with the *Days of Heaven* narrative. The League worked to defend farmers' interests against rapacious banks and commodity (grain) dealers at milling centers in, for example, Minneapolis. In 1916, the League gained control of the North Dakota legislature, and also elected the state's governor. For a capsule history, see www.answers.com/topic/nonpartisan-league (accessed May 26, 2010).
30. The trope of nature's indifference reappears, and with greater urgency, in *The Thin Red Line* (1998).
31. On a related topic, see Paul Virilio, *War and Cinema: The Logistics of Perception,* trans. Patrick Camiller (London: Verso, 1989), 1, concerning the use of photographic surveillance in the major wars of the last century: "On board an aeroplane, the camera's peephole served as an indirect sighting device complementing those attached to the weapons of mass destruction."
32. Steam tractors could be fired with anything combustible, but coal was the most efficient fuel and commonly used. In the short scene here, a shovelful of coal is thrown into the tractor's firebox.
33. Chion, *Film: A Sound Art,* 8; see also 454.
34. Ibid., 459.
35. Rick Altman, "The Material Heterogeneity of Recorded Sound," in *Sound Theory, Sound Practice,* ed. Rick Altman (New York: Routledge, 1992), 23. He clarifies: "Or rather, it

[every hearing] concretizes a particular story among the many that could be told about that event" (ibid.); and: "It is perhaps useful, in an image-oriented world, to think of the microphone as a 'sound-camera,' a collection device for sound that shares many of the characteristics of familiar image-collection devices" (26).

36. Malick's decision to mount a wind-driven generator atop the farmer's house is hardly a matter of historical accuracy in set dressing; indeed, it is quite unlikely that many farms, even well-off ones, would have had electricity in 1916. The use of low-voltage wind generators only became common on the Great Plains as a result of the Roosevelt administration's Rural Electrification Administration (REA), which got underway during the Great Depression.

37. Sergei M. Eisenstein, Vsevolod I. Pudovkin, and Grigori V. Alexandrov, "A Statement" (1928), trans. Jay Leyda, in *Film Sound: Theory and Practice,* ed. Elisabeth Weis and John Belton (New York: Columbia University Press, 1985), 84–85. As regards the impact of the sound of the wind charger (in the absence of its sight) and the issue of asynchronous sound, Béla Balázs, "Theory of the Film: Sound" (1945), in Leyda, ed., *Film Sound,* 120, suggests that "asynchronous sound (that is, when there is a discrepancy between the things heard and the things seen in the film) can acquire considerable importance. If the sound or voice is not tied up with the picture of its source, it may grow beyond the dimensions of the latter. Then it is no longer the voice or sound of some chance thing, but appears as a pronouncement of universal validity. . . . The surest means by which a director can convey the pathos or symbolical significance of sound or voice is precisely to use it asynchronously."

38. Béla Balázs, "Theory of the Film: Sound," 116. He continues: "Only when the sound film will have resolved noise into its elements, segregated individual, intimate voices, and made them speak to us separately in vocal, acoustic close-ups; when these isolated detail-sounds will be collated again into purposeful order by sound-montage, will the sound film have become a new art" (116–17).

39. *Constellation* is an astronomical term that Adorno borrowed from Walter Benjamin, by which he meant, in the words of Martin Jay (*Adorno* [Cambridge, MA: Harvard University Press, 1984], 14–15), "a juxtaposed rather than integrated cluster of changing elements that resist reduction to a common denominator, essential core, or generative first principle." The astronomical constellation posits a relation on the basis of observable proximity. But at the same time, the relation has a certain metonymic or even arbitrary quality (why link *these* stars and not those?). Nonetheless, once the relation is demonstrated, something heretofore invisible becomes apparent, and an insight is produced.

40. Ibid., 14: Jay summarizes force field as "a relational interplay of attractions and aversions that [constitutes] the dynamic, transmutational structure of a complex phenomenon." Cf. Susan Buck-Morss, *The Origin of Negative Dialectics: Theodor W. Adorno, Walter Benjamin, and the Frankfurt Institute* (New York: Free Press, 1977), 96: Adorno's "central effort was to discover the truth of the social totality (which could never be experienced in itself) as it quite literally *appeared* within the object in a particular configuration" (original emphasis). For a detailed discussion of Adorno's constellational thought, see ibid., 96–110; and Simon Jarvis, *Adorno: A Critical Introduction* (New York: Routledge, 1998), 175–92.

41. Christian Metz, "Aural Objects," trans. Georgia Gurrien, in *Film Sound: Theory and Practice,* ed. Elisabeth Weis and John Belton (New York: Columbia University Press, 1985), 154–61. See also James Wierzbicki, "Sound as Music in the Films of Terrence Malick," in Patterson, ed., *Cinema of Terrence Malick,* 113. Wierzbicki provides a close reading of the sound design of the film's opening credits and first scene, and of the extended climax involving the plague of locusts and burning of the crops.
42. Michel Chion, *The Thin Red Line,* trans. Trista Selous (London: BFI Publishing, 2004), 18. See also Michel Chion, *Audio-Vision: Sound on Screen,* ed. and trans. Claudia Gorbman (New York: Columbia University Press, 1994), 155: "The sound of noises, for a long time relegated to the background like a troublesome relative in the attic, has therefore benefited from the recent improvements in definition brought by Dolby. Noises are reintroducing an acute feeling of the materiality of things and beings, and they herald a sensory cinema that rejoins a basic tendency of . . . the silent cinema." See Chion, *Film: A Sound Art,* 117–45, for an extended discussion of what Dolby permits. Dolby "multitrack sound allows for vastly more present audio impressions of nature, largely by opening up the audio field to the high treble: the rustle of insects, the buzzing of flies, the high tweets of certain birds, the audio background of landscapes acquires more presence, even if it is still far from perfect fidelity to nature. A key film for this recognition of the possibilities of Dolby was Terrence Malick's drama *Days of Heaven*" (132). See also Gianluca Sergi, *The Dolby Era: Film Sound in Contemporary Hollywood* (Manchester, UK: Manchester University Press, 2004).

    Days of Heaven also made use of new technical advances in cameras; parts of the film were shot using the Panaglide, which preceded the development of the Steadicam. According to cinematographer Nestor Almendros, *Days of Heaven* was the first film to employ this camera. Its use is particularly notable in the scene in the river, where the camera circles around Bill and Abby wading (25:11–26:59), and later during the extended locust and fire sequence (01:10:34–01:15:16). See Almendros, *A Man with a Camera,* 176–77; reprinted in the booklet accompanying the DVD release, 25–27.
43. Chion, *Thin Red Line,* 18.
44. Ibid., 9.
45. Ibid., 42.
46. See Chion, *Film: A Time Art,* 266, and what he terms a "temporal vector."
47. The titles of this and other set pieces are from the CD soundtrack recording, *Ennio Morricone: Gli avvoltoi hanno fame (Two Mules for Sister Sara) & I giorni del cielo (Days of Heaven),* Legend CD16 (1994).
48. Richard Power, "Listening to the Aquarium: The Symbolic Use of Music in *Days of Heaven,*" in Patterson, ed., *Cinema of Terrence Malick,* 103–11, provides an often quite different account from mine of the film's score. While I readily acknowledge a number of his insights, I disagree with a number of his fundamental points. For example, Power argues for precisely defined signification as regards the types of music in the film. Thus, he suggests that listeners will hear "Aquarium" as a classical piece and therefore as representative of upper-class social strata ("*The Aquarium* is played only three times *[sic]* during the film, and its association with the upper class adds considerable meaning to these scenes"; 105), whereas the guitar piece "Enderlin" or the Cajun-style "Swamp

Dance" is folk music, "music of the working class" (104). In my view, to establish a dialectic of so absolute a character, as regards both the music itself and the way it will be heard, significantly and inappropriately limits the semiotic richness of the score as a whole and Morricone's music in particular.

49. Unfortunately, this acoustic detail is not retained on the DVD rerelease; it can, however, be heard on the soundtrack album. Nor was this sound effect audible in the screening of an original 35mm print of *Days of Heaven,* at the Walker Art Center in Minneapolis (May 2011).
50. Voltaire, "Treatise on Tolerance (On the Occasion of the Death of Jean Calas)," in *Candide and Other Writings,* ed. Haskell M. Block (New York: Modern Library, 1956), 369.
51. Power, "Listening to the Aquarium," 109, incorrectly identifies this music cue as "The Return."
52. Ibid., 110, provides a useful summary of the music. Power divides the formal structure into four distinct parts. Most of my discussion moves in a somewhat different direction.
53. Walter Benjamin, "Goethe's Elective Affinities," trans. Stanley Corngold, in *Selected Writings,* vol. 1: *1913–1926,* ed. Marcus Bullock and Michael W. Jennings (Cambridge, MA: Belknap Press of Harvard University Press, 1996), 356. Consider also Joan McGettigan, "*Days of Heaven* and the Myth of the West," in Patterson, ed., *Cinema of Terrence Malick,* 53: "The familiar, vast landscape, the source of so many western characters' hopes and dreams, is shown to be just that—a dream, a kind of heavenly apparition shared by the characters and the viewers, amorphous and unsustainable. Malick does not so much disprove the myth of the West as demonstrate our need for it and reinforce our desire for it." See also John Orr, "Terrence Malick and Arthur Penn: The Western Re-Myth," ibid., 63–76. Robert Zaller, "Raising the Seventies: The Early Films of Terrence Malick," *Boulevard* 15, nos. 1–2 (1999): 148, suggests that Malick "opens up the American vista in a way that makes the stolid grandeur of a John Ford taxidermic."
54. Theodor Adorno, *Negative Dialectics,* trans. E. B. Ashton (New York: Continuum, 1983), 6.
55. Adorno, *Aesthetic Theory,* 261.
56. Theodor W. Adorno, *Ästhetische Theorie,* in *Gesammelte Schriften,* ed. Gretel Adorno and Rolf Tiedemann, 20 vols. in 23 (Frankfurt am Main: Suhrkamp Verlag, 1970), 7:98.
57. Adorno, *Aesthetic Theory,* 81–82.
58. Adorno, *Beethoven,* 6 (original emphasis).
59. Adorno, *Aesthetic Theory,* 62.

CONCLUSION

1. Theodor W. Adorno, *Dream Notes,* ed. Christoph Gödde and Henri Lonitz, trans. Rodney Livingstone (Cambridge: Polity, 2007), vi. The dreams in this collection date from January 1934 to April 1969, the last of which was less than five months before his death.
2. Ibid., 28–29.
3. Theodor W. Adorno, *Introduction to the Sociology of Music,* trans. E. B. Ashton (New York: Continuum, 1988), 71–72.

4. Theodor W. Adorno, "Bourgeois Opera," trans. David J. Levin, in Adorno, *Sound Figures* (Stanford: Stanford University Press, 1999), 18.
5. Precisely this point is emphasized by Ingmar Bergman's 1975 *Magic Flute* film adaptation, in particular the several close-ups of the smiling face of a young, clearly enchanted child (in fact Bergman's granddaughter) during the overture and at later points in the opera. The social need for magic, broadly defined, remains intact, to judge from a great deal of modern literature (science fiction, *Harry Potter, Lord of the Rings*), film and television (from *Star Wars* to *Battlestar Galactica*), and video games—to say nothing of the centrality of music to these narratives. The modern world is disillusioned (Adorno cites Prospero laying aside his wand), and its human subjects sense the lack. No accident that in this essay Adorno draws numerous parallels between opera history and the modern history of film, incorporating in the process consideration of each medium's technologies.
6. Adorno, "Bourgeois Opera," 28–29.
7. Ibid., 23.
8. Ibid., 25.
9. Adorno, *Dream Notes*, 28–29.
10. Adorno, *Introduction to the Sociology of Music*, 71–72.
11. I'm borrowing from the opening line of *Negative Dialectics*, to wit: "Philosophy, which once seemed obsolete, lives on because the moment to realize it was missed" (Theodor W. Adorno, *Negative Dialectics*, trans. E. B. Ashton [New York: Continuum, 1983], 3).
12. Theodor W. Adorno, "Mahler," in *Quasi una fantasia: Essays on Modern Music*, trans. Rodney Livingstone (London: Verso, 1992), 84.
13. Theodor W. Adorno, *Mahler: A Musical Physiognomy*, trans. Edmund Jephcott (Chicago: University of Chicago Press, 1992), 6: "It is music's nature to overreach itself. Utopia finds refuge in its no man's land."
14. Ibid.
15. Rose Rosengard Subotnik, "The Historical Structure: Adorno's 'French' Model for the Criticism of Nineteenth-Century Music," in *Developing Variations: Style and Ideology in Western Music* (Minneapolis: University of Minnesota Press, 1991), 208.
16. Adorno, *Mahler: A Musical Physiognomy*, 6.
17. Ibid., 7.
18. Ibid., 14.
19. Ibid., 35.
20. Theodor W. Adorno, "On the Fetish-Character in Music and the Regression of Listening," in *Essays on Music*, ed. Richard Leppert (Berkeley: University of California Press, 2002), 293; and, in the same volume, "On the Social Situation of Music," trans. Wes Blomster, 395.
21. Adorno, "On the Fetish-Character in Music," 315. See also Theodor W. Adorno, *Aesthetic Theory*, ed. Gretel Adorno and Rolf Tiedemann, trans. Robert Hullot-Kentor (Minneapolis: University of Minneapolis Press, 1997), 41: "Mahler's music is progressive just by its clumsy and at the same time objective refusal of the neo-romantic intoxication with sound, but this refusal was in its own time scandalous, modern perhaps in the same way as were the simplifications of van Gogh and the fauves vis-à-vis impressionism."

22. Adorno, *Mahler: A Musical Physiognomy*, 36.

23. Ibid., 17: "If the Other is not to be sold off, it must be sought incognito, among lost things."

24. Adorno, "Mahler," 96: "The expression of suffering, his own and of those who have to bear the burdens, no longer knuckles under at the behest of the sovereign subject which insists that things must be so and not otherwise. This is the source of the offence he gives."

25. Adorno, *Mahler: A Musical Physiognomy*, 38: The art work, "chained to culture, seeks to burst the chain and show compassion for the derelict residue; in Mahler each measure is an opening of arms." Cf. 39: "Not despite the kitsch to which it is drawn is Mahler's music great, but because its construction untied the tongue of kitsch, unfetters the longing that is merely exploited by the commerce that kitsch serves." See further 61–62.

26. What Adorno once said of Berg holds true for Mahler: "The greatest works of art do not exclude the lower depths, but kindle the flame of utopia on the smoking ruins of the past" (Adorno, "Alban Berg," trans. Rodney Livingstone, in *Sound Figures*, 79).

27. Theodor W. Adorno, "Marginalia on Mahler," trans. Susan H. Gillespie, in *Essays on Music*, ed. Richard Leppert (Berkeley: University of California Press, 2002), 617. Cf. Adorno, *Mahler: A Musical Physiognomy*, 166–67, the final lines of this monograph, where Adorno returns to the *"Rewelge"* (reveille): "Mahler's music has sympathized with the social outcasts who vainly stretch out their hands to the collective. . . . Only those cast from the ranks, trampled underfoot, the lost outpost, the one buried 'where the shining trumpets blow,' the poor 'drummer boy,' those wholly unfree for Mahler embody freedom. Bereft of promises, his symphonies are ballads of the defeated, for 'Nacht is jetzt schon bald'—soon the night will fall."

28. See, for example, the excellent account by Peter Franklin, *Mahler: Symphony No. 3* (Cambridge: Cambridge University Press, 1991), 46–49 and 59–65.

29. Constantin Flores, *Gustav Mahler: The Symphonies*, trans. Vernon Wicker (Portland, OR: Amadeus Press, 1993), 102.

30. See Franklin, *Mahler: Symphony No. 3*, 63, regarding a poem, "Der Postillon" by Nikolaus Lenau (1802–50), that Mahler claimed to have had in mind when composing the movement. The verse is in quatrains, sixteen stanzas in all; the text makes repeated reference to the speed of travel and to the sounding of the posthorn. The coach driver eventually stops by a country churchyard to honor a friend buried there, and plays for him his favorite tunes. The poem, in English translation, is available online at www.bartleby.com/270/8/221.html (accessed May 27, 2014).

31. And yet, as ever, the dialectical nature of spirituality itself must be factored in. In 1937, Herbert Marcuse referenced the phrase "affirmative culture" to designate the role, pervasively assigned to cultural practices in late modernity, of cheering (by aestheticizing) for the status quo. By this means, culture (in the utopian sense of what might be, as opposed to what is) is neutralized. Affirmative culture, he suggested, insisted on the soul's nobility, but precisely because it cost very little to do so—and with the added advantage that appeals to the soul's nobility could serve as a safety valve to release social pressures demanding change. Locating humanity in the soul, in other words, all too conveniently leaves intact the material reality that debases the body. According to the

operating principles of affirmative culture, "Humanity becomes an inner state. Freedom, goodness, and beauty become spiritual qualities. . . . [Affirmative] culture speaks of the dignity of 'man' without concerning itself with a concretely more dignified status for men" (Herbert Marcuse, "The Affirmative Character of Culture," in *Negations: Essays in Critical Theory,* trans. Jeremy J. Shapiro [Boston: Beacon Press, 1968], 103). See also on this point Adorno, *Introduction to the Sociology of Music,* 42–43.

32. See in particular the detailed account of its compositional history, revisions, and musical unfolding in relation to its program and textual source (specifically, Emerson's poem *The Sphinx*) by Matthew McDonald, "Silent Narration? Elements of Narrative in Ives's *The Unanswered Question,*" *Nineteenth Century Music* 27, no. 3 (2004): 263–86. My reading of the composition's semiotics differs slightly from that of McDonald.
33. Ibid., 271n23.
34. Ralph Waldo Emerson, *Collected Poems and Translations,* compiled by Harold Bloom and Paul Kane (New York: Penguin, 1994), 5–8. The poem is also readily available online. Several key stanzas are quoted and explicated in McDonald, "Silent Narration?," 282.
35. Charles Ives, "Foreword," in *The Unanswered Question* [full score for chamber orchestra] (New York: Southern Music Publishing, 1953), 2. All subsequent citations of Ives's instructions are from this page.
36. In the revision carried out between 1930 and 1935, Ives slightly altered the trumpet part; originally, the five notes comprising the question remained the same for each of the seven iterations. His later revision alternated the final note of the motive, originally a C-natural, between C and B-natural, in this order: C-B-C-B-C-B-B. See H. Wiley Hitchcock and Noel Zahler, "Just What *Is* Ives's Unanswered Question?" *Notes: Quarterly Journal of the Music Library Association* 44, no. 3 (1988): 437–43.
37. The reference is to Mount Monadnock in New Hampshire, to which Emerson frequently referred and which he liked to climb, as did Thoreau.
38. See Thomas Harrison, *1910: The Emancipation of Dissonance* (Berkeley: University of California Press, 1996)—highly recommended.
39. James Jones, *The Thin Red Line: A Novel* (New York: Scribner, 1962).
40. *The Thin Red Line* (Fox War Classics, 2002), DTS.
41. Michel Chion, *The Thin Red Line,* trans. Trista Selous (London: British Film Institute, 2004), 60. Chion's small monograph is one of the most consistently insightful accounts of the film among the many published. The Ives episode is discussed on pp. 9–12, 36–37, and 60–61. See also Stacy Peebles, "The Other World of War: Terrence Malick's Adaptation of *The Thin Red Line,*" in *The Cinema of Terrence Malick: Poetic Visions of America,* ed. Hannah Patterson, 2nd ed. (London: Wallflower Press, 2007), 152–63, incorporating a discussion of Malick's indebtedness to Emerson.

BIBLIOGRAPHY

Abbate, Carolyn. *In Search of Opera*. Princeton: Princeton University Press, 2001.

Adorno, Theodor W. *Aesthetic Theory*. Edited by Gretel Adorno and Rolf Tiedemann; translated by Robert Hullot-Kentor. Minneapolis: University of Minnesota Press, 1997.

———. *Ästhetische Theorie*. Vol. 7 of *Gesammelte Schriften*, 20 vols. in 23, edited by Gretel Adorno and Rolf Tiedemann. Frankfurt am Main: Suhrkamp Verlag, 1970–86.

———. "Alban Berg." In *Sound Figures*, trans. Rodney Livingstone, 69–79. Stanford: Stanford University Press, 1999.

———. "Analytical Study of the *NBC Music Appreciation* Hour." In *Current of Music: Elements of a Radio Theory*, ed. Robert Hullot-Kentor, 163–215. Cambridge: Polity, 2009.

———. *Beethoven: The Philosophy of Music*. Edited by Rolf Tiedemann; translated by Edmund Jephcott. Stanford: Stanford University Press, 1998.

———. "Bourgeois Opera." Translated by David J. Levin. In *Sound Figures*, 15–28. Stanford: Stanford University Press, 1999.

———. "Commodity Music Analysed." In *Quasi una fantasia: Essays on Modern Music*, trans. Rodney Livingstone, 17–52. London: Verso, 1992.

———. *Current of Music: Elements of a Radio Theory*. Edited by Robert Hullot-Kentor. Cambridge: Polity, 2009.

———. "The Curves of the Needle." Translated by Thomas Y. Levin. In *Essays on Music*, ed. Richard Leppert, 271–76. Berkeley: University of California Press, 2002.

———. *Dream Notes*. Edited by Christoph Gödde and Henri Lonitz; translated by Rodney Livingstone. Cambridge: Polity, 2007.

———. "The Form of the Phonograph Record." Translated by Thomas Y. Levin. In *Essays on Music*, ed. Richard Leppert, 277–82. Berkeley: University of California Press, 2002.

———. *Introduction to the Sociology of Music.* Translated by E. B. Ashton. New York: Continuum, 1988.

———. "Is Art Lighthearted?" In *Notes to Literature,* ed. Rolf Tiedemann, trans. Shierry Weber Nicholsen, 2:247–53. New York: Columbia University Press, 1991–92.

———. "Mahler." In *Quasi una fantasia: Essays on Modern Music,* trans. Rodney Livingstone, 81–110. London: Verso, 1992.

———. *Mahler: A Musical Physiognomy.* Translated by Edmund Jephcott. Chicago: University of Chicago Press, 1992.

———. "Marginalia on Mahler." Translated by Susan H. Gillespie. In *Essays on Music,* ed. Richard Leppert, 612–18. Berkeley: University of California Press, 2002.

———. "Memorandum: Music in Radio." Mimeograph, 1938. Paul Lazarsfeld Papers, Columbia University Archive, New York.

———. *Minima Moralia: Reflections from Damaged Life.* Translated by E. F. N. Jephcott. London: Verso, 1978.

———. "The Natural History of the Theatre." In *Quasi una fantasia: Essays in Modern Music,* trans. Rodney Livinstone, 65–78. London: Verso, 1992.

———. *Negative Dialectics.* Translated by E. B. Ashton. New York: Continuum, 1983.

———. "On Some Relationships between Music and Painting." Translated by Susan H. Gillespie. *Musical Quarterly* 79, no. 1 (1995): 66–79.

———. "On the Contemporary Relationship of Philosophy and Music." Translated by Susan H. Gillespie. In *Essays on Music,* ed, Richard Leppert, 135–61. Berkeley: University of California Press, 2002.

———. "On the Fetish-Character in Music and the Regression of Listening." In *Essays on Music,* ed. Richard Leppert, 288–317. Berkeley: University of California Press, 2002.

———. "On the Social Situation of Music." Translated by Wes Blomster. In *Essays on Music,* ed. Richard Leppert, 391–436. Berkeley: University of California Press, 2002.

———. "Opera and the Long-playing Record." Translated by Thomas Y. Levin. In *Essays on Music,* ed. Richard Leppert, 283–87. Berkeley: University of California Press, 2002.

———. *Philosophy of New Music.* Edited and translated by Robert Hullot-Kentor. Minneapolis: University of Minnesota Press, 2006.

———. "Radio Physiognomics." In *Current of Music: Elements of a Radio Theory,* ed. Robert Hullot-Kentnor, 41–132. Cambridge: Polity, 2009.

———. "The Radio Symphony." In *Essays on Music,* ed. Richard Leppert, 251–70. Berkeley: University of California Press, 2002.

———. "The Schema of Mass Culture." Translated by Nicholas Walker. In *The Culture Industry: Selected Essays on Mass Culture,* ed. J. M. Bernstein, 299–335. London: Routledge, 1991.

———. *Towards a Theory of Musical Reproduction: Notes, a Draft, and Two Schemata.* Edited by Henri Lonitz; translated by Wieland Hoban. Cambridge: Polity, 2006.

Adorno, Theodor W., and Hanns Eisler. *Composing for the Films.* [1947] London: Athlone Press, 1994. Translated into the German as *Komposition für den Film* and published in *Gesammelte Schriften,* ed. Rolf Tiedemann et al., 15:7–155. Frankfurt am Main: Suhrkamp Verlag, 1976.

Almendros, Nestor. *A Man with a Camera.* Translated by Rachel Phillips Belash. New York: Farrar, Straus & Giroux, 1984.

Altman, Rick. "The Material Heterogeneity of Recorded Sound." In Rick Altman, ed., *Sound Theory, Sound Practice,* 15–36. New York: Routledge, 1992.

Anderson, Donald R. "The West of Frederick Jackson Turner in Three American Plays." *Journal of American Culture* 23, no. 3 (2000): 89–97.

Anonymous. *1923 Catalogue of Victor Records.* Camden, NJ: Victor Talking Machine Company, 1923.

———. *1925 Catalogue of Victor Records.* Camden, NJ: Victor Talking Machine Company, 1925.

———. *Mood Music.* Orange, NJ: Thomas A. Edison, Inc., 1921.

———. "The Talking Phonograph." *Scientific American* 37 (December 22, 1877): 384–85.

Antokoletz, Elliott, in collaboration with Juana Canabal Antokoletz. *Musical Symbolism in the Operas of Debussy and Bartók: Trauma, Gender, and the Unfolding of the Unconscious.* New York: Oxford University Press, 2004.

Ariès, Philippe. *Centuries of Childhood: A Social History of Family Life.* Translated by Robert Baldick. New York: Vintage Books, 1962.

Ashbrook, William. *The Operas of Puccini.* New York: Oxford University Press, 1968.

Ashbrook, William, and Harold Powers. *Puccini's "Turandot": The End of the Great Tradition.* Princeton: Princeton University Press, 1991.

Atlas, Allan W. "Belasco and Puccini: 'Old Dog Tray' and the Zuni Indians." *Musical Quarterly* 75, no. 3 (1991): 362–98.

———. "*Lontano-Tornare-Redenzione:* Verbal Leitmotifs and Their Musical Resonance in Puccini's *La fanciulla del West.*" *Studi Musicali* 21, no. 2 (1992): 359–97.

Attali, Jacques. *Noise: The Political Economy of Music.* Translated by Brian Massumi. Minneapolis: University of Minnesota Press, 1985.

Baker, Evan. *From the Score to the Stage: An Illustrated History of Continental Opera Production and Staging.* Chicago: University of Chicago Press, 2013.

Balázs, Béla. *Early Film Theory: Visible Man and the Spirit of Film.* Edited by Erica Carter; translated by Rodney Livingstone. New York: Berghahn Books, 2010.

———. *Theory of the Film: Character and Growth of a New Art.* [1949] Reprint New York: Dover, 1970.

———. "Theory of the Film: Sound" (1945). In *Film Sound: Theory and Practice,* ed. Elisabeth Weis and John Belton, 116–25. New York: Columbia University Press, 1985.

———. "Visible Man or the Culture of Film." In *Early Film Theory: Visible Man and the Spirit of Film,* ed. Erica Carter, trans. Rodney Livingstone, 1–90. New York: Berghahn Books, 2010.

Barthes, Roland. "Rhetoric of the Image." In *Image—Music—Text,* trans. Stephen Heath, 32–51. New York: Hill & Wang, 1977.

Bartók, Béla. *Bluebeard's Castle* [sound recording]. Libretto translation by Christopher Hassall. Deutsche Grammophon CD 289 447 040-2, 1998.

———. *Herzog Blaubarts Burg* [full score]. Vienna: Universal-Edition, 1963.

———. *Herzog Blaubarts Burg* [piano-vocal score]. Vienna: Universal-Edition, 1921.

Behrens, Roger. "On Music in Nature and Nature in Music." *Issues in Contemporary Culture and Aesthetics* 5 (1997): 17–26.

Belasco, David. *The Girl of the Golden West: A Play in Four Acts.* New York: Samuel French, 1915, 1933.

———. *The Girl of the Golden West: Novelized from the Play*. New York: Grosset & Dunlap, 1911.
———. *Six Plays*. Boston: Little, Brown, 1929.
———. *The Theatre through Its Stage Door*. Edited by Louis V. Defoe. New York: Harper & Brothers, 1919.
Benjamin, Walter. "Goethe's Elective Affinities." Translated by Stanley Corngold. In *Selected Writings*, vol. 1: *1913–1926*, ed. Marcus Bullock and Michael W. Jennings, 297–360. Cambridge, MA.: Belknap Press of Harvard University Press, 1996.
———. "On the Concept of History." Translated by Harry Zohn. In *Selected Writings*, vol. 4: *1938–1940*, ed. Howard Eiland and Michael W. Jennings, 389–400. Cambridge, MA: Belknap Press of Harvard University Press, 2006.
Bergström, Ingvar. *Dutch Still-Life Painting in the Seventeenth Century*. Translated by Christina Hedström and Gerald Taylor. London: Faber & Faber, 1956.
Billington, Ray Allen. *Land of Savagery, Land of Promise: The European Image of the American Frontier in the Nineteenth Century*. New York: Norton, 1981.
Birchard, Robert S. *Cecil B. DeMille's Hollywood*. Lexington: University of Kentucky Press, 2004.
Bizet, Georges. *Les pêcheurs de perles* [piano-vocal score]. 1863. Reprint edited by Michel Poupet. Paris: Editions Choudans, 1975.
———. *Les pêcheurs de perles* [sound recording]. Angel SBLX-3856, 1978; rereleased on CD, Classics for Pleasure B000003X6Y, 1994.
Blank, Les, and James Bogan, eds. *Burden of Dreams: Screenplay, Journals, Reviews, Photographs*. Berkeley, CA: North Atlantic Books, 1984.
Blum, Cinzia Sartini. *The Other Modernism: F. T. Marinetti's Futurist Fiction of Power*. Berkeley: University of California Press, 1996.
Bolig, John Richard. *The Recordings of Enrico Caruso: A Discography*. Dover: Eldridge Reeves Johnson Memorial, Delaware State Museum, 1973.
Brandon, Ruth. *Being Divine: A Biography of Sarah Bernhardt*. London: Secker & Warburg, 1991.
Brooks, Peter. "Body and Voice in Melodrama and Opera." In Mary Ann Smart, ed., *Siren Songs: Representations of Gender and Sexuality in Opera*, 118–35. Princeton: Princeton University Press, 2000.
Brown, Clive. "Ornaments: Late 18th Century and the 19th." *Grove Music Online*.
Brown, Royal S. *Overtones and Undertones: Reading Film Music*. Berkeley: University of California Press, 1994.
Buck-Morss, Susan. *The Origin of Negative Dialectics: Theodor W. Adorno, Walter Benjamin, and the Frankfurt Institute*. New York: Free Press, 1977.
Cachopo, João Pedro. "Tales of a Technologically Mediated Passion: Re-reading Beineix's *Diva* (1981), Herzog's *Fitzcarraldo* (1982), and Fellini's *E la nave va* (1983)." *Kinetophone* [online journal] 1 (2014): 59–81.
Caltvedt, Lester. "Herzog's *Fitzcarraldo* and the Rubber Era." *Film & History* 18, no. 4 (1988): 74–84.
Carner, Mosco. *Puccini: A Critical Biography*. 3rd ed. London: Duckworth, 1992.
Cavell, Stanley. *A Pitch of Philosophy: Autobiographical Exercises*. Cambridge, MA: Harvard University Press, 1994.

———. *The World Viewed: Reflections on the Ontology of Film*. Enlarged ed. Cambridge, MA: Harvard University Press, 1979.

Certeau, Michel de. *The Practice of Everyday Life*. Translated by Steven Rendall. Berkeley: University of California Press, 1984.

Chion, Michel. *Audio-Vision: Sound on Screen*. Edited and translated by Claudia Gorbman. New York: Columbia University Press, 1994.

———. *Film, a Sound Art*. Translated by Claudia Gorbman. New York: Columbia University Press, 2009.

———. *The Thin Red Line*. Translated by Trista Selous. London: British Film Institute, 2004.

———. *The Voice in Cinema*. Edited and translated by Claudia Gorbman. New York: Columbia University Press, 1999.

Citron, Marcia J. *Opera on Screen*. New Haven: Yale University Press, 2000.

Clément, Catherine. *Opera, or the Undoing of Women*. Translated by Betsy Wing. Minneapolis: University of Minnesota Press, 1988.

Cohen, Hubert. "The Genesis of *Days of Heaven*." *Cinema Journal* 42, no. 4 (2003): 46–62.

Collier, Richard. *The River That God Forgot: The Story of the Amazon River Rubber Boom*. New York: Dutton, 1968.

Connor, Steven. *Dumbstruck: A Cultural History of Ventriloquism*. New York: Oxford University Press, 2000.

Conrad, Peter. *A Song of Love and Death: The Meaning of Opera*. New York: Poseidon Press, 1987.

Cousins, Mark. "Praising *The New World*." In Hannah Patterson, ed., *The Cinema of Terrence Malick: Poetic Visions of America*, 2nd ed., 192–98. London: Wallflower Press, 2007.

Cowling, Mary. *The Artist as Anthropologist: The Representation of Type and Character in Victorian Art*. Cambridge: Cambridge University Press, 1989.

Crofts, Charlotte. "From the 'Hegemony of the Eye' to the 'Hierarchy of Perception': The Reconfiguration of Sound and Image in Terrence Malick's *Days of Heaven*." *Journal of Media Practice* 2, no. 1 (2001): 19–29.

Darcy, Warren. "*Creatio ex nihilo:* The Genesis, Structure, and Meaning of the *Rheingold* Prelude." *Nineteenth Century Music* 13, no. 2 (1989): 79–100.

Davidson, John E. "As Others Put Plays upon the Stage: *Aguirre*, Neocolonialism, and the New German Cinema." *New German Critique* 60 (1993): 101–30.

———. "Contacting the Other: Traces of Migrational Colonialism and the Imperial Agent in Werner Herzog's *Fitzcarraldo*." *Film & History* 24, nos. 3–4 (1994): 66–83.

Day, Timothy. *A Century of Recorded Music: Listening to Musical History*. New Haven: Yale University Press, 2000.

Days of Heaven. 1978. Directed by Terrence Malick. DVD 2010, The Criterion Collection.

Deleuze, Gilles. *Cinema 2: The Time-Image*. Translated by Hugh Tomlinson and Robert Galeta. Minneapolis: University of Minnesota Press, 1991.

DeMille, Cecil B. *The Autobiography of Cecil B. DeMille*. Edited by Donald Hayne. Englewood Cliffs, NJ: Prentice-Hall, 1959.

Deverell, William. "'Niagara Magnified': Finding Emerson, Muir, and Adams in Yosemite." In Amy Scott, ed., *Yosemite: Art of an American Icon*, 9–21. Berkeley: University of California Press, 2007.

Dizikes, John. *Opera in America: A Cultural History.* New Haven: Yale University Press, 1993.

Doane, Mary Ann. "The Indexical and the Concept of Medium Specificity." *differences: A Journal of Feminist Cultural Studies* 18, no. 1 (2007): 128–52.

Dolkart, Ronald H. "Civilization's Aria: Film as Lore and Opera as Metaphor in Werner Herzog's *Fitzcarraldo.*" *Journal of Latin American Lore* 11, no. 2 (1985): 125–41.

———. "Elitelore at the Opera: The Teatro Colón of Buenos Aires." *Journal of Latin American Lore* 9, no. 2 (1983): 231–50.

Donougho, Martin. "West of Eden: Malick's *Days of Heaven.*" *Post Script* 5, no. 1 (1985): 17–30.

Douglas, Mary. *Purity and Danger: An Analysis of Concepts of Pollution and Taboo.* Harmondsworth, UK: Penguin Books, 1970.

Dunn, David. "Nature, Sound Art, and the Sacred." In David Rothenberg and Marta Ulvaeus, eds., *The Book of Music and Nature,* 97–107. Middletown, CT: Wesleyan University Press, 2001.

Edison, Thomas. *The Papers of Thomas A. Edison.* Vol. 3: *Menlo Park: The Early Years, April 1876–December 1877.* Edited by Robert A. Rosenberg et al. Baltimore: Johns Hopkins University Press, 1994.

———. *The Papers of Thomas A. Edison.* Vol. 4: *The Wizard of Menlo Park, 1878.* Edited by Paul B. Israel et al. Baltimore: Johns Hopkins University Press, 1998.

Edison and Music. Orange, NJ: Thomas A. Edison, 1919.

Eisenstein, Sergei. *Nonindifferent Nature.* Translated by Herbert Marshall. Cambridge: Cambridge University Press, 1987.

Eisenstein, Sergei, Vsevolod I. Pudovkin, and Grigori V. Alexandrov. "A Statement" (1928). Translated by Jay Leyda. In Elisabeth Weis and John Belton, eds., *Film Sound: Theory and Practice,* 83–85. New York: Columbia University Press, 1985.

Elias, Norbert. *The Civilizing Process.* Vol. 1: *The History of Manners.* Translated by Edmund Jephcott. New York: Pantheon Books, 1978.

———. *Time: An Essay.* Translated by Edmund Jephcott. Oxford: Blackwell, 1992.

Emerson, Ralph Waldo. *Collected Poems and Translations.* Compiled by Harold Bloom and Paul Kane. New York: Penguin Books, 1994.

Encyclopedic Discography of Victor Recordings. Online at http://victor.library.ucsb.edu/.

Engh, Barbara. "After 'His Master's Voice.'" *new formations* 38 (1999): 54–63.

Ennio Morricone: Gli avvoltoi hanno fame (Two Mules for Sister Sara) & I giorni del cielo (Days of Heaven) [sound recording]. Legend CD16. 1994.

Estabrook, Margaret A. "Minstrel Jake Wallace and 'The Girl of the Golden West.'" *California History* 64, no. 2 (1985): 118–21.

Fabrizio, Timothy C., and George F. Paul. *The Talking Machine: An Illustrated Compendium, 1877–1929.* 2nd ed., rev. and enlarged. Atglen, PA: Schiffer, 2005.

Fairtile, Linda B. "*Duetto a tre:* Franco Alfano's Completion of *Turandot.*" *Cambridge Opera Journal* 16, no. 2 (2004): 163–85.

"Fanciulla Turns 100." Online at www.bu.edu/buniverse/view/?v=2BU6vnTx.

Faulkner, William. *The Mansion.* New York: Vintage Books, 1959.

Favia-Artsay, Aida. *Caruso on Records.* Valhalla, NY: The Historic Record, 1965.

Fille du Far West, La. Paris: Editions Premières Loges, 1995.

Fitzcarraldo. 1982. Directed by Werner Herzog. DVD 1999, Anchor Bay Entertainment, DV10938.

Flinn, Caryl. "Undoing Act 5: History, Bodies, and Operatic Remains—Kluge's *The Power of Emotion*." Chapter 4 in *The New German Cinema: Music, History, and the Matter of Style*, 138–69. Berkeley: University of California Press, 2004.

Flores, Constantin. *Gustav Mahler: The Symphonies*. Translated by Vernon Wicker. Portland, OR: Amadeus Press, 1993.

Foreman, Lewis. *Systematic Discography*. North Haven, CT: Linnet Books, 1974.

Foucault, Michel. *Discipline and Punish: The Birth of the Prison*. Translated by Alan Sheridan. New York: Vintage Books, 1979.

———. *The Order of Things: An Archaeology of the Human Sciences*. New York: Vintage Books, 1966.

Franklin, Peter. *Mahler: Symphony No. 3*. Cambridge: Cambridge University Press, 1991.

Freestone, J., and H. J. Drummond. *Enrico Caruso: His Recorded Legacy*. London: Sidgwick & Jackson, 1960.

Freud, Sigmund. *Civilization and Its Discontents*. Translated by James Strachey. New York: Norton, 1961.

———. "Mourning and Melancholia." In *On Murder, Mourning, and Melancholia*, trans. Shaun Whiteside, 201–18. London: Penguin Books, 2005.

Freund, John C. "First Production of Puccini's Opera." *Musical America* 13, no. 6 (December 17, 1910): 1–4.

Friedheim, Philip. "Wagner and the Aesthetics of the Scream." *Nineteenth Century Music* 7, no. 1 (1983): 63–70.

Frigyesi, Judit. "In Search of Meaning in Context: Bartók's *Duke Bluebeard's Castle*." *Current Musicology* 70 (2000): 5–31.

Frow, George L. *The Edison Disc Phonographs and the Diamond Discs: A History with Illustrations*. Rev. ed. Los Angeles: Mulholland Press, 2001.

Furstenau, Marc, and Leslie MacAvoy. "Terrence Malick's Heideggerian Cinema: War and the Question of Being in *The Thin Red Line*." In Hannah Patterson, ed., *The Cinema of Terrence Malick: Poetic Visions of America*, 2nd ed., 179–91. London: Wallflower Press, 2007.

Gay, Peter. *The Naked Heart*. Vol. 4 of *The Bourgeois Experience (Victoria to Freud)*. New York: Norton, 1996.

Gelatt, Roland. *The Fabulous Phonograph, 1877–1977*. 2nd rev. ed. New York: Macmillan, 1977.

Girard, Michele. *Puccini: His International Art*. Translated by Laura Basini. Chicago: University of Chicago Press, 2000.

Gitelman, Lisa. *Always Already New: Media, History, and the Data of Culture*. Cambridge, MA: MIT Press, 2006.

———. *Scripts, Grooves, and Writing Machines: Representing Technology in the Edison Era*. Stanford: Stanford University Press, 1999.

Goethe, Johann Wolfgang von. *The Sorrows of Young Werther and Selected Writings*. Translated by Catherine Hutter. New York: New American Library, 1962.

Goetzmann, William H., and William N. Goetzmann. *The West of the Imagination*. New York: Norton, 1986.

Gombrich, Ernst H. "Conditions of Illusion." In *Art and Illusion: A Study in the Psychology of Pictorial Representations*, 203–41. Princeton: Princeton University Press, 1960.

Goodwin, Michael. "Up the River with Werner Herzog." In Les Blank and James Bogan, eds., *Burden of Dreams: Screenplay, Journals, Reviews, Photographs,* 212–34. Berkeley: North Atlantic Books, 1984.

Gordon, George, Lord Byron. *Childe Harold's Pilgrimage: A Romaunt.* 3 vols. London: J. Murray, 1812–18.

Grand Opera with a Victrola. Arranged by Albert E. Wier. Published with record annotations by courtesy of the Victor Talking Machine Company. New York: D. Appleton, 1915–16.

Greenwald, Helen M. "Realism on the Opera Stage: Belasco, Puccini, and the California Sunset." In Mark A. Radice, ed., *Opera in Context: Essays on Historical Staging from the Late Renaissance to the Time of Puccini,* 279–96, 364–70. Portland, OR: Amadeus Press, 1998.

Groos, Arthur, and Roger Parker. *Giacomo Puccini: La bohème.* Cambridge: Cambridge University Press, 1986.

Grover-Friedlander, Michal. *Vocal Apparitions: The Attraction of Cinema to Opera.* Princeton: Princeton University Press, 2005.

Gunning, Tom. "Doing for the Eye What the Phonograph Does for the Ear." In Richard Abel and Rick Altman, eds., *The Sounds of Early Cinema,* 13–31. Bloomington: Indiana University Press, 2001.

Habib, André. "Ruin, Archive, and the Time of Cinema: Peter Delpeut's 'Lyrical Nitrate.'" *SubStance* 35, no. 2, issue 110 (2006): 120–39.

———. "Thinking in Ruins: Around the Films of Bill Morrison." *Offscreen* 8, no. 11 (November 2004), online at www.horschamp.qc.ca/new_offscreen/cinematic_ruins.html.

Hall, Roger A. *Performing the American Frontier, 1870–1906.* Cambridge: Cambridge University Press, 2001.

Hall, Stuart. "Ethnicity: Identity and Difference." *Radical America* 23, no. 4 (1989): 9–20.

Harrison, Thomas. *1910: The Emancipation of Dissonance.* Berkeley: University of California Press, 1996.

Hartmann, Louis. *Theatre Lighting: A Manual of the Stage Switchboard.* New York: D. Appleton, 1930.

Henkel, Guido. "Werner Herzog the Real Fitzcarraldo." *DVD Review* (November 1, 1999), online review (no longer active).

Herzog, Werner. *Conquest of the Useless: Reflections from the Making of "Fitzcarraldo."* Translated by Krishna Winston. New York: Ecco, 2010.

———. *Fitzcarraldo: The Original Story.* Translated by Martje Herzog and Alan Greenberg. San Francisco: Fjord Press, 1982.

———. *Herzog on Herzog.* Edited by Paul Cronin. London: Faber & Faber, 2002.

———. "The Minnesota Declaration: Truth and Fact in Documentary Cinema." In *Herzog on Herzog,* ed. Paul Cronin, 301–2. London: Faber & Faber, 2002.

Hillman, Roger. *Unsettling Scores: German Film, Music, and Ideology.* Bloomington: Indiana University Press, 2005.

Hitchcock, H. Wiley, and Noel Zahler. "Just What *Is* Ives's Unanswered Question?" *Notes: Quarterly Journal of the Music Library Association* 44, no. 3 (1988): 437–43.

Hoeckner, Berthold. "Wagner and the Origin of Evil." *Opera Quarterly* 23, nos. 2–3 (2008): 151–83.

Horkheimer, Max, and Theodor W. Adorno. *Dialectic of Enlightenment: Philosophical Fragments.* Edited by Gunzelin Schmid Noerr; translated by Edmund Jephcott. Stanford: Stanford University Press, 2002.

Inverne, James. "Beginning of the End." *Time Magazine World,* August 18, 2002. Online at www.time.com/time/magazine/article/0,9171,338591,00.html.

Ives, Charles. "Foreword." In *The Unanswered Question* [full score for chamber orchestra], 2. New York: Southern Music Publishing, 1953.

Jarvis, Simon. *Adorno: A Critical Introduction.* New York: Routledge, 1998.

Jay, Martin. *Adorno.* Cambridge, MA: Harvard University Press, 1984.

Joe, Joengwon, and Rose Theresa, eds. *Between Opera and Cinema.* New York: Routledge, 2002.

Johnson, James H. *Listening in Paris: A Cultural History.* Berkeley: University of California Press, 1996.

Johnson, Michael L. *Hunger for the Wild: America's Obsession with the Untamed West.* Lawrence: University Press of Kansas, 2007.

Jones, James. *The Thin Red Line: A Novel.* New York: Scribner, 1962.

Kane, Brian. *Sound Unseen: Acousmatic Sound in Theory and Practice.* New York: Oxford University Press, 2014.

Katz, Mark. *Capturing Sound: How Technology Has Changed Music.* Rev. ed. Berkeley: University of California Press, 2010.

Kendall, Stuart. "The Tragic Indiscernibility of *Days of Heaven.*" In Thomas Deane Tucker and Stuart Kendall, eds., *Terrence Malick: Film and Philosophy,* 148–64. New York: Continuum, 2011.

Kenney, William Howard. *Recorded Music in American Life: The Photograph and Popular Memory, 1890–1945.* New York: Oxford University Press, 1999.

Kittler, Friedrich A. *Gramophone, Film, Typewriter.* Translated by Geoffrey Winthrop-Young and Michael Wutz. Stanford: Stanford University Press, 1999.

Kluge, Alexander. *Die Macht der Gefühle.* Frankfurt am Main: Zweitausendeins, 1984.

Koepnick, Lutz P. "Colonial Forestry: Sylvan Politics in Werner Herzog's *Aguirre* and *Fitzcarraldo.*" *New German Critique* 60 (Fall 1993): 133–59.

Koestenbaum, Wayne. *The Queen's Throat: Opera, Homosexuality, and the Mystery of Desire.* New York: Poseidon Press, 1993.

Kraft, James P. *Stage to Studio: Musicians and the Sound Revolution, 1890–1950.* Baltimore: Johns Hopkins University Press, 1996.

Kramer, Lawrence. *After the Lovedeath: Sexual Violence and the Making of Culture.* Berkeley: University of California Press, 1997.

———. *Expression and Truth: On the Music of Knowledge.* Berkeley: University of California Press, 2012.

———. *Opera and Modern Culture: Wagner and Strauss.* Berkeley: University of California Press, 2004.

———. "Opera: Two or Three Things I Know about Her." In Mary Ann Smart, ed., *Siren Songs: Representations of Gender and Sexuality in Opera,* 186–203. Princeton: Princeton University Press, 2000.

———. "Philosophizing Musically: Reconsidering Music and Ideas." *Journal of the Royal Musical Association* 139, no. 2 (2014): 387–404.

Kurutz, Gary F. "Yosemite on Glass." In Amy Scott, ed., *Yosemite: Art of an American Icon*, 54–89. Berkeley: University of California Press, 2007.

Langman, Larry. *A Guide to Silent Westerns*. New York: Greenwood Press, 1992.

Latto, Anne. "Innocents Abroad: The Young Woman's Voice in *Badlands* and *Days of Heaven*, with an Afterward on *The New World*." In Hanna Patterson, ed., *The Cinema of Terrence Malick: Poetic Visions of America*, 2nd ed., 88–102. London: Wallflower Press, 2007.

Leafstedt, Carl S. *Inside Bluebeard's Castle: Music and Drama in Béla Bartók's Opera*. New York: Oxford University Press, 1999.

Lefebvre, Henri. *The Production of Space*. Translated by Donald Nicholson-Smith. Malden, MA: Blackwell, 1991.

Leppert, Richard. "Gender Sonics: The Voice of Patsy Cline." In Raymond Knapp, Steven Baur, and Jacqueline Warwick, eds., *Musicological Identities: Essays in Honor of Susan McClary*, 191–203. Aldershot, UK: Ashgate, 2008.

———. *Music and Image: Domesticity, Ideology and Socio-Cultural Formation in Eighteenth-Century England*. Cambridge: Cambridge University Press, 1989.

Leppert, Richard, and George Lipsitz. "'Everybody's Lonesome for Somebody': Age, the Body, and Experience in the Music of Hank Williams." *Popular Music* 9, no. 3 (1990): 259–74.

Lockhart, Ellen. "Photo-Opera: *La fanciulla del West* and the Staging Souvenir." *Cambridge Opera Journal* 23, no. 3 (2011): 145–66.

Lothar, Rudolph. *Die Sprechmaschine: Ein technisch-ästhetischer Versuch*. Leipzig: Feuer, 1924.

Lowe, Donald M. *The History of Bourgeois Perception*. Chicago: University of Chicago Press, 1982.

Maehder, Jürgen. "Studi sul carattere di frammento della *Turandot* di Giacomo Puccini." *Quaderni pucciniani* 2 (1985): 79–163.

Mallach, Alan. *The Autumn of Italian Opera: From Verismo to Modernism, 1890–1915*. Boston: Northeastern University Press, 2007.

Marcuse, Herbert. "The Affirmative Character of Culture." In *Negations: Essays in Critical Theory*, trans. Jeremy J. Shapiro, 88–133. Boston: Beacon Press, 1968.

———. "Remarks on a Redefinition of Culture." In *Science and Culture: A Study of Cohesive and Disjunctive Forces*, ed. Gerald Holton, 218–35. Boston: Houghton Mifflin, 1965.

Marker, Lisa-Lone. *David Belasco: Naturalisn in the American Theatre*. Princeton: Princeton University Press, 1975.

Martin, Adrian. "Approaching *The New World*." In Hannah Patterson, ed., *The Cinema of Terrence Malick: Poetic Visions of America*, 2nd ed., 212–21. London: Wallflower Press, 2007.

Martin, George. "Verdi Onstage in the Unites States: *Ernani*." *Opera Quarterly* 20, no. 2 (Spring 2003): 171–96.

Marvin, Roberta Montemorra. "Verdian Opera Burlesqued: A Glimpse into Mid-Victorian Theatrical Culture." *Cambridge Opera Journal* 15, no. 1 (2003): 33–66.

McCann, Ben. "'Enjoying the Scenery': Landscape and the Fetishisation of Nature in *Badlands* and *Days of Heaven*." In Hannah Patterson, ed., *The Cinema of Terrence Malick: Poetic Visions of America*, 2nd ed., 77–87. London: Wallflower Press, 2007.

McClary, Susan. *Feminine Endings: Music, Gender, Sexuality*. Minneapolis: University of Minnesota Press, 2002.

McDonald, Matthew. "Silent Narration? Elements of Narrative in Ives's *The Unanswered Question*." *Nineteenth Century Music* 27, no. 3 (2004): 263–86.

McGettigan, Joan. "*Days of Heaven* and the Myth of the West." In Hannah Patterson, ed., *The Cinema of Terrence Malick: Poetic Visions of America*, 2nd ed., 52–62. London: Wallflower Press, 2007.

———. "Interpreting a Man's World: Female Voices in *Badlands* and *Days of Heaven*." *Journal of Film & Video* 52, no. 4 (2001): 33–43.

Mean, Christopher Curtis. *Charles Garnier's Paris Opéra: Architechtural Empathy and the Renaissance of French Classicism*. New York: Architectural History Foundation; Cambridge, MA: MIT Press, 1991.

Metz, Christian. "Aural Objects." Translated by Georgia Gurrien. In Elisabeth Weis and John Belton, eds., *Film Sound: Theory and Practice*, 154–61. New York: Columbia University Press, 1985.

Michaels, Lloyd. *Terrence Malick*. Urbana: University of Illinois Press, 2009.

Millard, Andre. *America on Record: A History of Recorded Sound*. 2nd ed. Cambridge: Cambridge University Press, 2005.

Mitchell, Lee Clark. *Westerns: Making the Man in Fiction and Film*. Chicago: University of Chicago Press, 1996.

———. *Witnesses to a Vanishing America: The Nineteenth-Century Response*. Princeton: Princeton University Press, 1981.

Morrison, James. "Making Worlds, Making Pictures: Terrence Malick's *The New World*." In Hannah Patterson, ed., *The Cinema of Terrence Malick: Poetic Visions of America*, 2nd ed., 199–211. London: Wallflower Press, 2007.

Morrison, James, and Thomas Schur. *The Films of Terrence Malick*. Westport, CT: Praeger, 2003.

Morton, David. *Off the Record: The Technology and Culture of Sound Recording in America*. New Brunswick, NJ: Rutgers University Press, 2000.

Mottram, Ron. "All Things Shining: The Struggle for Wholeness, Redemption, and Transcendence in the Films of Terrence Malick." In Hannah Patterson, ed., *The Cinema of Terrence Malick: Poetic Visions of America*, 2nd ed., 14–26. London: Wallflower Press, 2007.

Mowitt, John. "The Sound of Music in the Era of Its Electronic Reproducibility." In Richard Leppert and Susan McClary, eds., *Music and Society: The Politics of Composition, Performance, and Reception*, 173–97. Cambridge: Cambridge University Press, 1987.

Muir, John. *Nature Writings: The Story of My Boyhood and Youth; My First Summer in the Sierra; The Mountains of California; Stickeen; Selected Essays*. New York: Library of America, 1997.

Musser, Charles. "Engaging with Reality: Documentary." In Geoffrey Nowell-Smith, ed., *The Oxford History of World Cinema*, 322–33. Oxford: Oxford University Press, 1996.

Nelson, Byron. "The Isolated Heroine and the Loss of Community in Puccini's Belasco Operas." *Yearbook of Interdisciplinary Studies in the Fine Arts* 2 (1990): 385–407.

New Victor Records. Victor Talking Machine Company monthly catalogues.

The New World. 2005. Directed by Terrence Malick. DVD 2008, New Line Home Video.

Ogden, Kate Nearpass. "California as Kingdom Come." In Amy Scott, ed., *Yosemite: Art of an American Icon*, 23–53. Berkeley: University of California Press, 2007.

Olwig, Kenneth R. "Reinventing Common Nature: Yosemite and Mount Rushmore—A Meandering Tale of a Double Nature." In William Cronon, ed., *Uncommon Ground: Rethinking the Human Place in Nature,* 379–408. New York: Norton, 1996.

Orr, John. "Terrence Malick and Arthur Penn: The Western Re-Myth." In Hannah Patterson, ed., *The Cinema of Terrence Malick: Poetic Visions of America,* 2nd ed., 63–76. London: Wallflower Press, 2007.

Paetzold, Heinz. "Adorno's Notion of Natural Beauty: A Reconsideration." In Tom Huhn and Lambert Zuidervaart, eds., *The Semblance of Subjectivity: Essays in Adorno's Aesthetic Theory,* 213–35. Cambridge, MA: MIT Press, 1997.

Parker, Roger. *Remaking the Song: Operatic Visions and Revisions from Handel to Berio.* Berkeley: University of California Press, 2006.

Peebles, Stacy. "The Other World of War: Terrence Malick's Adaptation of *The Thin Red Line.*" In Hannah Patterson, ed., *The Cinema of Terrence Malick: Poetic Visions of America,* 2nd ed., 152–63. London: Wallflower Press, 2007.

Petric, Vlada. Review: "*Days of Heaven.*" *Film Quarterly* 32, no. 2 (1978–79): 37–45.

Petts, Leonard. *The Story of "Nipper" and the "His Master's Voice" Picture Painted by Francis Barraud.* Bournemouth, UK: Talking Machine Review International, 1973/1983.

Phillips-Matz, Mary Jane. "Puccini's America." In William Weaver and Simonetta Puccini, eds., *The Puccini Companion,* 202–27. New York: Norton, 2000.

Power, Richard. "Listening to the Aquarium: The Symbolic Use of Music in *Days of Heaven.*" In Hannah Patterson, ed., *The Cinema of Terrence Malick: Poetic Visions of America,* 2nd ed., 103–11. London: Wallflower Press, 2007.

Presser, Beat, ed. and photog. *Werner Herzog.* Berlin: Jovis Verlag and Arte Edition, 2002.

Proctor, James D. "Whose Nature? The Contested Moral Terrain of Ancient Forests." In William Cronon, ed., *Uncommon Ground: Rethinking the Human Place in Nature,* 269–97. New York: Norton, 1996.

Puccini, Giacomo. *La bohème* [full score]. Milan: Ricordi, 1920/1999.

———. *La bohème: Vocal Score.* Mineola, NY: Dover, 2000.

———. *La fanciulla del West* [full score]. Mineola, NY: Dover, 1997.

———. *The Girl of the Golden West* [libretto]. New York: F. Rullman, 1910.

———. *Turandot.* 1999. DVD recording, RCA 74321–60917–2.

Puccini, Giacomo, and Luciano Berio. *Turandot.* 2003. DVD recording, TDK Recording Media Europe, DVUS-OPTURSF.

Randall, Annie J., and Rosalind Gray Davis. *Puccini and the Girl: History and Reception of "The Girl of the Golden West."* Chicago: University of Chicago Press, 2005.

Repphun, Eric. "Look Out through My Eyes: The Enchantments of Terrence Malick." *Sydney Studies in Religion* 9 (2009): 13–24.

Riis, Jacob A. *How the Other Half Lives: Studies among the Tenements of New York.* 2nd ed. Edited by David Leviatin. [1890] New York: Bedford/St. Martin's, 2010.

Rijsdijk, Ian. "The Belvedere and the Bunkhouse: Space and Place in *Days of Heaven.*" In Thomas Deane Tucker and Stuart Kendall, eds., *Terrence Malick: Film and Philosophy,* 126–47. New York: Continuum, 2011.

Rilke, Rainer Maria. *An Unofficial Rilke: Poems 1912–1926.* Edited and translated by Michael Hamburger. London: Anvil, 1981.

Robinson, Francis. *Caruso: His Life in Pictures*. New York: Studio Publications in association with Thomas Y. Crowell, 1957.

Robinson, Paul. *Opera and Ideas: From Mozart to Strauss*. New York: Harper & Row, 1985.

Rogers, Holly. "Fitzcarraldo's Search for Aguirre: Music and Text in the Amazonian Films of Werner Herzog." *Journal of the Royal Musical Association* 129 (2004): 77–99.

Rousseau, Jean-Jacques. *The First and Second Discourses*. Edited by Roger D. Masters; translated by Roger D. and Judith R. Masters. New York: St. Martin's, 1964.

Russolo, Luigi. *The Art of Noises*. Monographs in Musicology, no. 6. Translated by Barclay Brown. New York: Pendragon, 1986.

Rybin, Steven. "Voicing Meaning: On Terrence Malick's Characters." In Thomas Deane Tucker and Stuart Kendall, eds., *Terrence Malick: Film and Philosophy*, 13–39. New York: Continuum, 2011.

Saint-Saëns, Camille. *Le carnaval des animaux: Grande fantaisie zoologique*. Paris: Editions Dumond, 1922.

Schaeffer, Pierre. *Traité des objets musicaux*. Paris: Editions du Seuil, 1966.

Schauffler, Robert Haven. "Canned Music—The Phonograph Fan." *Collier's: The National Weekly* 67 (April 23, 1921): 10–11, 23–24.

———. "Canned Music—The Player-Piano Fan." *Collier's: The National Weekly* 67 (March 26, 1921): 11–12, 30.

Schneider, Norbert. *The Art of the Still Life: Still Life Painting in the Early Modern Period*. Translated by Hugh Beyer. Cologne: Benedickt Taschen Verlag, 1990.

Schopenhauer, Arthur. *The World as Will and Representation*. 2 vols. (1819/1859). Translated by Richard E. Aquila, in collaboration with David Carus. New York: Pearson Longman, 2008–10.

Schwartz, Arman. "Puccini, in the Distance." *Cambridge Opera Journal* 23, no. 3 (2012): 167–89.

Schwartzman, Arnold. *Phono-Graphics: The Visual Paraphernalia of the Talking Machine*. San Francisco: Chronicle Books, 1993.

Selfridge-Field, Eleanor. "Experiments with Melody and Meter, or the Effects of Music: The Edison-Bingham Music Research." *Musical Quarterly* 81, no. 2 (1997): 291–310.

Seligman, Vincent. *Puccini among Friends*. New York: Macmillan, 1938.

Senici, Emanuele. *Landscape and Gender in Italian Opera: The Alpine Virgin from Bellini to Puccini*. Cambridge: Cambridge University Press, 2005.

Sennett, Richard. *The Fall of Public Man: On the Social Psychology of Capitalism*. New York: Vintage Books, 1978.

Sergi, Gianluca. *The Dolby Era: Film Sound in Contemporary Hollywood*. Manchester, UK: Manchester University Press, 2004.

Sheean, Vincent. *Oscar Hammerstein I: The Life and Exploits of an Impressario*. New York: Simon & Schuster, 1956.

Sieglohr, Ulrike. "Excess and Yearning: The Operatic in Werner Schroeter's Cinema." In Jeremy Tambling, ed., *A Night in at the Opera: Media Representations of Opera*, 195–217. London: John Libbey, 1994.

Silverman, Kaja. *The Acoustic Mirror: The Female Voice in Psychoanalysis and Cinema*. Bloomington: Indiana University Press, 1988.

Simmel, Georg. "Kant and Goethe: On the History of the Modern *Weltanschauung*." Translated by Josef Bleicher. *Theory, Culture, and Society* 24, no. 6 (2007): 159–91.

———. "The Philosophy of Landscape." Translated by Josef Bleicher. *Theory, Culture, and Society* 24, nos. 7–8 (2007): 20–29.

Sinnerbrink, Robert. "Song of the Earth: Cinematic Romanticism in Malick's *The New World*." In Thomas Deane Tucker and Stuart Kendall, eds., *Terrence Malick: Film and Philosophy*, 179–96. New York: Continuum, 2011.

Sitney, P. Adams. "Landscape in the Cinema: The Rhythms of the World and the Camera." In Salim Kemal and Ivan Gaskell, eds., *Landscape, Natural Beauty, and the Arts*, 103–26. Cambridge: Cambridge University Press, 1993.

Smith, Henry Nash. *Virgin Land: The American West as Symbol and Myth*. Cambridge, MA: Harvard University Press, 1970.

Smith, Jacob. *Eco-Sonic Media*. Oakland: University of California Press, 2015.

Solie, Ruth. "Fictions of the Opera Box." In *Music in Other Words: Victorian Conversations*, 187–218. Berkeley: University of California Press, 2004.

Sontag, Susan. "Notes on 'Camp.'" In *Against Interpretation and Other Essays*, 275–92. New York: Noonday Press/Farrar, Straus & Giroux, 1966.

Sousa, John Philip. "The Menace of Mechanical Music." *Appleton's Magazine* 8 (1906): 278–84.

Specht, Richard. *Giacomo Puccini: The Man, His Life, His Work*. Translated by Catherine Alison Phillips. London: J. M. Dent and Sons, 1933.

Speck, Jules. *La fille du West: Opéra en trois actes*. Paris: G. Ricordi, c. 1911–12.

Stanyek, Jason, and Benjamin Piekut. "Deadness: Technologies of the Intermundane." *TDR: The Drama Review* 54, no. 1 (2010): 14–38.

Stendhal [Marie-Henri Beyle]. *Life of Rossini*. Translated by Richard N. Coe. Seattle: University of Washington Press, 1972.

———. *Vie de Rossini*. Paris: Michel Lévy Frères, 1854.

Sterne, Jonathan. *The Audible Past: Cultural Origins of Sound Reproduction*. Durham, NC: Duke University Press, 2003.

Stuart, Roxana. "Uncle Giacomo's Cabin: David Belasco's Direction of *La fanciulla del West*." In John L. DiGaetani and Josef P. Sirefman, eds., *Opera and the Golden West: The Past, Present, and Future of Opera in the U.S.A.*, 140–48. Rutherford, NJ: Fairleigh Dickinson University Press, 1994.

Subotnik, Rose Rosengard. "The Historical Structure: Adorno's 'French' Model for the Criticism of Nineteenth-Century Music." In *Developing Variations: Style and Ideology in Western Music*, 206–38. Minneapolis: University of Minnesota Press, 1991.

Suisman, David. *Selling Sounds: The Commercial Revolution in American Music*. Cambridge, MA: Harvard University Press, 2009.

Sullivan, Scott A. *The Dutch Gamepiece*. Totowa, NJ: Allanheld & Schram, 1984.

———. "Rembrandt's *Self-Portrait with a Dead Bittern*." *Art Bulletin* 62 (1980): 236–43.

Tambling, Jeremy. *Opera, Ideology, and Film*. New York: St. Martin's Press, 1987.

———. "Towards a Psychopathology of Opera." *Cambridge Opera Journal* 9, no. 3 (1997): 263–79.

Taussig, Michael. *Mimesis and Alterity: A Particular History of the Senses*. New York: Routledge, 1993.

Taylor, Timothy D. "The Commodification of Music at the Dawn of the Era of 'Mechanical Music.'" *Ethnomusicology* 51, no. 2 (2007): 281–305.

Taylor, Timothy D., Mark Katz, and Tony Grajeda, eds. *Music, Sound, and Technology in America: A Documentary History of Early Phonograph, Cinema, and Radio.* Durham, NC: Duke University Press, 2012.

The Thin Red Line. 1998. Directed by Terrence Malick. DVD 2002, Fox War Classics, 2002. DTS.

Thompson, Emily. "Machines, Music, and the Quest for Fidelity: Marketing the Edison Phonograph in America, 1877–1925." *Musical Quarterly* 79, no. 1 (1995): 131–71.

———. *The Soundscape of Modernity: Architectural Acoustics and the Culture of Listening in America, 1900–1933.* Cambridge, MA: MIT Press, 2002.

Thomson, Virgil. *The Musical Scene.* New York: Alfred A. Knopf, 1945.

Tocqueville, Alexis de. "Two Weeks in the Wilderness." In *Democracy in America and Two Essays on America,* trans. Gerald E. Bevan, 875–927. London: Penguin Books, 2003.

Turner, Frederick Jackson. "The Significance of the Frontier in American History." 1893. Online at http://xroads.virginia.edu/~Hyper/TURNER/chapter1.html.

Uvietta, Marco. "'É l'ora della prova': Berio's Finale for Puccini's *Turandot.*" Translated by Cormac Newark and Arman Schwartz. *Cambridge Opera Journal* 16, no. 2 (2004): 187–238.

Vázsonyi, Nicholas. "*Bluebeard's Castle:* The Spirit of Cinema from the Spirit of Opera." *Hungarian Quarterly* 46, no. 178 (2005): 132–44; and online at www.hungarianquarterly.com/no178/17.shtml.

The Victor Book of the Opera. 3rd ed. Camden, NJ: Victor Talking Machine Company, 1912.

The Victrola Book of the Opera. 4th ed. Camden, NJ: Victor Talking Machine Company, 1917.

The Victrola Book of the Opera. 5th ed. Camden, NJ: Victor Talking Machine Company, 1919.

The Victrola Book of the Opera. 7th ed. Camden, NJ: Victor Talking Machine Company, 1924.

The Victrola Book of the Opera. 8th ed. Camden, NJ: Victor Talking Machine Company, 1929.

Virilio, Paul. *War and Cinema: The Logistics of Perception.* Translated by Patrick Camiller. London: Verso, 1989.

Voltaire. "Treatise on Tolerance On the Occasion of the Death of Jean Calas." In *Candide and Other Writings,* ed. Haskell M. Block, 357–72. New York: Modern Library, 1956.

Wagner, Richard. *My Life.* 2 vols. New York: Dodd, Mead, 1911.

Walden, Elizabeth. "Whereof One Cannot Speak: Terrence Malick's *The New World.*" In Thomas Deane Tucker and Stuart Kendall, eds., *Terrence Malick: Film and Philosophy,* 197–210. New York: Continuum, 2011.

Warfield, Patrick. "John Philip Sousa and *The Menace of Mechanical Music.*" *Journal of the Society for American Music* 3, no. 4 (2009): 431–63.

Wattenberg, Richard. *Early-Twentieth-Century Frontier Dramas on Broadway: Situating the Western Experience in Performing Arts.* New York: Palgrave Macmillan, 2011.

Weber, James N. *The Talking Machine: The Advertising History of the Berliner Gramophone and Victor Talking Machine.* Midland, ONT: Adio, 1997.

Weber, Joseph N. "Canned Music—Is It Taking the Romance from Our Lives?" *Musician,* November 1930, 7–8.

Welch, Walter L., and Leah Brodbeck Stenzel Burt. *From Tinfoil to Stereo: The Acoustic Years of the Recording Industry, 1877–1929.* Gainsville: University of Florida Press, 1994.

Wierzbicki, James. "Sound as Music in the Films of Terrence Malick." In Hannah Patterson, ed., *The Cinema of Terrence Malick: Poetic Visions of America*, 2nd ed., 112–24. London: Wallflower Press, 2007.

Williams, Raymond. *Keywords: A Vocabulary of Culture and Society*. Rev. ed. New York: Oxford University Press, 1983.

Wilson, Alexandra. "Modernism and the Machine Woman in Puccini's *Turandot*." *Music and Letters* 86, no. 3 (2005): 432–51.

Winter, William. *The Life of David Belasco*. 2 vols. New York: Moffat, Yard, 1918.

Wolin, Richard. "Utopia, Mimesis, and Reconciliation: A Redemptive Critique of Adorno's *Aesthetic Theory*." *Representations* 32 (Fall 1990): 33–49.

Woolf, Virginia. "Mr. Bennett and Mrs. Brown." In *Collected Essays*, ed. Leonard Woolf, 1:319–37. London: Hogarth, 1966.

Zaller, Robert. "Raising the Seventies: The Early Films of Terrence Malick." *Boulevard* 15, nos. 1–2 (1999): 141–55.

Žižek, Slavoj, and Mladen Dolar. *Opera's Second Death*. New York: Routledge, 2002.

INDEX

Italic page numbers refer to figures and musical examples. Songs are listed by title.